On Moral Capital

Xiaoxi Wang

On Moral Capital

译林出版社

Springer

Xiaoxi Wang
Philosophy Department
Nanjing Normal University
Nanjing
China

Translated by Yaohong Chen
Proofread by Rene Morenski

"Funded by the Jiangsu Province Fund for Social Science"

"Funded by the Priority Academic Program Development of Jiangsu Higher Education Institutions"

ISBN 978-3-662-45543-2 ISBN 978-3-662-45544-9 (eBook)
DOI 10.1007/978-3-662-45544-9

Library of Congress Control Number: 2014954885

Springer Heidelberg New York Dordrecht London

Printed on acid-free paper

Springer is part of Springer Science+Business Media (www.springer.com)

Foreword

Can morality create profits for businesses? To this often controversial question, my answer is yes. Moral capital exists for a reason, and morality, as a productive force or a spiritual factor of production, plays a unique and irreplaceable spiritual role in business operations. To prove my point, I have been engaged in the systematic theoretical research of moral capital since the 1990s. In recent years, based on previous academic analyses, I have primarily studied the application of moral capital, trying to illustrate that morality is an important asset for businesses and that moral capital is a significant spiritual capital for business operations. Only by constantly developing moral capital can businesses seize the initiative in a landscape of fierce competition, thus harvesting more profits and benefits.

This book contains a series of research results (most of which have been published) and is divided into four chapters. Chapter 1 ("The Theoretical Basis of Moral Capital") discusses the logical relations between morality and economics as well as between morality and profit-making. It thereby lays a theoretical foundation for the existence of moral capital. Chapter 2 ("The Theory of Moral Capital") mainly interprets the concepts, formation, and mechanisms of moral capital. At the same time, it illustrates the point that morality, as a spiritual factor of capital (or a kind of spiritual capital), clings to and affects physical capital through its unique economic role. In this way, this book tries to construct a theoretical system for moral capital. Chapter 3 ("The Traditional Theory of Moral Capital in Chinese Intellectual History") primarily describes economic morality, especially the economic roles played by morality throughout traditional Chinese intellectual history, providing food for thought on how businesses can create and accumulate moral capital. Chapter 4 ("The Roles Played by Moral Capital in Business Operations") mainly discusses the special economic roles played by morality and the basic approaches and strategies for businesses to create moral capital in order to provide them with a unique basis for decision-making. The annex ("Moral Capital and its Evaluation Index System") was developed on the basis of a wide range of social investigations carried out over the years and summarizes aspects that I believe are of significance in terms of reference and enlightenment for the development of corporate culture and morality, as well as for the creation and assessment of the moral capital of businesses.

I would like to offer my sincere appreciation to the Jiangsu Philosophy of Social Science Planning Leading Group for approving the translation and publication of the book through expert review, to President Gu Aibin, Vice President Xie Shanqing, and Book Business Department Deputy Director Chen Ye et al. of Yilin Press for their great support, to translator Ms. Chen Yaohong and proofreader Rene Morenski for their hard work in the English translation of the book, to the authors whose research findings were quoted by me herein, to my colleagues who worked together with me to study relevant topics, and finally to my wife, Professor and Dean Guo Jianxin of the Humanities and Social Sciences Department of Nanjing Audit University who shares my academic research fields and goals and enhances me in each of our academic discussions and (occasional) arguments.

Although I have been constantly improving my studies on moral capital over the years and thus have the confidence to respond to various questions and criticism, there still may inevitably be some mistakes or omissions in the points I have raised. Any criticism and corrections from researchers and readers are welcome.

Contents

About the Author

Xiaoxi Wang PhD, entitled to Special Government Allowances of the State Council, is a professor, doctoral supervisor, Academic Committee member, and the Economic Ethics Institution Director of Nanjing Normal University. He currently acts as the Vice President of the China National Association for Ethical Studies (CNAES), President of the China Association of Economic Ethics, and Director of the Renmin University of China Ethical and Moral Development Research Center Economic Ethics Institution, one of China's 100 key humanities and social science research centers as designated by the Ministry of Education. As a leading expert in the General History of the Chinese Economic Ethics Thought Research Program, a major project put out to tender by the National Social Science Fund, he is an editorial board member of journals like *Chinese Social Science Digest, Studies in Ethics* and *Morality and Civilization*, and the *Chief Editor of the Chinese Economy Ethics Yearbook*. His main works include *Economic Ethics in China, Moral Capital and Economic Ethics* (self-selection), *General Theory of Ethics* (chief editor), *Modern Western Philosophy of Life* (chief editor) and *60 Years of Ethics in China* (co-author). His *The Traditional Economic Ethics Thought of China* has been translated into Korean. In the *2011 Chinese Outstanding Scholars in the Humanities and Social Sciences: A Report* published by the Chinese University Alumni Alliance, Wang Xiaoxi was named as part of the *List of Outstanding Chinese Scholars in the Humanities and Social Sciences*, which was published for the third time.

Chapter 1
The Theoretical Basis of Moral Capital

Abstract This chapter discusses the logical relationship between morality and economy as well as the relationship between morality and profit-making from different perspectives. It thereby lays a theoretical foundation for the existence of moral capital.

1.1 Morality Makes a "Real Economy"[1]

An economy cannot be separated from people. As a special form of social interest based on interaction and development, it reflects the essence of interpersonal relationships, or interpersonal interest relationships. According to Marx, a "real economy" can constantly train and develop man, and constantly handle interpersonal relationships. He pointed out that, "Real economy—saving—consists of the saving of labor time (minimum (and minimization of) production costs); but this saving is identical to the development of productive force. Hence, this is in no way an abstinence from consumption, but rather the development of power, of production capabilities. Therefore, both production capacity and the means of consumption will grow. The capability to consume is a condition of consumption and hence its primary means, and this capability is the development of an individual potential, a force of production." In other words, the economy is focused on man, morality, and the coexistence of the two, and essentially, it is based more around morality than input, output, or benefit. In my opinion, if it is totally separated from morality, the economy cannot be correctly understood and grasped, for in concept, it is not entirely about materials or material activities—morality also holds a crucial position. In addition, various economic phenomena reveal that morality is closely connected to property rights, which act as the key to opening the door of the economy, with productive labor as the core or precondition of economic activities, and with distribution and exchange to ensure continuous economic performance.

---

[1] *Studies on Ethics*, Issue 5, 2011.

X. Wang, *On Moral Capital*, DOI 10.1007/978-3-662-45544-9_1

1.1.1 Property Rights and Morality

Property rights, as an important precondition of economic activities, are the logical starting point for all economic activity, and the basis of economic benefit. However, without morality, property rights can hardly play their special economic role. Therefore, property right morality needs to be the first lesson for studying either the economy or property rights and their basic virtues.

In the sense of philosophical ethics, property rights, that is, "the rights to own property," "are the sum total of various rights owned by people on a given property or asset in a given society as well as the relationship between a given material and its user, and a way to affirm the existence of man within society."[2] Some think that property rights are just a basis for economic activity, or at most a kind of legal provision or legal relation, things which are not necessarily connected with morality. In fact, property rights mean not only owning or using property but also appreciating property in order to expand property rights, which is one of the most fundamental economic behaviors and concepts required to continue economic activity and develop society. During the process of property appreciation and property right expansion, property right morality plays an indispensable role.

1.1.1.1 The Rationality of Property Rights is Itself a Moral Phenomenon

We must understand clearly that the concepts of "who owns property rights" and "who should own property rights" are totally different. Consequently, during the process of property appreciation and property right expansion, the manifestations and nature of labor (and labor relations) are different. Under capitalism, where property rights are owned by the bourgeoisie, the nature of capital determines that social labor is "alienated," and the labor relationship between capitalists and workers is the embodiment of opposite and irreconcilable class relations. That is, under capitalism, property rights are the most representative reflection of morality in the form of economy. In a society with increasingly improved positive morality, the concept of "who should own property rights" will be increasingly clear and scientific. During China's period of socialist economic reform, significant achievements were made in terms of clarifying property rights, confirming the roles played by economic activities, and minimizing exploitation and inequality, which was reflected well in the timeliness and advancement of the socialist system and socialist morality.

[2] *Collected Works of Karl Marx and Friedrich Engels*, Vol. 31, People's Publishing House, 1998, p. 107.

1.1.1.2 Property Right Clarification Makes it Possible to Minimize Resource Consumption While Maximizing Benefits, Thus Realizing a Moral Economy

Property rights clarification is a basic requirement of economic morality, and requires a clear definition of "who should own property rights." When property rights are determined, people can exclusively and independently occupy, use, profit from, and dispose of a given property or resources. This will stimulate people's economic initiative and creativity, thus minimizing the cost of economic activities. On the other hand, when people have no clear idea about who can benefit from production and transactions, or how profits arising from economic activity can be shared, their initiative to participate in economic activity will naturally decrease. Without property rights determination as part of market transactions, rivalries over ownership are likely to occur, which will inevitably lead to low resource efficiency and social chaos. Although the unclear utilization and benefit distribution of property rights will not necessarily cause rivalries or external conflicts, they will surely discourage people from trying their best to maximize the effect of property rights through labor or transactions, which is, objectively, a waste of resources and an amoral economic behavior (Luo 2003).

1.1.1.3 Property Right Transactions Need Morality, as well as Property Rights, to Determine the Moral Principles of Transactions

A part of property rights are handled via transactions. The success or mutual benefits arising from a property right transaction largely depends on the rationality of the transaction rules applied, specially, ones that satisfy the basic requirements of the transaction. Therefore, a property right transaction can normally only be conducted based on scientific and reasonable transaction rules, of which moral rules, which reflect the basic requirements of the transaction, must be the most fundamental and representative of fairness. Meanwhile, property rights determine the moral principles of transactions. Property rights, as long as they are reasonable and moral, are supposed to be handled in a fair and reasonable manner. Based on clear and reasonable property rights determination, all parties involved in a transaction are entitled to decide whether to conclude the transaction or not, and the bargaining within the process of decision-making will make the transaction more reasonable and fair. On the contrary, if the property right determination is not clear, or is clear but not reasonable, some infringement is likely to take place. Sometimes, infringement is even labeled as being "rational" or "moral," which can make property right transactions deceptive.

In general, healthy property right morality will "effectively adjust and regulate interpersonal property right relationships, reduce conflicts arising from property right transactions, promote cooperation and improve cooperation efficiency related to property rights. In this way, an optimal distribution of property right resources is promoted, and the efficiency of property right transactions is improved (Luo 2003)."

1.1.2 The Nature of Productive Labor Lies in Moral Sublimation

Productive labor is manifested in the practical activities of human beings to produce the most basic materials for survival and development. It creates not only wealth but also human qualities, especially moral qualities, and its nature lies in the perfect demonstration and sublimation of morality. In fact, productive labor is direct evidence of morality being part of the economy.

1.1.2.1 Productive Labor Affirms the Existence of Man and the Value Thereof

Productive labor cannot be separated from human activity. It is the process of material production in which laborers (who are acting of their own free will) use certain means of production as the subject of their labor. The process and fruits of labor not only speak volumes for the substantive characteristics of man but also demonstrate the reason for man's existence and the purpose of man's survival. Productive labor acts as the foundation and logical starting point of human morality. In a materialistic capitalist society, laborers' existence and meaning cannot be affirmed through their productive labor. Furthermore, their productive labor and the fruits thereof become the means or tools of an alien power to oppress them and destroy their human nature. Even though, as part of the "capital" of the capitalist, workers, through productive labor, are transformed into "wage laborers." As Marx said, "On the one hand, the process of production constantly converts material wealth into capital, into means of creating more wealth and means of enjoyment for the capitalist. On the other hand, the laborer, on quitting the process, remains what he was on entering it, a source of wealth, but devoid of all means of making that wealth his own. Since, before entering the process, his own labor has already been alienated from himself by the sale of his labor-power, which has been appropriated by the capitalist and incorporated with capital, it must, during the process, be realized in a product that does not belong to him. Since the process of production is also the process by which the capitalist consumes the power of labor, the product of the laborer is constantly converted, not only into commodities but also into capital, into value that sucks up the value-creating power, into means of subsistence that buy the person of the laborer, into means of production that command the producers. The laborer therefore constantly produces material, objective wealth, but in the form of capital, of an alien power that dominates and exploits him; and the capitalist just as constantly produces labor-power, but in the form of a subjective source of wealth, separated from the objects in and by which it alone can be realized; in short, he produces the laborer, but as a wage laborer."[3] It can be seen that in an unreasonable social system, productive labor violates human morality. Of course, from the macroscopic perspective of historical development, human productive labor is always the source of power that drives social development and human progress. The phenomenon that productive labor goes against human morality has only been caused by unreasonable social systems, the change of which is thus a fundamental approach or means to sublimate human morality.

1.1.2.2 Basic Human Rights and Moral Values are Established Based on Labor

"Labor, at the same time as creating its commodity value, is also endowed with unique social and moral values. From the perspective of ethics, this is where the significance of human morality lies. Since labor and its fruits can be endowed with the moral values of man, labor itself becomes a basic right of human beings (or to be more precisely, of qualified mature laborers). Such a right is of general value and significance to the very right to existence—a basic way for laborers to exist, and also to the special value and significance of moral rights—a way for laborers to express their personality, dignity and honor, and for them to be recognized by society (Wan 2000a)." On the other side of the coin, those who do not work will lose their basic right to exist, as well as their moral values with the very meaning of existence at their core. In fact, the realization of human rights and moral values is closely connected with labor. First, labor is the only way to obtain due human benefits, including both physical and spiritual benefits. For the former, the basic material conditions for man to survive have to do with labor performance; while for the latter, all manner of political rights, the right to enjoy culture, acquire reputation, and even express opinions cannot be separated from human attitudes toward labor and the fruits thereof. Second, labor is the only form able to demonstrate the lofty realm of life and moral consciousness of man, and to illustrate the existence of man's values. Those who waste their life or reap without sowing should feel guilty for themselves and for the society in general, and the society itself would of course despise their irresponsible and negative attitude toward life.

1.1.2.3 Productive Labor Develops Good Human Qualities

Productive labor is the most complex and the most basic human activity to conquer nature. During the process of productive labor, the qualities of laborers are constantly sublimated. As Marx said, during the process of production, laborers will, at the same time as changing objective conditions, also change themselves. Specifically,

[3] *Collected Works of Karl Marx and Friedrich Engels,* Vol. 44, People's Publishing House, 2001, pp. 658–659.

first, laborers will develop the quality of pursuing truth: to work smoothly and gain ideal benefits, laborers must constantly explore the very nature of truth and develop scientific technologies. Meanwhile, they must firmly reject pseudoscience in order to make productive labor meet the requirements of human development. Second, productive labor, which cannot be realized without the intelligence, ability, and wealth of laborers, calls for the laborers' willingness to pay, work hard, and even sacrifice, and it requires the spirit of perseverance and struggle to develop intelligence, ability, and wealth. Third, productive labor is not only the most common but also the most arduous human activity that changes nature and creates wealth. It thus requires cooperation among laborers as well as joint efforts by them to improve the efficiency of productive labor. In modern times, productive labor has even higher requirements and is more likely to develop the spirit of seeking truth, struggle, and cooperation.

1.1.2.4 Productive Labor Generates Moral Rules and Influences the Harmony and Development of Social Relations

Since productive labor is a collective human activity, harmonious cooperation among laborers is required. Meanwhile, with the development of socialized mass production, the division of labor has become more detailed as laborers have become more interdependent in their work. Each laborer thus plays an important role within productive labor relationships. Moreover, productive labor is connected with society through various direct or indirect relationships that affect productive labor to some extent. Therefore, moral rules, which coordinate such relations, are bound to come into being in the process of production.

Smooth productive labor needs the restriction and guidance of moral rules. With the increasing socialization of productive labor, its harmonious progress will objectively and necessarily promote smooth interpersonal relationships within society at large. As the foundation and core of social moral rules, when applied to productive labor, this will produce rules in various fields of social production and social life, thus propelling the harmonious development of the whole society.

1.1.3 Justice and Equality are the Sustainable Basis of Distribution and Exchange

Distribution and exchange, as major economic phenomena, are important economic behaviors necessary for human beings to exist and society to develop. To put this in a different way, without them, the chains holding social production and social life together will break, paralyzing both social production and social life. Justice and equality are the basis of distribution and exchange. In a certain sense, equitable distribution and exchange are the precondition for the sustainable development of social behaviors.

1.1.3.1 About Distribution

Generally speaking, in any society, distribution can be divided into the distribution of the means of production and the distribution of the means of livelihood. The former, which mainly manifests itself as the distribution of production conditions, has a direct bearing on the speed and benefit of production and reproduction, and at the same time, directly influences the production and distribution of the means of livelihood. It is related to the ownership system and to property rights, the rationality of which directly determines the conditions and basis for the existence of justice and equity. If the ownership system and property rights cannot meet the requirements of social and historical development, or even go against its processes, the means of production cannot be distributed in a just and equal way. It can be said that in a society with unjust ownership and property rights systems, the justice and equity of distribution must be incomplete or even false. The latter, as a moral economic phenomenon, is very complex because of its diversified distribution bases and models of the current distribution situation,[4] various subjects of distribution, and strictly specific distribution principles and policies. In the context of complex distribution of the means of livelihood, the rationality of distribution does not lie in the amount distributed; rather it is realized by correctly grasping the subject of distribution and the corresponding interest relationships, scientifically understanding and correctly determining distribution basis and models, and correctly developing just and equal distribution principles and policies. That is, fully embodying the due justice and equity of today's economic morality is the basic concept and principle of the distribution of our means of livelihood in China. Moral-based distribution is a modern distribution model with moral meaning. The famous Chinese economist Professor Li Yining once put forward the concept of the "three distributions," namely, a primary income distribution as per market rules, a secondary income distribution as per government policies, and a tertiary distribution as per morality. For example, individual voluntary payments, contributions, and donations all belong to moral-based distributions, which play the special roles of easing and even resolving conflicts, and maintaining social justice and equality (Wang 1998a).

It can be seen that distribution, as an economic phenomenon, is more of a moral entity calling for justice and equality. It needs to be pointed out that "within a society, equal distribution must reflect the universal demands of social morality, but can in no way be separated from the realistic economic conditions of society by taking social morality as the only value basis. On the contrary, real equal distribution is realized based on the principle of equal rights and obligations, instead of merely being based on the principle of rights or the principle of obligations, which is biased. That is, equal distribution must reflect economic justice, systematic justice and ethical

---

[4] China claims the distribution system gives priority to labor-based distribution and allows the coexistence of other distribution modes. "Other distribution modes" include labor fruits-based distribution and distribution modes based on production factors, such as technology, information, capital or shares, and intangible assets.

justice at the same time; otherwise, it would be partial and biased, and thus unjust (Lu and Xiao 2002)."

1.1.3.2 About Exchange

Exchange, together with distribution, is an important part in sustainable economic activities, which are interdependent. Like distribution, exchange also requires justice and equality. Superficially, exchange is about the exchange of products via currency as the universal equivalent; on a more basic level, it is about the exchange of interpersonal interests, or of the "particular natural needs" of man. Objectively, therefore, exchange requires justice and equality. According to Marx, "Now, as regards the content outside the act of exchange (an act which constitutes the positing as well as the proving of the exchange values and of the subjects as exchangers), this content, which falls outside the specifically economic form, can only be: (1) The natural particularity of the commodity being exchanged. (2) The particular natural need of the exchangers, or, both together, the different values of the commodities being exchanged. The content of the exchange, which lies altogether outside its economic character, far from endangering the social equality of individuals, rather makes their natural differences into the basis of their social equality. If individual A had the same needs as individual B, and if both had realized their labor in the same object, then no relation whatever would exist between them; considering only their production, they would not be different individuals at all. Both have the need to breathe; for both the air exists as atmosphere; this brings them into no social contact; as breathing individuals they relate to one another only as natural bodies, not as persons. Only the differences between their needs and between their production gives rise to exchange, and to their social equation in terms of this exchange; these natural differences are therefore the precondition of their social equality in the act of exchange, and of this relation in general, in which they relate to one another as productive. Regarded from the standpoint of the natural difference between them, individual A exists as the owner of a particular value for individual B, and individual B as the owner of a value for individual A. In this respect, their natural differences again put them reciprocally into a relationship of equality. In this respect however, they are not indifferent to one another, but rather integrate with one another, have need of one another. In this way, individual B, as objectified in the commodity, is a need of individual A, and vice versa; as such, they stand not only in an equal, but also in a social, relation to one another."[5]

Of course, the justice and equality that are objectively required in an exchange are different from those that are actually realized in an exchange. That is, to realize an exchange and create benefits through an exchange, a series of codes of conduct standing for justice and equality are needed to restrict human behavior during an exchange. In a certain sense, without moral exchange, there would be no normal

[5] *Collected Works of Karl Marx and Friedrich Engels, Vol. 30, People's Publishing House, 1995, p. 197.*

and reasonable exchange and, thus, no normal productive labor and economic development. In other words, moral exchange is the foundation of normal exchange and the soul of normal economic development.

1.2 Is the Purpose of Morality Spiritual or Material?[6]

"What is the purpose of morality?" This is a simple as well as complex question. It is simple because it is really a nonissue—the answer is morality, which is useful and makes people learn to behave and earn more profit. It is complex because there are different answers to why morality is useful, how to behave, and what profit is, and it is hard to decide which is right.

A related question is "why do human beings need morality?" In fact, this is not difficult to answer, and the answer also gives an answer to "what the purpose of morality is." However, there are also different answers, some of which are widely divergent. Objective idealists hold that spirit, something already preexistent in the objective world, determines the existence of man and human society, thus determining the existence of morality. Hegel, who epitomized objective idealism, believed that human society, together with morality, is externalized from an absolute spirit, and that the existence of morality, as a part of human free will, is based on the existence of man. In the opinion of Hegel, free will is manifested in the three progressive spiritual phenomena of abstraction, morality, and ethics, wherein morality is the subjective and due rule of self-existence; therefore, morality exists based on the existence of man (although Hegel held that the real manifestation of the absolute spirit of human nature is in fact ethics). Furthermore, Hegel believed that the purpose of morality is to elucidate man, as well as man's very existence. Subjective idealists (or rationalists) widely believe that morality is determined by human "good will," and is born from human "conscience." "Humanity as an end in itself" is the main moral concept put forward by Kant. For him, a person must be rational, or moral, and a person is born with "good will"; therefore, the purpose of morality is to arouse and elucidate morality when manifested as "good will." "Men at their birth are naturally good" is a traditional Chinese subjective moral philosophy, according to which, the purpose of morality is to develop human benevolence and thus really embody human nature. However, neither objective idealists nor rationalists have found out the final purpose of morality. Without a clear final purpose, the theory of the purpose of morality is groundless. Influenced by foreign philosophical thought, the theory that man is naturally imbued with a moral sense has been dominant. Yet, there has also been the opposite opinion, mostly held by old materialists, that the purpose of morality is to make profit, and some even equate profit with morality. This is likely to make the purpose of morality itself unmoral, for when profit is made at the cost of ignoring or abandoning morality, unmoral behavior is bound to occur.

---

[6] The goal of morality is both spiritual and material, *Chinese Social Sciences Today, Philosophy Scholars Personal Column,* Dec. 23, 2013. This is original and unabridged.

According to the realistic ideas of Chinese theorists, I think it is very important to clarify the purpose of morality. Currently, there are two opposite opinions among Chinese theorists. One is that the purpose of morality is to expand the spiritual realm of man so that people will voluntarily fulfill their legal obligations. This opinion is, of course, correct. But how do we judge people's spiritual realm and why should we fulfill moral responsibilities consciously? The other opinion is that the purpose of morality is to make profit, and some even equate profit with morality. For this opinion, the question is how to make and use profit. If the question cannot be correctly answered, when man puts profit and enjoyment first, profit will be a synonym for morality. In fact, if we do not think from the perspective of socioeconomic development, we cannot answer the questions. That is to say, when morality is separated from profit, since "morality is human-oriented not material-oriented," talking about morality will be entirely theoretical, even hypocritical. Nevertheless, when morality is equated with profit, morality's essential purpose, namely perfecting humans and harmonizing interpersonal relationships, is ignored.

The purpose of morality is both spiritual and material.

From the perspective of Marxism, the purpose of morality is to "restore the human world and relationships to man himself." Much like the purpose of communist morality at advanced stage of socialism, this also applies to the present stage of properly understanding and grasping the purpose of morality. Restoration of the "human world" to man himself means that members of society should have a noble spirit; that in a perfect society, "individual creation and free development are no longer meaningless"; that "each person has a proportionate position," that is, "each person can freely develop his/her nature as a human" and "live a real human life in which all conditions and needs for living can be satisfied"; and that labor is no longer just a way to make a living but is a primary living necessity. In some sense, restoring people to the human world is also restoring human relationships, for the human world is composed of both people and human relationships. According to Marxism, the reason for "restoring human relationships to man himself" is determined by the human essence, since, "the human essence is no abstraction inherent in each single individual. In its reality it is the ensemble of all social relations." That is, humans are "individuals within their given historical conditions and relationships" and "the human essence is expressed in the social relationships of man." In short, man is not substantive, but rather an ensemble of human relationships. Therefore, "restoring the human world to man himself" necessarily requires the restoration of "human relationships"—harmonious human relationships. In this aspect, the purpose of morality emphasizes human perfection and harmonious human relationships, as well as human wisdom and spirit. In a strict macroscopic sense, the purpose of morality, according to Marxism, also stresses human perfection and harmonious human relationships, which is the purpose of morality that reflects the unity of spiritual benefits and material benefits. Furthermore, the ultimate goal of emphasizing human perfection and harmonious human relationships is to promote economic and social development. In fact, moral consciousness is evaluated based on human perfection and harmonious human relationships, and more importantly, on morality's ultimate functions and efficiency in promoting economic and social development, and also on the reasons and basis for the existence of morality.

1.3 Economic Morals and Their Functions[7]

Strictly speaking, the word "virtue" is neutral within the theoretical system of ethics and the context of daily discourse. It is manifested as a moral cognition of moral subjects, in the state of moral practice and in the tendency of moral habits. To put it in another way, virtues can be divided into moral and immoral virtues. However, in customary ethical discourse, "virtue" is a commendatory term that is defined as the noble state of moral subjects, and within the habits and tendency of beneficence.

Although virtues have been defined in many ways, economic morals, as a basic element of economic ethics, have rarely been technically defined, either at home or abroad. Indeed, compared with the "abundant" interpretations of the relationship between economy and morality, those of economic morals are quite "poor." Even though by interpreting, analyzing, and summarizing the intellectual achievements made by former researchers we can reach a comprehensive understanding of man's recognition, as well as the history, of economic morals. Based on such achievements, we can define and interpret economic morals in the modern sense and ultimately prove that economic morals are an enduring economic quality with noble value orientation that performs economic functions.

1.3.1 Ideological Origins of Economic Morals

From ancient Chinese intellectual history, it can be seen that ancient ideologists primarily understood economic morals according to the relationships between economy and morality, profit, and justice. There are four main ideological origins of economic morals.

First, economic morals refer to appropriate economic behavior.

Yan Ying of the Spring and Autumn Period thought that "morality is the basis of profit (or economy)."[8] In this case, morality means that making profit should be moderated with reasonable returns. According to Yan, "when wealth is abundant, morality is needed to limit wealth so that people will not indulge too much—excess wealth will lead to disasters"[9] and "morality is primarily about giving, which is noble."[10]

Second, economic morals include both economy-related morality and morality-based economy.

---

[7] *Morality and Civilization, 2008, Issue 6.*

[8] *Zuo Zhuan, the 10th year of Duke Zhao.*

[9] *Zuo Zhuan, the 28th year of Duke Xiang.*

[10] *Zuo Zhuan, the 10th year of Duke Zhao.*

Confucius of the Pre-Qin Period once said, "People living a poor and humble life in a rich and just country are shameful; and those living a rich and noble life in a poor and unjust country are also shameful."[11] In the opinion of Confucius, economic development requires both justice and morality, and a just and moral society will surely be rich; otherwise, it will be shameful. In other words, economy, profit, and moral virtues are all complementary and integrated.

Advocating moralism and utilitarianism respectively, Confucianism and Mohism reach a consensus in terms of their understanding of economic morals. Mohism representative Mo Tzu held that in the utilitarian system, economic morals are an approach to make profits, or where profits are made based on morality, thus organically integrating the concepts of profit and morality. He thought, "Morality is profit."[12] That is to say that real morality must be profitable, for it is defined by profit. When morality is equated with profit, economic morals are an approach to make profit, or at least those profits that have been received through morality.

Third, economic morals are virtues of both man and society.

A representative of this view is Dong Zhongshu of the Han dynasty. According to Dong, "Man is born with both morality and the nature of pursuing profit, with the former to meet spiritual needs and the latter to meet material needs. A man without morality cannot be really happy, and without profit he cannot survive." From the perspective of economic morals, the unity of morality and profit, and of spiritual and material needs, actually represents the interdependence between the economy and morality, or between profit and morality, which is necessary for man and the society at large. In other words, economic morals, in the final analysis, are virtues of both man and society.[13]

Fourth, economic morals represent economic morality as a heavenly principle.

Zhu Xi of the Song dynasty held that "the theory of morality and profit is the primary theory that Confucians should understand."[14] According to him, "profit is a material need of man,"[15] while "morality is a heavenly principle" and "noble people always put morality first, because putting profits first will definitely harm morality."[16] From the above, it can be seen that economic morals are economic morality as a heavenly principle.

Throughout Western intellectual history as well, economic morals have never been technically defined. Economic morals are just occasionally discussed from different angles when interpreting economic theories or thoughts concerning economic ethics. There are three main points of view on economic morals.

First, economic morals mean economic freedom.

Throughout Western intellectual history, it has been widely believed that economic morals rest on economic freedoms, for only freedom can encourage economic bodies to play their roles to the full, ensure fair transactions, and maximize

[11] *The Analects of Confucius Taibo.*

[12] *Mo Tzu Classics.*

[13] *Luxuriant Dew of the Spring and Autumn Annals, Materials Needs Prevail Over Morality.*

[14] *Collected Works by Chu Hsi, Vol. 24.*

[15] *Variorum of the Analects of Confucius, Ethics and Benevolence.*

[16] *Zhuzi's Language Category, Vol. 51.*

profits. A representative of this point of view is Adam Smith, the founder of free market economics, whose thinking has long influenced the development of Western economics. The core of Smith's economic theory is "laissez-faire." He believed that "every individual necessarily labors to render the annual revenues of society as great as he can. He generally neither intends to promote the public interest, nor knows how much he is promoting it.… He intends only his own gain, and he is in this, as in many other cases, led by an invisible hand to promote an end which was no part of his intention. Nor is it always the worse for society that it was no part of his intention. By pursuing his own interest he frequently promotes that of the society more effectually than when he really intends to promote it. I have never known much good done by those who affected to trade for the public good." In the view of Smith, man in nature is self-interested, which, objectively, will promote public benefits (Zhang 2001). He also thought that "a business which is beneficial to society shall be free to compete," "it is the vanity, not the ease, or the pleasure, which interests us" and "the sense of honor and dishonor arouses the diligence of human beings, encouraging them to create the miracles of moral and material civilization." Smith pointed out that restrictions, no matter in what form, will hinder the pursuit of self-interest, and thus in turn the increase and equal distribution of social wealth (Zhang 2007a). Therefore, the best economic policy is allowing complete freedom of personal activities, including free employment, free competition, free trade, free exchange, and free transaction without any human interference (Gu 2005).

Second, economic morals refer to good and evil economic behavior.

Modern British economist and ethicist Bernard Mandeville held that in all societies, being good is the responsibility of each social member; therefore, virtues shall be encouraged and vices shall be opposed. He also claimed that behaviors that pursue self-interest, something that lies in the very nature of human beings, are vices (such as greed, waste, extravagance, and vanity) that nonetheless contribute to social benefit and human development for all arts, skills, and industries. Economic and social properties are to a large extent created by the vices and defects of man, and the harshness of other basic elements such as air. According to him, needs, greed, envy, ambition, and other similar human characteristics all contribute great achievements, and therefore, the fundamental incentive for people to work hard is not the spirit of benefiting the public, but rather their various desires. Bernard Mandeville did not encourage vices, but he claimed that economic development is promoted by both virtues and vices (Zhang 2007b).

Third, economic morals mean providing services to each other.

The French postclassical economist Frederic Bastiat wrote in his work *Economic Harmonious* that economic morals are economic harmony and exchange embodied in "services," and "in a capitalist society where harmony is built on exchange, the content of such services is to provide service to each other. Service is an effort made to satisfy the desires of others. During such exchanges, people can help each other by working for each other and providing services to each other. Human social life requires constantly avoiding pain and pursuing the pleasure of being satisfied, which can only be realized through exchange. On the premise of free exchange, the efforts made by each person can be exchanged for services to satisfy their own desires. When one works to satisfy the desires of another person, one both provides and receives service at the same time, which forms the exchange of two services (Wu and Zhang 2007)."

At home and abroad, the definitions of economic morals can enlighten us toward different perspectives, both theoretically and practically. Their focus varies from the morality of economic behavior to the functionality of economic behavior, from the moderation of economic behavior to the forms and benefits of economic behavior, as well as many other considerations besides.

1.3.2 The Meaning of Economic Morals

First and foremost, we must clearly understand that economic morals are not the simple and mechanical combination of the economy and moral character/morality. Like the front and back of a coin, the economy and moral character/morality reflect the two sides of a social phenomenon. I once pointed out in a paper that the economy is not merely about the input and output, or the quantity of materials; actually, it cannot be separated from ethics. Any economy, which is incomprehensible and cannot exist without ethics, must be moral (Wang 2011). Seen from the relation between the market economy and morality, the claim that "a market economy is a moral economy" is objectively and practically well founded. The existence and resolution of the basic moral conflict between self-interest and altruism can well illustrate the inseparability between the economy and morality. In the socialist market economy, generalized moral education and moral rules are needed to fulfill the objective moral obligation in economic activities.

Economic morals, as a social phenomenon, can be understood from the following six aspects.

1.3.2.1 Economic Morals Are a Value Orientation and a Noble Economic Behavior

As previously stated, all kinds of economic behavior are of certain objective value orientations, either good or evil. In this book, the value orientations of economic behavior are of goodness, and are, as a minimum, manifested in making legitimate personal profit and benefiting society as far as possible. In this sense, making personal profit and benefiting society are not necessarily contradictory; instead, they are unified, interdependent, and complementary, which reflects the noble moral state of economic behavior. For economic entities (companies) or individuals, it is natural that they should put their own interests first. The point is that they should make profit in the course of serving society, whereas mercenary or beggar-thy-neighbor behavior is unmoral and will be despised.

1.3.2.2 Economic Morals Are Moral Obligations That Should be Taken by the Economic Body

For any economic body (a company or an individual), its formation, existence, development, and prosperity cannot be realized without social support. To be specific, there are three kinds of support: The intelligent support from society which provides the economic body with the necessary cultural knowledge and professional skills to exist; the policy support from the government which builds the basis and creates conditions for economic activity; and the mutual support from economic bodies to realize a harmony of interests and of cooperation, thus laying the foundation for mutual trust, a basic element required for even the simplest transactions. Besides, a company cannot normally carry out economic activities without the concern and support of the society. Therefore, any economic body will objectively take the moral responsibility for others and for society. In other words, accepting the moral responsibility for others and for society is the essence of the economic body's existence. In this light, the economic body is, to some extent, the moral entity. An economic body refusing to be responsible for others and society will lose its reasons and conditions for existence, and will surely be despised and abandoned by society.

1.3.2.3 Economic Morals Are the Moral Rules of the Economy

Economic morals are reflected by the spiritual state and moral behavior of the economic body, and are based on an understanding of the moral responsibility of the economy and the identification and execution of the economic morality criteria system. In fact, economic morals are the economic behavior of systematically implementing the requirements of moral rules. In any aspect of any economic activity, morality acts as a yardstick by which what should and should not be done can be judged. In this way, complex economic behavior can create maximum economic benefits in a normative, ordered, and rational way. Economic morality criteria are a spiritual element of the economy, and the internal basis and core content of economic activities.

1.3.2.4 Economic Morals Are the Moral and Personal Development of the Economic Agent

Economic activities do not exist without man or interpersonal relationships. The moral responsibilities and moral criteria system required in economic activities can only be put into practice with the participation of moral economic agents who can turn moral responsibilities and requirements into action. In other words, a moral economy can only be built by moral people. Therefore, man, as the economic body, needs to voluntarily develop morality as part of the process of participating in economic activities, thus really understanding the significance of morality within the economy and proving the existence and value of economic morality through effective and rational economic behavior.

1.3.2.5 Economic Morals Are Enduring Economic Qualities

The achievements of economic activities are ultimately reflected in their results. Product quality, resulting from economic activities, is determined to some extent by the moral quality of the economic agent. Since the degree of human-centered design, the responsibility for consumers contained within products, and the fulfillment of commitments made to consumers are all closely connected to the value orientation and moral consciousness of man, the lack or absence of basic moral consciousness is bound to affect product quality. Therefore, high-quality products must contain morality. An enduring economic quality means not only high product quality but also the stable and habitual morals of the economic agent. Only in this way can economic activities become a dynamic part of noble economic qualities and manifest the nature of economic morals.

1.3.2.6 Economic Morals Mean Economic Freedom

Economic freedom is an independent economic behavior which is formed based on the equality between economic relations and economic interest relations, while being based on certain economic laws and conforming to economic liberalism.

Economic freedom can be understood from the following aspects. First, the freedom to work, that is, laborers are free to control their working time, to decide what to do, and to achieve the economic goals they have set themselves,[17] on the premise that they can consciously reach achievable "survival indexes." Otherwise, they cannot realize their optimal economic benefits. Second, the freedom to transact, that is, laborers are free to decide when, how, and where to transact and who to transact with. As a basic form and means of the modern economy, transactions are made for the purposes of realizing material exchange, maximizing benefits, and obtaining better production and living conditions to expand reproduction. Third, the freedom to invest and consume; that is, investors are free to decide their own fields of investment, and to consume their investment returns. Investment is the key means and form of economic activities, with the purpose of obtaining more benefits, and in some sense, consumption itself is also a kind of investment. It can thus be said that rational consumption is rational investment.

[17] In this case, survival indexes refer to the physical condition, educational level, psychological quality, moral consciousness, etc. of man. As objective and subjective survival conditions and the efforts made to survive vary from person to person, the survival indexes of different persons are different.

It shall be pointed out that economic freedom is not unlimited—it has its internal basis and requirements. There are certain requirements for realizing economic freedom.

The first requirement is grasping economic laws. Proprietors, by only having a rudimentary grasp of basic economic laws, especially those of the fields that they are engaged in, could take the initiative in conducting economic activities. When describing the process of progressing from the realm of necessity to the realm of freedom, Marx pointed out that "with his development, the realm of natural necessity expands, because his wants increase; but at the same time the forces of production increase, by which these wants are satisfied. The freedom in this field cannot consist of anything else but of the fact that socialized man, the associated producers, regulate their interchange with nature in a rational way and bring it under their common control, instead of being ruled by it as by some blind power; that they accomplish their task with the least expenditure of energy and under conditions most adequate to their human nature and most worthy of it. Nevertheless, it always remains a realm of necessity. Beyond it begins that development of human power, which is its own end, the true realm of freedom, which, however, can flourish only upon that realm of necessity as its basis. The shortening of the working day is its fundamental premise."[18] Since freedom means recognizing necessity and changing the objective world, in order to realize economic freedom it is necessary to really understand the economy and conduct economic activities in accordance with the laws and basic rules of the economy. It is most certainly wrong to think that economic freedom is unlimited; in fact, unrestricted economic behaviors are not free, but limited, even restricted.

The second requirement is building an awareness of responsibility in business operation. Economic freedom and economic responsibilities are dialectically united; that is, economic freedom is achieved upon the basis of economic responsibilities. To be free in their economic activities, proprietors must build an awareness of responsibility, since all their economic activities are social and can only be conducted with the support of society. If development laws and requirements of society are ignored, if the benefits of stakeholders are disregarded, then objectively speaking, normal social relations, especially social cooperative relations, will be destroyed. And in this case, economic activities, which cannot be supported by society or cannot be conducted via normal social relations, are not free. Therefore, to achieve economic freedom, it is necessary to undertake the corresponding economic responsibilities, so that rational economic concepts and behavior can comply with people's inner economic will and desires. History has proved that irresponsible economic behavior, or economic desires and actions representing an unlimited reflection of economic will, are impracticable. One viewpoint is that for companies as economic bodies, "the most important and practical way to undertake their responsibilities is through realizing cleaner production" and by "trying to lower material and energy

[18] *Collected Works of Karl Marx and Friedrich Engels, Vol. 7, People's Publishing House, 2009, p. 927.*

consumption and realizing pollution-free production," thus constantly "promoting the improvement of environmental conditions (Liu 2004)." It is an insightful opinion—cleaner production not only promotes the economic development of society but also constantly improves the operating philosophy and economic performance of companies. It can be said that cleaner production is rational and efficient, and is thus economically free.

The third requirement is improving laws, regulations, and policies. To rationally limit economic freedom within economic activities, it is necessary to take the following three measures. First, improve the legal system to protect the proprietor's right of participating in economic activities. Second, remove man-made policy interference, especially government interference, which requires the government to make clear their functions and play their due roles, to create a sound operating environment through effective policies, laws, and regulations, and to guide proprietors to operate freely under fierce economic competition, thus realizing efficient business operation. Third, enhance the cooperation between proprietors, for all economic activities are social. In order to conduct efficient economic activities, and thereby having the complete initiative in terms of business operation, proprietors must make the most of various social relation resources and use various contributing factors directly or indirectly; otherwise, the business activities of proprietors will be passive and constrained. Therefore, proprietors need to cooperate in good faith, in order to create an economic condition which is beneficial to the rapid and harmonious development of the economy.

In conclusion, economic morals are the due moral responsibility, noble value orientation, and enduring economic qualities of economic behavior.

1.3.3 Functions of Economic Morals

The elements of economic morals, like economic morality philosophy, economic value orientation, and enduring economic qualities, all play their special roles within economic activities. Generally speaking, the functions of economic morals mainly include the following.

1.3.3.1 Purifying the Social Environment

Economic morals mean that the economic agent has an economic moral philosophy, economic value orientation, and economic qualities required by the times. The behavior of the moral economic agent is bound to influence the whole process of economic behavior, including people's rational attitude toward economic behavior in production, exchange, distribution, consumption, sales, service, and fruition, thus promoting harmonious economic development, and furthermore improving the moral quality of society as a whole, both in terms of production and in terms of realizing real social harmony. In a socialist market economy, economic morality is specially needed to purify the social environment. "Professor Paul Anthony Samuelson of the Massachusetts Institute of Technology, winner of the Nobel Economics Prize in 1970 once answered a Chinese journalist: 'At present, nothing can replace the market to organize complex and large scale economies. But the problem is that the market has neither heart nor brain, so it cannot feel or think'. Coincidentally, Professor Harry Markowitz of the City University of New York, winner of the Nobel Economics Prize in 1990 said similar words to a Chinese journalist, 'The market has neither heart nor brain, so we cannot expect it to consciously realize its inherent social inequality, let alone expect it to correct such inequality.'" "The market economy needs different hearts and brains, and morality plays the role of the heart and brain, both of which are indispensable (Xiao 1995)." We can say that economic morals reflect the development of the market economy, and what is more, they act as an important spiritual basis and a social condition for the purification of the social environment. From another perspective, economic behavior lacking in economic morals, such as venality, fraudulence, and falsification, will hinder the normal conduction of economic activities and degenerate morality.

1.3.3.2 Enhancing Economic Force

Economic force, as one of the forces pushing forward economic development, can be understood and developed from both material and spiritual aspects. Materially speaking, material and technology are the basis for economic development; however, they cannot play their roles without the participation of economic agents (laborers or labor originators). Spiritually, economic morals play a special irreplaceable role in economic development. On the one hand, they set correct value orientation and goals for economic behavior as "an invisible rational hand or rational force to realize the rational management of all capital invested in production and guide the economic agent to maximize profit (Wang et al. 2005a)," thus powering economic activities in an invisible but forceful way. On the other hand, economic morals can constantly increase the moral quality of the economic body, thus arousing labor enthusiasm and promoting material and technology to fully play their roles. "If man cannot exist as a real or complete man, or exists passively or even reactively, no matter how advanced technology and equipment are and how abundant resources are, his productivity is bound to stay low (Wang 2000)." On the other hand, "arousing laborers' enthusiasm in production largely depends on solving interpersonal conflicts in relation to production, and on appropriately handling relations concerning status and the material interests of man (Liu 1998)." Obviously, economic morals can reconcile various internal and external benefit-based relationships in economic organizations like companies, synergizing the power of economic force, and thus ensure effective economic development.

1.3.3.3 Improving Material Development

Material development, supported by spiritual, political, and systematic development, lays the foundation for socialist development. Economic morals, as an important part of spiritual development, play a unique role in improving material development. On the one hand, economic morals create a spiritual environment for material development. All materials are created by man, and it is undeniable that technology plays an important role in determining the quality of materials (goods). However, we shall also see that technology is not the only index by which the final quality of materials (goods) should be judged—except for durability and effectiveness, human-centered design, namely how a material (good) can meet the real needs of man, actually plays a much bigger role in determining the quality of materials (goods). In today's world, where commercial competition is increasingly fierce, almost all companies are trying to find out the "secret" of building time-honored brands. From the successful experience of world famous businesses like Starbucks, Coca-Cola, BMW, Sony, Kodak, and McDonald's, it is not hard to discover that although their approaches to success are different, they follow the same law, namely always caring about the inner needs and value propositions of consumers, and creating human-centered experience to meet consumers' deeper needs. For example, Starbucks does not only provide coffee but also a "third space" between work and home; Coca-Cola spreads the idea of "infinite happiness," which speaks for the value of freedom and energy; Sony always engages in providing consumers with the latest and coolest audiovisual enjoyment for the purposes of creating happiness through technology; for Kodak, behind cameras and film, it is actually all about selling "moments in time" and "moments forever"; and when speaking of McDonald's, aside from delicious hamburgers and fries, people will "taste" the company's life philosophy of "laugh every day (Ma 2005)." Therefore, in some sense, economic morals are the soul of materials. On the other side, economic morals energize material development. Materials are developed based on collective intelligence and power, which requires conscious cooperation. Also, economic morals are an important condition for promoting material development through building harmonious interpersonal relationships, and guiding people to support each other and realizing win–win or multi-win situations. When commenting on *In Search Of Excellence,* R. Edward Freeman and Daniel. R. Gilbert Jr. pointed out that "the secret of excellent companies is understanding the values and ethics of employees and combining them with their corporate strategies (Zhou 1999)," which means that corporate development and profit increase depend on harmonious ethical relations based on correct values.

1.3.3.4 Benchmarking Economic Behavior

The most direct goal of economic behavior is material benefits; however, how to create or realize material benefits (through means and approaches) is a very complex process. Economic morals are the benchmark for all kinds of economic behavior. "In many cases, customer service and product quality are the goals, and profit is only a by-product (Zhou 1999)." As Merck Chairman George W. Merch said, "We try never to forget that medicine is for the people. It is not about the profits. The profits follow, and if we have remembered that, they have never failed to appear. The better we have remembered it, the larger they have been (James and Jerry 2003)." Obviously, as long as we try to realize the consistency of economic purposes and moral purposes, and the unity of moral philosophy and material philosophy, and adhere to taking moral rules as the rules of conduct, then the process of creating materials will definitely be rational and efficient. Professor James C. Collins and Professor Jerry I. Porras of Stanford University once took 18 truly exceptional and long-lasting companies (each has a successful history of at least 45 years) and studied each in direct comparison to one of its top competitors. They examined the companies for 6 years and found that "long-lasting companies pursue profits. But they also pursue visions with a wider range and a more profound significance.... Visionary companies make profits while pursuing visions. They have done both (James and Jerry 1996)."

Meanwhile, economic morals are the basis for the value identification of all rational and ordered economic activities. From form to content, economic activities vary a lot. The unity of economic concepts, economic goals, and the means of economic morality is determined by the unity of value orientation, and the basis of value identification is economic morals. In this regard, contemporary German scholar P. Koslowski said that in a market economy, "the economy is controlled by both economic laws and by people. In human wishes and choices, there is always a choir composed of expectations, standards, opinions and moral concepts that all play their roles (Koslowski 1996)."

1.3.3.5 Reconciliation of Economic Interest Relations

Morals are about relations. Hence, economic morals, which can be understood as the moral requirements and habits needed to build up harmonious economic relations, especially economic interest relations, are about economic relations. In economic activities, the economic agent has its own economic purpose whose realms, methods of realization, forms of presentation and functions are different, even fundamentally different. Some differences are minor, and are even the main characteristics and conditions of economic development, but some are a result of rivals' immoral beggar-thy-neighbor economic concepts and measures, the existence and development of which are bound to affect the benefit and development of the rivals, and ultimately affect the economic agents involved. Economic morals have the function of reconciling various economic activities to realize win–win or multi-win situations. In fact, in economically developed organizations and areas, the existing economic morals such as justice, fairness, integrity, and cooperation have been reconciling the interests of stakeholders. As Stephen R. Covey said that "only basic morality can give life to interpersonal skills,"[19] only economic morals can provide the necessary skills to maintain a harmonious relationship among stakeholders.

1.4 Pareto Optimality and its Moral Basis[20]

Since China launched its economic reforms in 1979, the country has been attracting the attention of the world with its rapid economic development. As the world's second largest economy, to maintain an optimal economic state and sound economic development, China should develop modern economic concepts based upon Pareto optimality and its profound moral basis.

Pareto optimality is a state of allocation of resources in which it is impossible to make any one individual better off without making at least one individual worse off during the process of allocating a certain amount of allocable resources to a set of individuals. Given an initial allocation of goods among a set of individuals, a change to a different allocation that makes at least one individual better off without making any other individual worse off is called a Pareto improvement. From the above, it can be seen that when Pareto optimality is realized, no further Pareto improvement can be made; and Pareto improvement is the optimal route and approach to realize Pareto optimality. Actually, "behind Pareto optimality is a moral restraint; that is to say, resource allocation is optimized when it is impossible and meaningless to make any one individual better off without making at least one individual worse off. When Pareto optimality has not been realized, Pareto improvement can be carried out to make at least one individual better off without making any other individual worse off (Yang 2003)."

"Pareto optimality is, of course, an economic principle concerning efficiency. It reveals that when Pareto optimality is achieved in an economy, the utilization of social resources and distribution of wealth reach a balance, which means there is no surplus or shortage, and thus efficiency and social welfare are maximized. It is worth noting that the realization of Pareto optimality requires not only economic principles, but also some basic morals. In other words, we can say that only when certain social moral principles are followed can Pareto optimality be realized (Tang 2005)." In fact, without morality, no economy can realize Pareto optimality—when morality is the shortest board of the economy, economic development will be largely limited. In many cases, the lack of morality primarily led to economic stagnation or setbacks, and the credit crisis or sudden collapse of famous and even time-honored companies. Therefore, morality is an important basis and condition for obtaining Pareto optimality. First, Pareto optimality is the optimality of economic justice. To realize Pareto optimality in resource allocation and human

---

[19] Stephen R. Covey. The Seven Habits of Highly Effective People: Restoring the Character Ethic. p. 21.

[20] In Search of the Moral Basis of Pareto Optimality, *Chinese Social Sciences Today, Philosophy Scholars' Personal Column*, Nov. 18, 2013.

equality, the means and goals must be just. The purpose of Pareto improvement is obtaining the optimal and most appropriate resource allocation. This requires respecting labor, being concerned with and realizing the due interests of man, and implementing just resource allocation without waste. In the process of market exchange with optimized resource allocation, justice plays the role of maximizing benefits; without justice, production is divorced from contribution, which destroys the laborers' enthusiasm for the next round of production, reduces the input of productive resources, and objectively hinders the creation of social wealth. In this case, the realization of Pareto optimality will be groundless. Second, Pareto optimality is about cooperation and mutual benefit. Pareto optimality describes the optimal state of resource allocation, the realization of which depends on optimizing laborers' enthusiasm for labor through optimal resource allocation, and the teamwork and dedication of laborers. In a market mechanism, the allocation of resources, especially productive resources, is always accompanied by competition. Actually, in a rational sense, competition is beneficial for the optimality of resource allocation. Therefore, stakeholders need to support and promote each other to realize win–win or multi-win situations. Third, Pareto optimality requires integrity. Resources are allocated to a set of individuals or organizations as per certain rules, in the process of which, the disclosure of information, like resource reserve, allocation basis, allocation methods, and allocation results, is required in order to reduce the cost of transactions. The acquisition and identification of information is also required, along with negotiation and supervision, as well as information regarding breaches, thus optimizing the results of resource allocation. In a society where integrity is overwhelmed by fraud and cheating, people have to spend a lot of energy, time, and money on preventing and solving disputes. As a result of this, lots of resources cannot be used in productive activities and a lot of social wealth cannot be created (Tang 2005). Fourth, Pareto optimality is the optimality of human-centered product or economic gain design. Products or economic gains are the resources for the existence and reproduction of man. The more such resources can meet the needs of man, the more they can improve his living and production quality, and the more they can promote the economic development of society.

1.5 The Economic Value of Morality[21]

The economic value of morality has been a controversial topic since the latter half of the twentieth century. In the 1960s, researchers in developed countries such as the USA brought up the issue of corporate social responsibility. This attracted increasing concern, as some economists argued that corporate behavior is always for-profit, and hence tried to resist the call for corporate social responsibility coming from the academic world and other sectors of society. In the 1970s, some phi-

[21] Originally published on *Social Sciences in China,* Issue 4, 2011; reprinted on *Xinhua Digest,* Issue 23, 2011; reprinted on Ethics, Issue 10, 2011.

losophers decided to break through disciplinary boundaries by introducing moral theories into commerce, thus laying the foundation for the development of business ethics (De George 1987). Later, the Enron Scandal in 2002, and the financial crisis which swept across the world in 2008, forced Western academics to readdress the role of morality within economics, as well as the economic value of morality.

In the early 1990s, when China proclaimed the establishment of the socialist market economy, academics had a fierce debate over the economic value of morality. The debate was dominated by two opposing views: one that morality is useless and the other that morality is omnipotent. The former holds that the market economy can progress naturally without the help of morality, while the latter holds that morality is the key to everything: it not only promotes the construction of the market economy but also leads its very development. Although both views involve the economic and social functions of morality, neither takes into account the economic value of morality in the strict sense of business ethics. Even so, the argument promoted the formation and development of China's business ethics as an independent discipline.[22] In the mid-1990s, some researchers put forward the idea that "the market economy is a moral economy," thinking that market economy is rule-based, and morality is all about rules and regulations. "Actually, regulating the market economy is about regulating the behaviors of economic agents, which includes individuals, communities and society at large (Xia 1995)." Before long, economists were arguing over the relationship between morality and economics.[23] Opinions like "morality is useless" and "economics is immoral" were criticized by economists and ethicists alike. To some extent though, an academic consensus was reached that "the market economy is a moral economy."[24] A representative view from economist Wei Sen is that "it is a form of moral color-blindness if one fails to see that market institutions have an ethical dimension and that the market works with the support of morality (Wei 2002)"; as a result, "dialogue should be

[22] In China, the study on business ethics as a discipline started from the early 1990s. Since then, a number of papers discussing the subject of business ethics, economic morality, the economic significance of the economy, the consistency between the commodity economy and moral progress, the relation between profit making and morality, the traditional Chinese business ethics, etc. have sprung out, and works studying theories concerning business ethics have also come out. In the past 20 years, the disciplinary system of business ethics has been basically constructed in China.

[23] Representative works appearing during the controversy: Fan Gang, Morality in the Eyes of Economists, *Economic News,* Dec. 8, 1994; Liu Fushou, Shouldn't Economists be Moral? *Exploration and Free Views,* Issue 7, 1995; Jia Chunxin, Could Economics Divorce from Morality? *Finance and Economics,* Issue 6, 1995, Fan Gang, "Immoral" Economics, *Reading,* Issue 6, 1998; Sheng Hong, Morality, Utility and Others, *Reading,* Issue 7, 1998; Yao Xinyong, The Moral Mistakes in "Immoral" Economics, *Reading*, Issue 11, 1998; Luo Weidong, Economics and Morality—Rethinking of Some Economic Trends, *Zhejiang Academic Journal,* Issue 5, 2001, etc.

[24] Representative works interpreting the significance of morality in the economy or economics during the period from mid-1990s to early twenty-first century: *Economics and Ethics* (Li Yining, Sanlian Bookstore, 1995), Morality: A Significant Variable in the Study of Economic Activities and Economics (Zhang Jun, *Social Sciences in China*, Issue 2, 1999), The Moral Dimension of the Market Economy (Wan Junren, *Social Sciences in China*, Issue 2, 2000), How Economists be Moral (Xu Dajian, *Morality and Civilization*, Issue 5, 2002), etc.

resumed between modern economics and contemporary ethics (Wei 2003)." From the history of Western economic thought, it can be found that "moral economics" is by no means a new concept. Keynes himself once said, "Economics is essentially a moral science, not a natural science."[25] The Nobel laureate Amartya Kumar Sen also clearly stated that "the separation of economics and ethics has resulted in the immiserization of welfare economics, and greatly weakened the basis of descriptive economics and forecasting economics" and "as the gap between modern economics and ethics grows wider, modern economics has faced serious immiserization (Sen 2000)." From the above, it can be seen that economics cannot ignore morality, and hence neither can the study of economics.

The academic study of the economic value of morality, currently experiencing steady development, needs to be taken further and to adopt a broader scope, both at home and abroad. The reason is that on the one hand, the existing economic discourse system rejects such study, while on the other hand traditional ethics cannot effectively analyze modern economic behavior. If we break down the problem of the economic value of morality into the two sub-issues of whether morality has economic value and how to turn morality into economic value, then mainstream academia will surely give a definite answer to the former but cannot give a satisfactory answer to the latter. Based on the positive effect morality can have on the modern market economy, this book tries to investigate the economic value of morality as a special productive resource. It then goes on to interpret the positive role played by morality during its transformation into economic value and examines the reasonable transformation limits, thus fostering the further development and adjustment of China's socialist market economy.

1.5.1 Morality is a Productive Spiritual Resource That Can Create Economic Value

All value is ultimately created through production, and so it is with the economic value of morality. Therefore, it is necessary to analyze how morality is involved in the creation of value during the production process. This can then be used as the background for academics to put forward the concept of[26] "moral productivity."

[25] Quoted from Wei Sen, The Nature of Economics and Economics in the Perspective of Philosophy, *Economics*, Vol. 6, Issue 3, Apr. 2007.

[26] Morality, as a kind of consciousness, affects the attitude of laborers as a productive force towards production; adjusts the relations between the elements of productivity; saves living labor and means of production; and ultimately improves labor productivity. As economist Chen Caihong said, "Ideologies like morality are of indispensable great value for the progress of human society," and "as a 'useful' ideology, morality has really, as being proved by history and reality, helped human society to save various costs and increase benefits" (Chen Caihong, Morality and Utility—An Understanding on and a Choice Faced by Modern Economics, *Southeast Academic Research,* Issue 6, 2001). In *The Market of Virtue,* Michael Baurmann put forward the concept of "moral productivity." He did not specially interpret the expression, only saying that it is the role played by morality in economic behavior (*The Market of Virtue,* translated by Xiao Jun and Huang Chengye,

Production theory is always a focus of concern for researchers. Even though researchers will hold different opinions, they generally agree on the importance of spiritual elements in production. Adam Smith described straightforward productive power as "mere bodily labor" in *The Wealth of Nations,* but in *The Theory of Moral Sentiments,* he also stressed the significance of morality in production. Liszt and Storch stressed that production cannot lead to wealth without the physical power, intelligence, and morality of human beings (Jing 2003). Marx's general production theory emphasizes that spiritual production, including morality, is indispensable to production, and that it directly influences and restricts the direction of "special production."[27] In fact, the formation of material productive forces relies on the use of mental strength, which includes morality. "As a productive force, human beings are also natural objects, alive with awareness, and labor itself is the manifestation of productive forces";[28] therefore, "without human beings as a 'subjective productive force' and the conceptual orientation thereof, productive forces will just be 'dead productive forces' rather than 'living social productive forces' (Wang 1998b)." Morality, as a special productive force, is the "subjective productive force" of living labor, and the spiritual support and soul of the value provided by these material productive forces. During the course of creating value, morality does not play a direct or explicit role, but rather exerts an indirect or implicit influence. It permeates the production process and materializes in the objective outcomes of living labor. For this problem, we can analyze it from both macroscopic and microcosmic perspectives, as well as from both static and dynamic perspectives.

First, let us look at the role morality plays in production from macroscopic and microcosmic perspectives.

Macroscopically, or from the perspective of society in general, morality can create a good environment for production, as well as provide the necessary social conditions for the development of production. At the same time, it is also able to reduce the associated "social cost." Modern socialized mass production is a kind of comprehensive social production, rather than mere material production. Morality, as an intrinsic spiritual element of production, has its own special role to play, a role which has nonetheless been long ignored.[29] During the value creation process of

---

China Social Sciences Publishing House, 2003). I agree with the concept of "moral productivity," which indicates the role played by morality in the process of value creation. It should be pointed out that "moral productivity," in this case, means a spiritual element which plays a special role in the process of materials production, not a real, existing entity.

[27] Marx's production theory falls into "special production theory" and "general production theory." The former means the production of materials, while the latter refers to production and reproduction of the whole human society including the production of materials, man, spirit, and social relations. See Yu Wujin, Maxist Philosophy as a Comprehensive Production Theory, *Philosophical Researches,* Issue 8, 2003.

[28] *Collected Works of Karl Marx and Friedrich Engels,* Vol. 5, People's Publishing House, 2009, p. 235.

[29] Material production guides other types of production as their basis, and on the contrary, other types of production will, to different degrees, affect and restrict the development of material production. Morality penetrates into other types of production in different ways and affects materials production indirectly.

production, morality can be seen within a product's design philosophy, in order to achieve convenience, durability, and efficiency. It thus plays a role in defining the function of a product, and will materialize in high-quality products that are made to meet the demands of human beings. Furthermore, as a kind of standard or yardstick, it is also involved in the stipulation of production conditions and labor composition in the form of living labor. As a "non-institutional constraint"[30] of production, morality is necessary for improving product quality and reducing social production costs. Of course, the morality involved in creating value must be consensus-based; otherwise, it would be impossible for morality to play its part.

Microcosmically, morality participates in creating value through the spiritual power and support it gives to laborers as individuals. First of all, morality, which reflects the ideal relationship between people in social life, is the embodiment of ethical values; morality guides people to act in a way that enables them to reach a rational survival mode through cognition and practice. Second, morality also reveals the rational development of people, as well as the rational development trends of society as a whole. Laborers, as the primary productive force, need to establish their value in life while following reasonable moral rules, thus adapting themselves to social development. Third, reflecting the individual quality and feelings of laborers, morality acts as a stabilizer to influence a laborer's attitude toward his or her work. Without basic moral sentiments, the "living labor" will merely become an instrumental "dead productive force." Of course, the individual moral "preference" can only create value when it acts directly as a social moral. Therefore, only morals that have been internalized into the values of laborers and have become part of the moral rules that guide their behavior, can genuinely be said to have created value. Occasional moral consciousness and moral impulses can hardly be converted into constant behavior.

Now, we examine the role morality plays in production from static and dynamic perspectives.

Statically, morality participates in creating value in two ways. First, it participates in the forming of a social productive force. "Every productive force is an acquired force, the product of previous activity. Thus the productive forces are the result of man's practical energy, but that energy is in turn circumscribed by the conditions in which man is placed by the productive forces already acquired, by the form of society which exists before him, which he does not create, which is

[30] In this case, "noninstitutional" factors refer to rules and regulations coming into being gradually in people's social life in a long period of time, such as customs, ethics, morals, cultural tradition, values, concepts, and ideologies which impose nonmandatory restriction on human behavior. Douglass C. North held that in the restraint system of human behavior, informal institutions play a very important role—even in the most developed economic system, formal institutions only constitute a very small part of the general restraints determining human behavior, and most of the behavior space for human behavior selection is restrained by informal institutions. See Douglass C. North, *Institutions, Institutional Change and Economic Performance,* translated by Liu Shouying, Shanghai Sanlian Bookstore, 1994, p. 140.

the product of the preceding generation."[31] Those "social forms," representing the common behavior of people involved in social production, undoubtedly include morality as a form of social awareness. Second, morality is embodied within value as a product of labor.[32] "In the labor-process, man's activity, with the help of the instruments of labor, effects an alteration, designed from the commencement, in the material worked upon. The process disappears in the product, the latter is a use-value, Nature's material adapted by a change of form to the wants of man. Labor has incorporated itself with its subject: the former is materialized, the latter transformed. That which in the laborer appeared as movement, now appears in the product as a fixed quality without motion. The blacksmith forges and the product is a forging."[33] Engels pointed out that labor "still contains the third element which the economist does not think about—I mean the mental element of invention, of thought, alongside the physical element of sheer labor." During the process of production, as a manifestation of living labor, the "spiritual element of invention and thought" is materialized, and obviously, the "spiritual element" here will also contain morality. Morality cannot directly change the natural attributes or the subject of labor, nor can it directly sculpt the attributes of the product of labor, and hence it cannot directly create the value within a product. However, through the approach taken by the laborers, morality can act on other factors of production to create specific attributes or optimize functions of the product. In this way, production can better satisfy the demands of the consumer and play a role in creating value. In short, the process through which morality participates in creating value is the process through which laborers input moral values into the product of their labor in order to better meet the demands of the consumer. In this sense, the reasonable limit of the consumers' demands is one of the bases on which to judge the reasonable limit for morality's ability to participate in "creating value."

Dynamically, the way in which morality participates in creating value is a process. It has been stated that the means of production mark the level of development of productive forces, while the morality of the laborers involved are also a further indicator. First of all, the level of productive forces shall be measured by a static constitution of production factors, and also by the integration effects of production factors—this refers to a reasonable and effective organization of laborers, production means, and the nature of the labor involved. These thus play a joint role within the overall production process. However, the reasonable allocation of production factors cannot be realized without some form of standard for morality. As previously mentioned, morality affects production efficiency by affecting worker behavior, while a higher moral standard can also enhance worker responsibility. Furthermore, morality determines the ways in which laborers, production

[31] *Collected Works of Karl Marx and Friedrich Engels,* Vol. 10, People's Publishing House, 2009, p. 43.

[32] *Collected Works of Karl Marx and Friedrich Engels,* Vol. 1, People's Publishing House, 2009, p. 67.

[33] *Collected Works of Karl Marx and Friedrich Engels,* Vol. 5, People's Publishing House, 2009, p. 211.

means, and products can mutually influence each other, as well as influencing the reasonableness of such combinations. Morality thus plays a role in improving both production means and the finished product itself. Moreover, morality is a powerful tool for coordinating interpersonal relationships and creating a spiritual bond to optimize labor relations. Harmonious internal relations within a labor community can effectively reduce "friction consumption" and work as a "lubricant" to maintain these relations. Modern socialized mass production is based on a complex social division of labor and value exchange; even the simplest production process involves multiple instances of cooperation. A rational sense of morality helps laborers to establish a concept of cooperative competition, something that will improve production efficiency and create more social wealth, thus pushing social production and social interaction toward a more reasonable direction. Finally, the level of productive forces is not equal to the effectiveness of temporary production. If value is created at the cost of sacrificing long-term interests such as environmental ethics or ecological morality, the process is fundamentally destructive to productive forces. Only when morality is positively correlated to rational goals of social development can it truly create value.

In conclusion, morality is an indispensible spiritual element of modern mass production. As an embodiment of value and a regulatory system for ethical relations, morality is a key part of the social production process. Production effectiveness and economic benefit are all closely connected with morality. In this sense, it can be said that the role played by morality in creating value can be converted into "productive resources." That is to say, morality can become a productive spiritual force for creating economic value.

1.5.2 The Unique Role Played by Moral Capital in the Increment of Value and the Restraint of Capital

As a kind of spiritual resource, morality, which consists primarily of moral rules, values, and social customs, plays a unique role in the creation of value. As far as economic activities are concerned, all moral elements conducive to making profit can be classified as spiritual resources. Given the unique role played by morality in the creation and the increment of value, some researchers even raise morality to the height of moral capital.[34]

[34] Domestic scholars Luo Weidong and Wang Zeying mentioned the concept of moral capital in 1998 and 1999, respectively. See Luo Weidong, The Economic Functions of Morality, *Journal of Zhejiang Provincial Party School,* Issue 1, 1998; and Wang Zeying and Liu Xiangbo, How Moral Capital Pulls out the Market Economy from the Dilemma of Low Efficiency, *Hunan Normal University Social Sciences Journal*, Issue 5, 1999. In 2000, I systematically interpreted the concept of "moral capital" in *Moral Capital,* which attracted the attention of the academic circle. See *The Business Ethics in China Yearbook* (2000–2009). Later, I discussed the mode of action and reasons of existence of moral capital in a series of papers. See *Moral Capital* and Business Ethics (*Selected Works of Wang Xiaoxi*), People's Publishing House, 2009. In 2003, Spanish scholar Alejo G. Sison published The Moral Capital Of Leaders: Why Virtue Matters (translated and published by Central

It should be noted that the "capital" in moral capital does not refer to the classical concept of capital as discussed by Marx, but rather falls within the scope of general capital.[35] Social morality guides, normalizes, restrains, and coordinates production in its own unique way, promoting an increase in economic value. Therefore, according to the general concept of capital, morality, as a spiritual element with a direct effect on value, does indeed have capital attributes. In other words, moral capital reflects the capital of production factors within the scope of general capital, rather than acting in line with the classical concept of capital working as an analysis tool to reflect or criticize the capitalist social system and its economic relations, as posited in Marx's theories on political economics. In his view, capital is not an object, but rather a value that in turn creates surplus value. Capital belongs to the category of the economy, and furthermore the category of economic relations. It presents the theory that capital exploits the differences in wage labor between the capitalist classes and the working classes. Moral capital deems morality to be a kind of valuable productive source, enabling people to analyze the special role played by morality in the increment of value. This is the difference between the concept of moral capital and that of Marx's classical capital, and also the starting point for understanding the theoretical space and logistical boundaries of moral capital. Economist Luo Weidong explicitly defines the economic functions and effects of morality as "moral capital"—"The economic functions of morality and capital are similar—they combine economic activities and create considerable benefits. We can borrow Bourdieu's broad concept of capital to call morality 'moral capital' (Luo 1998)." From the perspective of social utility, moral capital is not only a spiritual element that can promote and maintain the importance of value but also a value orientation containing rational social concepts which can realize the win–win situation of combined economic and social benefits.

Morality as a spiritual resource has the dual values of regulation and purpose. For the former, morality regulates and restrains people through rationality, and helps them realize their goals in a way that is beneficial for social development. However, morality is much more than just an instrumental form of rationality. In addition to the increment of value, moral capital can also restrain capital to a certain extent. Therefore, morality as a spiritual resource is the combination of "morality in the form of capital" and "moral capital."

Morality can increase value in the following three aspects.

First, morality improves value through being able to activate physical capital. The nature of capital lies in constant movement, a phenomenon through which value

---

Compilation & Translation Press in 2005), in which he systematically expounded the mode of action, development, and management of moral capital. Although we discussed moral capital from different perspectives, I agree with the opinion of Sison, that is, moral capital can guide, regulate, restrict and reconcile economic behavior, ensure the rationality of production and operating activities, and maximize economic benefits. I think that moral capital generalizes the economic value of morality in the scope of general capital; it emphasizes on the unique roles played by morality in increasing economic benefits.

[35] Capital generally means the value of capital derived from value creation of living labor. All material and spiritual elements affecting the roles played by living labor during the process of value creation and increment are of the attributes of capital.

is created and increased. Morality can activate physical capital in a number of ways. First, it accelerates the speed of movement of physical capital. Through setting moral standards for organizational institutions and harnessing people's potential, morality optimizes resource distribution and vitalizes tangible assets, while also encouraging manufacturers to produce things in a more proactive way. Furthermore, morality can be constantly manifested and accumulated in physical capital, and be turned into capital stock in the form of corporate reputation and brand competitiveness, improving the added value of tangible assets. Finally, morality can drive technological progress and promote the commercialization of technical outcomes.

Second, morality reduces transaction costs by optimizing the "neighborhood effect." In a business environment characterized by amoral companies, low social integrity and a chaotic market order, various speculative behaviors, even illegal behaviors, are very likely to propagate. Therefore, "morality matters a lot.... It can lower transaction costs and promote economic growth (Zhang 1999)." In particular, morality can optimize economic activity, turning certain inefficient "neighborhood effects" into effective ones. Allen E. Buchanan mentioned in *Ethics, Efficiency, and the Market* that "critics of the market have been quick to point out the pervasiveness and seriousness of neighborhood effects, or externalities, as a key source of the market's failure to achieve efficient outcomes". During a company's decision-making process, morality clears up inefficient "neighborhood effects" by internalizing negative externalities based on the consideration of detrimental third-party effects. He also pointed out that "positive externalities (beneficial third-party effects) are also inefficient." "This is similar to the way vaccination not only benefits those who have been vaccinated but also those who have not, since the overall probability of infection is lowered (Allen 1991)." Through strengthening an individual's sense of responsibility, morality can encourage individuals in a market economy environment to control their behavior autonomously, encouraging them to act in a relatively uniform way which can thus preclude the possibility of "free riding (Douglass 1991)." For example, Douglass C. North thought that "these concepts make people restrict their behavior in such a way that they do not become free riders." It can be seen that morality can not only reduce, and even remove, the design costs of "formal institutions" but also minimize unnecessary "transaction costs," and ultimately establish a harmonious transaction environment.

Third, morality can help appreciate financial capital through regulating and guiding the market. In a capital market development, morality plays the role of regulating the market to realize a more rational operation model. At present, both international and domestic capital markets need further regulation, since moral deficiencies and a faulty credit system in the financial sector have greatly influenced the efficient operation of modern financial systems.[36] "Injecting" moral resources into financial capital, or enhancing moral restraint, can improve the morality level of financial professionals, make certain that third-party rating agencies can issue audit reports in a fair and nonpartial way, and guarantee the authenticity and credibility

[36] For the financial crisis sweeping across the world in 2008, one of the main reasons is the lack of moral capital in the financial field. See Wang Xiaoxi and Zhang Zhidan, China's Ethical Responsibility in the Financial Crisis, *China Education Daily* (Theory), Dec. 4, 2008.

of information. Additionally, morality is helpful in regulating the management of listed companies, eradicating international transactions, and guiding the rational flow of financial capital, thus appreciating financial capital as well as creating social benefits. On July 31, 2011, the *Financial Times* launched eight FTSE4GOOD "moral indexes" at the London Stock Exchange in the UK. When explaining the idea of "moral indexes," the *Financial Times* CEO Mark Makepeace said, "While choosing investees, investors show a strong preference toward companies with a sense of social responsibility. Recently, investment in such companies has quadrupled (Liu 2001)." The launch of "moral indexes" is the prime example to illustrate that morality can regulate and guide the capital market.

1.5.3 Business Operations: Putting Morality's Economic Value into Practice

During the development of the market economy, morality's economic value is mainly reflected in the moral operation of companies. Therefore, the operating activities of companies are a manifestation of morality's economic value. In the socialist market economy, companies are the subjects of economic activity, and they need to build their morality to realize moral operation while pursuing their goal of economic benefit.[37] It was said by economist Zhang Jun that, "although a company produces 'private goods', its productive forces are 'public goods'. The motive of self-interest alone cannot ensure the efficiency of a company; it also needs moral values such as team spirit and corporate culture, the establishment of which is closely related to morality (Zhang 1999)." Therefore, the management of a company should realize that morality is the core competitiveness of that company, something that can guarantee its sustainable development.

Corporate moral operations represent a concept that is rich in content, and including moral management, moral marketing, and moral leadership. Only with multidimensional moral operation models can companies maximize the value of their human resources, fully mobilize the potential of their employees, improve their products' market share, and ultimately establish their core competitiveness.

1.5.3.1 Moral Management and Human Resources Development

In the history of management theory both at home and abroad, human resources was not considered as an important asset until modern times. Modern business theorist Daniel A. Wren holds that the value of human resources lies primarily in two aspects. First, industrial psychology tries to establish a scientific foundation for personnel management within companies, and as a result, the career design of "making

[37] "Moral operation" does not mean the morality of operation, but moral corporate business activities.

the best use of everyone" replaces the original plan of choosing "first-class workers." Second, in contrast to conventional personnel management, modern human resources management puts more stress on strategic design (Daniel 2000). From the history of management theory as described by Wren, it can be found that developing the intellectual potential and multidimensional qualities of employees lies at the core of modern business management practices. Business management activities focusing on human resources management contain a significant number of regulated and purposive moral considerations, which I shall call "moral management." Essentially, such moral management is a kind of human-oriented moral management, which can maximize the value of human resources and establish a company's core competitiveness. Its functions are reflected in the following aspects.

First, in terms of organizational structures, moral management can expand an employee's freedom to work, since flexible moral management is conducive to the establishment of flexible organizational structures. Conventional management holds that a narrow management scope ensures management's rigorous control of subordinates. Correspondingly, a very professional organizational structure can also be confronted with the significant drawbacks of rigid organization, low human-oriented management and a lack of vitality. However, modern management thinks that a wider management scope helps to increase organizational efficiency, while a "flat" organizational design can avoid over-professionalization of departments so that a flexible team-based organization can replace the rigid departmental division (Stephen 1997). A wider management scope and a diversified department design can expand the space within which employees are free to work. Moral management can help companies to continuously adapt to the external environment, and help them recognize and handle various emergencies, thus improving internal human relations at the same time.

Next, in terms of management activities, moral management can stimulate people's creative potential, thus improving a company's innovative capabilities. In conventional business management, management activities only focus on the low-level needs of people as an object of management, and ignore their high-level needs. In contrast, modern business management focuses on the comprehensive development of people. It meets the high-level needs of people in terms of their self-realization, while also arousing the creative potential of people at a higher level.

Finally, in terms of the relationship between moral management and a company's performance and efficiency, moral management can improve an individual's abilities through promoting teamwork, something that is conducive to improving overall efficiency and performance. Peter Ferdinand Drucker holds that in new organizations, "the responsibilities of traditional departments will change greatly to include standard maintenance, personnel training and work allocation, rather than just handling business," and that this transformation would require teams to "reach higher levels of self-discipline and bear more responsibilities in terms of maintaining interpersonal relationships and communication." Teamwork is established based on organizational goals and functions, as well as the cohesion of morality and cooperation (Peter 1999). In some sense, the morality of cooperation plays a more important role in increasing the efficiency of teamwork. It helps create a healthy social environment within a team, and at the same time greatly lowers internal "friction costs" and improves efficiency and performance. All of these are very important for companies in the modern market economy. Practice has proven that a team-based organization held together by morality tends to be more stable and efficient.

1.5.3.2 Moral Marketing and Market Share

Marketing is the process of value exchange between companies and consumers. Philip Kotler believes that modern marketing comprises a huge marketing network, the process sequence of which includes five steps—inbound logistics, operations, outbound logistics, sales, and service, and that its support system consists of four parts—purchasing, technical development, human resources management, and company infrastructure (Philip 1997). On the whole, modern business marketing activities mainly involve three kinds of relationships, namely, intercompany relationships, interdepartmental relationships, and the relationship between companies and consumers.

During the process of marketing, a successful company must build harmonious relationships between its various stakeholders. The marketing activities of a company are conducted to meet the demands of consumers, but more importantly, to build trust between the company and its stakeholders based on integrity. This trust of relationship maintains a mutually beneficial relationship and helps the company to improve competitiveness. In this sense, we can say that trust-based business marketing is actually a kind of moral marketing strategy, which can improve the market share of a company through the following approaches.

First, moral marketing builds brand competitiveness. P. Koslowski wrote in *The Principles of Ethical Economics,* "In today's economy, non-material activities grow much faster than material activities, and the culture of a service-oriented economy grows faster than the material production of an industrial economy. The symbolic and non-material values used to assess commodities have become material values through the saturation of materials (Koslowski 1997)." Therefore, in the market economy, product marketing is actually a form of cultural marketing, the functions of which rest on convincing consumers to acknowledge the cultural values of a commodity. Once the values are established, consumers will accept products as a symbol of cultural values, and develop habitual, even dependent buying behaviors. Therefore, a successful company can always build a stable trust relationship with its consumers through the promotion of product culture and values, thus establishing its brand competitiveness.

Second, moral marketing builds corporate reputation. Corporate reputation is a kind of intangible asset, and represents the consumer trust accumulated during a long-term relationship. Moral marketing can improve corporate reputation from the following three aspects: building a long-term trust relationship between companies and suppliers, which lowers transaction costs and ensures cost-effective transactions; building a trust relationship between companies and consumers, which is embodied in consumer satisfaction toward the functionality, quality, and sales service of a company's products; and building an honest and faithful social image to exploit potential consumer demand through improved reputation.

Third, moral marketing improves organizational performance. Modern marketing is a marketing network formed by a number of value chains, including purchasing, supply chain, technical research and development (R&D), human resources management, support systems, and many more. The marketing network allocates resources according to marketing activities, in order to ensure that companies can provide consumers with the best services and most satisfactory products in the shortest time. In terms of marketing activities, interdepartmental cooperation plays a vital role in guaranteeing a smooth exchange of ideas, creating benefits for stakeholders, and finally improving the overall organizational performance. For example, technical R&D cannot be conducted without the market information fed back by the sales department. In fact, a sincere partnership is a prerequisite for an internal exchange of market information. Sufficient information exchange is the basis for building mutual trust, which creates benefits for stakeholders and ensures genuine cooperation. Therefore, a satisfactory commodity, though seemingly just reflecting its functionality, price, and after-sales service, is actually a manifestation of morals.

1.5.3.3 Moral Leadership and Corporate Development

Leaders and managers are two totally different concepts. In *Management,* Stephen P. Robbins defined them as follows: "managers are appointed, and they have legitimate power to reward and punish; their ability to influence is based on the formal authority inherent in their positions. In contrast, leaders may be appointed, or may emerge from within a group; they can influence others to perform beyond the actions dictated by formal authority," and "leaders are people who are able to influence others and who possess managerial authority (Stephen 1997)." Real leaders play professional roles, and more importantly, have a personal charisma, so "in the case of charismatic authority, it is the charismatically qualified leader who is obeyed by virtue of personal trust in his abilities, his heroism or his exemplary qualities so far as they fall within the scope of the individual's belief in his charisma (Max 1997)." Personal charisma does not grow from a particular position, but rather from some kind of moral leadership. Georges Enderle, while analyzing different leadership behaviors, developed the following typical moral internalization scheme: positionality–role personality–responsibility. He thinks that real leadership behavior is moral leadership with moral attributes. Moral leadership exists for two reasons: externally, "the development trend of the modern market economy is that non-economic factors, namely social and cultural ones (including moral factors), have increasingly penetrated into various aspects of economic activities, and now exhibit an increasing influence. They have even influenced entrepreneurs, whether unconsciously or subconsciously (Zhang 2005)." Internally, "leaders enjoy a certain freedom in their behavior within an organization due to their decision-making power. The larger this behavior space is, the more important they are in distributing resources (potential), the heavier the responsibility they bear, and the greater the significance of leadership ethics is for the functional relationships within a company."[38] For enterprises, the moral leadership of entrepreneurs is of direct or indirect economic value. Moral leadership behavior is one of the sources of increased value, and a spiritual manifestation of business ethics that pushes forward the sustainable development of an enterprise.

The internal relations between the moral leadership of entrepreneurs and the development of an enterprise can mainly be summarized in three aspects.

First, moral leadership arouses the entrepreneurial spirit of both entrepreneurs and employees, providing inexhaustible spiritual power for corporate development. In a market economy, leaders generally fulfill the roles of command, coordination, and motivation, which, in terms of leadership ethics, are referred to as leading, maintaining unity, and being a "key player," respectively.[39] Moral leaders can arouse the entrepreneurship of managers and employees, injecting inexhaustible spiritual power into corporate development.[40] Moral leaders, while encouraging their subordinates to achieve organizational goals, will also discuss business development strategies with them, greatly stimulating their creativity.

Second, moral leadership improves the leadership skills of entrepreneurs by cultivating a team spirit. A company cannot develop without good teamwork, which largely depends on the moral leadership of entrepreneurs. In *The Moral Capital of Leaders,* Alejo G. Sison pointed out, "Leadership is a two-way transformative and intrinsically moral relationship between a leader and his followers. The two parties involved in a leadership relationship—the leader and the followers—morally transform and elevate each other through their interaction. Thus, ethical leadership becomes the primary conduit through which not only people, but also the organization for which these people work, become ethical. Leadership nurtures personal ethics, allowing it to grow and encompass an auspicious organizational culture." It can, thus, be seen that "the core of leadership is ethics (Alejo 2005)." A leader without a strong sense of morality can hardly be a real leader in charge of a first-class team. Practice has proven that entrepreneurs with a history of great achievement and personal charisma, to the extent of being capable of influencing the public at large, are not only the symbols of corporate culture but also the spiritual leaders of corporate teams.

Third, moral leadership encourages companies to bear social responsibility, creating a healthy social environment for corporate development. According to Peter

[38] Horst Steinmann Albert Lohr, *Business Ethics,* p. 152.

[39] Horst Steinmann Albert Lohr, *Business Ethics*, p. 152.

[40] *In Why has Japan 'succeeded'? Western Technology and the Japanese Ethos* (Sichuan People's Publishing House, 1982), Michio Morishima from London School of Economics and Political Science discusses the Japanese ethos in the behavior model built based on regulations. In *Governing the Market* (Enterprise Management Publishing House, 1994), Robert Wade stresses the role played by "Confucian ethics" in Japan's commercialism. Another Japanese economist Masahiko Aoki interprets the teamwork, professional ethics, and code of conduct of the Japanese with the logic of the Game Theory in his book Information, *Motivation and Negotiation in Japanese Economy* (Commercial Press 1994). Those sources provide abundant research results for economists studying issues relating to the leadership of morality in economic activities. See Zhang Jun, Morality: A Significant Variable in the Study of Economic Activities and Economics, *Social Sciences in China*, Issue 2, 1999.

Pratley, "market demand forces enterprises to lower costs, adjust strategies, reduce investment and cut jobs. Even when faced with enormous market pressure, entrepreneurs must take morality seriously. Corporate managers can only achieve performance by integrating moral requests into corporate policy (Peter 1999)." Moral leadership requires entrepreneurs to be responsible for society at large, and not just that within their companies. According to *The Growth and Development of Chinese Entrepreneurs: A Special Investigative Report 2007,* among the 4586 investigated entrepreneurs, more than 90 % thought that "an excellent entrepreneur must have a strong sense of social responsibility."[41] It can be seen that more and more entrepreneurs have realized the importance of social responsibility, to the extent that it has now become a key criterion for successful entrepreneurs. Entrepreneurs with a good sense of social responsibility and with the "flood of morality flowing within (Wen 2009)" them, will lead their companies to be more responsible for society. This in turn will certainly improve the level of corporate capital stock, as well as create a healthy social environment and improve public opinion, all of which will be very helpful for further corporate development.

1.5.4 Discussion

This section focuses on the positive relationship between social morality and economic behaviors. First, it tries to remedy the defects found in existing research in terms of the externalization and representation of the economic value of morality. It does this by analyzing the complicated interaction and inherent law between morality and its economic value. Beyond this, it examines the dual nature of moral values and discusses the process of business operations, in order to find a cognitive model and an analytical framework to explain phenomena concerning economic ethics. All the efforts above aim at correcting the theoretical prejudice currently being displayed toward the economic value of morality (a prejudice caused by today's knowledge structure and disciplinary standpoints), and finally resolve the differences in the relationship between economy and morality. I believe that, even though analyzing and demonstrating morality's economic value with the above framework cannot cover all aspects of business ethics, it can nonetheless illuminate the primary aspects, something conducive to preventing the "extrinsic nature" currently found in economic ethics research from being too negative and one-sided.

It must be pointed out that although this book highlights the positive economic value of morality based on the above three aspects, this does not mean that I have ignored or denied the limitations thereof. On the contrary, I know very well that to correctly understand "morality's economic value," the basic theoretical premise is to find out "what kind of morality under what circumstance has economic value"; otherwise, our understanding of morality's economic value will land in the mire of

[41] http://business.sohu.com/20070415/n249440719.shtml.

The Growth and Development of Chinese Entrepreneurs: A Special Investigation Report 2007, Apr. 15, 2007, http://business.sohu.com/20070415/n249440719.shtml.

pan-moralism, due to blurred confines and conditions. That is, only when morality is internalized into the self-consciousness of economic agents and becomes a part of the production process can it become a kind of spiritual productivity that creates value. In addition, only when conforming to the laws of social development can morals positively influence economic activities; otherwise, they will merely hinder rather than promote economic development. Morals in daily life do not necessarily create economic value directly, and only those meeting certain preconditions are able to do so.

First, only when an abundant supply of moral resources is arranged by the basic economic system of society can morality create and increase value. Among various kinds of morality, social morality is most likely to fulfill this role. This means that abundant and stably supplied moral resources are a prerequisite for morality's ability to create and increase value. Under the arrangement of society's basic economic system, morality is transformed into economic value. Generally speaking, the arrangement of this economic system not only acts as an indicator for the flow of social benefit but also contains certain ethical principles and moral goals. Only economic systems and policies based on moral considerations can create proper economic benefits.

Next, a normative market development can only be realized within a just and credible moral environment. This is the precondition for moral operation. In a rule-based market economy, transactions are conducted according to certain rules. To realize the normal operation of the market economy, certain ethical principles and standards must be involved in the design and arrangement of such rules, and the most important principle is that of market justice. Generally, a trading system built on market justice is required in order to establish consumer trust. However, a market system does not always lead to consumer trust. Only when macroscopic market justice and microcosmic market integrity are acting together, is it possible to build up a trust relationship system based on the principle of justice. In this case, it would be fair to say that the "moral indexes" of a market environment are qualified, thus guaranteeing a smooth market development. If not, the market will be purely for profit, and the nature of morality in the market would turn from investment to speculation, meaning amoral market sentiment could penetrate into companies, breaking up their cohesion and making moral operation impossible. What would be even worse is that companies following "moral operation" would become the victims of morality. Therefore, a market with a moral environment in good order lays a foundation for the realization of "moral operation." In the view of Michael Baurmann, the economic market cannot survive for a long time without morality, because "when a society, regardless of the conditions of modern economic life, allows the free pursuit of self-interest, it will lead to a development tendency towards disintegration of the foundation of society, and ultimate self-destruction (Michael 2003)."

Finally, only when companies or other economic agents are willing to take on basic social responsibilities and fulfill their obligations as stakeholders, can morality create better job performance and production efficiency. Generally speaking, in the operational management of a company, there exists a network structure of stakeholders. To maximize the benefits of these stakeholders, a sense of social responsibility is needed as a basic principle to guide the construction of the network. In particular, the sense of social responsibility within a company can activate and integrate all elements of management and turn various "job requirements" into a sense of responsibility and obligation, thus improving job performance and production efficiency. In contrast, for a company lacking a sense of social responsibility, operational management will deteriorate into mere "job management," destabilizing the stakeholder network. For example, the primary cause of the global economic crisis triggered by the US subprime mortgage disaster was the financial institutions' lack of the sense of social responsibility.

For modern economic life, morality will create economic value, either naturally or spontaneously; otherwise, the economic value and value transformation of morality cannot be realized or maintained. Furthermore, in a society without a sound social operating mechanism, morality could not play its economic role, and we would witness an abnormal social phenomenon where moral people suffer losses but amoral people would make a lot of money. Actually, such a possibility can also remind us to pay attention to morality and its economic value within these complicated social processes.

In conclusion, morality's economic value is a complex theoretical question, and also a major practical question. From the perspective of ethics, all economic behaviors are human behaviors, and hence contain a certain morality. Even "amoral" economics can take egoism as its ethical basis and moral prerequisite. Discussing the economic value of morality is mainly aimed at solving the problem of ethical egoism in economics in order to provide a theoretical analytical framework that can transcend ethical egoism. This should enable us to guide economic rationality based on unreasonable values, and replace these with reasonable moral reasons, thus heading toward a more sound and rational social development.

1.6 Morality Creating Profits is Not the Materialization of Morality

In the series of my published works regarding business ethics, I claim that morality can create profits, which, according to some scholars, may be interpreted as advocating the materialization of morality. However, this is obviously not the case. The fact is that they are visibly different—underlining morality's functions of guidance and restriction is totally different from turning morality into a physical material.

In fact, the materialization of morality is a false concept. According to the fundamental ideas of modern natural science, the word "material" does not have a specific definition. In different disciplines, especially in the natural and social sciences, a material is signified and described differently; but generally, it refers to a substance with a given volume and weight. From the perspective of natural science, a material is composed of elementary particles like molecules, atoms, electrons, and ions; while from the perspective of social science, a material is, according to Lenin, a philosophical concept which indicates objective reality, which has objective reality as its essential characteristic, and which does not exist upon our feelings, but can be copied, photographed, and reflected by our feelings.

In this sense, the materialization of morality, or turning morality as a spiritual phenomenon into a material, is technically impossible. Moreover, materials in the objective world are all chemical materials, or mixtures thereof, and morality as a spiritual phenomenon could never have chemical properties. Besides, materials always exist in certain states of matter, and all materials in the objective world, from huge ones like the universe and celestial bodies to very tiny ones like molecules, atoms, and electrons vary a lot in their three basic states—solid, liquid, and gaseous state. None of these properties can be applied to the concept of morality. In other words, any "field" accessible to materials has nothing to do with morality. It can therefore be concluded that morality cannot be materialized, and it is impossible for morality to exist as a material.

As for the oft-cited transformation from the spiritual (including moral spirits) to the material, this actually refers to the "externalization" (affecting the shapes and characteristics) of spirits into materials, or the "externalization" of moral spirit, which plays the role of guidance and restriction, into materials with moral attributes. For example, when red stoneware is made into a teacup (teapot), it is impossible for something transformed from morality to exist as an ingredient. However, the shape, characteristics, and quality of the teacup (teapot) are designed to meet the needs of man and society, and its practicability and durability largely depend on the producer's moral concepts of caring for consumer needs and being responsible for his or her consumers. In addition, the market share of the teacup (teapot) also often depends on the moral spirit contained therein, or its externalization degree of moral spirit.

Therefore, morality-creating profits actually mean morality, through guidance and restriction, helping companies to obtain more benefits or profits, but does not suggest the materialization of morality. In fact, the concept of "moral capital" I have put forward and demonstrated contains two meanings. First, when a type or a category of products are produced to meet the needs of man and the society, such products will be favored by the market and become more and more popular. Second, when reconciling the relationship between the producer and the stakeholder, human-oriented or moral measures need to be taken, for only moral measures can, on the one hand, reduce, even remove, the friction cost caused by information block or conflicts of interest, and on the other hand, arouse the enthusiasm of employees and reduce the required labor time per unit product, thus reducing product costs. Third, in the sales process, a high level of integrity lies in fulfilling the promises made to consumers, which will in turn build consumer trust and expand the market share of products. At the same time, this will promote product sales and cash flow. It can thus be seen that guiding the production and sales of products using morality is an important basis and condition for making more profits. Besides, morality also plays the role of restraining any improper behavior on the part of the proprietor, in order to guarantee that the company will not decline or collapse due to immoral production or sales practices. This is a precondition for the company to make profits. It also needs to be pointed out that in my concept of "moral productivity," morality is not a kind of material productivity, but a spiritual element of productivity, a kind of spiritual productivity.

According to Marx, machines, as a kind of dead productivity, must be activated by subjective spiritual productivity in order to become labor productivity. That is, although productivity is manifested as materials, the human spiritual state, especially moral consciousness, is the element that affects laborers' value orientation and labor enthusiasm. Their cognition, improvement, and utilization of tools (machines) are the main features of productivity; and their ecological consciousness is the key to developing and utilizing interdisciplinary subject resources. Therefore, to improve productivity levels, it is necessary to improve the moral consciousness of laborers, thus advancing the optimal existence and function of productivity elements.

1.7 Internal Combination of Ethics and the Economy[42]

In recent years, the relationship between ethics and the economy has been a major concern for the emerging interdisciplinary subject of business ethics. However, although the concept of "business ethics" has been widely used, related theoretical problems like "what business ethics is" have not been clearly solved yet, meaning the relationship between the economy and ethics is not clear, neither practically nor theoretically. Given this background, this section tries to clarify the logical relationship between the economy and ethics, and the interdependence between the two. Namely, the fact that in the economic sphere, the economy cannot be interpreted without morality, and that morality also cannot be interpreted without the economy.

1.7.1 The Birth and Significance of Business Morality

In the late 1970s, business ethics was born as a new discipline in the USA. Soon afterward, this discipline took root in Europe and China throughout the 1980s and 1990s (De George 1987; Wang et al. 2005b). Due to differences in historical and cultural traditions, business organization and political conditions, these geographical areas adopted different models and approaches in developing business ethics. However, in the view of many scholars, the appearance of the concept of "business ethics" in these areas presents a characteristic of universal meaning; that is to say, the combination of the economy and ethics, and the birth of business ethics, actually reflect a new academic attitude and a theoretical supposition from economic society and the intelligentsia after experiencing various business "scandals" in the latter half of the twentieth century.

However, in spite of the wide and constant development of business ethics movements worldwide, and in spite of the rapid development of business ethics in interdisciplinary exchanges, thus far, the internal combination of ethics and the economy still lacks a clear value gist and a systematic theoretical framework to provide an

[42] *Philosophical Researches*, Issue 6, 2007.

intellectual basis for its legality. The reason is that avoiding studying the metatheories of business ethics has delayed the formation of any general theories thereof, and hindered the development of business ethics as a discipline. In this context, "problem- and action-oriented" business ethics is popular among economic ethicists. As the president of the International Society of Business, Economics, and Ethics Georges Enderle said, "My proposal is not a general theory of business ethics, which, according to me, is still too early to be put forward. It is rather a conceptual understanding of business ethics which advocates a 'top-down' method by integrating a number of basic characteristics, and focusing on a method for 'problem-and action-oriented' business ethics (Georges 2002)." The famous American economic ethicist Richard T. De George also mentioned that business ethics aims at providing a problem-oriented systematic action framework to integrate the knowledge of various principles, thus changing the ethical qualities of economic behavior at different levels (De George 1987). It needs to be pointed out that such a framework has not been formed today.

The reason why there are still no general theories regarding business ethics is the lack of interdisciplinary dialogues, which is fundamentally caused by the interdisciplinary barriers existing at a deeper level. In 2002, Norman E. Bowie, professor at the departments of strategic management and philosophy at the University of Minnesota wrote *Business Ethics, Philosophy, and the Next 25 Years* at the invitation of *Business Ethics Quarterly* where he acted as a governing board member to celebrate its tenth anniversary. In the article, he said that no discipline could provide a systematic knowledge framework and a powerful theoretical basis for business ethics in the way that moral philosophy can. However, American moral philosophers seem to be reluctant to engage in the study of business ethics, and management professors cannot solve profound theoretical problems in most cases due to their lack of ethical knowledge. Moral philosophers study business ethics based on a collection of traditional mainstream ethical knowledge such as utilitarianism, deontology, and virtue ethics, and they only take business ethics phenomena as the theoretical externalization and empirical materials of such traditional knowledge (Bowie 2000). This will ultimately mean that issues concerning business ethics will usually fall into the scope of traditional ethics.

In this sense, if we cannot find an intellectual basis for the internal combination of ethics and the economy to help us promote the formation of general theories on business ethics, the legality of the disciplinary knowledge of business ethics will be questioned, and business ethics will lose its independence due to the intervention of theories from other disciplines. As an immediate consequence, many special issues appearing in different economic sectors often cannot find any theoretical support or intellectual basis when they are in a dilemma, and it will not be practical to solve such issues using broad or microscopic theories. Therefore, without the necessary theoretical basis, the approach to put the rational-seeming "problem-oriented" action framework into practice will turn into a strategic pattern dominated in turn by different action plans. As a result, a unified action framework cannot be formed, which is in fact something primarily caused by a lack of general theories. However, the primary cause of the tension between the practice and general theories of business ethics is the tension between the principles relating to business ethics—there are barriers between the logical thinking models and the knowledge standpoints, as well as barriers between the different principles. As Amartya Sen said in *On Ethics and Economics,* economic theories avoid analyzing deep-seated rules and ignore the roles played by ethics when practically describing human behavior. This leads to a severe immiserization of modern economics (Sen 2003). Besides, such barriers can also cause controversy surrounding the question of "should economists study morality or not?"

1.7.2 The Economy's Endogenous Morality and its Structure

According to Marxist moral genetics, moral phenomena in human society cannot be independently interpreted without their corresponding economic living conditions; and likewise, morality is required in any economic system. The endogenous morality of the economy can primarily be seen in maintaining the rules and supporting the values of a given economy. We can understand the endogenous morality of the economy from the following four aspects.

1.7.2.1 Coexistential Relationship

De George believed that business ethics could be understood from the two perspectives: business morality and academic research. The difference between the two lies in the fact that the former influences economic life through general moral principles or rules, such as "do not lie," "do not steal," and "do not cheat." In this sense, morality exists outside economic life, and moral principles and rules are applied within the economic sphere in the same way as they are applied in other social spheres. The latter, on the other hand, tries to implant an ethical way of behaving into economic activities through a framework shared by economics and ethics, in order to increase ethical qualities at different behavioral levels and improve economic life as well (De George 1987). In my view, this is just the perspective from which modern society views issues concerning business ethics: in the former case, morality looks on the economy; while in the latter case, they form an interaction. Generally speaking, social structure can be considered as a social relationship system built according to certain rules, while the socioeconomic structure is the way that laborers jointly conduct an economic activity with economic relationships as the subject. However, an economic relationship not only stands for an economic attribute but also contains, in the sense of social relations, the shared basis of various social relations. These include the principles of reconciliation (like the principle to reconcile moral values), collective consciousness, and personalized character, all of which are preconditions for the existence of ethical relations. In economic relationships, ethical relationships exist objectively under the reconciliation rules of moral values. Correspondingly, in an economic structure, there also exists a moral structure system determined by ethical relations. Modern business ethics is the very conscientiousness and practice of such an interdependent structure, and can be referred to as an economic organism.

1.7.2.2 Joint Efforts in Mechanism Construction

Although the moral structural system exists objectively within the socioeconomic structure as a necessary condition, this does not mean that it is bound to be affected by the consciousness of the social subject. The social subject is prominently reflected by the phenomenon that in economics, the moral structural system is suspended as a fixed value or as a constant assumption. According to the realistic relationship between the economy and morality, "it is the process that an economic relationship separates itself from social and cultural norms which makes for the formation of a stronger economic law (Koslowski 1997)." In this case, morality is only a doctrine which is chosen, or which provides a value selection theory. It must dress itself up, waiting to be selected by the "majesty of economy" at will. However, the independence of the economic relation is hindered by the realistic operating mechanisms of the market economy—the negative externality of the market and the production and distribution of public products unavoidably lead to market failures, and political interference is limited (government failures). As it turns out, even a perfect system design and arrangement cannot remove the inherent defects of the market mechanism. Moreover, in any market, the external conditions suspended in the market mechanism have started to change gradually. The structural variation or fine-tuning of society will change the operating routes of the original market mechanism, and this restructuring of the mechanism requires the efforts of all parties involved. In this sense, morality not only reconciles the conflicts of interest but also participates in the amendment of those fixed values and assumptions. The market mechanism needs to take advice from morality and integrate this into its own operating mechanism. Therefore, morality shall participate in the construction of the market operating mechanism, rather than existing within the mechanism as a limiting condition.

1.7.2.3 Common Development in Practice

"Concurrence in practice" actually relates to the possibility of moral behavior in economic life. Before the age described in *The Protestant Ethic and the Spirit of Capitalism* by Max Weber, the evaluation of practical economic success, from the perspective of individual or social success, was inferior to that of morality, which means moral values were self-sufficient. In the age described by Weber, economic behavior and moral behavior were unified from an asocial success perspective. Making profits was considered as a binding duty given by God—it was rational and, most importantly, it was morally positive. Consequently, economic behavior became a part of good morals. After the age described by Weber, the evaluation of individual and social economic success precedes that of morality. From inferiority to rationality, and on to positivity, economic behavior has gradually climbed up to a superior position in terms of social success. While at the same time, the position of moral evaluation has declined. Given the above, in modern times, the combination of the economy and morality, practically, will be different from before: it will focus more on economic diversification and decentralization at the level of behavioral motives, and more importantly, the motives of economic behavior will be considered as a complex structure rather than a simple hierarchy. Meanwhile, from the perspective of the results of economic behavior, moral evaluation, while still acknowledging the rationality and goodwill of economic behavior, also restrains economic behavior and keeps its independence and priority at a higher value level.

1.7.2.4 Value Sharing

The concept of economic rationality, marked by amoralism, is popular in modern Western economics. Economic rationality identifies economic and moral behavior as facts and values, respectively, and based on the incommensurability between facts and values rejects moral values. However, in the view of the famous American professor of logistics Hilary Putnam, the difference between facts and values is only relevant when discussing metaphysics, and in reality, it is very hard for us to define something as a mere fact or a mere value. He used the word "tanged" to describe the relationship between facts and values, and outlined that some moral values can even form the basis of scientific practice (including economic practice (Putnam 2003)). In fact, unlike the viewpoint that economic phenomena are facts, and moral phenomena are values, as held by many economists, the correct relationship between facts and values is that economic phenomena are facts containing values, whereas moral phenomena are values containing facts. Therefore, from a knowledge sociology perspective, it is groundless to say that the economy is "value free" or "value-neutral." However, in the context that economics does not select or judge values, which thus constitute a value standpoint, we cannot say that values are contained within the economy. In fact, many assumptions and presuppositions in economics exist upon moral values. Economics must illustrate its contribution to social development and its attitude toward values such as freedom, equality, and justice. In this way, morality and the economy are not just facts and values within the economic sphere; instead, they need to clarify their own standpoints and share some facts and values on the basis of dialogue and consensus. As Hilary Putnam said, "It is wrong to think that the parts of life concerning human prosperity (mainly economic prosperity—citation) and related rules (moral rules—citation) are incompatible. They shall be considered as interdependent parts of a complex relation system within a wider scope based on a theoretical consensus which is both responsive and responsible (Putnam 2003)."

The above four characteristics constitute a structural description of the internal combination of the economy and morality. In modern times, an in-depth combination of economy and morality can only be understood when all these four characteristics are taken into consideration. In this sense, morality exists within the economy as part of a certain structure, and from social existence through to social consciousness, it manifests itself progressively as four hierarchies: structure–mechanism–behavior–values. These maintain the rules and support the values needed for a healthy economy. However, the understanding of the economy's endogenous morality and its structure depend on the ethical consciousness of individuals or society, something that always has a direct bearing on the presence or absence of morality in the economic sphere. Morality's presence or absence is a condition for its existence in the economy in terms of self-existence or self-creation.

1.7.3 Morality Outside the Economy

If morality is an endogenous element of the economy, then objectively, moral value attributes must be contained in all economic activities. In that case, morality, which maintains the rules and supports the values of a society, will undoubtedly cling to the economy. As a result, in a market economy, the so-called rational economic behavior, which is always for-profit, is bound to cultivate or breed a consciousness of self-interested moral values. The problem is what the source of the value of moral criticism against rational economic behavior and market economy system is, which, in turn, poses another question: whether the endogenous moral values in a given economy can grow into or evolve into an "alien" force of moral introspection. In fact, this is related to the compatibility between the economy and morality. Is the endogenous morality of an economy limited in terms of its rationality? Is the endogenous morality of an economy qualified to comprehensively evaluate the economy?

Economic imperialism, despite the criticism it receives from all sides, is undeniably controlling our times with its strong social control and powerful knowledge ideology. As the famous economist Karl Polanyi said, "Such an institution could not exist for any length of time without annihilating the human and natural substance of society; it would have physically destroyed man and transformed his surroundings into a wilderness. Inevitably, society took measures to protect itself, but whatever measures it took impaired the self-regulation of the market, disorganized industrial life, and thus endangered society in yet another way. It was this dilemma which forced the development of the market system into a definite groove and finally disrupted the social organization it was based upon it (Karl 1999)." If the opinion of Polanyi is acceptable, it means that society is inlaid within the market, and thus the market constitutes a value basis of society, rather than the other way round. Consequently, the values advocated in economic spheres will stay above the values of society as a whole. Based on its actual ability to control the market that it derives from, modern economics has constructed a corresponding knowledge ideology and hegemonic discourse. In *On Ethics and Economics,* Amartya Sen points out, "Generally speaking, in mainstream economics, there are two ways to define rational behavior. The first way is considering rationality as the internal consistency of choices, and the second way is equating rationality with the maximization of self-interest (Sen 2003)." In economics, rational behavior defined in these ways is equated with actual human behavior. Thus, genuine human behavior is expanded from an internal consistency to an external consistency of self-interest maximization that interprets all forms of human behavior (Sen 2003). In this way, rational behavior maximizing self-interest becomes the basis for interpreting other human behavior, including political, moral, and legal behavior.

However, the real-life complexity of human behavior indicates that, although other forms of human behavior are ultimately controlled by economic behavior, they themselves retain their bottom line in values, which, according to the relationship between the economy and morality, can be interpreted from the following aspects. First, the compatibility between moral values in a political system and those in an economic system is limited. In the political system, values contained in freedom and equality are much more abundant than those in the economic system. If the values contained in freedom and equality are only understood through the rules of the market economy, the inequality of results caused by the inequality of origins will be reasonable from an economic point of view. However, political justice tries to restrict such economic freedom to ensure that "the least advantaged are benefited (Wan 2000b)" in apolitical democracy . Second, the bottom line can interpret the conflicts between values in the economic system and those in history and culture. In the opinion of institutional economics, the institutions in any economy can be divided into formal institutions and informal institutions. The reason why advanced economic institutions (formal institutions) cannot play the roles expected of them after being transplanted into a society is that they conflict with the informal institutions of society. Generally speaking, informal institutions refer to historical and cultural traditions, especially moral traditions which contain an understanding of some basic values in a given cultural community and their stands.

In this very sense, no economies can exist without the cultural values, traditions, and necessary political conditions provided by their society. However, the value stands of the above, which form the environmental conditions of the market economy, do not in fact accord with the logic and value stand of the economy, which creates value conflicts between the market economy and other social subsystems, something which is inevitable during the expansion of a market economy in terms of its behavior and value consciousness. Among such conflicts, the conflict between internal business morality and external business morality is the most obvious one. In short, when there are irreconcilable conflicts between internal business morality and external business morality, as based on the value stands of the whole society, the latter will call for the restructuring and adjustment of the former, so as to build new social value structures and orders.

From the above, we can see that internal business morality and external business morality are different. The former, meaning the moral attributes of all economic activities, exists objectively in all forms of economic behavior and adheres to the economy; while the latter is the adjustment and transcendence of the former. Such an adjustment takes the concept that "morality is the form of social consciousness and social norms" as its core value, which keeps morality from completely adhering to the economy. That is, moral values created in the economic sphere are no longer the unique identification of morality. In my view, understanding the values and value stand of external business morality is the source of value of the moral criticism of the corresponding economy. In this case, are internal business morality and external business morality totally different? What is the relationship between them? In my view, all social ideologies built upon a material economy have value adjustments and organization mechanisms within the universal sense of society. From the perspective of the relationship between the economy and morality, the mechanism is the essence of the interaction of internal and external business moralities. Social ideologies with values of universal social norms like morality, laws, and religions, once being given the utility and standing for the whole society, will integrate with the values of other social subsystems, forming universal value stands, and the norms thereof, for the whole society. This explains exactly why the compatibility between the economy and morality reflects internal business morality, and why the conflicts between them reflect external business morality. In other words, if the economy can adjust the value structure of its internal business morality upon its external business morality, while taking the value stand of whole society as a whole, the combination of internal and external business morality is indeed possible.

1.7.4 Economic Significance and Value Realization of Morality

The significance of discussing the internal combination of the economy and morality is that, based on a scientific understanding of the internal relationship between the economy and morality and the existing moral resources, we can design a special way economy–morality combination to gain a new understanding of the role of morality in improving economic development. In this sense, the concepts of "moral productivity" and "moral capital," which act as value dynamics for social reproduction and as a source of value investment respectively, are introduced herein.

"Moral productivity" is an abbreviation for the concept that "morality is a kind spiritual productivity." Representing the spirituality of social labor productivity, moral productivity is the spiritual and value element of material productivity, often manifesting itself as a moral consciousness structure, moral value consensus, and common ways of moral behavior, which form a key part of social labor productivity. As a kind of spiritual productivity, moral productivity provides a basis for and supplements material productivity. This in turn acts on moral productivity in the same way. In the past, philosophers have considered moral productivity as a generalization of the concept of "the omnipotence of morality," in terms of productivity, and refuted the existence of moral productivity as a kind of spiritual productivity based on the general distinction between the spiritual and the material. Can we find the concept of spiritual productivity based on the intention of spiritual productivity within Marxism?

In *The German Ideology,* Marx and Engels discussed the production of the social relationship between the "four aspects of the primary historical relationships," namely, "the production of material life itself"—the production of material means of production, "required reproduction," "the production of life," and "a certain mode of cooperation." They actually discussed the material aspect of the history of productive forces, but since "the sum of productive forces achieved by man determines the social situation," they had to "always combine human history with the history of industry and exchange in order to study and discuss."[43] It can be seen that classical authors, though emphasizing the decisive effect of the material aspect of the sum of productive forces, did not replace the material aspect of the sum of productive forces with the entity concept of "material production." In the context of this work, Marx always put each concrete form of production, even consciousness-related production, into a social and historical context to study. Thus, when Marx talked about different forms of production being separated by the division of labor, he meant social production, which is "a kind of social force formed by the joint activity of different individuals—an expanded productive force." In this sense, we cannot find pure, independent, and substantive forms of social labor in real-life material and spiritual production. Therefore, in the opinion of Marx, material production and spiritual production are just two categories of the division of labor within the same production—namely social production, which reflects the material and spiritual aspects of social production. It is important to note that classical authors thought this is exactly why capitalism causes the division of labor to bring about an "immobilization and alienation of social activities" which shall, therefore, be sublated.

In fact, it is the interaction between material production and spiritual production that gives social production the ability to express different types of production status. "Therefore, without the penetration of spiritual elements, materials as the productive forces of other materials can only exist as materials (Wang 2002)." Some Soviet scholars in the early 1980s thought that "spiritual production can be defined as the production of consciousness conducted by a group of internally organized people specially separated—the ideological classes of society—in a special social form (Novikova 1988)." In other words, morality as a kind of spiritual productivity is a type of special "production of consciousness" conducted by the intellectual and political classes in a certain society. Such "production of consciousness" conducted by certain ideological classes reflects the external moral requirements of the social production system. It is based on the regulation of adjustment to the value stands of overall social development on the internal moral structure of social productivity, aiming at actively guiding the healthy development of social productivity to meet human and social needs.

However, how do we combine moral productivity with social production to create economic profits? To answer this requires taking morality as a value source of invisible assets within investment. In economics, one of the preconditions of investment is making profit, and thus the object to be invested can be considered as the asset needed to create value or appreciate. Therefore, we need to consider morality as a kind of capital available for value investing and then come to the concept of "moral capital."

[43] *Collected Works of Karl Marx and Friedrich Engels*, Vol. 3, People's Publishing House, 1960, pp. 33–34.

As morality's ability to create social wealth in production, moral capital refers to moral concepts and behavior that can create profits and benefits. At the same time of maintaining and incrementing economic value, moral capital, unlike other types of capital, has the final goal of realizing mutual economic and social benefits (Wang et al. 2005a). The economic roles played by moral capital can be understood from the following aspects:

1. Moral capital must first of all be a kind of "value investing realized," which means the economic agent has a clear understanding of the moral conditions of economic activities and the available moral resources, and is able to consciously use such moral resources in various aspects of production. In a market economy, moral capital prominently manifests itself as the cultural development of the business community, focusing on building a behavioral model with universal restriction and regulatory guidance. The value realization of moral capital, in terms of social benefits, will improve the social image of companies, strengthen consumers' sense of identity of corporate culture, and enhance corporate reputation. In a company, especially in the sector of human resources, the realization of moral capital plays the roles of improving employees' moral quality, promoting harmonious interpersonal relationships among employees, enhancing the overall cohesion of the company, and strengthening the sense of responsibility of employees. Besides, moral capital can also, at a spiritual level, improve the enthusiasm and creativity of technical personnel to accelerate the realization of rational R&D and production, thus promoting the scientific application of patents and franchises.
2. Moral capital is an effective solution to market failure. For external business problems (principally external negative effects), the realization of moral capital can fill some of the gaps in economic regulation. For a company, its external negative problems can be solved through economic measures—internalizing such external problems so that the company itself pays for the cost of the problems. However, this solution, while having a certain value, tends to make the company turn external value evaluation into no more than a process for internal income analysis. In this way, social responsibility is simply quantified as an economic standard. If there are certain responsibilities which cannot be quantified, or some responsibilities that are superior to an economic task in the sense of value, the solution of internalizing external problems shall be used in a limited way. On the contrary, moral capital pre-considers external problems from the perspective of motivational decision-making: different economic plans are considered in a similar manner according to particular value standards. In this way, the cost is taken into account in advance, which further internalizes social costs; meanwhile, during the process of decision making, companies can measure the value priority of responsibilities in advance, according to different action plans. Therefore, moral capital can fundamentally solve external business problems.

In terms of public products, moral capital can, in a certain sense, prevent the behavior of "free riding" from occurring, thus ensuring the production and social supply of public products. Amartya Sen once pointed out that there are three ways to solve the problem of public product production: first, establishing publicly owned companies; second, developing economic policies and systems; and third, companies considering the production of public products as a motivation for decision making. In the view of Sen, the former two ways come with a large social cost, which will, in turn, fall on the public, becoming an additional social burden. Thus, the third way is the best solution; namely, the production of public products becoming a motivational factor in decision making, which thus ensures that the production of public products does not become a problem. However, if companies produce public products without making profits, or even produce them at a loss, most of them will not get involved. Therefore, it needs to be pointed out that companies investing moral capital in production can actually obtain spiritual benefits from physical assets which seem to be unprofitable, since this is an optimal selection made by the companies to build reputation, improve popularity, and appreciate both tangible and intangible assets.

References

Alejo, G. S. (2005). *The moral capital of leaders* (pp. 49–50; translated by W. Yu & M. Ding). Central Compilation & Translation Press.

Allen, E. B. (1991). *Ethics, efficiency, and the market* (p. 31; translated by S. Liao, et al.). China Social Sciences Publishing House.

Amartya, S. (2000). *On ethics and economics* (p. 13, 18, 79; translated by Y. Wang & W. Wang). Commercial Press.

Amartya, S. (2003). *On ethics and economics* (pp. 13, 16–26; translated by Y. Wang & W. Wang Wenyu) Commercial Press.

Bowie, N. E. (2000). Business ethics, philosophy, and the next 25 years. *Business Ethics Quarterly, 10*(1), 7–20.

Daniel, A. W. (2000). *The history of management thought* (pp. 556–557; translated by R. Zhao et al.). China Social Sciences Publishing House.

De George, R. T. (1987). The status of business ethics: Past and future. *Journal Business Ethics, 6*(3), 201, 263–267, 381–389.

Douglass, C. N. (1991). *Structure and change in economic history,* (p. 50; translated by Y. Chen et al.). Shanghai Sanlian Bookstore.

Georges, E. (2002). *Action-oriented business ethics* (p. 53; translated by G. Gao, X. Wu et al.) Shanghai Academy of Social Sciences Press.

Gu, S. (2005). *Basic theory of liberalism* (p. 243). Central Compilation & Translation Press.

James C. C., & Jerry, I. P. (1996). *Built to last* (p. 70). Xinhua Publishing House.

James, C. C., & Jerry, I. P. (2003). *Built to last* (p. 5). China CITIC Press.

Jing, Z. (2003). On economic source of Marx's spiritual production theory. *Theory and Reform,* (2).

Karl, P. (1999). *Great transformation: The political and economic origins of our time* (pp. 59–60; translated by S. Huang et al.). Yuan-Liou Publishing Co., Ltd.

Koslowski, P. (1996). *Ethics of capitalism* (p. 3). China Social Sciences Publishing House.

Koslowski, P. (1997). *The principles of ethical economics* (p. 4, 123; translated by Y. Sun). China Social Sciences Publishing House.

Liu, G. (1998). *On social productive forces* (p. 106). People's Publishing House.

Liu, G. (12 July 2001). UN launches "Moral Indexes,". *Beijing Youth Daily.*

Liu, X. (2004). *Moral discourse between man and nature: The process of environmental ethics and the introspection on it* (pp. 139–140). Hunan Normal University Press.

Lu, F., & Xiao, W. (2002). *Introduction to applied ethics* (p. 151). Contemporary China Publishing House.
Luo, N. (2003). Market economy, moral rights and property right ethics. *Studies on Ethics*, (2).
Luo, W. (1998). The economic functions of morality. *Journal of Zhejiang Provincial Party School,* (1).
Ma, L. (2005). *Marketing experience—meeting human needs* (pp. 1–2). Capital University of Economics and Business.
Max, W. (1997). *Economy and society* (p. 241; translated by R. Lin). Commercial Press.
Michael, B. (2003). *The market of virtue* (p. 28; translated by J. Xiao and C. Huang). China Social Sciences Publishing House.
Novikova, L.I. (1988). *The spiritual production. A social-philosophical aspect of the problem of spiritual activity* (p. 148; translated by Q. An). Beijing Normal University Press.
Peter, F. D. (1999). *The coming of the new organization* (pp. 6–7). China Renmin University Press, Harvard Business School Press.
Peter, P. (1999). *The essence of business ethics* (p. 107; translated by C. Hong, L. Hong, & G. Wu). China CITIC Press.
Philip, K. (1997). *Marketing management: Analysis, planning, implementation, and control* (Version 12; p. 44). Tsinghua University Press.
Putnam, H. (2003). For ethics and economics without the dichotomies. *Review of Political Economy,* 15(3), 396, 412.
Stephen, P. R. (1997). *Management* (pp. 236–240, 412; translated by W. Huang et al.). China Renmin University Press.
Tang, K. (2005). The footstone to build a harmonious society: The virtuous interaction between the economy and morality and their harmonious development. *A Study on the Theories of Mao Zedong and Deng Xiaoping,* (6).
Wan, J. (2000a). *The dimension of morality—introduction to modern business ethics* (p. 236). Guangdong People's Publishing House.
Wan, J. (2000b). The market economy and democratic politics: From the perspective of business ethics. *Philosophical Researches*, (4).
Wang, X. (1998a). *Business ethics and corporate development* (p. 48). Nanjing Normal University Press.
Wang, X. (1998b). The second study on "Morality is a Dynamic Productive Force,". *Jiangsu Social Sciences,* (3).
Wang, X. (2000). Moral capital. *Jiangsu Social Sciences,* (3).
Wang, X. (2002). *Economic morals* (p. 130). People's Publishing House.
Wang, X. (2011). The disciplinary basis of business ethics. *East China Normal University Journal,* (2).
Wang, X. et al. (2005a). *Moral capital theory* (pp. 2–9). People's Publishing House.
Wang, X., Zhu, J., & Wang, J. et al. (2005b) Business ethics in China: Two decades. Nanjing Normal University Press.
Wei, S. (2002). *Economics and Ethics* (p. 69). Shanghai People's Publishing House.
Wei, S. (2003). Rational choices made in the game between ethics and the market. *A Study on the Theories of Mao Zedong and Deng Xiaoping,* (1).
Wei, S. (2007). The nature of economics and economics in the perspective of philosophy. *Economics,* 6(3).
Wen, J. (4 Feb. 2009). See China in the light of her development—Speech at the University of Cambridge. *People's Daily.*
Wu, Y., & Zhang, J. (2007). *Foreign economic intellectual history* (p. 152). High Education Press.
Xia, W. (1995). The market economy is a moral economy. *Expanding Horizons,* (3).
Xiao, W. (1995). Market economy is moral economy. *Expanding Horizons,* (3).
Yang, C. (2003). Market and conscientiousness—The morality of the market economy. *Philosophical Researches,* (3).
Zhang, H. (2001). *Business ethics* (pp. 7–8). Sun Yat-Sen University Press.
Zhang, H. (2005). *A study on business ethics and its scope* (p. 265). Sun Yat-Sen University Press.

Zhang, J. (1999). Morality: A significant variable in the study of economic activities and economics. *Social Sciences in China*, (2).
Zhang, X. (2007a). *18 lessons on the intellectual history of western ethics* (pp. 112–123). Shanghai People's Publishing House.
Zhang, X. (2007b). *18 lessons on the intellectual history of western business ethics* (p. 75). Shanghai People's Publishing House.
Zhou, Z. (1999). Combination of management and ethics: The profound reform of management philosophy. *Nankai Journal* (Philosophy and Social Science), (3).

Chapter 2
The Theory of Moral Capital

Abstract This chapter mainly interprets the concept, formation, and mechanism of the action of moral capital. Furthermore, it illustrates the point that morality, as a spiritual element of capital or a kind of spiritual capital, clings to physical capital while affecting physical capital by playing a unique economic role, thus trying to construct a theoretical system of moral capital.

2.1 The Concept and Value Realization of Moral Capital[1]

Capital has a variety of forms, including physical capital, money capital, and human capital. Of these, human capital plays a decisive role in economic development (Zhao 1999). The American economist Theodore William Schultz, winner of the Nobel Prize for Economics, once pointed out that "in an economy possessing land and reproducible material capital like the production technology possibly owned by the US, but restricted by such problems that nobody can get any professional experience, that no one has ever received any school education, that no one has any economic information except the information in his own living area, that everyone is restricted by his living environment, and that people have a life expectancy of 40 years, the economic production of the economy will surely drop tragically. Without human investment to prominently improve human ability, low-level output will surely co-exist with extremely rigid economic organizations (Theodore 1990a)." However, human capital, which is directly connected with moral capital, prevents human capital from obtaining benefits. The improvement of human creativity and working skills depend on the correct value orientation, scientific moral spirit, and moral practice of people in society. Therefore, in the process of economic development, morality is certainly an important asset invested in production. "Why did the most developed countries in the world, including the US and some European countries, after developing the market economy for several hundred years, suddenly find that they did not know what the economy is at all, as if they were still at the medieval medical level before the foundation of modern medicine (Lu 1999)?" One of

[1] Originally titled as Moral Capital, *Jiangsu Social Sciences*, Issue 3, 2000 and Ethics, Issue 8, 2000. The paper has been included in *Moral Capital and Business Ethics* (Selected Works of Wang Xiaoxi), People's Publishing House, 2009.

X. Wang, *On Moral Capital*, DOI 10.1007/978-3-662-45544-9_2

the main reasons is that they have never really understood the special roles played by morality in the economy.

2.1.1 Capital and Moral Capital

Capital, as an economic concept, is the value that creates surplus value under capitalism. The economic system of capitalism determines that capital, in the form of substances and thoughts, is a kind of value that creates profits. In modern times, "capital is a kind of capability which can be invested into production to create social wealth (Wang 1999)." "Scientifically, ethics has the function of encouraging people to constantly improve themselves, and at the same time, continually cherish and improve the interpersonal relationships within co-existence, so as to build a better living environment based on the concept of rational existence, pushing forward sustainable social development. Where the function is applied in production, human quality, especially moral quality, will naturally be improved, which will surely lead to self-motivation and harmonious cooperation. Consequently, the functions and benefits of tangible assets are maximized and labor productivity is thus increased." In this sense, moral capital is a kind of capital (Wang 1999). Of course, it must be pointed out that only scientific morality can become a kind of capital in production.

2.1.1.1 Moral Capital is Intangible: It Is the Spiritual Aspect of Human Capital and the Spiritual Element of Physical Capital

Moral capital has the following characteristics:

First, man, as the subject of production, is the core capital that plays its roles, and makes profits as a result of that production. If man only participates in production as a kind of physical capital,[2] complete production cannot be realized, and thus profits and benefits cannot be made. In fact, things can only be assets or resources, rather than capital, if man is not involved. Man that participates in production as labor is more than an "economic man." In the theory of traditional economics, the subject of economic activities is abstracted as the "economic man" who acts as a precondition for economic analysis. Economic man is defined as a man driven by the motivation of self-interest to pursue the maximization of self-interest. The fact is, in actual economic activities, that the subject thereof is the "moral man," bringing with him economic, social, and environmental responsibilities, whose content is much richer than the "economic man."[3] Therefore, in terms of production, man is certainly controlled by certain consciousness and guided by certain values. The moral consciousness of man directly affects and restricts his enthusiasm and energy release.

---

[2] It is only a hypothesis for illustration. Man becomes "living labor" as long as he participates in production.

[3] This is one of the conclusions of the opinions of American economic ethicists made by Lu Xiaohe (See Lu 1999).

Second, the benefits and profits made by physical capital in production largely depend on the value orientation of laborers and their responsibility for themselves and society. In recent years, Haier has gradually expanded its market share in Europe, and one of the reasons, as explained by foreign distributors, is that Haier products have begun to reflect the requirements and respect the habits of European consumers. For example, Haier washers have now totally occupied the stores of some foreign dealers who used to only sell Japanese washers. In the final analysis, this is Haier's responsibility for the interests of itself, of China, and of European consumers that have expanded its washers' market share in Europe and created more benefits and profits. This shows that moral capital is of greater significance than physical capital in terms of profit making. At the same time of making substances a kind of capital, morality activates physical capital further, and is thus the basis of profit making.

2.1.1.2 The Roles of Penetration, Guidance, and Restriction Played by Moral Capital

First, moral capital has penetrated into various aspects and levels of production rather than existing independently, and it plays roles based on its unique and independent value function. In a certain sense, production is a process in which human thoughts or spirits are materialized. History has proved that in a nation that ignores education and morality, production is obviously blind, having only the purpose of survival, and thus cannot create more benefits or profits. On the contrary, if the purpose of production is of a noble value orientation, the sense of responsibility of the laborers involved will penetrate into production. In addition, the rational spirit of being responsible for any legitimate interest runs through all aspects of distribution, exchange, and consumption. Therefore, aside from an increase in profits, expanded reproduction will be realized at the stage of updating, and the rationality of expanded reproduction will be further improved. In this sense, morality has become a major intension and a requirement of production, and an important condition of profit making through production, all of which can be realized in a socialist market economy.

Second, moral capital is a kind of "spiritual capital" or "knowledge capital." With advancement (idealism) or orientation, morality's involvement in production as a kind of capital will surely form a power, one that cannot be replaced by other kinds of capital. As an invisible "hand of rationality" or "power of rationality," morality realizes the rational operation of all kinds of capital involved in production, guiding people to maximize profits. The concept of "some people and some regions in China should be allowed to get rich before others so that these people and regions can lead the way to common prosperity for all "as put forward by Deng Xiaoping, is the goal of the economic development and socialist moral development of China. Moral ideals in the economy promote rapid economic development, and realize the legitimate interests of individuals and the common interests of the whole nation at the same time, which is the concentrated expression of the relevant functions, especially the orientation of socialist moral capital.

Third, moral capital plays a unique reconciliatory and restrictive role. Production requires harmonious interpersonal relationships, as well as rational systems and norms, which is another special content as well as an action model for moral capital involved in production. Essentially, the socialist market economy is based on laws and norms, something that is not a natural result. "Being" and "should be" are very different concepts. Only when morality plays its special role as a kind of capital, can the socialist market economy work normally instead of becoming out of order. The reconciliation of morality, on the one hand, promotes the rationality of social production relationships and interpersonal cooperation, and on the other hand, impels the institutionalization of morality. Consequently, benefits are maximized in every aspect of production, and various types of capital that participate in production supplement each other and maximize profits. There are reasons for some entrepreneurs to believe that harmonious interpersonal relationships are also a kind of capital, and that rational institutions create profits.

2.1.1.3 The Formation of Moral Capital is Slow and Arduous

The formation of moral capital is a unique process. First, moral capital forms as a result of the improvement in moral cognition and moral consciousness. One of the preconditions for moral capital to play its part in production is that man, as the subject of productive activities, must fully understand what morality is and what scientific morality is, and at the same time, guide his behavior using moral responsibility. However, moral consciousness cannot be developed overnight; it comes into being through the constant deepening of moral cognition, the cultivation of moral will, and the gradual strengthening of moral belief. Therefore, the improvement of moral cognition and consciousness is a slow and long-term process.

Second, the formation of moral capital is a systematic work, needing the joint efforts of schools, families, and society at large, especially in terms of enhanced education concerning social morals, professional ethics, and family virtues. Additionally, the formation of moral capital also relies on economic, technical, cultural, and educational development, the low level of which will certainly affect the improvement of people's moral cognition and consciousness. In a company, the formation of moral capital requires both "hardware" and "software" development. Hardware development refers to working environment and conditions; while software development means improving management and operating systems, building a sound moral and cultural environment, enhancing moral education, and taking various effective measures to improve employees' moral consciousness and the company's overall moral quality.

Third, the formation of moral capital is an arduous process. In the socialist market economy, the coexistence of various economic sectors is likely to lead to different values and value orientations. Meanwhile, different moral opinions in the West have been constantly influencing people's social life, which makes the formation of moral capital more complex. For example, some companies' immoral behavior, such as cheating and fraud, is closely connected with their value positioning of putting profits first, and making profits at the cost of sacrificing the interests of others. Therefore, during the formation of moral capital, we need to separate good values from bad ones, and encourage good behavior while correcting the bad, thus making scientific morality an important force in production.

2.1.2 *Moral Capital Creates Value*

As stated above, moral capital plays a role in various aspects of production. It improves product quality while shortening the necessary labor time per product. As a kind of rational intangible capital, moral capital, after participating in production, keeps creating tangible benefits and improving itself at the same time.[4] The fact that moral capital creates value can be understood from the following aspects.

2.1.2.1 Human Moral Quality and Productivity

An improvement in productivity is marked by substances, but determined by man. I once pointed out that man in terms of socialist productivity exists under the identity of "master," thus dominating both society and nature. Therefore, although man exists primarily as a living substance, his quality directly determines his creative labor and the speed of economic development. If man cannot exist as a real or complete man, or exist passively or even reactively, no matter how advanced the technology and equipment are, or how abundant the resources are, his productivity will certainly stay low. However, human quality is complex and diverse—it includes a combination of physical, psychological, cultural, ideological, political, and moral qualities, among which, moral quality is the fundamental one. Man, only by fully realizing his existence and the significance thereof, and by clarifying a noble value orientation for his existence, can build up a spirit of constant self-motivation and create the basic conditions for productivity development (Wang 1994). To be specific, "only with improved moral consciousness and cognition, higher comprehensive qualities, and fully motivated enthusiasm and initiative, could people consciously improve their professional ability, management level, and efficiency, and actively gain cultural knowledge and technology to improve their means of production, production technology, labor organization, and operating management. This can also lead to further innovations in production. In this way, the quantity, quality, and economic benefits of products will be greatly improved, and the development of productivity will be greatly promoted (Wei 2000)." We, therefore, have reasons to believe that

[4] With the constant development and improvement of social relations of production, moral capital participating in production is also developed and improved. Since scientific morality is always determined by the material conditions of social life, the development and improvement of the relations of production will certainly promote the constant development and improvement of morality. Beside, only in socialist production could morality keep developing rather than turning into "moral doctrine."

the moral consciousness and quality of man are also important elements of productivity, and that scientific moral quality will surely create more benefits and interests in production.

At the same time as determining human quality, especially moral quality, productivity is affected by a combination of various internal productivity elements and their levels of rationality. The reconciliation of various internal productivity elements is not a simple reconciliation between man and substances. Substances are possessed and controlled by man; therefore, the relationship between substances and man is, in essence, the reconciliation of the relationships of production, rights, and status between one man and another. If laborers can freely and independently control the means of labor, realizing their rational combination with the object of labor, interpersonal relationships and interpersonal interest relationships can be rationally reconciled, which will undoubtedly greatly improve man to cognize, improve, and develop the means and object of his labor (Wang 1994).

2.1.2.2 Management Morality and Business Vitality

Management, in essence, is about the management of man, and Taylorism, which takes workers as machines, will never meet the development requirements of modern businesses in China. "A company not respecting human rights and dignity drastically underestimates the personality and vitality of workers, and is thus only a source of revenue for the exchange of labor and money, while rejecting human nature (Wang 1999)." In the socialist market economy, such companies will gradually lose their time and space to exist.

Modern management should be human-centered, and fully reflect the morality of management, which is the only way to unite workers to realize normal business operations.

First, we must equate human dignity in order to vitalize workers. One of the basic goals of business managers is making their workers have a unified cognition of company development and arousing the enthusiasm of their workers in order to reach the developmental targets. However, the realization of this goal requires developing the workers' sense of ownership over the company. The problem lies in how to keep the balance between the leadership of the business managers and the development of workers' ownership over the company. In my opinion, business managers should be leaders with the attitude of workers. In other words, they not only carry out the overall planning and effective commanding but also try to advocate the human dignity of workers—they should tell workers that all staff members of the company, regardless of their positions, are equal. Therefore, managers should first of all respect their workers—aside from serving workers, they should ask for their opinions, turning "managing workers" into "managing with workers." That is, the management goals, content, methods, and measures of managers contain the wisdom of all members of staff, and thus the company actually operates under an ideological guidance of all staff members. For companies with poor performance, one of the main reasons is that managers always put themselves high in the position of "leaders," and workers are merely passively controlled by management. Such a wide gap between managers and workers dampens the enthusiasm of workers. Once the balance of management is upset, the validity and profits of the company will vanish, pushing the company into a dead end.

Second, interests must be fostered in order to create more interest. Vital interests are the core concern of workers. Their enthusiasm derives from the maximization of their vital interests, and the equal realization of their interests. Therefore, to manage workers, a manager must first respect the interests of his workers. A qualified manager will put the interests of workers and the reconciliation of such interests foremost. In a company, the realization of workers' interests (the proportions of obtained interests in relation to corporate interests and in due interests) and the equality of reconciliation of workers' interests are always proportional to the future profit realization of the company. A worker whose legitimate interests cannot be obtained in a normal way cannot commit himself to work. Therefore, when the interests of workers are distributed irrationally or seriously unequally, even the most capable manager cannot avoid ultimate failure.

Third, managers take the lead in work. In a company, the image of its managers is directly connected with its fate. A responsible manager will bring hope to workers, so that even in case of temporary difficulty or frustration, workers will work hard as a team. On the contrary, a manager who makes workers feel hopeless despite their payment, and who always puts his self-interest first, will seriously destroy his workers' enthusiasm. An irresponsible manager is actually a burden on the company, for his behavior improves product costs and lowers the company's interests. Therefore, in a socialist market economy, regardless of the nature of the company, managers should be fully aware that their behaviors are silent orders and an invisible leverage, which directly affect the benefits and profits of the company.

2.1.2.3 Moral Content and Product Quality

All products are spiritualized substances. First, all products are designed based on the technological and cultural cognition and technical approaches of man. Therefore, the requirements of beer bottles are different from those of other kinds of bottles, bicycles vary from brand to brand, and so on. It can be said that each category of product has its unique culture and technical materialization. Second, all products are the materialization of the moral consciousness and quality of man, and the moral content of products determines the final product quality. Besides, the characteristics of products, aside from technological and cultural elements, largely depend on the morality contained therein. The morality and moral content of a product mainly consist of the human-centered design of the product, the responsibility contained therein, and the fundamental philosophy of product manufacturing.

First, human-centered product design is concerned with the physiological and psychological needs of man. "It shall, on the one hand, focus on the natural attributes of man, so that new products can technically meet practical human needs; and on the other hand, absorb artistic ideas in line with the spiritual human need to create aesthetic product appearance for the consumer's enjoyment," thus "making products safe, reliable, comfortable, nice-looking and economical (Hu 1994)." For example, when making a glass cup, the vacuum cup is the best choice, since it is insulated. This makes users feel safe, comfortable, and satisfied. So although such cups are much more expensive than common glass cups, there are still consumers willing to pay the extra money for them. It tells us that the more a product meets the physiological and psychological needs of consumers, the more salable and profitable it is.

Second, product design is different from product manufacturing. That is to say, a design, no matter how excellent, cannot necessarily be transformed into products. To realize this transformation, a sense of responsibility must penetrate each aspect of production. Strictly speaking, a company aiming at building itself into a famous brand will always say no to nonconforming products. Even if nonconforming products are found, they shall never be sold to consumers. In China, many famous companies once destroyed nonconforming products for the purpose of showing society that all their products are qualified, and reminded employees to keep in mind that the manufacture of qualified products needed their responsibility and conscience.

There are reasons that some famous foreign and domestic companies are trusted by consumers. Just from the high quality of their products, consumers can see the rational spirit, and the preciseness and responsibility of their employees. Therefore, it is natural that the products of such companies would be salable and popular even without advertisements.

Third, corporate profits rest not only on product quality but also on the business philosophy of high quality and reasonable prices. The "tap water philosophy" used by Panasonic is the secret to its success worldwide. Panasonic set the goal of making better products with lower prices, just like producing tap water. This is a concentrated expression of the sense of responsibility for consumers. Product prices do not increase with an increase in product quality, but product quality nonetheless improves without any impact on price. In fact, the self-motivation and sense of responsibility of employees can, objectively, improve efficiency while comparatively lowering product costs.

2.1.2.4 Reputation and Market Share

It is undoubtedly true that reputation makes money. When summarizing the capitalist spirit, the famous German scholar Max Weber said, "Never forget that credit is money. If someone has lent me money and didn't ask for it back when it was due, he lent me the profits arising therefrom, or we can say that he gave me the profits that I could have made from the loan in that period of time. If a man with good credit borrows a lot and makes good use of the loans, he can make a lot of money therefrom (Weber 1987)." He also said, "Those good at making money will be the owners of others' wallets. Those known for always paying money on time can gather all the spare money from their friends, anytime anywhere." This opinion also applies to the production and operation of companies. When consumers trust the products of a company and are willing to buy them, they are giving money to the company. In Germany, from large corporations like Benz to small and medium sized enterprises (SMEs), they all believe that they are not only selling products but also credit. For them, selling credit is more important than selling products.[5]

In China, many famous companies know the relationship between credit and market share very well, as well as that between market share and profits, and they take credit as an important part of their existence. On the one hand, they penetrate credit into the whole process of production, in order to ensure product quality. On the other, they build up credit in sales and service, so that credit becomes their basis for profit maximization. They know that once credit is lost, the conditions and reasons for them to exist in the first place will disappear. The "super nanny service" provided by Jiangsu Chunlan, the "entire care-free service" by Shanxi Bole Group, and the "12345" service norm developed by Little Swan, have all created satisfactory social and economic benefits. Several years ago, a newspaper once published an article titled *Morality Creates Order*, which recorded the news that a fridge plant received increasing orders while its peers were all facing a slump. The reason was that the plant adhered to the principle of "not selling nonconforming products," which helped it win consumer trust and a bigger market share. It tells us that though corporate credit is priceless, it can create enormous economic benefits.

2.2 Dependence and Independence of Moral Capital[6]

The theoretical research of "moral capital" has been widely and actively echoed by the theoretical cycle. The emergence of the concept of "moral capital," as a natural outcome of the combination of the economy and ethics, derives from the super economic analysis of the traditional concept of capital. To better define the concept of moral capital and clarify confusion arising from it, this section will, from the perspective of capital's duality, renew long preconceived ideas about capital in a more complete and wider sense. At the same time, it will systematically expound the theory of "moral capital" as a new concept to help people greatly understand it.

2.2.1 The Dependence of Moral Capital

Due to its own characteristics, moral capital must rely on physical capital—it cannot exist independently or work normally without physical capital. Physical capital is a kind of value entity, which, with integrated values and use values, distributes

[5] See *Yangtze Evening News*, October 28, 1998, second page (A).

[6] Originally titled as The Third Study on Moral Capital (co-written by Zhu Huiyu), *Jiangsu Social Sciences*, Issue 6, 2002; reprinted fully in *Ethics*, Issue 2, 2003. This paper has been included in Moral Capital and Business Ethics (*Selected Works of Wang Xiaoxi*), People's Publishing House, 2009.

certain benefits to it owners. It mainly includes entity capital, financial capital, and equity capital. Having a scientific picture of the dependence of moral capital is not only a basic requirement to understand the concept of moral capital deeply but also a basis for moral capital to perform its unique roles. The dependence of moral capital can be understood from the following aspects:

2.2.1.1 The Direct Purpose of Moral Capital Management is Promoting the Appreciation of Physical Capital

The direct purpose of capital management is obtaining appreciation, as is the direct purpose of moral capital management. However, the difference is that moral capital appreciation manifests as the appreciation of physical capital. If capital management is limited by metaphysical thought, it will certainly be abandoned after losing its technical effectiveness. For this reason, some scholars pointed out that "the use-value of physical capital is embodied in physical capital; therefore, to obtain the use-value of moral capital, it is necessary to combine intangible capital with physical capital (Lei and Liu 1999)." This means that intangible capital (including moral capital) can only realize its actual value after being materialized into physical capital. Of course, the "materialization" herein is different from the "materialization" put forward by György Lukacs. In this case, "materialization" refers to moral capital that plays its unique roles by participating in the whole process of capital management, thus constantly promoting the maintenance of value and the increase of physical capital. When talking about cultural capital (including moral capital),[7] Bourdieu believes that a transformation is an inevitable necessity. He writes, "Capital depends on the field in which it functions,[8] and at the cost of the more or less expensive transformations, which are the precondition for its efficacy in the field."[9] The essence of the transformation is that moral capital ultimately facilitates the appreciation of physical capital to produce the type of effective power within the area and process. At the same time, Bourdieu criticizes the partial opinions of "economism" and "semiotics," and confirms the possibility of the transformation from intangible capital to physical capital. In fact, only by playing its unique roles could moral capital, which relies on physical capital, ultimately transform into

[7] Bourdieu thought that to scientifically "explain the structure and functions of the social world," we should "introduce all forms of capital," and divide capital into the three basic forms of "economic capital," "cultural capital," and "social capital." According to his interpretation, moral capital, in a certain sense, is included in "cultural capital" (see Bourdieu *Cultural Capital and Social Alchemy:An Interview with Bourdieu*, translated by Bao Yaming, People's Publishing House, 1997, pp. 189–211).

[8] Bourdieu said, "From the perspective of analysis, a field may be defined as a network or a structure formed by the objective relations between different places" (see *Cultural Capital and Social Alchemy:An Interview with Bourdieu*, translated by Bao YamingBourdieu People's Publishing House, 1997, p. 142).

[9] *Cultural Capital and Social Alchemy:An Interview with Bourdieu*, translated by Bao Yaming, People's Publishing House, 1997, p. 192.

physical capital or ultimately promote the appreciation of physical capital at a substantial level of value. In this way, moral capital obtains the practical significance of its existence, thus can be acknowledged and valued by society. Physical capital management also internally requires moral capital. After penetrating into physical capital, moral capital will play its unique roles, maximizing physical capital and facilitating its appreciation. It can be said that the dependence of moral capital is essentially embodied in its promoting the appreciation of physical capital, thus realizing its spiritual and material value.

2.2.1.2 The Input of Moral Capital Depends on the Input of Physical Capital

The input of moral capital, as a precondition of the scientific management of moral capital, depends on the input of physical capital. In other words, the input of moral capital is accompanied by the consumption of physical capital, including various human, physical, and financial resources. Specifically speaking, physical capital works on moral capital in the following ways: first, effective moral education is provided to employees to improve their moral quality, thus realizing the effective input of moral capital. It mainly takes place in four areas: families, schools, relevant organizations, and society. Moreover, the realization of effective education requires the participation of material means—various material or physical educational resources are invested and consumed. Second, morality is put into practice. Only by applying morality to real situations could employees internalize moral principles and rules as moral beliefs, thus realizing the effective input of moral capital. In fact, morality as a spirit requires practice and must be put into practice to realize its values. However, moral behavior, no matter how noble it is, cannot be realized without the participation of a physical intermediary. Morality only existing in thought is meaningless and cannot even be labeled as "moral behavior." During the process of putting morality into practice, a physical intermediary always gets involved in the form of physical capital, namely, human, physical, and financial resources. Third, a social moral environment is built. The input of moral capital requires an improvement in man and moral quality, thus requiring a social moral environment that contains a soft moral environment and a hard moral environment. On the one hand, the construction of the former includes creating a social moral atmosphere, as well as building a social moral assessment system, and a social credit system. The latter includes constructing human-centered public utilities, creating public artworks advocating morality, etc. Needless to say, both conditions require human, physical, and financial input of companies. Without such input, the construction of the moral environment will certainly be unrealistic due to the lack of physical support. In fact, aside from acknowledging that moral capital can be inherited and passed, more importantly, we should realize that essentially, the input of moral capital certainly relies on the input of physical capital, which is independent of moral capital. It can be said that the particularity of moral capital in terms of its input fully reflects its dependence.

2.2.1.3 The Value Realization of Moral Capital Depends on the Management of the Original Capital

All kinds of capital must exist in mobility, which is a key feature of capital. The maintenance of value and the increase of physical capital can only be realized during the process of capital management. Likewise, the unique value of moral capital can only be realized when it is present in mobility. The difference is that moral capital cannot participate in capital management to realize its value independently without physical capital; it must participate in the management of the original capital, that is, the capital management with physical capital as the subject. In *The Second Study on Moral Capital*, I point out, "the management mechanism of moral capital, essentially, is playing roles in the process of production, exchange, distribution and consumption (Wang and Yang 2002)." It can be said that the production, exchange, distribution, and consumption based on physical economic goods is the process to realize the maintenance of value and the increase of physical capital, and also the process in which moral capital plays its roles and realizes its values. During production, moral capital "ensures win-win production results, human-centered means of production, and ecological products." In exchange, moral capital "corrects the wrong motives of exchange caused by the irrational pursuit of profits, overcomes the ethical defects in exchange, and internalizes the negative external effects of exchange results." In distribution, moral capital ensures a more reasonable distribution. In consumption, moral capital makes consuming behavior more rational, thus promoting sustainable and steady economic development (Wang and Yang 2002). Of course, moral capital can only play the above roles with the participation of physical capital; otherwise, moral capital is powerless and certainly cannot realize its values. In fact, the main values of moral capital is directly participating in the management of physical capital and playing its unique roles in various aspects, thus ultimately realizing the appreciation of physical capital and itself in different dimensions. The reliance of moral capital on the management of physical capital is a main expression of its dependence.

2.2.1.4 The Normal Management of Moral Capital Depends on the Support of Relevant Elements

The smooth management of moral capital depends on the support and guarantee of relevant elements. From microcosmic, mesoscopic, and macroscopic perspectives, we can see that the moral qualities of humans, the conditions of business ethics, and the social environment are the three elements supporting and guaranteeing the normal management of moral capital. First, at the microlevel, moral capital does not exist without man and his moral qualities. The management of moral capital is certainly human-centered, so capital management without the participation of man is meaningless and nonexistent. Particularly, in a mature market economy, business development, and the management of moral capital necessarily call for modern entrepreneurs with a high moral quality. It can be said that man and moral capital are naturally inseparable, and the combination of moral capital and man as well as his moral quality is a necessary requirement for the existence and value realization of moral capital. Second, at the meso-level, moral capital's participation in capital management as well as realization of the maintenance of value and increase of physical capital are closely related to the ethical improvement of relevant social organizations. In reality, a company with low moral quality will surely ignore the functions of morality and overlook the due position of moral capital. The support and guarantee of business ethics, especially management ethics, lay a foundation for moral capital to fully play its roles. The improvement of management ethics enables companies to develop and manage moral capital in a more scientific and conscious manner during economic practices. In other words, the improvement of business ethics (especially management ethics) and the functioning of moral capital are interdependent. At the macro-level, the appearance of moral capital is determined by the support of the social environment. When economic and social development reaches a certain level, and with the support of social norms (such as laws, regulations, and policies), it is possible for moral capital to emerge and play its roles. In a society whose systems allow immoral behavior to create profits, morality is certainly ignored, making it impossible for moral capital to play its roles.

2.2.2 The Independence of Moral Capital

While participating in the various operating aspects of the modern market economy, moral capital always stays in line with the management of physical capital. By running through the entire process of managing physical capital, moral capital plays its unique roles in production, exchange, distribution, and consumption, thus realizing its inherent value. In addition to dependence, moral capital also features independence due to its particularity unlike traditional capital. In fact, such particularity makes moral capital independent from other types of capital. Only by managing moral capital, which is based on a scientific analysis of its particularity, are we truly able to realize the value of moral capital and make moral capital fully play its roles.

2.2.2.1 The Input of Moral Capital is Universal

The independence of moral capital, in terms of input, manifests as a unique universality. From the theoretical and practical perspectives, we can see that unlike the input of other kinds of capital, which is limited in certain companies, industries, and fields, the input of moral capital is universal—companies, regardless of their natures and types, input moral capital in their business operation consciously or unconsciously. Besides, companies are required to add moral capital into their business operation constantly to manage moral capital in a more optimal way. Without sufficient input, moral capital cannot fully play its roles. Furthermore, a company ignoring the significance of moral capital will gradually lose the various tangible and intangible benefits brought by its previous input of moral capital. There are two reasons. Objectively, the external pressure from the social environment forces companies to input moral capital constantly. To maximize its benefits, a company must input moral capital according to the actual situation and use it in a scientific matter, thus making it fully play its roles for economic activities. In the Prisoner's Dilemma of game theory, each prisoner has two strategies and a strictly dominant individual strategy, that is, no matter what strategy is taken by B, A can maximize his benefits (the benefits of A is higher than those of B) through this strategy. "However, if both prisoners take another strategy (a more cooperative strategy) rather than the strictly dominant strategy, their goals can actually be achieved in a bigger way (Sen 2001)." Likewise, external restrictions from the social environment and internal requirements for the realization of self-interest force companies to behave more cooperatively and credibly in real economic activities. In a general sense, there are necessary objective reasons for companies to input and add moral capital constantly. Subjectively, while pursuing material benefits, companies also have spiritual pursuits that are especially of moral realms. The existence of a company is of both economic and spiritual significance. In society, it plays a certain moral role while simultaneously undertaking certain moral obligations. A company is composed of man while man has his own different kinds of unique pursuits, among which, those at higher levels are all related to mortality. Therefore, man in society and companies consisting of man, while simultaneously pursuing material benefits, can input moral capital consciously and independently.

2.2.2.2 Moral Capital has the Function of Optimization

The independence of moral capital, in terms of capital management, is embodied in its function of optimization. That is, the management of moral capital can activate physical capital, facilitate the realization of the "neighborhood effect (Buchanan 1991)" of efficiency, and encourage companies to realize economies of scale in a wider sense.

First, the optimization function of moral capital manifests as activating physical capital.

While expounding the general formula for capital, Marx begins by stating, "The circulation of commodities is the starting-point of capital. The production of commodities, their circulation, and that more developed form of their circulation called commerce, these form the historical groundwork from which it rises. The modern history of capital dates from the creation in the 16th century of a world-embracing commerce and a world-embracing market."[10] Capital in ceaseless mobility is "alive" and thus can be called "capital." With the function of optimization, moral capital activates physical capital to improve its mobility and circulation rate. Besides, by enhancing the cohesion among employees and their sense of ownership over their companies, moral capital promotes the rational management of physical

[10] *Collected Works of Karl Marx and Friedrich Engels*, Vol. 23, People's Publishing House, 1972, p. 169.

capital. Moreover, by improving corporate reputation, moral capital activates the original assets of companies. In short, when working with physical capital, moral capital can play its role of optimization, which is commonly known as "activating tangible assets with intangible assets." In addition, the involvement of moral capital in economic activities can prevent the occurrence of decreasing marginal revenue. As reflected by real economic performance, under certain circumstances, decreasing marginal revenue did not occur, which is explained as the results of technical progress based on the New Growth Theory appearing after the 1980s. However, it is irrefutable that moral capital is certainly another reason. First, technical progress enables people to buy machines with a higher technical content at the same cost of money capital. When efficiency is greatly improved, insufficient utilization of machines and decreasing capital revenue can be avoided. Similarly, the participation of moral capital in economic activities can also improve efficiency, thus preventing the occurrence of decreasing capital revenue. Second, moral capital, at a deeper level, determines the direction of technical progress and the degree of technical application. The management of moral capital influences man, thus influencing the development and utilization of technology. In fact, when human moral quality is improved, scientific research will be more active, the transformation from technology to products will be smoother and the utilization of technical products will be more rational. In other words, the higher the moral capital management level is, the better moral capital can play its roles, and the higher the possibility of economic growth.

Second, the optimization function of moral capital manifests as the efficiency of "neighborhood effects."

In the process of circulation, moral capital is of universal and efficient neighborhood effects. In particular, morality can optimize economic activities, making some inefficient neighborhood effects become efficient. Allen E. Buchanan mentions in *Ethics, Efficiency, and the Market* that "externalities critics of the market, have been quick to point out the pervasiveness and seriousness of neighborhood effects, or externalities, as a key source of the market's failure to achieve efficient outcomes (Buchanan 1991)." It is true that negative externalities will lead to inefficient economic activities. "More of the chemical is produced than would be produced if the total costs of production, including the costs to breathers of polluted air, were taken into account in establishing the equilibrium price for the product (Buchanan 1991)." Moral capital can reawaken people to pay attention to third-party costs which have been ignored, making them view and solve related problems from a more responsible and forward-looking perspective, thus avoiding the occurrence of inefficient neighborhood effects. Besides, "positive externalities (beneficial third-party effects) are also inefficient." It is like a vaccination, which not only benefits those who have been vaccinated but also those who have not, as the probability of infection is lowered (Buchanan 1991). This can be called "free riding." However, the neighborhood effects of moral capital are not only efficient but also can play active roles in the circulation of moral capital, thus optimizing externalities and preventing "free riding." When studying systems and their transformation with economic methodology, Douglass C. North mentions, "I'm talking about values instilled by families and education. They make people restrict their behaviors so that they would not be free riders (Douglass 1991)." He also believes that the optimal solution to the problem of "free riding" is using the power of ethics and morality, which is economical, practical, and workable. Therefore, managing morality as a kind of capital to make it play its unique roles is the most economical and practical solution to the problem of "free riding."

Third, the optimization function of moral capital manifests as promoting companies to realize economies of scale.

The management of moral capital helps companies to realize moderate capital expansion both internally and externally, thus realizing economies of scale. The "economies of scale" essentially means that "in the context that other conditions remain unchanged, as input increases, the output greatly increases." "The main reason for the formation of economies of scale is cost reduction (Qin 2000)." In a company, internally, good management of moral capital can develop employees' sense of ownership over the company and arouse their enthusiasm, thus increasing productivity with a low cost and expanding the scale of production and output at the same time. Moreover, by virtue of its good social image and existing brand(s), as well as its original reputation and popularity, it can guide consumers to acknowledge and trust its new products and brand(s) and accelerate market positioning and consumer acceptance of its new products and brand(s). Thus, it can realize the branding, serialization, and large-scale production of products while lowering the costs arising from guiding consumers to accept new products and brand(s). In this way, its economies of scale with external expansion are realized. Externally speaking, on the one hand, the company wins the trust of its partners, and thus builds a sound, long-term, and stable partnership that is based on an advanced corporate culture and a good reputation brought by moral capital. On the other hand, morality helps the company widely spread its brand(s). By transferring its image or brand(s) with compensation instead of inputting physical capital (which is the ritual of economic expansion), it can expand its economic scale in a short matter of time, thus realizing the economies of scale.

2.2.2.3 Moral Capital Regulates and Guides the Capital Market

First, moral capital regulates the capital market to make it rational.

In the capital market, the independence of moral capital manifests as a regulator of the capital market, making it rational. It is true that China's capital market still needs further regulation—investor litigation and compensation systems are still defective and illegal fund raising is still rampant. Particularly, after the Yinguangxia scandal broke, investors started to have grave doubts about the independence and justice of some intermediaries and the credit of some listed companies. We cannot deny that in some sense, China's stock market is financing-oriented, and the capital market is predominated by speculation rather than investment. Therefore, our goal is to build a sound, investment-oriented capital market. To realize this goal, the first problem that must be solved is information asymmetry in the capital market. The great economist George Akerlof points out that in the market for lemons (used-goods market), serious information asymmetry will lead to adverse selection illustrated by the price curve in general economic theory,[11] and ultimately greatly restrain market vitality. The key to solve the problem of information asymmetry and prevent China's capital market from turning into an awkward "market for lemons" is morality. It has been theoretically and practically proven that moral capital management can effectively solve this problem. In fact, the participation of moral capital in economic activities is helpful in developing the professional ethics of the jobholders of intermediaries. With moral intermediaries, financial and audit reports will be issued independently and justly to guarantee that information obtained by investors are true and reliable. At the same time, the economic activities of listed companies will be regulated to ensure legal, sound, and rational business operations. In this way, investors will have a clear picture of listed companies, and their doubts caused by information asymmetry will be removed. Once the problem of information asymmetry is solved, the capital market will see less deception and cheating, and investment will prevail over speculation. As a result, the capital market will walk into prosperity.

Second, moral capital guides investors to invest in companies with a sense of social responsibility.

In the capital market, the independence of moral capital also manifests as guidance for investors. In addition to working with physical capital, moral capital, a kind of capital that is as important as physical capital, has found a new way to play its unique roles in the form of moral indexes. On July 31, 2011, Financial Times launched eight FTSE4GOOD "moral indexes" at London Stock Exchange in the UK. When explaining the idea of "moral indexes," the CEO of Financial Times, Mark Makepeace indicates that the indexes were launched at the request of investors. He states, "While choosing investees, investors showed a strong preference to companies with a sense of social responsibility. Recently, investment on such companies has quadrupled (Liu 2001)." Moral indexes judge and select companies based on certain standards. They encourage investors to invest in companies that have a sense of social responsibility and high moral quality, which makes the management of moral capital more practical and feasible. Superficially, the change of moral indexes guides investors; however, in actuality, companies' management of moral capital is the real source of power behind it. In new economic conditions, for a company, "it is the PE ratio rather than capital and assets that determine its corporate value; while the PE ratio is determined by a price-to-eyeball ratio, or 'attention', rather than the expectation of investors (Zhang 2000)." Since the "attention" is largely determined by the moral indexes of companies, those performing well in the input and management of moral capital tend to have higher moral indexes, thus attracting more investors and obtaining higher economic returns. This manifests as

---

[11] In general economic theory, the interpretation of price curve is that for a commodity, when it price increase, its market demand decreases, and there will be fewer buyers; when its price decreases, it is market demand increases, and there will be more buyers. If in a market, the information of the buyer and seller is serious asymmetric, adverse selection will occur, that is, the commodity price decreases, the market demand decreases and there are fewer buyers.

higher aggregate financing and share prices. On the contrary, companies that ignore or even despise morality will have low "moral indexes." If they are unable to attract investors, they will consequently suffer from a slump in share price.

2.2.2.4 The Value Realization of Moral Capital is Multi-dimensional

The value realization of moral capital is multi-dimensional. It is determined by the dependence of moral capital that the direct goal of moral capital is facilitating the appreciation of physical capital. However, the appreciation of physical capital or material economic goods is not the only value embodiment of moral capital. In fact, through scientific management, moral capital can realize its value in different dimensions. First, moral capital realizes its value by facilitating the maintenance of value and the increase of material economic goods. With scientific management, moral capital can fully play its roles to realize the maintenance of value and the increase of physical capital, including entity capital, financial capital, and equity capital. This is the motive power that drives moral capital to exist and participate in capital management. Second, moral capital realizes its value through its own value progress. On the one hand, such progress mainly lies in the improvement of various expressly stated moral norm systems, and the rationality and feasibility of expressly stated moral regulations and rules. On the other hand, it lies in the constant assimilation between not expressly stated moral spirits, moral beliefs and moral concepts. Third, moral capital realizes its value by facilitating the appreciation of intangible capital. Intangible capital means "capitalized immaterial assets that are controlled by specific subjects that can continuously play their roles in production, management and service, and that can bring economic benefits to their owners in a certain period of time (Lei and Liu 1999)." The social benefits brought by moral capital will improve corporate image, strengthen consumers' sense of identity of corporate culture and enhance corporate reputation. In a company, especially in the sector of human resources, the realization of moral capital plays the roles of improving employees' moral quality, promoting the harmonious interpersonal relationship among employees, enhancing the overall cohesion of the company, and strengthening the sense of responsibility of employees. In addition, moral capital can, at the spiritual level, improve the enthusiasm and creativity of technical personnel to accelerate the realization of rational R&D and production, thus promoting the scientific application of patents and franchises.

2.2.2.5 Benefits Generated by Moral Capital are Long Lasting and Durable

Relative to other kinds of capital, moral capital requires a greater length of time to create benefits, but its positive influence will also last longer. In *Moral Capital*, I systematically expounded why it takes a relatively long time for moral capital to create benefits. This time, I will also talk about the long-lasting effects of the benefits of moral capital, which will accordingly affect companies over a longer period time.

First, since the "the formation of moral capital is slow and arduous," and it needs a "special process" for moral capital to create benefits, it is only natural that moral capital requires an extensive amount of time to create benefits (Wang 2000b). We must note that the formation and improvement of virtues of positive significance, as well as the improvement of people's moral quality and consciousness are relatively long processes; therefore, compared with the formation of other kinds of capital that of moral capital will take a longer time. Moreover, the value realization of moral capital in various dimensions is a more complex and slower process. Second, moral capital creates long-term benefits. Moral capital penetrates into physical capital and realizes it value by building brands. Once a brand is built, its "sustainable and steady development, advantageous production status, huge economic value and high social reputation (Wang 1997)" will bring long-term economic benefits to the company. It has been discovered that a good corporate image can bring long-lasting and long-term benefits to companies. On the contrary, companies ignoring moral capital tend to be hit by deadly blows. Here is an example. On November 28, 2001, S&P lowered Enron's rating to B−, and Moody's lowered its rating to B2, while also indicating the possibility of a further de-rating. In just one day, Enron suffered an 85 % slide (Zhang 2002). It is true that it takes a longer time for moral capital to create benefits relative to other kinds of capital, but its benefits last a longer time. In a company, when the input and management of moral capital are ignored, or the functions of moral capital in economic activities are denied, the company is bound to suffer from a catastrophe.

2.3 The Economic Interpretation of Moral Capital[12]

A few years ago, in *Moral Capital* (Wang 2000b), I originally put forward and expounded the concept of "moral capital." In the later *The Second Study on Moral Capital*, and *The Third Study on Moral Capital*, I made a further study and analysis of "moral capital." The topic attracted the attention of the academic circle, and the echoing, questioning and discussion of some scholars brought the study on moral capital to a deeper level. This section will have a deeper exploration of moral capital from the perspective of economics, thus better revealing the rational intension of moral capital.

[12] Originally titled as The Fourth Study on Moral Capital (co-written by Hua Guihong), *Jiangsu Social Sciences*, Issue 6, 2004; reprinted fully in *Ethics*, Copied Newspaper and Periodicals of Renmin University of China, Issue 2, 2003. This paper has been included in Moral Capital and Business Ethics (*Selected Works of Wang Xiaoxi*), People's Publishing House, 2009.

2.3.1 Capital in a Broad Sense and Moral Capital

"Capital" is a very important word in economics. Unless particularly specified, the general attribute of capital refers to the ability to participate in the production of commodities and services and create social wealth. To be specific, capital is obtained via investment. Every kind of investment is made primarily to improve the economic agent's ability to create wealth in the future. Investment is considered flows while the result thereof (e.g., capital) is considered stocks. In other words, capital is the embodiment of the ability to create wealth in the future—the ability deriving from the accumulation of investment. Therefore, capital reflects the ability to create wealth, which constitutes the fundamental intension and essential attribute of capital in the modern society.

Then, what is the extension of capital? Based on the intension that "capital is the ability to create social wealth," the extension of capital, as considered by traditional theory, can be physical capital and monetary capital that is materialized or monetized, or has a kind of immaterialized existence, such as "human capital," which has been widely accepted.[13] It can be a tangible ability that is physical, financial, and human in nature, as well as an intangible ability that can create social wealth. That is, aside from widely accepted tangible capital, such as physical, monetary, and human capital, capital also includes intangible capital. Intangible capital mainly includes "knowledge capital," which acts as the core corporate competitiveness in management; "social capital," which is a key component of sociology; and "moral capital," which is the topic to be discussed herein. These kinds of intangible capital have general attributes of capital, for they all exist in general production and can improve the economic agent's ability to create social wealth.

The concept of "moral capital" is put forward according to the concept of capital in a broad sense which exists based on capital's general attribute of "creating social wealth as a kind of ability."

In the history of Western economic thought, the emergence and evolution of the broad concept of capital started from the emergence and evolution of the thought of human capital. Therefore, we can understand moral capital according to the theory of capital in a broad sense based on the concept and theory of human capital.

In fact, before Theodore William Schultz and Gary Stanley Becker, some economists, such as William Petty, Adam Smith, J. H. Von Thunen, Irving Fisher, and Alfred Marshall, had considered man as a kind of capital. However, since human capital was seldom included in the formal and core content of economics, capital at one time only referred to physical capital and monetary (financial) capital. Therefore, in

[13] Since William Petty, who was called "the father of English political economy" by Marx, the roles played by human power in economic management and development have been a focus of economics. One of Petty's wisdoms is "labor is the father and active principle of wealth, as lands are the mother." Petty did not say "labor is the father, as lands are the mother" and used "active." He meant something. Of course, modern human capital theory was developed by Theodore William Schultz. In the perspective of human capital theory, human capital is a human ability to create wealth, and the ability herein means knowledge, skills, physical conditions, etc.

the history of Western economics, American economists Theodore William Schultz and Gary Stanley Becker founded the formal theory of human capital after World War II and won the Nobel Prize in Economics for their study on human capital. According to Schultz, an objective existence that can "provide economic value of productive services is a kind of capital (Theodore 1990a)." With improved knowledge, skills and comprehensive quality, man can internally improve production capacity, increase productivity, and provide productive services; therefore, it can tentatively be said that human capital exists (and shall be included) in capital in a broad sense.

In China, "capital" has long been understood from the perspective of the relations of production. According to Marxist political economics, capital is the value created by surplus value. It is not materials, but the certain relations of production between capitalists and workers; while the means of production, as the materialization of such relations, thus become capital. Since the content of capital progresses with social progress, it is natural that the relations represented by capital are advantageous in the capitalist society than in the feudal society. However, the "shell" of socialist relations of production will ultimately be broken because it cannot stop the expansion of the revolutionary relations of production that grow internally.

In fact, the concept of capital that we know from the perspective of the relations of production is just a part of the Marxist concept of capital. In *Outlines of the Critique of Political Economy (Drafted 1857–1858)*, an important achievement made by Marx in the 1950s about his re-study of the political economy, he points out, "The saving of labor time is equal to an increase of free time, i.e. time for the full development of the individual, which in turn reacts back upon the productive power of labor as itself the greatest productive power. From the standpoint of the direct production process, it can be regarded as the production of fixed capital, with this fixed capital being man himself."[14] In section (c) "The production of means of production increases as the increase of labor productivity. The free time in the capitalist society and communist society," Marx writes, "The direct production process itself here appears only as a moment. The conditions and objectifications of the process are themselves equally moments of it, and its only subjects are the individuals, but individuals in mutual relationships, which they equally reproduce and produce anew. The constant process of their own movement, in which they renew themselves even as they renew the world of wealth they create."[15]

In our opinion, the conclusion that "this fixed capital being man himself" is undoubtedly the further expansion of Marx's definition of capital. Obviously, Marx landed at this conclusion by taking the abstract of capitalist relations of production and replacing it with the premise of the direct production process. He called "man" who fully plays his roles in the direct production process as "fixed capital." As a kind of capital, human capital makes the intension and extension of capital in economic development extending to capital in a broad sense with human capital as

[14] *Collected Works of Karl Marx and Friedrich Engels*, Vol. 46 (II), People's Publishing House,1980, p. 225.

[15] *Collected Works of Karl Marx and Friedrich Engels*, Vol. 46 (II), People's Publishing House, 1980, p. 226.

the core. Marshall once said, "Capital is principally composed of knowledge and organizations.... Knowledge is our most powerful engine of production."[16] From the perspective of the subsequent ability of economic development—the accumulation of capital, Schultz points out, "The concept of human capital has laid a foundation for the accumulation of capital in a broad sense (Theodore 1990a)."

For moral capital, from the standpoint of academic compatibility, we can consider that in the view of capital in a broad sense, labor is an element in the utilization of labor where "labor is the Father and active principle of wealth"; is a kind of ability that "can provide economic value of productive services"; and is an element that constitutes a kind of "fixed capital being man himself." Furthermore, morality is the "spiritual aspect of human capital and the spiritual intension of physical capital (Wang 2002)." Since "capital is principally composed of knowledge and organizations," morality, as man's cognition and understanding of his own improvement, of principles for harmonious interpersonal relationships, and of human behavior norms, is man's "knowledge" and adaptive capacity regarding himself and the social environment, and of course, an organic component of capital. Therefore, the content as a theoretical system of moral capital shall also exist as an organic component of the "theory of capital accumulation in a broad sense." In capital theories, the theory of moral capital shall hold a place.

2.3.2 Moral Resource as an Institutional Resource

To become capital, a substance, or a kind of existence must have the general attributes of "resources." Is morality a resource?

As we know, morality is man's cognition and understanding of his own improvement, of principles for harmonious interpersonal relationships and of human behavior norms, and is the social ethical norms and principles abided by economic agents. Undoubtedly, according to the theoretical frame of new institutional economics, institutions are norms and rules that constrain people's transaction behavior. Thus, morality is an institution. Different from a "formal constraint" like law, morality is an "informal constraint."[17] When taking about morality, we must talk

---

[16] Marshall, *Principles of Economics* (I), Commercial Press, 1981, p. 157.

[17] In new institutional economics, law and morality are considered as "formal constraint" and "informal constraint," which, in our view, is not proper. According to the logic of new institutional economics, formal constraints are a series of norms and rules (from laws to independent agreements) created by man consciously. Based on the method of exclusion, morality (a kind of ideology) was classified as an informal constraint. This surly means that morality is not a norm created by man consciously to constrain his behavior, which does not agree with the real management and development conditions of social economies. A sound moral system does not form naturally. On the contrary, it needs to be designed, built and maintained, and it even needs a "punishment" system consciously built to push forward the construction of a sound moral system. In real social life, the construction of the social moral constraint system is by no means progressive and unconscious. Moral development is an important part of socialist cultural and ideological development, and denying morality's character as a formal constraint is, in some sense, denying the importance of morality in social and economic activities. Therefore, we think it is necessary to re-study the

about institutions, for institutions that include law and morality are actually also resources for the development of the social economy.

In general, "resources" in "resource allocation" refers to scarce resources such as land (natural resources), capital (physical capital), and human resources. We believe that institutions, with their special attributes, are very important elements and resources for economic development.[18] Resources can be divided into two categories: resources existing independently, such as land, capital, and human resources; and resources existing dependently, like technology, organizations, morality, and institutions.

Then, under which category do institutions fall?

First, all resources are considered as input. In any social production process, institutions or rules are a kind of important "input." Without certain orderly rules, production can only be Robinson's production, and the sociality of the production process (including the sociality of family production and operation) certainly requires the participation of orderly rules adapting to such production process, regardless of whether the rules are formal regulatory restrictions (laws and regulations) or informal social conventions (morals and customs).

Second, all resources are used at costs. Therefore, in different production processes and transactions, institutions and rules are introduced and developed with different costs. As Douglass C. North states, "resources are consumed to define and protect property rights and fulfill contracts (Douglass 1994)." The development of institutions provides primitive institutional resources for the production process, while the introduction of new institutions marks the change and innovation of institutions. No matter what, development or introduction of institutions, the process is accompanied by the consumption of noninstitutional resources. More specifically, when the microcosmic economic agent develops or changes its institutions, a certain amount of direct costs will arise, while the change of macroscopic social institutions actually means the benefit adjustment and restructuring among socioeconomic agents, which, in most cases, will generate a certain amount of social costs. Therefore, generally speaking, institutions are scarce resources obtained at costs, and the allocation and application thereof are also realized at costs.

Third, the most important thing is that different ways of allocation of different resources lead to different economic performances, and the differences between different institutional resources will affect economic performance.

At the microlevel, the core of transaction cost theory in new Western institutional economics is analyzing how institutions and institutional changes determine and affect the transaction cost level in the world of nonzero transaction costs. Indeed, institutions significantly affect the transaction cost level and thus affect economic

classification of "formal constraints" and "informal constraints." In this book, the issue is not discussed profoundly. As for the theoretical research on "formal constraints" and "informal constraints," please see Douglass C. North, *Institutions, Institutional Change and Economic Performance*, Shanghai Sanlian Bookstore, 1994.

[18] For the analysis on the special attributes of institutional resources, please see Effective Supply and Economic Development, Nanjing Normal University Press, Chapter V "Innovation and Economic Progress," 2000, pp. 183–191.

efficiency. The well-known Coase theorem explains the close relation between the efficiency of resource allocation and (property right) institutions. Institutions affect transaction costs by increasing or decreasing the value of main parameters, such as uncertainties, externalities and opportunistic behavior. It is worth noting that institutions can also affect transaction costs by changing the means of the transaction. Generally, it is believed that companies are the substitutions of the price mechanism. The establishment of companies greatly reduces transaction costs, thus improving the efficiency of resource allocation. However, the establishment of companies will not necessarily lead to an improvement in efficiency, for alike companies with the same noninstitutional resources are different in efficiency, and the separation and revocation of companies will sometimes lead to the improvement of efficiency. In fact, the establishment and change of companies are, essentially, about turning external market transactions into internal corporate transactions. The rationality of internal transaction institutions and rules determines the transaction cost level, and it also affects the rationality of corporate organizations, causing the X-efficiency or X-inefficiency of resource allocation.[19] In *Moral Capital*, I analyzed the X-efficiency or X-inefficiency of resource allocation from the perspective of "the value realization of moral capital." From the aspects of "human moral quality and productivity," "management morality and corporate vitality," "moral content and product quality," and "credit and market share," I expound how morality affects the efficiency of resource allocation in details (Wang 2000b).

At the macro-level, different institutional frameworks will greatly affect economic development. One of the very famous points of North is that "the development of an efficient economic organization in Western Europe accounts for the rise of the West." "An efficient organization entails the establishment of institutional arrangements and property rights that create an incentive to channel individual economic effort into activities that bring the private rate of return close to the social rate of return (Douglass and Robert 1998)." The effects of institutions and rules on economic development and efficiency have a more solid foundation and a more powerful precondition than organizations. The purpose of North's statement is to refute the opinion that "technical innovation is the primary reason for the economic development of the West," which was held by many economic historians. Of course, we cannot agree with the opinion of North completely, even though his opinion has greatly enlightened us. He made the mistake of "hypercorrection": for the economic development of a country, institutional resources are as important as other available resources. Without sound institutions and orderly rules, regardless of the abundance and massive input of other resources, the production possibility frontier of the country cannot be sustainably expanded, and its overall efficiency of resource allocation can hardly be increased. The lack of institutions will seriously constrain economic development. On the contrary, the change and innovation of institutions will greatly

[19] In *Institutions, Institutional Change and Economic Performance*, Douglass C. North points out that the effect of institutions on economic performance is much complex than its mere or main effect on the constitution of transaction cost level. In fact, the interaction among skills, institutions, organizations, transformation costs and transaction costs is mutual and crossed.

regulate the utilization of other resources, thus becoming an important source of economic development.

From the above analysis of the resource attribute of institutions, we can see that morality, as a part of institutions, is also a resource.

Since the production of a certain non-Robinson's social economy can only take place with the regulation of particular norms and rules, a certain moral system is necessary. What's more, it takes a certain amount of time for moral rules to form and adapt to the development of a certain economy. We can consider the change of morality as the most formidable "slow variable" in social change. Besides, the formation of moral rules is not a thing in itself, which forms without any input. On the contrary, the formation and operation of the moral system, the improvement of moral quality, as well as social and cultural progress all need to be realized. In other words, the moral system is constructed at the cost of a lot of resources. Once the moral system is built, it will start to play its unique roles at the micro and macro-levels. A sound moral system shall first act as an effective social constraint and a very effective "incentive mechanism," which will constrain "opportunistic" motivation and behavior, and control "moral hazards" to reduce the efficiency loss of socio-economic resource allocation caused by "opportunistic behavior. On the contrary, without an effective moral system, "opportunistic" motivation and behavior will run rampant and out of our control. There is no need for us to accurately estimate the loss of social resource allocation caused by the lack of morality and credit during the socioeconomic transformation period—the loss is tremendous. From the macroscopic perspective, the economic downturns occurring over the past 20 years are more or less related to people ignoring the functions of morality, consciously or unconsciously. From the microscopic perspective, in most cases, the falling of companies in competitions is related to the lack of morality and credit.

In the socioeconomic system or institutional arrangement system, law and morality work together. Therefore, when talking about institutional resources, it is necessary to pay attention to the relations and differences between the roles (including processes and results) played by law and morality. In short, in the field of the economic analysis of law (or law and economics), a lot of research concerning the effects of law on socioeconomic development and the efficiency of the legal system has been made. The research results show that law, by protecting property rights, preventing intimidation, resolving differences, and reducing the loss caused by non-cooperation, lowers transaction costs and thus improves the efficiency of resource allocation and pushes forward economic development. It is worth noting that compared with law, morality shall be considered as a more important and economical (economically efficient) resource. During the process of transaction, in addition to abiding by the law, it is more important to build a good reputation to obtain more market value resources. It can be said that credit and integrity play a more important role than law in realizing the prosperity of a company. In a society beset by a general lack of credit and integrity, the phenomenon of "law fails where violators are legion" may happen. Regarding this, Mao Yushi once said, "A covenant must be made on a credible and reliable basis. Legal protection without the precondition of credit can hardly, and even cannot guarantee the fulfillment of the covenant

(Mao 2003)." In fact, even in the eyes of economic analysis researchers, law is a "luxury." In the regulation of socioeconomic rules, the formulation and application of laws are very costly. Let alone the cost of legislation, for the application of laws, as said by Robert B. Cooter and Thomas Ulen, "no one knows how much social wealth has been spent to solve social disputes (Mao 2003)."

Relative to law, morality (as non-mandatory, introspective, positively incentive social norms and rules) is a more precious and economical resource for social development. As physical, monetary, and human resources that can become capital resources, moral capital is also a social resource—moral capital resource, which plays an essential role in greatly improving the economic efficiency in the entire process of reproduction and the transaction of a social economy with orderly and efficient development.

2.3.3 The Economic Logic that Moral Source can Become Moral Capital

Why can moral resource be called "moral capital"? To answer this question, an economically logical and reasonable explanation is needed.

We have demonstrated repeatedly that during the process of creating wealth, namely, the entire process of reproduction (including production, exchange, distribution, and consumption), morality plays its unique roles everywhere. The economy is filled with "morals" characterized by "dependence," "independence," "penetration," and "guidance (Wang 2002)." Furthermore, demonstrating that "the economy is filled with morals" is not enough to prove the existence and functions of moral capital; we still need to empirically analyze the roles played by morality in socioeconomic development. That is, we need to focus on demonstrating the indispensability of moral capital in socioeconomic development and expounding the unique roles played by moral capital in promoting social production and social wealth creation.

First, unrestrained reproduction and transaction processes are accompanied by extremely high costs.

In the process of reproduction, interpersonal relationship is maintained at the cost of certain resource consumption. In new institutional economics, such a cost is called "transaction cost." In this case, "transaction," in a broad sense, means interpersonal interaction. In economics, the intension of "transaction" is much more profound than that of "exchange." In some sense, the transaction process is the reproduction process in a broad sense. The reason is that their essences are both interpersonal interactions and relationships, which occur during the process of creating wealth. Generally, transaction costs include three parts: the costs of collecting information, of negotiation and signing contracts, and of fulfilling contracts. If transactions are conducted under the condition of limited information and rationality, not to mention the costs of information collection, unrestrained transaction progress will be out of order, and the transaction process and results will be uncertain. The most typical results, as profoundly revealed by information economics, are "adverse selection" and "moral hazards." Given the above, it is necessary to introduce constraint and incentive mechanisms. Moral constraint and motivation are indispensable in economic activities.

Second, morality is a constrain mechanism that can effectively reduce opportunistic behavior.

In a transaction production, the motivation and future behavior of every party involved are uncertain to some extent. Therefore, a major source where transaction costs arise from is the moral hazard behavior that damages the interest of the parties involved. It is true that in real economic life, man's nature is self-interest. In this case, without effective moral constraints, opportunistic behavior that attempts to be "free riding" will prevail, obstructing the progress of transactions due to extremely high transaction costs.

In general, morality takes on productivity during the process of reducing the consumption of physical resources or transaction costs that arise from interpersonal interactions. Morality and law, as institutional resources, work together to constrain the parties involved in a transaction. Undoubtedly, with effective constraints during the transaction process, transaction costs will drop significantly, which reflects the key role played by morality.

Third, the altruism of morality constructs the self-discipline mechanism and incentive mechanism of parties involved in the transaction.

It can be said that morality, as other economic resources, penetrates into the entire process of economic development. By constructing an effective self-discipline mechanism for the parties involved in a transaction, it reduces the transaction costs, improves the efficiency of resource allocation, and accelerates wealth creation. From the process, it obtains the ability to create social wealth like other capital resources, thus obtaining the general attributes of capital.

Morality effectively constrains parties involved in the transaction, which makes it a kind of capital. Under the constraint of moral norms and rules, parties concerned transact in accordance with agreed transaction rules. Essentially, morality is embodied as "responsibility"; therefore, when moral rules, followed by parties concerned (economic men), participate in the transaction with self-interest purposes, the self-interest purposes and altruistic behaviors are unified. In this way, the interests of the parties involved are satisfied. In fact, in an orderly market economy, under the constraint of moral rules, one party can only realize its own goals by first meeting the needs of the other party. Confucius once said, "What you do not wish for yourself, do not do to others." Similarly, what you do wish for yourself, do to others first. Only when producers provide buyers with commodities or services that meet buyers' effective needs (the behavior is essentially altruistic) are they able to realize the value of their commodities and services, and thus realize their own subjective benefits.

Furthermore, we can say in an orderly market economy, altruistic (responsible) behavior leads to more altruistic results. Behind altruistic (responsible) behavior are moral norms and rules, moral constraints and incentives, and the unique roles that are effectively played by moral capital. In short, morality, with its constraints and incentive functions, prevents the "moral hazard" in the transaction process, reduces the uncertainties caused by human factors and lowers transaction costs. In this way, on the one hand, it improves the efficiency of resource allocation and accelerates the creation of social creation, and, on the other hand, obtains the general attributes of capital, thus becoming a precious institutional resource. Ultimately, it becomes moral capital—a kind of capital in a broad sense.

2.4 The Concept and Functions of Moral Capital in History and the Contemporary World[20]

"Moral capital" is a new and controversial concept.[21] The focus of controversy is that "moral capital" can be a judgment—"morality is a kind of capital," and the judgment implies two basic concepts, namely, "morality as a kind of capital" and "capital in the form of morality," which seem to deviate from people's traditional understanding of "morality" and "capital." However, I believe that the concept of "moral capital" is a new intension of "morality" and "capital" in the context of the contemporary world. This section aims at discussing the formation of the concept of "moral capital" and its contemporary significance, thus profoundly illustrating the special roles played by morality as an instrument in economic development.

2.4.1 From "Morality as an End" to "Morality as an Instrument"

The primary difference between "morality as a kind of capital" and "morality in the general sense" lies in the understanding of their functions. Generally speaking, morality[22] has two functions: first, it functions as an end—morality, through defining the significance and ends of the existence of man and society, delegates responsibility to the moral subject based on what should be done and provides moral constraints in the form of rules; and second, the function as an instrument—on the basis

[20] Originally titled as The Fifth Study on Moral Capital (co-written by Li Zhixiang), *Jiangsu Social Sciences*, Issue 5, 2006; reprinted fully in *Ethics*, Issue 10, 2006. This paper has been included in Moral Capital and Business Ethics (*Selected Works of Wang Xiaoxi*), People's Publishing House, 2009.

[21] See the series of papers of Wang Xiaoxi for the research on "moral capital," including, Moral Capital, *Jiangsu Social Sciences*, Issue 3, 2000; The Second Study on Moral Capital, *Jiangsu Social Sciences*, Issue 1, 2002; The Third Study on Moral Capital, *Jiangsu Social Sciences*, Issue 6, 20023; The Fourth Study on Moral Capital, *Jiangsu Social Sciences*, Issue 6, 2004; and Wang Xiaoxi et al., *Moral Capital Theory*, People's Publishing House, 2005. For the controversy over "moral capital," please see The Capitalist Characteristics of Morality (Zheng Gencheng, Luo Jiancheng, et al., Journey of Zhuzhou Institute of Technology, Issue 5, 2002).

[22] In this case, morality means morality complying with the law of historical development in a certain historical period. Presently, it refers to morality in a scientific sense.

that the moral subject is responsible for what he should do, morality provides moral support to promote the existence and development of other things, thus presenting the reasons and value for its own existence.[23] In fact, in the economic sphere, capital has existed as an instrument to create profits. People do not accumulate capital for more capital, but for making profits. "Morality as a kind of capital" is used as an instrument to create profits; therefore, from "morality in the general sense" to "morality as a kind of capital," the main change is that morality's function as an instrument to create profits is highlighted.

It seems that taking morality as an instrument to create profits has deviated from people's traditional understanding on the functions of morality, for some hold that morality should be considered as an end rather than an instrument. However, the development of moral research has proved that acknowledging and highlighting morality's function, as an instrument in economic development, is one of the general trends of moral research and one of the basic requirements for the development of a modern society.

Traditionally, it is held that morality's function as an end is vastly superior to its function as an instrument and plays the decisive role. This can be understood from the following three aspects:

First, traditional moral research focused on the ultimate end and significance of an individual or a group of people, which establishes the dominance of morality as an end in society. Traditional ideologists mainly tried to answer the questions of what moral people are, what a moral life is, and what a moral society is. These questions share a single common core, that is, the ultimate end of man to exist and live. The answer given by Aristotle is "the highest good (Aristotle 1992)." In his opinion, all actions and choices are made to achieve good ends. Ends fall into different levels, so does good. Standing at the top of good, which is expected by people themselves, is the "highest good"—the ultimate end that ultimately constrains all other social behavior. Therefore, morality, taking "the highest good" as its primary content, is bound to play its role mainly as an end. In ancient Greece and Rome, and the Middle Ages, most ideologists followed the ethical ideology of Aristotle: a moral goal at the highest position is put forward at first, and then actions and choices are made in various aspects of society to realize a goal. Chinese Confucians thought in the same way: they stressed the importance of morality in every aspect of social life, believing that "morality is superior to interests" and "morality regulates the behavior of making interests."

Second, from the relationship between ethics and other social disciplines, it can be seen that the former stands high above the latter. Such a relationship indicates that the primary function of morality is defining the ultimate end of man to exist, and that of other disciplines is studying and providing various necessary means to realize the ultimate end. Aristotle held that politics, taking the highest good as its subject, "is the most sovereign and most authoritative science" that is "served by other sciences." Sciences, including tactics, money management, and oratory, all

[23] For the "dual functions of morality," please see Li Zhixiang, On the Dual Dimensions of the Research on Economic Ethics, *Studies on Ethics*, Issue 1, 2006.

belong to politics (Aristotle 1992). Ethics dominated over disciplines for a very long time; the late philosopher Epicurus even claimed that natural science should be the subordinate to ethics. He defined "good" as happiness, and wrote, "If we were not troubled by our suspicions of the phenomena of the sky and about death, and also by our failure to grasp the limits of pain and desires, we should have no need for natural science."[24] Adam Smith, who built his reputation based on *The Wealth of Nations*, actually studied economics under the title of "Professor of Moral Philosophy." It tells us that even in Britain in the eighteenth century, economics was still a branch of ethics. According to traditional Confucianism, the moral development of individuals was considered as the basis for the development of a country. This indicates that the study of ethics and morals was considered as the basic discipline of ethics, and other disciplines were used as instruments to promote moral development from the individual level to the family level and the societal level.

Third, morality as an instrument is closely related to morality as an end, that is, morality as an instrument is used to realize the moral ends rather than any ends. In traditional moral research, morality was also considered as an instrument. It is just that it was used to realize its own ends, instead of any other social ends. While defining "brave," Plato pointed out, "The brave man preserves [conservation] both in pain and pleasures and in desires and fears and does not expel it from his soul (Plato 1994)." Here, the "conservation in desires and fears" is a moral end, and "being brave" is a moral instrument that submits to and helps achieve the end. The thought of Plato coincides with Chinese Confucian thought. According to Confucius, "a brave man is a moral man at first."[25] In this case, bravery submits to morality and helps develop morality as an instrument.

In the modern society, social sciences are independent from general ethics. Claiming that "value" should be distinguished from "fact," social sciences keep value out of their fields to set their independent ends of development, thus eliminating the constraints of morality. In this case, the dominance of morality as an end is broken, and morality as an instrument gradually breaks free from the moral ends. That is, aside from serving the moral ends, morality as an instrument also services other independent disciplines.

In the field of politics, controversial Italian politician Machiavelli is the first one to put morality's function as an instrument ahead of its function as an end. In *The Prince*, he wrote that a successful prince must "be a fox to discover the snares and a lion to terrify the wolves (Machiavelli 1996)." In the sense of morality, a successful prince is neutral, that is, he could be good to bring happiness to his people or be evil to bring disasters to his people. Therefore, the quality of a successful prince is not constrained by morality, but is only a moral instrument. We can understand it like this: we advocate bravery (a lion to terrify the wolves) and wisdom (a fox to discover the snares) just because they are helpful in realizing a political end rather than a moral end. Therefore, the impact of Machiavellianism is that it completely

[24] [Greece] Epicurus and Lucretius, Epicureanism: Doctrine of Epicurus, translated by Bao Limin, China Social Sciences Publishing House, 2004, p. 39.

[25] *The Analects of Confucius·The Practice of Government.*

separates politics from ethics, "focusing on the measures taken to achieve ends no matter whether the ends are good or evil (Russell 2003)." Thus, a new approach was developed that combines ethics and politics—"political ethics," which differs from "ethical politics." "Ethical politics" pursues "politics following the nature of ethics," while "political ethics" pursues "ethics that meet the requirements of politics."

The Dutch philosopher Mandeville was another controversial figure for his thoughts about morality. In *The Fable of the Bees: or, Private Vices, Public Benefits*, he reveals, "So Vice is beneficial found, When it's by justice bound; Nay, where the people would be great, As necessary to the state, As hunger is to make 'em eat. Bare Virtue can't make Nations live, In splendor; they, that -would revive, A Golden Age, must be as free, For acorns, as for Honesty (Bernard 2002)." He was criticized because he, superficially, defended the rationality of vices, which may make vices more rampant. However, Mandeville later left researchers with the following question: what kind of morality do we need to create a materially prosperous society? Obviously, "virtue" in this case refers to a means to realize material prosperity.

Later, the thoughts of Machiavelli and Mandeville were developed into one of the dominant thoughts of empirical sociologists, namely, the principle of "value neutrality." This principle requires researchers to put value evaluation and moral emotions aside when analyzing a social phenomenon, namely, using empirical analysis to find out the ends caused by different means, regardless of whether the ends are moral or not. Max Weber said, "An empirical science cannot tell anyone what he *should* do—but rather what he can do—and under certain circumstances—what he *wishes* to do (Weber 2000)." Empirical sociologists try to expel moral evaluation, including the ultimate moral end, from empirical disciplines to ensure that the research of social sciences is scientific.

Influenced by the above ideological trend, economists also try to separate morality from economics, thus setting its own economic ends. Marshall expressed the opinion clearly. In *Principle of Economics*, he wrote, "But, for all that, the steadiest motive to ordinary business work is the desire for the pay which is the material reward of work. The pay may be on its way to be spent selfishly or unselfishly, for noble or base ends; and here the variety of human nature comes into play. But the motive is supplied by a definite amount of money: and it is this definite and exact money measurement of the steadiest motives in business life, which has enabled economics far to outrun every other branch of the study of man (Marshall 1994)." That is to say, the moral ends of spending the pay is not included in the study of economics, and only the obtainment of the pay, unrelated to morality, is the issue studied by economics. John Maynard Keynes and Lionel Robbins were the representatives supporting the opinion of Marshall. Keynes stated, "The function of political economy is to investigate facts and discover truths about them, not to prescribe rules of life. Economics laws are theorems of fact, not practical precepts. Political economy is, in other words, a science, not an art or a department of ethical enquiry. It is described as standing neutral between competing social schemes. It furnishes information as to the probable consequences of given lines of action, but does not itself pass moral judgment, or pronounce what ought or what ought not to be (Keynes 2001)." Robbins also pointed out, "Unfortunately, it does not seem logically possible to associate the two studies in any form but mere juxtaposition. Economics deals with ascertainable facts; and ethics with valuations and obligations (Lionel 2000)." Amartya Sen, winner of the Nobel Prize in Economics, made the following conclusion regarding this situation: "It can be said that with the development of modern economics, the importance of the methods of ethics has been seriously played down (Sen 2001)." In fact, separating morality from economics, which seems like disciplinary "purification," is actually the regression in the development of economics.

In economics, the principle of "value neutrality" actually only clears away morality as an end, but still keeps morality as an instrument. Economists disconnect morality as an end and morality as an instrument, making the latter serve the former. They do not care about the moral ends in the economic life, but rather have much concern for moral instruments, that is, they only care what morals are beneficial for economic development. Economists do not study why a quality or behavior is moral; they only study what morals should be advocated for the good of economic development. Adam Smith once studied the significance of moral instruments for economic development. He analyzed the virtue of "frugality" from the economic perspective of "what desires are beneficial for economic development," instead of from the ethical perspective of "what desires are necessary and reasonable." He clearly points out, "Frugality increases capital; while extravagance and recklessness diminish capital (Adam 1994)." Keynes later applied the same method when he reversed the early definition of "extravagance." The difference is that he used the theory of "effective demand" instead of "capital accumulation" as the instrument.

In intellectual history, Max Weber was a representative advocating morality as an instrument. In religious sociology, Weber mainly analyzed how morals deriving from religions affect the development of capitalism. In fact, it is a review of the roles played by religious morals in the development of capitalism. Weber found that different religions played different roles in the rising of capitalism. Some promoted the development of capitalism, while some were counterproductive. The reason is that some religions agreed with capitalism in ethical spirits, but some failed. The conclusion made by Weber is that Protestant ethics can promote the development of capitalism, for the "duties," such as abstinence and progressiveness, which are advocated by Protestant ethics, just constitute the spiritual cores of capitalists and salaried workers. He stated, "The ability of mental concentration, as well as the absolutely essential feeling of obligation to one's job, are here most often combined with a strict economy which calculates the possibility of high earnings, and a cool self-control and frugality which enormously increase performance. This provides the most favorable foundation for the conception of labor as an end in itself, as a calling which is necessary to capitalism: the chances of overcoming traditionalism are greatest on account of the religious upbringing (Weber 1992)."

Weber's Protestant ethics developed a brand new perspective: first, an amoral end is set, and then various moral elements, which are helpful in realizing this end, are found. In the theories of modern economics, institutional economics follows this view. After R.H. Coase conducted a study on corporate origination cost, institutional economists found that institutions are an important element pushing forward social and economic development. Douglass C. North pointed out, "The structures of political and economic organizations determine economic performance and the growth of knowledge and technology. The various forms of cooperation and competition in human development and their implementation, as well as the institutions organizing human activities are the very center of the economic history (Douglass 2005)." Then, what are "institutions"? In short, institutions are "the rules of interpersonal interaction." Undoubtedly, moral rules are the most basic among all rules of interpersonal interaction. Institutional economists analyze morality in the following way: they find the morals that can minimize the rational organization costs, thus promoting economic and social development. In *Trust: The Social Virtues and the Creation of Prosperity*, Francis Fukuyama identifies, "... a nation's well-being, as well as its ability to compete, is conditioned by a single, pervasive cultural characteristic: the level of trust inherent in society," which clearly shows the importance of trust as an institutional moral in social development.

The emergence of institutional economics provides a brand new method for ethical research to analyze morality. That is, considering morality as a necessary and effective means for economic development and highlighting morality's function as an instrument. The concept of "morality as a kind of capital" just came into being based on this method. In fact, morality's functions, as an end and as an instrument, cannot be completely separated, and they are not naturally mutually exclusive. Morality cannot exist without the ends, responsibility and constraints from its function as an end; on the contrary, morality cannot realize its practical value without the practical significance provided by its function as an instrument.

2.4.2 From "Physical Capital" to "Moral Capital"

Literally, the difference between "capital" and "moral morality" is that the former refers to capital in a general sense, covering capital in different forms; while the latter refers to capital in a special sense, covering only capital in the form of morality. Therefore, the significance of the concept of "moral capital" is narrowing the extension of capital to further specify its concept. However, from the development of the concept of "moral capital," we can see that it has a greatly profound significance: initially, "capital" did not refer to capital in a general sense, but capital in a special sense—capital in the form of materials. Therefore, when nonmaterial morality is included in capital by the concept of "moral capital," the extension of "capital" is not narrowed but expanded.

Since the emergence of classical political economics, "capital" has been a very important economic concept. Classical political economists, when analyzing the elements of economic activities, adopted the "trichotomy"—capital, labor, and land. Capital is provided by capitalists, and the income arising from such capital is profits; labor is provided by workers, and the income arising from such labor is wage; land is provided by landlords, and the income arising from such land is rent. However, with the development of modernization and industrialization, capital continuously flew into land, and capitalists constantly defeated landlords. As a result, the importance of land kept decreasing, and land as an element was merged into capital, thus "binary opposition" put forward by Marx formed in economic activities: the opposition between capital and labor, between capitalists and workers, and between profits and wage. In the eyes of later researchers, "capital," in the economic system, has at least the following three characteristics:

First, capital must be capable enough to support the entire process of profit creation, thus making the process manifest as the total capital of the process where capital realizes its appreciation. Although later researchers admit that capital is "resources invested in the market in the expectation of return (Lin 2005)," classical political economists and Marx all held that capital can create profits. What's more, it must create its own profits, and in the process of which, it must realize self-appreciation. Capital realizes self-appreciation by the following means. First, it acts as the elements of production, including the means of labor in the form of constant capital and the means of livelihood (labor) in the form of variable capital. Then, the elements interact with each other—labor, which is controlled by the means of livelihood, processes the subject of labor using the instruments of labor, thus producing profits-contained commodities. Superficially, profits are the outcome of the combination of various elements of production, but in actuality, the process of profit creation is just a "solo dance" of capital. Marx once clearly stated, "If now we take in turn each of the two different forms which self-expanding value successively assumes in the course of its life, we then arrive at these two propositions: Capital is money: Capital is commodities. In truth, however, value is here the active factor in a process, in which, while constantly assuming the form in turn of money and commodities, it at the same time changes in magnitude, differentiates itself by throwing off surplus value from itself; the original value, in other words, expands spontaneously. For the movement, in the course of which it adds surplus value, is its own movement, its expansion, therefore, is automatic expansion (Marx 2001)." Therefore, "capital," in the view of classical political economists and Marx, expands its value spontaneously and is the total of "constant capital" and "variable capital." The difference is classical political economists thought that the "spontaneous expansion of value" creates profits, while Marx thought it creates surplus value. The totality of capital determines that only things, which can independently create profits, can be called capital, and every necessary element for profit creation cannot be independently called capital. Specifically, profits cannot be created without the means of production, land, and labor, which are all not considered independent capital as none of them can create profits independently.

Second, capital manifests abstractly as money and concretely as various materials (elements of production). Abstract capital manifests as a certain amount of money at the start and end of a period, but in the entire process of profit creation, it must be embodied as various elements needed for profit creation. That is, it shall act as a certain amount of means of production (including the subject of labor and instrument of labor) and means of livelihood (including the necessities of life of workers), and then act as a certain amount of commodities. In this case, money, the means of production, and the means of livelihood, are all profits-contained final commodities, which symbolize and manifest as certain tangible materials. Hence, the "capital" understood by classical political economists and Marx is called "physical capital" by later researchers. It should be pointed out that intangible things, such as institutions, law, and culture, might be excluded from the scope of "physical capital." The concept of "physical capital" is closely related to that of "total capital." Their combination makes the process of profit creation a process in which tangible material wealth realizes its value expansion. Of course, Marx once pointed out that the essence of all economic goods is the interpersonal economic relationship. Put another way, an economic relationship must be embodied through tangible materials. Therefore, Marx's "physical capital" has profound intension.

Third, physical capital is of objective independence, which separates itself from its owners. Physical capital exists as "materials" independently of "man." Although all physical capital is owned, it can be independent from its owners. For the owners of physical capital, acquiring, occupying, and transferring physical capital only means the increase or decrease of external material wealth, and they themselves remain the same. Although Marx once stressed that "capitalists are the personalization of capital," the process of profit creation shows clearly that when physical capital constantly changes its forms during the expansion of its value, capitalists who see such expansion remain unchanged. The relative independence of physical capital indicates that only things existing independently of man can be capital; and those existing within man and cannot be separated from man are excluded from the scope of "capital."

Later researchers criticized the "capital" understood by classical political economists and Marx. They called it "traditional capital" or "physical capital." Human resource theorists raised an objection early. They thought if capital is mainly physical capital in the form of natural resources, and if capital is the major force pushing forward social and economic development, then, it is certain that the country with the most abundant natural resources will have the fastest economic development and create the most profits. However, the fact is some countries deficient in natural resources are economically developed, while many countries abundant in natural resources are still developing. Human resource theorists thus made the conclusion that the most important factor determining the economic growth of a country is not natural resources, machines or science, but population quality. As Schultz said, "The decisive factors of production in improving the welfare of poor people are *not* space, energy, and cropland; the decisive factor is the improvement in population quality (Theodore 1990b)." That is, compared with physical capital, human capital is more important.

Human capital theorists try to change people's traditional understanding of capital. They prefer to use marginal analysis method to understand capital. They list the various elements needed for profit creation, and then analyze the marginal investment and marginal income of each element. They believe that only when the marginal investment of an element of production can create profits, the element can be considered as a kind of capital. Schultz said, "I believe, the approach of investment needs to be determined to promote economic development. According to the approach, the amount of capital is increased by investment, and income is increased by adding the productive service of capital, which are the keys of economic growth....Thus, the accounting of all additional investments gives a complete and consistent explanation of the marginal changes in the stock of capital, of the marginal changes in the productive services from capital, of the marginal changes in income and the consequent income increase (Theodore 1990c)."

From the same perspective of capital, human resource theorists put forward the proposition that population quality is also a kind of capital, for the investment in population quality can also bring a certain amount of profits. The investment in health, children's education, adult education, and skill training can all create profits exceeding the cost. Schultz said, "My approach to population quality is to treat quality as a scarce resource, which implies that it has economic value and that its acquisition entails a cost. In analyzing human behavior that determines the type and amount of quality that is acquired over time, the key to the analysis is the relation between the returns from additional quality and the costs of acquiring it. When the returns exceed costs, the stock of population quality will be enhanced (Theodore 1990b)."

It should be noted that the concept of "investment in human capital" can actually be found in the thoughts of Marx. Variable capital, which creates surplus value, manifests as labor (human resource). Moreover, the concepts of "subject productivity," and "spiritual productivity," which were put forward by Marx, essentially focus on the roles played by man in the production process. Furthermore, the conclusion of "science and technology are part of the productive forces" made by Marx also contains the thought of human capital investment.

In the theory of human capital, population quality is considered as a kind of capital. Conceptually, human capital tries to change traditional capital from the following three aspects:

First, the concept of human capital tries to break free from the constraint of total capital, considering the necessary elements in the process of profit creation as capital. Physical capital can create profits and be embodied in elements of production, but human capital, as an element of production, cannot create profits. Although physical capital manifests as a certain amount of money abstractly, in the process of profit creation, as elements of production, it transfers materials into profits. The entire process of capital expansion is actually the transformation of capital in form. However, human capital that participates in the entire process of profit creation is only embodied in labor; and many elements of production, including the means of production, are not the physical embodiment of human capital. Therefore, the process of profit creation cannot reflect the value expansion of human capital. The reason why population capital is considered as a kind of capital is that in the condition that other elements of production remain relatively unchanged, the investment in population quality can create profits higher than the cost. Therefore, the concept of human capital opens the doors for analyzing the capitalization of various elements of production: every element in the process of profit creation may be considered as an independent object of investment, as long as the cost is lower than the profits.

Second, the concept of human capital tries to break the definition that capital is in the form of tangible materials, while incorporating intangible things. Physical capital, coming from natural resources, exists in the form of tangible materials, and human capital contains a lot of intangible elements. In the theory of human capital, population quality mainly includes the physical and psychological conditions, education level as well as knowledge and skills of man, among which, except the physical condition of man which has some characteristics of physical capital, the rest are totally intangible and conceptual. However, when they are considered by the theory of human capital to be profitable, they actually have broken free from the constraint of capital in form. That is, anything, no matter tangible or intangible, can be called capital as long as it creates profits.

Third, the concept of human capital tries to break the notion that capital is independent from man, considering things internalized as the elements of man as capital. Physical capital, independent from man, can be owned by anyone and can be transferred freely in legal ways, whereas, human capital, which is completely internalized as a part of its owners, cannot be separated from its owners. Due to this reason, human capital owners must participate in the process where human capital forms to improve their population quality. What is more, after the population capital of labor is formed, it cannot be freely transferred to another.

Human capital management theory, which is developed based on the theory of human capital, further expands the concept of human capital from the perspective of corporate management. It includes things contributing to improving the productivity of employees, such as talent recruitment, employee motivation, and skill training, in the scope of human capital. According to human capital management theory, any measure that can improve the productivity of employees can be considered as investment in human capital, which greatly develops the concept of human capital.

After the concept of capital was expanded by human capital, the theory of "cultural capital" emerged. Cultural capital theorists represented by Bourdieu found that culture is also a kind of capital. They pointed out that when individuals accept the value of the ruling class through schooling or other routes, they could create more wealth than uneducated ones in the market.[26] Bourdieu stated, "The special symbolic logic, which forms the distinction, provides people possessing a lot of cultural capital with an asylum to protect their physical and symbolic profits in addition: any specific cultural ability (for example, the ability to read in the world of illiteracy), because of its scarcity, can obtain its value according to its position in the distribution of cultural capital, and thus create obvious profits to its owners." The concept of "cultural capital" advocated by Bourdieu is very ideological: he believed that the profits created by cultural capital are actually the rewards from the ruling class on the ideological ground, for the purpose of spreading its cultural concepts to society. Later researchers threw out Bourdieu's view. Through the cost–benefit method, they found that the profits created by cultural capital are higher than the cost, and

[26] Translated by Bao Yaming (1997, p. 196, 192–201), *Cultural Capital and Social Alchemy:An Interview with Bourdieu*, translated by Bao Yaming, People's Publishing House, 1997, pp. 196, 192–201. In the view of Bourdieu, cultural capital exists in three forms, namely, in the form of personal culture concretely, in the form of cultural products objectively, and in the form of cultural institutions systematically.

thus made the conclusion that culture is a kind of capital. A cultural capital theorist once said, "In some sense, a cultural institution, which, like a certain language or the gendered division of labor, can create future profits for a society, and at the same time, create and maintain the high costs needed to be paid by it, which can be considered as a form of capital."[27]

"Cultural capital" and "human capital" are alike in many aspects, such as content. To some extent, they share the same content. According to Bourdieu, cultural capital has three forms.[28] The first form (embodied form) is thought as the content of human capital by later researchers. Moreover, in the development of the theory of human capital, cultural capital is included. In terms of form, they all emphasize conceptual and intangible things.

However, "cultural capital" and "human capital" differ from more aspects. The concept of "human capital" focuses on man, which is the carrier of capital—things related to man and productivity can be included in human capital; while the concept of "cultural capital" focuses on culture, which is considered as the content of capital—things taking culture as content and can help improve income (such as embodied personal cultural concepts, objectified cultural and art works, and institutionalized social cultural institutions) can be included in cultural capital. Moreover, human capital internalizes natural and social sciences and technologies into personal knowledge and skills, thus directly improving the productivity of workers; while cultural capital focuses on the humanities and cultural concepts, and manifests at the very beginning as the personalization, materialization and institutionalization of cultural values and concepts.

In fact, the theory of corporate culture took the lead in putting forward the thought but not the concept of cultural capital. The theory of corporate culture requires building the corporate cultural environment and calls for the implementation of such concepts as a social concept, a management concept and a marketing concept. However, the question remains—why should companies develop corporate culture? Undoubtedly, companies develop culture to obtain more profits instead of just for culture itself. In the eyes of entrepreneurs developing corporate culture, corporate culture is just a kind of capital—developing corporate culture is the investment of cultural capital, which will create profits higher than the cost. This thought happens to coincide with the opinions of cultural capital.

From "physical capital" to "human capital," such characteristics as totality, tangibility, and independence of capital were removed. From "human capital" to "cultural capital," the capitalization of culture was revealed. Thus, the foundation for developing the concept of moral capital is laid, for the core of culture is morality.

---

[27] Christopher Clague and Shoshana Grossbard- Shechtman, *Cultural Capital and Economic Development: An Introduction*, translated by Wu Dan. See Xue Xiaoyuan (editor) and Cao Rong (editor), *Globalizationand Cultural Capital*, China Social Sciences Publishing House, 2005, pp. 222, 223.

[28] Translated by Bao Yaming *Cultural Capital and Social Alchemy:An Interview with Bourdieu*, translated by Bao Yaming, People's Publishing House, (1997, pp. 196, 192–201). In the view of Bourdieu, cultural capital exists in three forms, namely, in the form of personal culture concretely, in the form of cultural products objectively, and in the form of cultural institutions systematically.

Including morality in the scope of capital is actually an inevitable result of the constant expansion of the concept of capital as well as a necessary requirement to make the economy the core of social life.

2.4.3 *Morality acts as an Instrument in Promoting Economic Development*

From "morality as an end" to "morality as an instrument," and from "physical capital" to "moral capital," moral capital is an innovative concept, which, however, is not a word game played on the basis of fantasy, but a conscious and theoretical understanding of the development of social practice. Behind the innovative concept are the strong requirements of social practice.

In traditional society, limited by science and technology, man could only obtain limited wealth from nature, and thus could only satisfy limited human needs. Limited wealth and needs determine the theoretical propositions in the historical context: people must, theoretically, demonstrate that human needs are limited and that among all human needs some are moral and thus desirable, and some are immoral and thus undesirable. In this case, morality as an end is required as a standard to judge limited needs and satisfaction. Of course, to obtain wealth to satisfy limited needs, moral instruments, such as diligence, frugality, and friendship, are also needed; but in the traditional society, these morals were undoubtedly at the edge of the moral system, subordinating to limited needs as morality as an end.

In modern society, as the development of science and technology, man almost can change nature as he wants, and the material wealth created by man has been growing nonstop. In the practical life with infinite wealth, man's desire for wealth is completely liberated, reaching a state of "everything desired is desirable." In this case, the demonstration of the morality of desires has been degraded to a minor theoretical issue as well as a major theoretical issue of how to maximize wealth to satisfy the maximum desires of man.

In the progress of modernization, through the value expansion of capital, the increase of wealth starts to hold the central position of the stage of history, and wealth and capital have obtained the right to re-interpret various social matters. First, they needed to recapture the economic positions, which were ethicized in the traditional society by stripping off the religious and moral coats of economic materials, restoring their economic nature. As a result, wealth and capital built a solid foundation called "physical capital." After consolidating their economic positions, wealth and capital extend their influence to the traditional noneconomic fields. In these fields, the increase of wealth and capital become the light of ether, radiating every sector of social life to re-interpret social matters according to their standard. In this case, various social matters take on different characteristics, which serve the increase of wealth and the creation of profit. Consequently, "economic man" is derived from "social man," and "politicians" are derived from "political rulers," and all human behavior can be "analyzed economically (Becker 1996)." The concepts of "human capital" and "cultural capital" are exactly an outcome of the process in which capital changes various social matters.

When capital involves noneconomic fields, morality is inevitably affected to some extent. In the trend of secularization, morality, though undertaking the noble mission of making the world meaningful, has to act as a kind of capital due to its special functions. Under the rule of material wealth and capital, morality can no longer abstractly stand high above all social matters; instead, like other social matters, it participates in the process of wealth creation and makes corresponding adjustments to make the greatest contribution to economic development. The concept of "moral capital" is the theorization of such change of morality.

Hence, the theoretical and practical significance of the concept of morality lies in that the concept agrees with the following reality: economic development is the core of today's social development. Development is the theme of today's world, and the core of development is economic development. Although in recent years, comprehensive development, which includes social development, has become a major social concern, but it is undeniable that the active force of comprehensive development is still economic development. Therefore, in real life, we should try to explore more elements and use all possible forces that can promote economic development. The concept of "moral capital" emerges as required by the times. It clarifies the function of morality as an instrument to promote economic development and tries to explore more moral elements in favor of economic development on a broader level.

As we can see, the existence of moral capital has been demonstrated practically and theoretically. Then, why are there still people unwilling to accept the concept of moral capital? I believe that it is because some researchers still have the following questions: is it moral to consider morality as a kind of capital? Will morality still be pure when it is considered as an instrument? Furthermore, will morality be deemed false if it is considered as a means to obtain economic profits?

Schultz faced the same questions when he advocated the concept of "human capital." He found that the main reason that some people could not accept the concepts of "human capital" and "investment in human capital" is that they thought it was demeaning to consider man as an object of investment. He stated, "Hence, to treat human beings as wealth that can be augmented by investment runs counter to deeply held values. It seems to reduce man once again to a mere material component, to something akin to property. And for man to look upon himself as a capital good, even if it did not impair his freedom, may seem to debase him. No less a person than J. S. Mill at one time insisted that the people of a country should not be looked upon as wealth because wealth existed only for the sake of people. But surely Mill was wrong; there is nothing in the concept of human wealth contrary to his idea that it exists only for the advantage of people. By investing in themselves, people can enlarge the range of choice available to them. It is one way free men can enhance their welfare (Theodore 1990c)." When the concept of "moral capital" faces the problems once faced by "cultural capital," our answer is as follows: like "cultural capital," "moral capital" will not diminish the freedom and personality of man, or the purity of morality; instead, it will promote the freedom and personality of man as well as the comprehensive development of morality.

First, considering morality as a kind of capital focuses on morality's function as an instrument and requires the development of moral elements promoting economic development. Thus, it is helpful in laying a real and solid foundation for moral development in economic life. Historical materialism has told us clearly that profits are the real foundation for the formation and development of morality. Morality serving the self-interest of individuals and the collective interests of society will be accepted at last, though the process may be long and hard; and morality ignoring the self-interest of individuals and the collective interests of society will be abandoned at last, although such morality may be advocated in an amount of time. History has shown that when moral requirements and benefit requirements are disjointed completely, hypocrites and double-dealers would run rampant. The theory of moral capital calls for morals, which play the role of capital and promote economic development. Therefore, such morals are useful in real life and are needed by economic life. Undoubtedly, the advocacy of such morals will not become the hotbed of hypocrites and double-dealers. Instead, it will encourage morality to perform better in real life. Therefore, considering morality as a kind of capital and exploring morals that promote economic development is the most effective way to realize the internal combination of the economy and morality.

Second, considering morality as a kind of capital only means paying attention to morality's function as an instrument and setting right the relationship between morality as an end and morality as an instrument. It does not mean that morality can only acts as capital. When Adam Smith put forward the concept of the "economic man," he did not mean to replace or deny the concept of the "social man." Likewise, the concept of "moral capital" does not replace or deny the concept of "general morality"; it merely emphasizes that morality is also a kind of capital that was ignored in ethical research. Undoubtedly, morality should and must act as both an end and an instrument. However, in today's society, which is dominated by economic development, morality's function as an instrument is more urgently required, although its function as an end is still very important. Therefore, putting forward the concept of moral capital is not denying morality's function as an end, but strengthening morality's function as an instrument on the basis of acknowledging its function as an end, thus providing strong moral support for economic development.

Third, considering morality as a kind of capital is emphasizing the consciousness of the economic agent in economic development as well as the rationality of the inter-economic agent relationship, which directly affects and constrains economic benefits and economic development speed. Therefore, considering morality as a kind of capital does not debase morality, or destroy the nobility and purity of morality; instead, it highlights the irreplaceable and special roles played by morality in economic development. The concept of "moral capital" is not related to the issue of "what morality is," and thus will not change the extension of the concept of morality. In fact, it is related to the issue of "what the functions of morality are" and focuses on morality's function as an instrument. In modern times, morality acting as an instrument to promote economic development is of course noble and pure. In fact, the concept of "moral capital," by expounding the functions of morality as a kind of capital, demonstrates the irreplaceability of moral capital in economic development, and at the same time, further defines and expands the practical significance of morality.

The development of the theory of moral capital and morality as an instrument is a "win-win situation" for economic and moral development. The investment in moral capital, on the one hand, will provide more resources for economic development; and on the other hand, will profoundly affect moral development. In the final analysis, the significance of the existence of morality not only lies in moral advocacy and consciousness but also, perhaps more importantly, in the special roles played by morality. What's more, it is morality's function as an instrument and the benefits created by moral capital that determine the truth and nobility of moral advocacy and the profundity and greatness of moral consciousness.

2.5 Moral Capital and its Development[29]—Comments on *The Moral Capital of Leaders* by Alejo G. Sison

After publishing *Moral Capital* in 2000, I published a series of papers studying moral capital together with my colleagues, and wrote the book *Moral Capital Theory*.[30] Such works demonstrate the concept, basis of existence, basic characteristics, mechanism of action, and forms of action of moral capital from various perspectives, while garnering attention from academic circles. Some scholars agree with the theory of moral capital, but some believe the existence of moral capital is groundless, and have challenged my opinion. Therefore, it is necessary to conduct a deeper study on moral capital. In *The Moral Capital of Leaders* (Sison 2005a) (translated by Yu Wenxuan and Ding Min), Alejo G. Sison expounds the intension, characteristics, management, and forms of action of moral capital from an original perspective. This book is of obvious significance in terms of theoretical enlightenment and practical reference value.

2.5.1 *What is Moral Capital?*

What is moral capital? On what grounds does moral capital exist? Such questions have been repeatedly illustrated in my study. According to the opposing opinions and questions from academic circles, and *The Moral Capital of Leaders* by Sison, I formed the following analysis:

[29] Originally titled as *The Sixth Study on Moral Capital*, Morality and Civilization, Issue 5, 2006; reprinted fully in *Ethics*, Issue 1, 2007. This paper has been included in Moral Capital and Business Ethics (*Selected Works of Wang Xiaoxi*), People's Publishing House, 2009.

[30] Moral Capital, *The Second Study on Moral Capital, The Third Study on Moral Capital, The Fourth Study on Moral Capital* and *The Fifth Study on Moral Capital* are published in *Jiangsu Social Sciences,* Issue 3, 2000; Issue 1, 2002; Issue 6, 2004 and Issue 5, 2006, respectively. The book Moral Capital Theory was published by the People's Publishing House in Feb. 2005.

2.5.1.1 Capital can be Interpreted in Different Dimensions in Different Social Contexts

By analyzing the concept of capital we can demonstrate that morality is a kind of capital. According to Marx, under capitalism, capital is the value that creates surplus value, which is the essence of capital. In *The Moral Capital of Leaders*, Sison ignores this classical idea of Marx, which thus limits his thought on moral capital. In a certain social institution, there are rational and irrational morals, and morals to be capital must be judged based on an analysis. Besides, not all capital is moral, or to say morals are not always of moral significance. Therefore, only in a just, equal and free socialist public ownership system could the real unity between moral capitalization and capital moralization be realized.

In Sison's book, we can see the characteristics of capital as the subject. He pointed out, "Capital was the productive part of wealth, the class of wealth that yielded revenue, the stock that was saved for future—as opposed to immediate—consumption" (p. 7). Moreover, "popular business usage understands capital to be synonymous with wealth, with wealth understood at a stock and not any specific kind or part of it. Among merchants and accountants, capital indicates the net value of wealth, the assets that remain once liabilities have been discharged" (p. 7).[31] In short, "Initially, capital is almost always associated with wealth and property." (p. 6) "But, wealth by itself does not behave as capital, nor is capital always enabled to yield income" (p. 8) because "it's not enough just to have resources, assets or wealth; it is also imperative that one be able to capitalize such wealth" (p. 10). That is, "wealth first needs to undergo a certain process of transformation or conversion into property, before it can actually function as capital" (p. 10). What is more, "the conditions for the transformation of wealth into property and capital undoubtedly exist in the physical asset, but the transformation itself is the result of human mind and integrity. In other words, without the intervention of human beings, neither property nor capital could exist as such, for our mental powers are essential in the transformative process of "propertization" and capitalization: the capturing and fixing of relevant socioeconomic information about resources. Yet, during much of the history of economic science, labor—the distinctively human contribution to the production of wealth—has surprisingly been conceived as a factor not only separate, but even diametrically opposed to capital. This was arguably Karl Marx's foremost contention" (p. 11).

Sison has profound insight into capital. He points out that wealth without unclear ownership, especially wealth with undefined ownership and institutional procedure cannot be capitalized. Wealth needs to be transformed into property before it can actually function as capital because it "permits one to identify, describe, capture, and organize in a user-friendly way the economically meaningful aspects of a resource" (p. 10). When wealth is transformed to capital, its value expands. However, it can only be realized through labor by wealth owners, taking credit as value orientation or the principle of conduct under certain ideological guidance. Sison tells us that on

[31] Opinions quoted from *The Moral Capital of Leaders* are marked with the page numbers directly.

the one hand, capital, though being money and materials, shall have clearly defined ownership; and on the other hand, capital can only function as capital when it is involved in the production process as arranged by man. Regrettably, in the book, Sison does not further discuss capital's essence in terms of relationships—he does not systematically and profoundly analyze the logical relationship between the spiritual level (such as thought and morality) and physical level of capital. This may be related to the guiding philosophy and fundamental ideas of Sison. Regardless, the book is still of great significance for the development of the theory of moral capital.

In fact, the essence of capital in terms of relationships indicates that in the private ownership system, it is certain that owners of wealth or assets invest their wealth or assets in production in order to make profits through the labor of others. In this process, they will maximize the wealth for the next round of investment, and at the same time, minimize the expenditure on reproduction. However, in socialist public ownership system, though the fundamental purpose of wealth owners is still making profits, the input and output of wealth are balanced and rational, and most importantly, wealth is always used for the benefits of the majority.

Even in private economic activities, the flow and utilization of wealth from the value increment of capital are guided and constrained by socialist constitutions.

The economic value of capital is realized with the participation of the spiritual elements of capital. Maybe Sison's contention that the capitalization of wealth is the result of the human mind and integrity is different from my opinion to some extent; however, we both agree on one thing—morality is a kind of capital. Sison also acknowledges the existence of intellectual, human, and social capital, thus the existence of moral capital is natural.

2.5.1.2 Is Moral Capital Equal to Virtue?

What is moral capital? In *Moral Capital*, I wrote that moral capital refers to the ability of capital to produce social wealth in the process of production, and the moral philosophy and behavior that can create profits and benefits (Wang 2000b). Sison defines moral capital in a different way. He believes moral capital as "excellence of character, or the possession and practice of a host of virtues appropriate for a human being within a particular sociocultural context. Nowadays, its meaning could also be expressed by the word "integrity," a trait suggesting wholeness and stability in a person as someone on whom others could depend or rely. Having virtues or an excellent character may be considered moral capital not only because they are a form of wealth, but also because they are productive capacities or powers that accumulate and develop in an individual, through proper investments of time, effort and other resources, including financial ones" (p. 41). Sison's definition of capital is of theoretical significance. First, he defines moral capital as "excellence of character" and believes moral capital can be expressed as "integrity," indirectly equating "excellence of character" with "integrity." This is a precise and appropriate hint (in a particular discourse context), for integrity (especially Sison's definition of "integrity" as "a trait suggesting wholeness and stability in a person as someone on whom others could depend or rely") is an important lever that promotes the value expansion of capital. Second, Sison believes that moral capital is "the possession and practice of a host of virtues appropriate for a human being within a particular sociocultural context." Expressions like "a particular sociocultural context" and "appropriate for a human being" were deliberately used, for virtues vary as the change of times and nationalities. Only in this way, the concept of "moral capital" would not be generalized. Third, Sison points out that moral capital is the "excellence of character." The reason is that moral capital, being a kind of wealth, is also a capacity or power with productivity, which is an important precondition or basis for the existence of moral capital. In fact, morals, virtues or excellent characters are only a kind of potential moral capital, or, at most, a moral asset has not participated in production yet. We cannot equate morals, virtues or excellent characters with moral capital. Therefore, Sison's definition of moral capital still needs to be questioned as it indicates conceptual expressions of "morality can be defined as moral capital" and "moral capital can be considered as morality," which are seriously flawed in wording and formulation.

2.5.1.3 The Manifestation and Noumenon of Moral Capital

In the concept of moral capital, morals are useful or scientific morals that are involved in the production process and the creation of social wealth. Such morals must be the ideal presentation of morality in social life, and thus moral capital is necessary in economic activities. Sison understands it in a special but reasonable way. He writes, "Happiness represents the definitive form of moral capital. Happiness is moral capital in its perfect state, where there is only pure gain or accumulation and loss is no longer possible. Even the use or consumption of this form of moral capital does not cause it to diminish, but on the contrary allows it to grow further. Once achieved, moral capital in the form of happiness is no longer subject to future risks and its value becomes more intrinsic than instrumental. The reason for wanting happiness—for accumulating moral capital in this form—is none other than happiness itself" (p. 189). Then, he quotes Aristotle, "A nominal agreement exists regarding happiness—a good, flourishing life—such as that which human beings ultimately seek in all their activities" (p. 190). Therefore, "In the optimum of happiness, there is only pure gain and enjoyment, without any risk of loss. The value of happiness as moral capital is substantive rather than instrumental" (pp. 195–196).

Sison considers happiness a manifestation of moral capital and points out that value is the noumenon of happiness. From this perspective, we can demonstrate, at a deeper level, that moral capital has good reasons to exist due to its aggressiveness and the functions of guidance and completeness.

Of course, happiness, in the scope of morality, is defined in different times and classes. Happiness, as a manifestation of moral capital, should be the "should-being" happiness pursued by people in a certain society.

2.5.1.4 The Perfectness of Moral Capital Determines the "positivity" of its Functions and Benefits

In economic development, the input of moral capital will not change with the increase or decrease of profits and benefits. The reason is that moral capital is a kind of spiritual capital, so once it exists, it means that the economic agent is of excellent morality, and physical or money capital has been managed according to a certain value orientation of the economic agent to achieve a good end. Otherwise, moral capital cannot exist. For this reason, there is no need to consider the retreat of moral capital, for it would always promote economic development. Physical and money capital will face low profits, or even a loss occasionally, but this has nothing to do with moral capital. In fact, when guided by the value orientation of a noble economic subject, moral capital will try to change the way and field of investment of physical and money capital, thus expanding the value of profits and interests. Moreover, when physical and money capital retreats from the original investment channel due to sluggish economy or bad management, moral capital always plays the role of guidance and coordination.

For the above, Sison shares my opinion, which he expresses clearly and reasonably. He believes, "moral capital does not share that ambivalence, or equal usefulness for the good or the bad, that the other forms of capital display" and "it can never be used to further evil purposes" (p. 46). For moral capital, "one distinguishing characteristic is that it will not cause any losses" (p. 130). He also states, "That is, virtue is a 'positive externality', a good that is non-rivalrous and non-excludable in its consumption. This means that whatever gain one makes in moral capital or virtue does not detract from any others', and it would actually cost everyone more if somebody were to be excluded or barred from the benefits of moral capital or virtue of himself. Likewise, if someone's virtue can only benefit himself, according to its attribute as 'public goods', it can be said that there is a lack of virtue. Market mechanisms alone could not provide it, since it would always be easier to freeload on the benefits of other people's virtue than to take the pains of developing it oneself" (pp. 216–217). Sison's conclusion that "market mechanisms alone could not provide it" is quite precise and appropriate. Virtues, as a kind of moral capital, cannot be transacted or exchanged, and will not be consumed or lost; they only play the role of promoting, reconciling, and perfecting economic development. When expounding "virtues as a kind of moral capital," Sison makes a logical flaw. He states, "Unlike human, intellectual, cultural or social capital that perfect the person in just a limited aspect—be it in health, knowledge, an aptitude or skill, or through an advantageous acquaintance or relation—moral capital is unique in that it perfects the human being as a whole person. Moral capital is onto what makes a person strong, or smart, or thrifty (instead of being liberal or generous); it is not even what makes a person successful in business. Rather, moral capital is what makes a person good as a human being. This doesn't mean that a person well-endowed with moral capital, by this very measure, is necessarily devoid of bodily strength, or health, or intelligence, or has to reject profit in business ventures. It only means that such a person would never readily sacrifice his moral excellence as a condition to gain health, knowledge, social connections, or profit" (p. 41). It seems that Sison considers moral capital as a kind of completely independent capital that is separate or even opposite of capital in other forms. This is rather one-sided and wrong. In fact, moral capital does not independently play it roles in economic activities—it penetrates into human behavior, physical capital, and management institutions to function (Wang 2000b). Meanwhile, capital in other forms, such as human, intellectual, cultural, and social capital cannot exist or function without the special roles played by moral capital. Moreover, moral capital promotes the health, knowledge, intelligence, and technical level of man. It is metaphysical to think that "moral capital is onto what makes a person strong, or smart, or thrifty; it is not even what makes a person successful in business." This opinion in Sison's book is actually self-contradictory.

2.5.1.5 The Significance of Moral Capital Lies in Actions

The significance of moral capital, which lies in actions, is an important contention of Sison in the book. He points out, "The key to developing moral capital consists in taking advantage of the dynamics among three operational levels found in the human being, namely, the level of actions, the level of habits and the level of character. Among these levels, actions are the elementary building blocks, and may be considered the basic currency of moral capital. This means that nothing in human agent acquires moral significance unless it issues into actions or comes as a consequence of actions" (p. 62). He also states, "That moral capital relies mainly on actions means, in the first place, that thoughts or ideas are not enough, no matter how indispensable they may be. Leadership, or the accrual of moral capital for oneself and one's organization, is not a theory but an art, a practice" (p. 84). Moreover, he specially stresses, "Moral capital is built upon actions, on the exercise of actions. This means it's not enough to have the capacities to act or to acts with sense" (p. 85). Moral capital is not built "on the mere possession of capacities for action" (p. 85).

The thoughts of Sison have revealed the important characteristics of moral capital—no matter how developed moral consciousness is and how systematic moral code is, morality cannot be capital without actions.

Here, we require a further analysis of the following question: "What does turning morality into action mean?" In his book, Sison does not answer this question, which, in my opinion, is caused by the lack of a rigorous, theoretical and logical analysis. Sison's contention that "moral capital is built upon actions" indicates that thoughts and ideas, or morality itself cannot become moral capital. We must know that once thoughts and ideas or morality are put into action, they become an element of moral capital. Therefore, it is appropriate to change "moral capital itself is not a theory" into "moral capital itself is not just a theory." Turning thoughts and ideas or morality into action is not a general moral activity; in fact, it also includes such economic activities as the formulation of production, management, sales services, and corporate institutions, which are conducted under the guidance of thoughts and ideas or morality. Morals, like being civilized and polite, taking pleasure in helping others and protecting the environment, without being related to economic activities, or playing particular roles in economic development, cannot become moral capital.

2.5.2 The Functions and Management of Moral Capital

In a series of papers concerning moral capital written by my colleagues and me, the functions and management of moral capital are discussed from different aspects. In terms of functions of moral capital, moral capital affects and determines the value orientation, attitude towards labor, and way of act of the economic agent or producer. Meanwhile, it also reconciles the relationship between various stakeholders in the process of economic development, thus maintaining the rational and harmonious relationships of the stakeholders with the special power of morality. During the process, moral capital also acquires the special ability of creating social wealth.

The primary function of moral capital is enhancing the morality of leaders. In *The Moral Capital of Leaders*, Sison focuses on "leadership." He believes that leadership grows from morality. "Leadership is a two-way transformative and intrinsically moral relationship between a leader and his followers. The two parties involved in a leadership relation—the leader and his followers—morally transform and elevate each other through their interaction. Thus, ethical leadership becomes the primary conduit through which not only persons, but also organizations for which these persons work, become ethical. Leadership nurtures personal ethics, allowing it to grow and configure an auspicious organizational culture" (p. 50). From the perspective of leadership, Sison stresses, "Ethics lies at the very heart of leadership" (p. 49). Sison tells us that a leader, when losing his morality, will lose the trust of his followers and his authority as well. Furthermore, leaders that lack morality certainly do not have charisma, and naturally cannot analyze and organize with the power of morality, let alone understanding how morality penetrates into economic activities to play its unique roles. Therefore, in the scope managed by a leader lacking morality, moral capital can hardly be utilized and even cannot play its role in economic activities. We must say that the theory of moral capital of leaders put forward by Sison is of great academic value and significance of guidance.

According to Sison, to have moral capital, a leader must first be moral. He writes, "A sine qua non condition for a good leader is that he be, at the same time, morally upright and professionally competent or effective" (p. 48). Second, a leader is required to lead in the forms of both stewardship and servant-leadership. "Stewardship reflects a significant reform on the thinking mode of leadership, for it emphasizes on an even deeper sense of responsibility of a leader for his followers." "A steward-leader should respect the right of his flowers to make decisions about their work, and also acknowledge their capacities of influencing the purposes, organization and institutions of the organization" (p. 51). "Servant-leadership is an even more revolutionary trend than stewardship, for it turns traditional leadership thinking, with its emphasis on a high-profile figure and his stellar interventions, upside down. A servant-leader should not only recognize the interests of others in the organization: he is also duty-bound to transcend his own self-interest to better serve the others' needs. His obligation is to provide those under his care with a chance to grow and develop as persons; he ought to furnish them with opportunities to gain, both materially and morally, through the work that they do in the organization" (pp. 51–51). Third, a leader must realize the importance of trust because "without this atmosphere of trust, no dialogue, no understanding, no cooperation, no commerce, no community would be possible." "The social cohesion that arises from the growth of trust, as we already know, lowers transaction costs, facilitates entrepreneurial initiatives and boosts economic competitiveness" (p. 52). Sison thoroughly analyzes the importance of morality for leadership. In his final analysis, to develop morality, or to accumulate more and better moral capital, a leader must be moral. He must respect his followers for they are equal in personality; he must put the benefits of his followers first; he must epitomize the wisdom of his followers; and, more importantly, he must be a moral model. Leaders that have a strong sense of hierarchy or enjoy playing politics must be mediocre and incompetent, and will certainly lack or lose moral capital.

The core role played by moral capital is improving the moral consciousness and determining the value orientation of the economic agent. The economy does not exist without man. All economic activities are the externalization and materialization of the thoughts and morals of man. Therefore, unlike other kinds of capital, moral capital must, first, solve the spiritual problems regarding capital, namely, improving the moral consciousness of man, perfecting the code of economic actions and determining the direction of action and value orientation of the economic agent. It can be said that in the absence of the economic agent's moral consciousness, there would be no moral capital, and other kinds of capital cannot smoothly acquire the profits and benefits they should make. "Without moral capital, capital in other forms is likely to turn from the advantages of a company into the source of its decline" (p. 56). Taking companies like Enron Corporation as an example, Sison illustrates that the loss of morality will lead to the loss of other kinds of capital. Likewise, in China, the lack of morality and credit has led to the decline or sudden collapse of some famous and even time-honored companies.

As I once demonstrated this contention in *Moral Capital*, moral capital directly improves product quality and lowers product costs, thus creating more profits. Here, I want to emphasize that, generally, moral capital ensures product quality. We must see that for a company, development is a process of operation in which many aspects and elements are involved; therefore, good product quality may lead to higher-than-expected or lower-than-expected benefits and profits. A company fulfilling its after-sales service commitments with integrity will certainly expand its market share and accelerate sales and capital flow, thus making more profits. At the same time, product quality is improved. On the contrary, if a company fails to fulfill its after-sales service commitments, its market share will shrink and its sales and capital flow will slow down. Consequently, fewer profits are acquired, and product quality is lowered, while product cost is increased.

2.5.3 Development and Enhancement of Moral Capital

The premise for the formation of moral capital is that the economic agent develops a certain level of moral consciousness and can guide or effect economic behavior in economic activities. Capital moral will not take shape when the economic agent just knows some knowledge about morality, or there are just standards about good and evil or moral code established in society. The reason is that if moral requirements have not become the self-consciousness of the economic agent, or have not played roles in economic activities to promote the increase of wealth, moral capital does not play its roles, and there is of course no moral capital. Therefore, developing moral consciousness is an important approach to developing and enhancing moral capital.

Moral capital, unlike physical capital, can only be enhanced by constant development. According to Sison, "Developing virtues is adding investment stocks in moral capital" (p. 155).

Sison says that actions are the basic currency of moral capital. He creatively believes that the development of habits can continuously increase moral capital. According to him, "Habits arise from the repetition of voluntary human actions." "If actions, which make up the basic currency of moral capital, constitute the principal in an account, habits correspond to their compound interests. Habits are the payoff in terms of moral capital for the repetition of voluntary human actions" (p. 97). It is reasonable to consider habits as a kind of moral capital. However, in the definition that states "habits are the payoff in terms of moral capital for the repetition of voluntary human actions," the expression of "voluntary human actions," in my view, is vague, and is likely to cause misunderstandings. It is better to reword it as "conscious human actions."

Sison holds that time and freedom are two requirements for the development of habits. "Time means a certain permanence or duration in being" (p. 111). In my view, taking time as a requirement is of no practical significance and can be ignored. Sison stresses, "Habits are always developed gradually as a result of the repetition of actions" (p. 111). This is indisputable, but taking time as a requirement is unnecessary and weak theoretically. In fact, by just slightly changing the perspective and wording of "habits are always developed gradually as a result of the repetition of actions," which is an object fact, we can change its focus from the length of time to the importance of the repeated forge and constant practice of actions, making the requirement theoretically strong. The second requirement is freedom. Sison divided freedom into physical, psychological and moral freedoms. Physical freedom "consists in an openness of one's nature and a capacity for movement." Psychological freedom "means whenever a person chooses, the determining factor in his choice is none other than himself, that is, his sovereign will." Moral freedom is "more powerful than the natural state of a person; it arises from personal virtue and moral habits" (p. 112). He adds, "Physical freedom and psychological freedom are 'negative freedoms'; freedoms from contrary physical forces and psychological forces. Moral freedom, on the other hand, is a 'positive freedom'" (p. 112).In addition, it is "a more powerful freedom." Sison uses the concepts of physical freedom and psychological freedom to outline and compare against moral freedom, a substantive characteristic of morality. However, the problem is, according to Sison's explanations of physical and psychological freedoms, the concepts of physical and psychological freedoms do not exist. In his final analysis, "negative freedom" is not freedom at all. I point out this problem to emphasize that real freedom is the freedom to grasp the objective law of natural and social development and act according to such law. Only in this way could we understand the relationship between the development of moral habits and freedom. In other words, only when an economic agent acquires freedom, or the so-called "moral freedom" according to the law of moral life, could he develop habits as moral capital.

To develop virtues, adding investment stocks in moral capital, Sison, on the basis of stressing that "the nature of habits represents a kind of moral capital superior than other activities" (p. 127), holds, "habits are not the decisive factor for the formation and development of moral capital," and "the character of man usually is more influential than habits" (p. 127). The reason is that character is built based on habits. "We could say that character or culture is like a bond in moral capital. Bonds are financial instruments that governments or corporations use in order to raise funds. An investor defers consumption and purchases a bond in the hope of receiving an income for a set number of years. Only after this period does he expect to recover the principal or the original amount of the loan" (p. 129). "Just like bonds, character and culture are the result of a long-term investment, usually of several years' worth of continued efforts on the part of agents. Once established, however, they no longer change easily, nor are they ordinarily susceptible to loss. They entail the barest minimum of risk. That is because character and culture embody the conscious and willful determination of one's freedom and reason in a motley set of deep-rooted and enduring habits. Unlike bonds, however, character and culture could enjoy high rates of return, income or interest, together with low risk. A person's habits, once securely entrenched in character, do not only enable him to perform ever more and better actions, but they also predispose him to acquire other habits similar to those he already has, and likewise increase their perfection" (p. 130).

In short, according to Sison, the development and enhancement of moral capital requires the development of moral habits, and the addition of investment stocks requires the development of character. This is a central issue regarding the formation of moral capital. From the perspectives of "habits" and "character," Sison demonstrates the development and enhancement of moral capital. His study is original and valuable.

A problem is that Sison only analyzes the development and enhancement of moral capital from the perspectives of personality (the personality of man or the company as man). At this point, his thoughts are undistributed. The development of habits and character requires the participation or cooperation of various elements, and some elements need special attention and need to be specially crafted. First, the possibility for the penetration of the moral concepts of capital in other forms is created. To manufacture a product, particular technical and cultural parameters are needed. What's more, particular moral concepts are also needed to affect or change products designed according to general technical and cultural parameters, making the product meet the production and living needs of man in a better way. Additionally, during the entire process of manufacturing, moral concepts can effectively play the role of guidance, regulation and supervision. Second, the mechanism of action of moral capital is studied and turned into operable procedures and institutions. Otherwise, even with the presence of noble moral consciousness and the "habits" and "character" that Sison mentions, morality cannot turn into moral capital. Third, action is required for the formation and development of moral capital, and "appropriate social and cultural background or community environment" are needed for turning morality into practice. Therefore, when studying the development and enhancement of moral capital, we cannot ignore the purification and perfection of social and cultural background and the social environment.

2.5.4 The Management of Moral Capital

Sison discusses the issue of moral capital management in his book. This is worth mentioning, theoretically or practically. Bad management of moral capital will lead to low profits, and even the loss of moral capital.

Sison points out that "the best strategy of moral capital management is investing the lifestyle of pursuing morality" (p. 194), "for a person, the lifestyle gives unity and texture to everything he does: the feelings he experience, the actions he performs, the habits he cultivates, and the unique character he forges; it lends structure and meaning to his existence" (p. 195). He also points out that the lifestyle of a company (or the history of a company) is like the lifestyle of a person. About this, his one insightful opinion is managing moral capital through the "lifestyle pursuing virtue." To manage moral capital, it is necessary to stock moral capital first. "Investing the lifestyle of pursuing morality" is actually about developing such virtues as justice, temperance, bravery and cautiousness in a wider sense, namely, in the sense of the all-round lifestyle of man or the company, thus creating the maximum or best "moral heritage."

According to Sison, to manage moral capital effectively, we must be able to measure moral capital. Sison mentions two "measurement strategies": "one consists in indirect measurement, which measures the absence or lack of moral capital and its consequences. The other engages in direct measurement which detects the presence of moral capital and its effects" (p. 205). On the one hand, Sison believes that indirect measurement, which measures the absence or lack of moral capital and its consequences, is the quantitative analysis of employee behavior (such as mobility, absenteeism and indolence) and illegal behavior (such as assault, attack, murder, pilferage, and embezzlement of corporate resources by accident or on purpose). On the other hand, he believes it is the qualitative analysis of negative factors like employees' life quality, happiness, faith, and value orientation, for knowing the lack of moral capital (pp. 206–208). It can be inferred that according to the analysis results, concepts and measures about how to avoid the consequence of the lack of moral capital and how to develop and enhance moral capital will come into being. Direct measurement is the qualitative analysis of the "qualification, royalty and satisfaction of human capital and corporate atmosphere of a company" (p. 211). To be specific, direct measurement includes measuring the social, environmental and ethical responsibilities of companies and individuals; measuring companies' ability to attract, motivate and retain talents; measuring companies' reputation which effectively retains a customer base and enhances the royalty and donation of employees; and measuring whether entrepreneurs "value teamwork, take customers as the center, appreciate fair competition, constantly make innovations and take initiative" (p. 212). According to Sison, the direct measurement of moral capital means quantitatively analyzing "human capital revenue, return on the investment in human capital, and the added value of human capital" (p. 219). By directly measuring moral capital, we can form a clear picture about the stock and lack of moral capital, thus accumulating experience as well as learning lessons. At the same time, we can effectively choose investment stocks of moral capital for the accumulation of moral capital currency.

Sison's moral capital management philosophy is a significant breakthrough in the field of modern corporate management. From a brand new perspective, he explores a new sector in modern corporate management.

Of course, the management of moral capital is a systematic work. A specific plan covering the content, methods and ways as well as objectives of moral capital management is needed. Moreover, strategies and measures regarding moral capital management need to be developed from the perspectives of moral concepts and practical operation, companies and individuals as well as correction and investment. In different countries, areas and companies, the requirements of moral management are different, even essentially. In this case, moral capital management plans need to be developed according to specific circumstances, thus realizing the efficient management of moral capital.

In China, there is an urgent need for taking stock of the moral capital of companies in an all-round way. It is necessary to analyze such moral capital profoundly as the management philosophy and objectives of companies, the moral quality of managers, the moral quality of employees, the moralization of corporate institutions, the morality contained in corporate culture, corporate moral environment, the human-centered design of products, the sincerity of intercompany cooperation, after-sales service commitments and their fulfillment, corporate social responsibility, corporate morality and moral capital management. Only in this way, could we accumulate more and better moral capital, make full use of the functions of moral capital and enhance the core competitiveness of modern companies constantly.

2.6 The Basic Forms of Moral Capital[32]

Over the past decade, I have made a series of studies on moral capital,[33] especially the functions of moral capital from multiple perspectives. Undoubtedly, "without moral capital, capital in other forms is likely to turn from the advantages of a com-

[32] Originally titled as The Seventh Study on Moral Capital, Morality and Civilization, *Ethics*, Issue 11, 2009. This paper has been included in Moral Capital and Business Ethics (*Selected Works of Wang Xiaoxi*), People's Publishing House, 2009.

[33] Before *The Seventh Study on Moral Capital*, I have published six papers and one monograph studying moral capital. Moral Capital (the concept and value realization of moral capital), *The*

pany into the source of its decline (Sison 2005b)." This has been repeatedly demonstrated by theories, history and reality. As a kind of special capital, moral capital not only has the characteristics of general capital but also has its own characteristics. According to nature, effects and functions, general capital can be divided into different forms, as can moral capital. In the very least, it exists in the forms of moral institutions, rational relationships, subject consciousness and moral products. Studying and expounding the four forms of moral capital will help us to understand moral capital and its forms of existence from a new perspective, thus better grasping the management mechanism of moral capital.

2.6.1 The Form of Moral Institutions

The form of moral institutions is a basic form of moral capital with fundamental significance. A society is filled with many norms and constraints, tangible or intangible. Institutions, which are tangible norms, play the role of guaranteeing economic development and business operation. Put another way, they ensure normal, regulatory and efficient economic development. No matter the means, institutions are formulated to service people and shall therefore be rational in value. Rational institutions cannot be separated from morality—they should be moralized as moral institutions. The institutionalization of morality, or the moralization of institutions, is actually a process of seeking the virtuous interaction between morality and institutions, rather than counter posing morality and institutions, which will lead to the extreme conclusion of "morality is not an institution, and an institution does not require morality."

In some sense, if a moral institution, by normalizing and constraining human behavior, can promote the increase of economic and social benefits, the institution is of significance to moral capital. Therefore, moral institutions are moral capital. In fact, moral capital in the form of moral institutions plays a decisive role in economic activities. Once an institution lacks morality, or becomes an instrument that destroys human nature and distorts human relationships, economic activities cannot yield expected benefits and even normal economic activities will be destroyed, no matter what measures are taken. The American economist Douglass C. North once said, "The structures of political and economic organizations determine economic performance and the growth of knowledge and technology. The various forms of

Second Study on Moral Capital (the effects and functions of moral capital, co-written by Yang Wenbing), *The Third Study on Moral Capital* (the dependence and independence of moral capital, co-written by Zhu Huiyu), *The Fourth Study on Moral Capital* (moral capital from the perspective of economics, co-written by Hua Guihong), and *The Fifth Study on Moral Capital* (the concept and functions of moral capital in the history and the contemporary world, co-written by Li Zhixiang) were published on Issue 3, 2000; Issue 1, 2002; Issue 6, 2002; Issue 6, 2004; and Issue 5, 2006 of *Jiangsu Social Sciences* respectively. The *Sixth Study on Moral Capital (Comments on The Moral Capital of Leaders by Sison)* was published on *Morality and Civilization*, Issue 5, 2006. Monograph *Moral Capital Theory* (co-written by Hua Guihong, Guo Jianxin et al.) was published by People's Publishing House in 2005.

cooperation and competition in human development and their implementation, as well as the institutions organizing human activities are the very center of the economic history (Douglass 2002)." We can derive from his thought that moral institutions play unique roles in economic activities.

An opinion, which has been long held, is that the market is unrelated to ethics, the economy is unrelated to morality and the institution is unrelated to humanity. In several centuries, some theorists claimed that a company is an "amoral" entity, thus it does not need to undertake moral responsibilities. However, today's society requires companies to undertake moral responsibilities, announcing the end of the era in which management and institutions were free from ethics. "Managers are starting to pay attention to corporate morality. They do not consider it as decorations or a special hobby, but an organic component of efficient management that is involved in every aspect of business operation (Lynn 2004)." In business management, this is the "return of value," which, in the context of Max Weber, is the return of "culture." According to Weber, actions are profit-driven, and culture, in the form of religions, determines the direction of actions. In my opinion, morality, in the form of institutions, guides actions to be rational. Then, what are the functions of institutionalized morality? In general, institutionalized morality imposes necessary constraints on human behavior; without such "necessary" constraints, it is difficult to realize free business operation. Essentially, moralized institutions mainly play two roles in business operation.[34]

First, for a company, externally, moralized institutions effectively constrain opportunistic behavior. In a transaction, the behavior of parties involved is uncertain, and in this case, an important source growing and increasing transaction costs is the behavior with "moral hazard" of one party, which will infringe the interests of the other party. Moral constitutions can constrain opportunistic behavior as "free riders." Therefore, the participation of necessary moral constraints in a transaction can lower transaction costs. Furthermore, the requirements of moral institutions constitute the self-discipline mechanism and incentive mechanism that works on parties involved in a transaction, thus lowering transaction costs and increasing mutual benefits.

Second, for a company, internally, the constraint of necessary moral institutions will improve labor efficiency, economic benefits and resource utilization, promoting the formation of a healthy, natural source ecology and social ecology. Therefore, "the ethical atmosphere built by managers is crucial for the success of the organization for which they work."[35] On the one hand, the constraint of moral institutions ensures human-centered product design and the fulfillment of after-sales service commitments. On the other hand, the constraint of moral institutions guarantees

[34] In this case, "business operation" is understood in a wide sense, including various business operation and the entire processes thereof. In some sense, "business operation" is a synonym of economic activities.

[35] [US] Dennis J. Moberg, Trustworthiness and Conscientiousness as Managerial Virtues. See [us] Daryl Koehn (editor) (2003, p. 195), *Trust and Business*, translated by Lu Xiaohe et al., Shanghai Academy of Social Sciences Press, 2003, p. 195.

the perfection of human nature and the realization of all-round and free human development. As Sison states, "The main end product or result of doing is not an independent artifact, but rather, an operative moral habit. And in the measure that what one acquires are virtues, the process of self-production is, at the same time, a process of self-perfection (Sison 2005b)." Sison expresses the opinion that rational corporate behavior not only creates goods but also promotes self-perfection. The basic precondition of rational corporate behavior is the constant improvement of moral institutions.

In today's world, among various economic, political, environmental and security issues, moral capital is a necessary element. However, how can we combine morality with corporate management institutions and economic decision-making? According to Paine, there are four questions, which present four modes. The four questions are as follows: What are our goals? What do we want to be? What do we own to others? What are our rights? The four corresponding modes are *goal*—whether the action serves a valuable goal; *principle*—whether the action follows relevant principles; *man*—whether the action respects the legal interests of people involved; *power*—whether we have the right to take the action (Lynn 2004). The process of following the above four modes to make decisions and formulate institutions is actually the process of realizing the institutionalization of morality, or creating moral capital. That is to say, the ultimate value pursuit of moral institutions is corporate responsibility or corporate morality. Sison defines corporate morality as "The main virtue to be practiced in the production of basic moral capital assets or currency is, therefore, that of justice: the constant and firm will to give to each of one's associates—or to every one of a firm's stakeholders—his due in accordance with law. Justice disposes the agent to respect the rights of others and to establish harmony in human relationships such that equity and the common good are promoted (Sison 2005b)." This is the essence of moral capital. For China, moral institutionalization means the institutionalization of such morals as patriotism, justice, integrity, humanity and friendship.

2.6.2 The Form of Rational Relationships

The form of rational relationships is a basic form of moral capital in the dimension of subjectivity. Morality, in the form of the rational relationships between man and man as well as man and society, directly determines the result and benefits of corporate economic activities. Through reconciling interpersonal relationships, moral capital in the form of rational relationships reduces "friction consumption," thus improving productivity and resource utilization. In the final analysis, it synergizes economic benefits.

First, the construction of the internal rational relationship of a company promotes the formation of moral capital. Such relationship reduces interpersonal "friction consumption," realizing interpersonal harmony. Morality reflecting rational interpersonal relationship acts as the lubricant for social relations. "Just because of the fact that they are trusted and loved, those who do not deserve our trust and love may be believable and lovely."[36] In fact, the interpersonal relationship guided by trust and love is a special moral force.

A company is composed of complex subjects. Subjects playing different roles interact and cooperate to form an entity. Within the company, there is a complex and clear-cut division of labor—even a simple product is made based on interpersonal cooperation. Therefore, employees are connected by both cooperation and competition, which, exist in each other. Particularly, in modern and intensive production, the rational interpersonal relationship helps employees develop the modern concept of competition—coopetition, which directly promotes rational and conscious production and transaction activities, increasing productivity and labor efficiency.

However, there are still companies which, having been affected by Western Taylorism for a long time, apply a material-centered instead of a human-centered management mode in management and production. For them, laborers are just "materials" or "talking instruments" inputted into production. In this case, companies are alienated into "a place that provides laborers in exchange for money (Wang 1999)." The personality of employees is derogated and their enthusiasm is destroyed. As a result, their optimal productivity cannot be realized. Nowadays, short-sighted companies who put materials in front of laborers have been gradually expelled from the market. On the contrary, many excellent companies, especially transnational corporations, take the interests of employees seriously. For example, workplaces are designed rationally according to the needs of employees, such as the needs of work, education and entertainment. By trying to meet human needs, which is a requirement for establishing rational interpersonal relationships, such companies have won the praise of society and have taken the lead in human-centered management. In fact, a company with rational management and competition is surely harmonious in interpersonal relationship, which makes the company more capable in making a profit.

Second, the external relationship includes intercompany relationships, and the relationship between companies and other social factors (individuals, groups and society). A harmonious external relationship helps companies to make the best use of shared resources to create profits. In fact, companies are also connected by the coopetition relationship. Cooperation is the basis for a win-win situation. For example, nowadays, competitive bidding has become a basic economic activity of companies to exist and develop. From the perspective of the owner, when a project is to be carried out by one company, he will divide the project into some subprojects and invite several companies to bid for the project. The introduction of the competition mechanism is helpful in controlling project quality, progress and costs. From the perspective of the bidders, they are given an opportunity for fair competition,

---

[36] [US] Fernando L. Flores and Robert C. Solomon, Rethinking Trust, See [us] Daryl Koehn (editor), (2003, p. 76)*Trust and Business*, translated by Lu Xiaohe et al., Shanghai Academy of Social Sciences Press, 2003, p. 76.

and winners of the subjects can, during the process of the project, cooperate with and learn from each other, and share profits. The example tells us that the unity of cooperation and competition is the unity of the moral man and the economic man. Upon the realization of such unity, the relationship between rivals will turn from the original win-lose, which is in opposition and exclusive, to win-win. Thus, a rational relationship is built between companies, and moral capital grows and develops. Consequently, corporate development is greatly encouraged.

The rational relationship between companies and society is also a form of moral capital. Through harmonious cooperation, various available resources are fully used, and the forces of different parties are effectively reconciled. In this way, the creation of material and spiritual wealth is maximized. Upon the hypothesis that our society is rational, companies are required to undertake necessary social moral responsibilities in the first place. Only in this way, the communication between companies and society can become the basis and condition of making a profit.

Of course, whether the internal and external relationships of a company can well play their roles depends on the sense of responsibility of the parties involved. There are mainly three views on corporate responsibilities. One is "profit first," that is, companies are for-profit, so they only need to undertake economic responsibilities, and other responsibilities shall be subject to or included in economic responsibilities. The second view is "theory first," namely, companies are legal persons with a moral personality, so their social responsibilities include responsibilities to the exclusion of direct economic responsibilities (such as responsibilities for environmental protection, the government and public, and consumers and employees). The third view is "reconciliation first," which calls for determining the social responsibilities of companies from the perspective of a dynamic social system. In fact, corporate social responsibility is a dynamic concept. We need to find the balance where companies undertake the right amount of responsibilities during the dynamic process. When companies undertake necessary social responsibilities, a rational relationship is built between companies and society that is based on which corporate images and reputations have a rising growth. Companies with and without good reputations hold quite different statuses in market competition. Reputation directly determines the future of a company. A good reputation helps a company to remain invincible in market competition. It can be said that a good corporate reputation lays the basis for trust and cooperation, and is the premise for building rational relationship and promoting profit making. As Sison states, "trust lowers transaction costs and is the key to solving the problem of corporate action (Sison 2005b)." The American scholar Francis Fukuyama studies trust, a kind of moral capital. He believes that when the sense of trust is widely developed in a social network, then the cooperation (transaction) between any social members in the network will cost less than that in a social network full of the sense of distrust (Fukuyama 1998).

Of course, we must notice that the formation and development of moral capital in the form of a rational relationship tends to be affected by many internal and external factors. Therefore, the management mechanism of such moral capital is more difficult and complex.

2.6.3 The Form of Subject Consciousness

The form of subject consciousness is also a basic form of moral capital in the dimension of subjectivity. Moral capital in the form of institutions and rational relationships focuses on complex intersubject interactions (such as relationship, environment, communication and competition), whereas moral capital in the form of subject consciousness is about the subject's noble value orientation and active attitudes towards life.

Man is the carrier of culture and is more the undertaker of morality. Moral capital in the form of subject consciousness is mainly embodied in subjects engaged in production, management and service activities. In fact, it is not very precise to say so. The subjects of economic activities are not only carriers (passive and mechanical) but also initiators (active and creative). In other words, people engaged in real economic activities are not what Gottfried Wilhelm Leibniz calls "monads," but what Engels calls "conscious people who act and pursue some purposes based on deliberation or just passion; everything happens for conscious purposes and expected goals."[37] Since human activities are not mere spontaneous impulsions, it can be said that the activities of economic agents must have purposes and targets.

Therefore, the problem is not whether human activities have purposes or not, but whether the purposes are rational or not, and what the standard is for making a judgment. According to the hypothesis of rational behavior or hypothesis of the rational man, which is the foothold and primary precondition of mainstream Western economics, behavior meeting the requirements of self-interest maximization (or Pareto optimality) is rational; otherwise, is irrational. The typical mode representing the logic hypothesis is the Prisoner's Dilemma in game theory. In fact, the Prisoner's Dilemma only judges individual rationality, but the result of individual rationality may lead to collective irrationality (Wang 2009). At the very least, collective rationality at different levels needs to be judged by morality. Therefore, to judge the rationality of economic activities, the participation of moral capital in the form of subject consciousness is necessary.[38]

First, moral capital in the form of subject consciousness determines the value orientation of the subject, thus determining his attitude towards labor and his labor enthusiasm. In this way, the value orientation of business activities can be determined. Moral capital in the form of subject consciousness reflects the subjective spiritual state and rational action of the economic agent. In case of the lack of such

[37] *Collected Works of Karl Marx and Friedrich Engels*, Vol. 4, People's Publishing House, 1995, p. 247.

[38] For the concept of rationality, different disciplines and schools have different definition. In my view, "real rationality," as quoted by Koslowski from Blaise Pascal, "it needs the tact of geometry and also the skills of wisdom" (see [Germany] Peter Koslowski, Some Principles of Ethical Economy, translated by Sun Yu, China Social Sciences Publishing House, 1997, p. 6). That is, the development of rationality needs both calculation and wisdom, and morality is the ultimate component. Or to say, rationality shall be understood from both economic and ethical perspectives.

moral capital, the benefits created by physical capital will drop dramatically, and at the same time, the construction and reproduction of other forms of moral capital, namely, the forms of rational relationships, of institutions and of moral products will be restricted fundamentally. The above mentioned subjective spiritual state and rational action of the economic agent intensively manifest as the spirit of responsibility, spirit of moral responsibility, and, especially, the spirit of social responsibility and justice of the economic agent. Once possessing moral capital in the form of subject consciousness, the economic agent will be highly capable of "reading" economic activities in order to review the relationship between himself, the subject of real communication and the economic subject. As Sison states, "It only means that such a person would never readily sacrifice his moral excellence as a condition to gain health, knowledge, social connections or profit (Sison 2005b)."

In the absence of moral capital in the form of subject consciousness, there will be no moral responsibility. The consequence is disastrous for individuals, collectives and even the world. From the Sanlu scandal to the financial crisis sweeping across the US, their domino effect has knocked over many innocent companies. Such examples have proved the ultimate and basic role played by moral capital in the form of subject consciousness. It is true that the Sanlu scandal and the financial crisis are not caused by individuals but groups; however, we must see that a group itself is a "personalized person." Therefore, a company drifting away from morality will certainly become a "lost lamb"—it is eager to find the way home, but it is unable to do so. Therefore, proprietors must learn how to use morality to make money rather than using money to make money, just like "scoring a success indirectly rather than directly" (*Sun Tzu's Art of War*). In 2008, when talking about the Sanlu scandal, Wen Jiabao said, "An entrepreneur must be moral. Each entrepreneur should have the blood of morality flowing inside and should undertake social responsibility. Society needs companies following the requirements of law and morality (Wen 2008)." Morality determines the value orientation, attitude towards labor, production purposes and enthusiasm of laborers. In fact, it is just a matter of asking the question of "Who are being served?" After the question is answered, there will be market, profits and development. In the market, economic agents with and without consciousness will have totally different results, and thus their fates are totally different.

Second, moral capital in the form of subject consciousness also determines the utilization and efficiency of resources. An economic agent with highly developed subject consciousness will conduct business activities in accordance with the requirements of scientific development, environmental protection and human-centered operation. In this way, the utilization and efficiency of resources will certainly be improved, promoting the expansion of economic benefits. What is more, the cascade effect and even snowball effect created will greatly promote the accumulation and increase of physical, money and moral capital.

It is worth mentioning that the moral quality of business leaders actually demonstrates and guides the development and utilization of moral capital, for they are the examples that workers follow. In other words, leaders are important moral capital in the form of subject consciousness. In *The Moral Capital of Leaders*, Sison states, "Leadership is a two-way transformative and intrinsically moral relationship between a leader and his followers. The two parties involved in a leadership relation—the leader and his followers—morally transform and elevate each other through their interaction. Thus, ethical leadership becomes the primary conduit through which not only persons, but also organizations for which these persons work, become ethical. Leadership nurtures personal ethics, allowing it to grow and configure an auspicious organizational culture (Sison 2005b)." Leaders lacking morality certainly do not have charisma and naturally cannot analyze and organize with the power of morality, let alone understand how morality penetrates into economic activities to play its unique roles and builds a virtuous external relationship. Therefore, in the scope managed by a leader lacking morality, moral capital can hardly (and even cannot) play its role in economic activities.

It should be pointed out that in "the form of subject consciousness," "subject" means not only individuals but also economic units. Each economic unit, with its philosophy of economic behavior and moral consciousness, can certainly play roles the same as (and even better than) man as moral capital in the form of subject consciousness.

2.6.4 The Form of Moral Products

The physical carriers of moral capital are moral products, relying on which moral capital finally realizes its value, and therefore, it is "a key leap" to realize the accumulation and value expansion of moral capital. It can be said, "From commodities to money, as I said elsewhere, commodity value makes a break-neck leap. If it fails, it is the commodity owner rather than the commodity that will be broken."[39] I once pointed out, "In recent years, Haier has gradually expanded its market share in the European market, and one of the reasons, as said by foreign dealers, is that the products of Haier meet the requirements and respect the habits of European consumers. For example, Haier washers have totally occupied the stores of some foreign dealers who only sold Japanese washers before. In the final analysis, it's Haier's responsibility for the interests of itself, of China, and of European consumers that expanded its washers' market share in Europe and created more benefits and profits (Wang 2000b)." When moral capital turns into materialized morality, or moral products, it is transformed into physical capital, helping companies to build business integrity and reputation and encouraging companies to grow stronger. Many foreign companies, especially American and European companies, build their business in this way. Paine believes, "Many companies take actions to enhance their reputation, or respond actively to the needs and interests of customers," and "executives of big businesses are talking about how to protect corporate reputation and brands, and entrepreneurs are talking about how to build reputation and brands (Lynn 2004)."

[39] In this case, the "break-neck leap" by Marx means commodities need to be sold to realize their value. Actually, moral capital in all forms is finally embodied in moral products, which will be meaningless without the "leap." In this sense, I call the manufacturing of moral capital as "a key leap" of moral capital in the production sphere.

Undoubtedly, moral capital in the form of moral products is directly related with the survival of a company, and with the transformation from moral capital to physical and economic capital. Therefore, many companies take providing customers with quality, efficient, reasonably priced, marketable, and human-centered commodities as their core task to stand steadily in fierce market competition. In this sense, it is reasonable to call "products with human-centered design" as the products of "ethical entities" or moral products.

Moral products, as the unity of moral capital and economic capital, have an aspect as materials (economic capital is hypothesized in advance) as well as an aspect as symbols (moral capital is hypothesized in advance). Such unity makes moral products different from common products. Particularly, moral products as symbols can be repeatedly used, during which, its value will be increased infinitely rather than being decreased. In general, common products are produced for use in production and daily life. Compared with common products, moral products can not only meet human needs but also create new benefits. Moreover, moral products play the role of expanding the market share and accelerating capital and money flows, thus maximizing benefits. Then, how are moral products, the materialized form of moral capital, made?

First, during the process of production, companies must try to meet "human needs,"[40] which is the basic principle for product design and manufacturing. In the context of increasing economic globalization, companies will face consumers with various habits, preferences and even special requirements from around the world. This requires companies to research and develop products meeting the real needs of consumers based on the principle of "consumers first."

Second, the spirit of putting the interests of consumers first must penetrate into all aspects of production. Products are "spiritualized" materials. On the one hand, "all products are designed based on the technological and cultural cognition and technical routes of man"; on the other hand, "all products are the materialization of the moral consciousness and quality of man (Wang 2000a)." Moral capital determines the existence of products, while products act as the carrier of moral capital.

In today's society, which calls for environmental protection due to environmental degradation, moral products must be ecological. That is, at the same time of being useful, moral products must not be harmful to consumers as well as those of the human and social environment. When studying the issue of efficiency, Li Yining raised some questions. "Can we say that social production is efficient no matter what we produce? If the products manufactured are harmful to human health and the environment, can we say social production is efficient? Can't we improve efficiency without producing such products (Li 1995)?" Following his thought, we can ask, "Can products play its roles and create benefits once they are manufactured?" Products actually include materials, introductions as services and human-centered services. For example, some products, even with high quality, still fail to find a market due to poor after-sales services. It tells us that in this market, which is a

---

[40] In this case, human needs refer to the physiological, psychological and social needs of man.

battleground without gunfire, moral products are crucial for the existence and development of companies.

In conclusion, analyzing and expounding moral capital from the perspective of typology undoubtedly can deepen our understanding of moral capital. It can be considered as a search on the precondition of moral capital management. In four basic forms, moral capital plays different roles and functions differently. Moral capital in the form of institutions mainly penetrates economic institutions; in the form of rational relationships principally exists in the interpersonal relationships of the economic sphere;[41] in the form of subjects mainly manifests in the economic agent; and in the form of moral products is primarily embodied in products. Therefore, the four forms of moral capital are the basic functioning forms of moral capital. Of course, the four forms are not completely separated. They are independently analyzed for the purpose of research. In fact, they penetrate into and affect each other. To be specific, from the perspective of the relationship among morality in the form of moral institutions (A), in the form of subject consciousness (B), in the form of rational relationships (C) and in the form of moral products (D), A guarantees the realization of B and C, B and C are the requirements for the optimal performance of A, C ensures the realization of D, and D is the embodiment and final outcome of A, B, and C. The four forms coexist in space and exist in sequence in time, which is a requirement for the virtuous management of moral capital. Just like the realization of truth is a process, the realization of moral capital is also a process, which I intend to analyze independently.

2.7 In What Sense Could Morality Become Capital?[42]

After publishing my studies on the theory of moral capital, I heard voices of agreement as well as of disagreement. Some thought the existence of moral capital is groundless and impossible, while some thought the theory of moral capital, as a breakthrough of the binary opposition between moral capital as an end and moral capital as an instrument, had ultimately revealed the functions of effects of moral capital. I insist that the existence of moral capital is well founded. Denying the existence of moral capital is denying the economic functions and effects of morality, which means denying the reason for the existence of morality.

It is worth pointing out that the concept of "capital" in moral capital is not the classical concept of capital put forward by Marx, but the concept of "production element capital"—the concept of capital in a broad sense. It is not an analysis tool that reflects or criticizes some social institutions or economic relations; it considers capital as a kind of valuable productive resource and outlines the special roles

[41] In this case, institutions are understood at the macro-, meso-, and microlevel, and do not only mean basic social institution at the macro-level.

[42] Originally titled as The Eighth Study on Moral Capital, *Morality and Civilization*, Issue 6, 2011.

played by morality in the expansion of economic value. Then, in what sense could morality exist as a kind of capital?

2.7.1 Morality is the Soul of Human-centered Product Design

For an enterprise, its economic development or revenue growth largely depends on the design and quality of its products for which, as determinants of market share and any increase or decrease in revenues, products greatly affect the profitability of the enterprise. Furthermore, the design and quality of products are all subject to technological constraints, social culture and morality. In general, technology determines the applicability, practicability, durability and convenience of products; social culture influences the style and appearance of products; and morality defines the degree of human-centered design and intrinsic value of products. Among these three factors, morality plays a decisive role. The reason is that the value of products lies in how well they can serve people; therefore, the more their styles and functionality are designed according to human needs,[43] the more they are endowed with morality, and hence the more popular they will be. For example, in China, the world's largest cell phone market, which has undergone increasingly fierce competition in recent years, some cell phone brands can still dominate the market through their long-standing popularity and high market share. One of the reasons for this, aside from focusing more on research and development (R&D) in terms of functionality and style of their products, is that manufacturers also seriously consider consumer demand throughout the whole process of product design and manufacturing, ultimately injecting more morality into their products. The importance of morality can also be proved by the sudden collapse of famous brands like the dairy producer Sanlu. When the demands and safety of consumers are ignored, morality is abandoned, which will invariably lead the brand to ruin. It can be seen from the above that the market share of products largely hinges on the moral principles followed by manufacturers, and the moral content within their products.

2.7.2 Morality is an Important Factor to Shorten Socially Necessary Labor Time per Product Unit

During the process of product manufacturing, due to the variance of production technology and processes, especially morality contained in products, the socially necessary labor time, which determines the costs of similar products, varies. In the information age, the convergence of production technology and processes tend to be

[43] In this case, human needs refer to the needs of human beings as determined by their natural attributes and social attributes. For the former, human beings have specific product requirements due to physiological reasons, while for the latter, human social activities require products to be helpful in improving interpersonal communication and quality of life.

higher and higher in level and shorter and shorter in time. Therefore, how to shorten socially necessary labor time per product unit has become a key for corporate competition. Whoever successfully shortens socially necessary labor time per product unit will be the winner of market competition, thus creating benefits and establishing its position. The shortening of socially necessary labor time per product unit largely depends on the penetration of morality during the process of production. Taylorism management is effective in shortening socially necessary labor time per product unit and was thereby prized as the only scripture for at one time. However, the point is that the management mode essentially ignores and even destroys human nature. It not only destroys the enthusiasm, initiative and creativity of employees but also causes the tension and even opposition between employers and employees. Under such a management mode, in case of interpersonal friction, labor will always be emotionally unstable, psychologically unbalanced and negatively go-slow. Consequently, productivity is low, which means a low socially necessary labor time per product unit. As time goes by, such a kind of management mode that lacks morality will gradually be replaced by human-centered management modes.

In the context of modern mass production, the product manufacturing of any company is actually a social behavior; therefore, effective social collaboration is required to maximize socially necessary labor time per product unit. Obviously, it depends on the improvement of overall social moral quality. Francis Fukuyama once pointed out that whether a country or region can configure effective and rationally operated corporate organizations and business forms is the key element that determines its sustainable economic development. The formation of such corporate organizations lies on the "spontaneous social force" of the interpersonal trust in society (Fukuyama 1998). It is true that in the context of modern production, companies compete while cooperating with each other. However, to realize win-win situations, cooperation is necessary. Honest cooperation has the power of preventing the cost increase caused by information blockade, meaningless friction and the undoing of benefits given to each other. For this reason, some scholars have claimed, "Morality is important!… It can lower transaction costs and promote economic development (Zhang 1999)." It can be said that in the condition of modern production, morality plays an indispensable role in shortening socially necessary labor time per product unit and creating more profits.

2.7.3 *Morality is the Source of Corporate Reputation*

There is no doubt that reputation, as the life of a company, plays a decisive role for the expansion of the market share. To develop reputation, aside from technology and culture, morals like integrity and the sense of responsibility are also crucial. A customer buys the products of a brand out of trust. During the process of use, the increase of trust largely depends on the moral content of products and the fulfillment of after-sales service commitments. The positive correlation between corporate morality and corporate reputation has been proved by the prosperity and decline of a large number of companies around the world. When a company, on the one hand, sincerely considers the real needs of consumers during product design and production, trying its best to meet such needs to maximize the benefits of consumers, and on the other hand, fulfills its commitments in sales and after-sales services, it will simultaneously build its reputation and expand its market share. On the contrary, if a company, no matter how famous it is, loses its morality in product design, production, sales or after-sales services, such as cutting corners, adulteration, exaggerating product functions, and making empty promises, its reputation will be seriously damaged. Consequently, its sales and profits will drop, which may ultimately lead to the collapse of the company. A world famous carmaker once experienced a trust crisis in China due to its lack of the sense of responsibility in after-sales service provisions. Events such as smashing the car with the hammer and dragging the car with the donkey happened successively in front of its consumers and the public. Its reputation was seriously damaged and its sales dropped sharply. Thanks to the great efforts of its headquarters, it finally went through the trust crisis at the cost of a long time and a lot of money. It can be seen that the sense of responsibility is the spiritual pillar of a company, and moral commitments and actions are necessary for the reputation building and maintenance as well as the creation of benefits and profits of the company.

2.7.4 *Morality is an Important Factor to Activate Tangible Capital and Increase the Capacities for the Multiplication of Capital*

The nature of capital lies in movement, through which value is created and incremented. In the process of movement, morality activates human and tangible capital to promote the increment of value. First, it accelerates the movement speed of physical capital. Through moralizing organizational institutions and arousing the potential of people, morality activates tangible capital, thus optimizing resource distribution and improving productivity. In a certain sense, the corporate institutional reforms carried out after the economic reform in 1979 is the embodiment of the moralization of corporate institutions. Through institutional reforms of property rights, the interest relationship between the state, companies, and individuals has become clearer, more just and more reasonable. This greatly aroused the enthusiasm of laborers and maximized resource utilization, leading to the rapid growth of economic benefits. Next, morality can be constantly materialized and accumulated in physical capital, and turns into capital stock in the form of corporate reputation and brand competitiveness, improving the value added of tangible assets. Finally, morality can drive technological progress and promote the commercialization of technical outcomes. As mentioned above, a responsible company surely has a good reputation, which helps expand its market share, thus increasing the value added of tangible capital and ultimately increasing profits. Finally, morality motivates human capital by improving the character, quality, and spiritual realm of the economic agent, thus becoming a capital source for the profit creation of companies and even the increase of wealth of the whole society. Only laborers with active value orientation and excellent professional ethics can become the "primary element of production." In this sense, moral capital and human capital are closely connected internally at both the theoretical and practical level (Wang 2011).

2.7.5 Morality Guides or Constrains Rational Consumption

In production and daily life, man consumes materials and spiritual wealth like culture. In the process of consumption, morality plays the role of guidance and constraint to prevent immoderate consumption and waste which may lead to ecological crises and environmental degradation. Rational consumption is moral. It mainly manifests as such consumption concepts and behavior as low-carbon consumption, moderate consumption, and ecological consumption. Low-carbon consumption is about minimizing consumption and emissions to protect the environment. Moderate consumption advocates rationally improving the consumption level, namely, it opposes excessive and luxury consumption and does not support parsimonious and hysteretic consumption. Instead, it tries to find a balance between the improvement of living standard and environmental protection. Ecological consumption opposes the predatory and destructive consumption, considering it as a kind of abnormal consumption that destroys natural and social ecology, which will ultimately hinder corporate profit creation and social wealth growth. Therefore, rational consumption is moral consumption that encourages the growth of social wealth. Only rational consumption under the guidance and constraint of morality could push forward production development and wealth growth.

It is worth pointing out that morality does not equal moral capital. That is, not all morals can be considered capital. First, only morals that are able to play economic roles and create benefits can be considered moral capital. In terms of the theories of capital, from the classical theory of capital of Marx, to the theories of capital in a broad sense, including the theories of human capital (Theodore 1990a), social capital (Zhao 1998) and cultural capital (Bourdieu 1997), our understanding on the concept of understanding has been changing. The British economist Marshall once said, "Capital is principally composed of knowledge and organizations… Knowledge is our most powerful engine of production (Marshall 1981)." The US socialist Nan Lin (2005, pp. 16–18) also pointed out that actions or choices have emerged as an important element of new theories of capital (Lin 2005). The concept of capital in a broad sense exists objectively. As Schultz, the father of the theory of human capital, writes, "If it can provide productive service with economic value, it's a kind of capital (Theodore 1990a)." However, in various theories of capital in a broad sense, no matter the theory of human capital, or cultural capital or social capital, capital can only play its roles based on the creativity of living labor. In this sense, modern theories of capital actually follow the classical theory of capital of Marx. Since the value of capital derives from the value creation of living labor, all material and spiritual elements playing roles in the formation and increment of value are of the attributes of capital. Therefore, capital is the value of the materials and spirits inputted in the production process to create profits or benefits—this is capital in general. Moral capital is the further expansion of capital in the broad sense or in the general theoretical basis; it is a special capital form separated from capital in the broad sense or capital in general. Non-physical moral capital is different from physical capital. It penetrates into human, knowledge, cultural, and social capital, and plays its special roles through capital in other forms. In capital in a broad sense or capital in general, no matter the attribute of labor contained in physical capital, or the spiritual elements contained in non-physical capital, as long as it is/they are related to the value end, then it/they can be considered as the value source of moral capital. In fact, scientific morality can play its roles in production by virtue of its special functions of guidance, regulation, constraint, and conciliation, thus promoting value expansion. Therefore, by forming the perspective of capital in a broad sense or capital in general, morality, as a spiritual element affecting the formation and increment of value, is of the obvious attributes of capital. For this reason, all moral elements that encourage living labor to create value added (profits), such as moral concepts, values, customs, norms, goodwill, and benevolence shall be considered as moral capital. The Chinese economist Luo Weidong once called the economic functions and effects of morality as moral capital. He thought that like capital, the economic functions and effects of morality participate in economic activities and create benefits. According to him, morality is not merely a spiritual element that promotes the maintenance and increment of value. Instead, it contributes to the creation of mutual social and economic benefits, thus working as an end that contains the rational spirits of society.[44] In this sense, all value elements reflecting the rational social spirits contained in physical and intangible capital can be included in the scope of moral capital.

Second, there is a logic boundary dividing morals as capital and morals known as capital. Putting forward and agreeing with the concept of moral capital does not mean believing in pan-moralism or the omnipotence of morality. The boundary of the field of productive activities is the boundary of the functions of morality. Historically, the concept of morality was closely connected with productive activities from the very beginning. With the development of human productive activities, modern capital has gradually developed new forms, such as human, social, cultural, and moral capital. Therefore, moral capital is the outcome of human productive activities. From the macro-sense of social development, considering morality as a kind of capital does not mean beautifying capital with morality, or turning morality into a hypocritical instrument for capital growth, but stressing that morality can and shall play its unique role in creating benefits and profits. In fact, while working as an instrument to create profits, morality also criticizes capital internally. In the modern society, the nature of capital is pursuing a surplus value or more profits, and human, social, cultural, and moral capital is helpful in realizing this purpose. On the one hand, capital always tries to take everything as an instrument to obtain surplus value or more profits; while on the other hand, capital configures man himself objectively through controlling resources, knowledge, culture, and morality in its unique way.

[44] "On the Economic Role of Morality". Journal of the Party School, Zhejiang Provincial Committee, CPC, 1998, no. 1.

Improved rational spirits, in turn, internally constrain the negative effects of capital, criticizing capital internally. In this aspect, moral capital has more obvious value orientation than capital in other forms. Morality can not only serve capital as a rational instrument but also constrain capital internally with its rational orientation of value in order to avoid the irrational expansion of capital's nature and the immoderate expansion of "capital logic." However, to play the dual roles of moral capital, it is necessary to turn the status of morality from "within itself" to "for itself" during the process of capital movement, which requires the management of moral capital in real economic activities. Specifically, we need to organically combine the business activities and moral practice of companies in the market economy, forming the special ethical culture and core competitiveness of companies.[45]

2.8 Why Does Moral Capital Exist?[46]—Response to Questions

After putting forward the concept of "moral capital" in the early twenty-first century, in the following years, I made a series of studies on the basis of the existence of moral capital and its mechanism of action, which have attracted the attention from home and abroad. These studies were agreed, criticized or questioned by many, which injected new vitality to academic controversy and greatly promoted my academic research. In this section, I will correct mistakes concerning commonsense issues and further expound my understanding of moral capital.

2.8.1 Moral Capital is Fundamentally Different from the "capital" Defined by Marx in Nature

Some thought that "in the view of Marx, the nature of capital is not materials, but productive relations, and every pore of capital is dirty" and "according to Marx, the combinations of morality and capital is unimaginable (Yaoming 2012)." It is indeed unimaginable if we combine socialist morality or good morality with the capital understood by Marx. However, the fact of the matter is that the concept of moral capital is not merely a simple combination of morality and capital. What's more, as I have pointed out in my published papers, the "capital" in the concept of moral capital is not the "capital" defined by Marx. I once wrote in a paper, "The 'capital' in moral capital doesn't mean the classical capital employed and discussed

[45] As Sison said, "Without moral capital, capital in other forms is likely to turn from the advantages of a company into the source of its decline." Alejo G. Sison, *The Moral Capital of Leaders*, translated by Yu Wenxuan and Ding Ming, Central Compilation & Translation Press, 2005, p. 56.

[46] Originally published on *Philosophical Trends*, Issue 3, 2013; reprinted on *Chinese Social Science Digest*, Issue 7, 2013 and *Ethics*, Issue 6, 2013.

by Marx; it generally falls in the scope of capital."[47] Social morality plays the roles of guidance, regulation, constraint and reconciliation in the process of production, promoting the expansion of economic value. Therefore, from the perspective of the general concept of capital, morality, as a spiritual element affecting the formation and increment of value, is of the attributes of capital. In other words, the concept of moral capital reflects capital as an element of production and is thus the concept of capital in a broad sense. It is not an analysis tool that reflects or criticizes some social institutions or economic relations as understood by Marx. According to Marx, capital is not materials; rather, it is the relationship between the capitalist class and the working class. Capital is about the economy, and more about economic relations. It presents the relation that capital exploits wage labor between the capitalist class and the working class. Differently, moral capital considers morality as a valuable productive resource and analyzes the special roles played by morality in the process of value expansion. This is a difference between the concept of moral capital and the concept of capital in the view of Marx, and the starting point to understand the theoretical space and logic boundary of moral capital. Economist Luo Weidong explicitly calls the economic functions and effects of morality as moral capital—"The economic functions of morality and capital are similar—they intervene economic activities and create considerable benefits. We can borrow Bourdieu's broad concept of capital to call morality 'moral capital'. From the perspective of social utility, moral capital is not only a spiritual element to promote the maintenance and increase of economic value, but also an orientation of value containing rational social spirits which can realize the win-win situations of economic and social benefits (Wang 2011)." It can be seen that moral capital is a kind of spiritual capital in the concept of capital in general, rather than an element of special capital, for the "capital" defined by Marx is not a synonym of morality. Therefore, moral capital does not fall into the scope of the capital criticized by Marx, but the scope of capital in general. Developing capital is not in conflict with developing morality, and the latter expands the stock of capital. Under socialism, only moral capital can be inputted in production to maximize the benefits of capital. In my opinion, there is no need to worry about if there will be conflict between moral capital and the nature of capital, for the nature of "capital" in the view of Marx and moral capital are different fundamentally; and capital in general is not in conflict with moral capital.

According to the above, we can say that moral capital is anything but the combination of morality and capital in the view of Marx. What is more, moral capital is not an artificial combination of morality and capital; instead, it is a phenomenon of economic ethics or the ethical economy.

In my opinion, denying the existence of morality using questions that I have answered in previous papers without an academic investigation and an analysis on my previous responses to questions is the reflection of typical academic dwarfism and academic fickleness. Presently, the concept of moral capital has been widely

[47] "Capital in general" means that the value of capital derives from the process in which living labor creates value. All material and spiritual elements playing roles in the formation and increment of value are of the attributes of capital.

applied to various theoretical research and economic agencies for the purpose of profoundly understanding and analyzing the modality of economic development. In fact, according to the theoretical development of the concept of moral capital, instead of discussing the existence of moral capital, what we should do is determine how to further improve, understand and apply the concept of moral capital and related theories. It is a consensus reached by economists from home and abroad that the content and forms of capital are diverse (including physical, money, human, and spiritual capital), and morality capital is the core or fundamental element of human and spiritual capital. Morality can undoubtedly play its unique role of value expansion in economic development, and its existence is well founded. It is written by a skeptic that "morality can only be understood as integrity and abiding the law in economic activities, as the human-oriented principle in production and management, or as public service activities in public relationships. It submits to and serves the end of profit maximization in economic activities (Yaoming 2012)." Is not the economic function of morality where "it submits to and serves the end of profit maximization in economic activities"? Since the answer is yes, how could we say morality has nothing to do with obtaining more profits? In fact, although "submits to and serves" is timidly expressed in "it submits to and serves the end of profit maximization in economic activities," from this perspective, it shows that without morality, negative effects will surely accompany the process of obtaining benefits.

2.8.2 Moral Capital and Moral Capitalization are not Logically Connected

Some believe that the concept of moral capital is "the capitalization of morality at the level of simple conceptual generalization (Zheng 2012)." Let me be clear, "The concept of 'moral capital' does not mean interpreting morality as a kind of 'capital (Zheng 2012),'" or capitalizing morality or equating morality with capital. As for the opinions that moral capital is "moralized capital" and moral capital is "naming capital with morality," I want to say that they do not have anything to do with the concept of moral capital. I put forward the concept of moral capital based on the special roles played by morality in economic development and profit creation, which is completely different from moral capitalization. In fact, moral capitalization means equating morality with capital and considering morality as a resource and an instrument to make money. This, of course, is blasphemous of morality. Morality is a spiritual element of capital—it cannot form capital independently; in fact, it depends on material elements to play its roles in economic activities. Therefore, positive moral capitalization is a subjective conjecture. What's more, as I mentioned above, capitalized morality is not the positive morality with which we are familiar.

Some scholars view "economics in a strict sense," where "capital" can be "measured" and "book kept." In my view, "moral capital" cannot be "measured" or "book kept." I also believe that the concept of "capital" in "moral capital" is quite different from the concept of "capital" defined in "Marxist political economics in a strict sense (Zheng 2012)." Here, I do not discuss whether there are differences between economics in a strict sense and economic in a non-strict sense, or between Marxist political economics in a strict sense and Marxist political economics in a non-strict sense. Instead, I would like to say that regardless of whether such differences exist or not, the "measurement" and "bookkeeping" of capital can be understood in a wider and deeper way in today's society. Absolute quantitative "measurement" and "bookkeeping" only exists in traditional economics. In modern economics, we do not just think of capital as just concerning materials and numbers. It must contain cultural elements, and in a certain social conditions, it must contain political elements. From the perspective that the ownership and investment of capital cannot be separated from man, interpersonal relationship and the (moral) value orientation of the subject of behavior, we can say that capital, in some sense, is also a moral entity—capital can be interpreted from the angle of morality. It is due to this reason that skeptics modified "economics" and "Marxist political economics" by adding "in a strict sense." In fact, in the process of economic development, people's value orientation, and attitude towards labor actually reflect how their moral consciousness directly affects product quality and the fulfillment of after-sales service commitments, thus directly affecting the market share of products, capital flow, and profit creation. Therefore, morality is an indispensable spiritual element for the formation of moral capital and an important spiritual condition for obtaining more profits. It has been widely accepted at home and abroad that morality is certainly contained in human capital and spiritual capital. Since morality is the core content of human and spiritual capital, we can say the concept that "morality is a kind of capital" is unique and logically reasonable. Those who cannot see it are, at least, scientifically illiterate and lacking common sense—they only see superficial phenomena and simply have no idea about interdisciplinary research.

2.8.3 Will the Concept of Moral Capital Cause Morality to Fall Victim to "Instrumentalization"?

Some believe that the concept of moral capital will cause morality to fall victim to "instrumentalization." I must clarify that analyzing the functions of morality does not mean morality is instrumentalized. Moreover, the "instrumentalization of morality" is a pseudo-proposition. To prove it, it is necessary to find out the reason for the existence of morality or the end of morality. Some will say that the end of morality is expanding people's spiritual realm so that they will fulfill their moral responsibilities consciously. This is correct. However, how do we judge people's spiritual realm? Why should we fulfill moral responsibilities consciously? I believe that if we do not think from the perspective of socioeconomic development, we cannot answer such questions. Therefore, morality exists because of its unique functions, including its functions in the economic sphere. There is no need to concern ourselves with whether morality's playing of its roles is considered as using morality as an instrument, for its utilization is the primary precondition and purpose for its existence. Some ethicists considered instrumental rationality as the vulgarization of moral instrumentalism, insisting that morality has nothing to do with obtaining more profits and stressing that "morality can only be human-based, rather than material based."[48] In my opinion, they are just hypocritical moral theorists.

In fact, as I have said, the instrumentalization of morality is a pseudo-proposition. When morals are only used as instruments to make money, they are not good morals, but evil morals, or even pseudo-morals. Sacrificing morality to make money is an abnormal phenomenon existing temporarily in a particular social context. If morals are considered as the terms or means of transactions, it means morality or conscience can be exchanged or transacted, which is of course unimaginable. I think people with common sense would never think like this. Moreover, studying and expounding the economic value of morality has no necessary logical relation with the instrumentalization of morality. Academic common sense tells us that during the process of capital management, morality certainly plays its unique role as a "rational instrument." However, instrumental rationality cannot be equated with the instrumentalization of morality. Confusing them by thinking that the concept of moral capital means morality is "tradable" is both illogical and vulgar.

2.8.4 Will Capital Make Money Unscrupulously, Causing Moral Leprosy due to the Emergence of the Theory of Moral Capital?

Some believe that due to the emergence of moral capital, capital will make money unscrupulously, causing moral leprosy. This is really a concern of some professional and unprofessional people. In fact, moral capital logically contains the requirements of morality. Therefore, the emergence of moral capital will not demoralize society; instead, at the time of regulating capital, moral capital will push forward the progress of society. Considering morality as a kind of capital does not mean beautifying capital with morality, or turning morality into a hypocritical instrument of capital growth. Moral capital plays dual roles in economic activities: on the one hand, it acts as an element or a means of capital to make profits; while on the other hand, it criticizes capital internally. The former role focuses on creating more profits or surplus value in a legal and moral way; the latter role means that capital, while pursuing surplus value, also configures man himself objectively. The improved spiritual and material quality will, in turn, internally constrain the negative effects of capital, criticizing capital internally. In this aspect, moral capital has a more obvious value orientation than capital in other forms. Morality can not only serve capital as a rational instrument but also internally constrain capital with its rational value orientation, making a capital investment rational and legal. Therefore, the emergence of moral capital will not make capital pursue profits unscrupulously, causing moral

[48] Actually, I put forward the concept of moral capital only for the purpose of stressing the morality's unique function of creating benefits and profits. Calling it as "being material centric" is far-fetched.

leprosy; instead, it stresses that capital investment cannot be completely separated from morality—capital must be moral.

2.8.5 *Is not Morality as a Normative Value Requirement Objectively Necessary?*

Some hold that "moral capital" is a normative value requirement, as "such normative value requirement, which is instrumental, considers 'morality' as a mere means. It is of probability without objective necessity, thus it cannot be considered as a general proposition—'morality' cannot become a value spirit in general (Yaoming 2012)." I cannot understand how this conclusion is derived. The fact is, from the perspective of scientific moral requirements, normative value requirements pursue and advocate generalization with objective necessity; they positively promote economic and social development. If normative value as an instrument aims at making "profits" and always puts "profits" first, "morality" itself is likely to be discarded. In this way, the relationship between morality and benefits is separated metaphysically. Some stress that morality is necessary for society, and it is human-based instead of material-based. Then, what does "human based" mean? In my opinion, it means promoting the development and perfection of man, which is "material based." The development and perfection of man is "material based" in a broad sense. There is also an opinion that the bone of contention regarding morality (the functions and end of morality) is always the ultimate value of morality. The reason is that "man [serves] as an end" and "man [serves] as a means," and the "end" and "means" included therein are not at the same logical level and value level. This is not a real scientific and philosophical view. If we still believe that the ultimate end of morality lies in "man as an end," we are just repeating the opinion of Kant. The reason is that "man as an end" and "man as a means" are dialectically unified. The fact is that the ultimate end of morality is developing and perfecting man, during which, man certainly plays his roles sufficiently and reasonably as a means. "Ends" certainly include "means"; and "means" is certainly taken to realize "ends." Ends without means and means without ends are all incomprehensible.

According to skeptics, to understand morality, "we must, first of all, grasp such basic concepts with transcendence as the ultimate value concern and the ultimate end of morality, human nature and human essence, or we will lose the soul and quintessence of morality (Yaoming 2012)." I believe these are empty words, which are theoretically groundless. What are the basic concepts of "transcendence" like the ultimate value concern, the ultimate end of morality, human nature and human essence? If we insist to consider "value rationality on the basis of absolute value ends" as "transcendence" or "morality," such morality is entirely imaginary. In my view, to understand "transcendence," we need to cognize the noumenon of morality under phenomena, and the noumenon is the "should-being" of man in social life. Based on the understanding of the "should-being," we then cognize moral responsibilities, moral norms and moral practice; otherwise, theories about the so-called "transcendence" will be empty words lacking logical thought.

In conclusion, good morals can, by virtue of their special functions, help economic activities to obtain higher efficiency and more profits. For this reason, the existence of moral capital is well founded. As Gao Yaoming states in *Questioning the Concept of Moral Capital*, "in fact, history has proved that civilized social graces and self-disciplined moral value spirit can greatly improve efficiency" and "it's rational to encourage companies to pursue profits in a moral way (Yaoming 2012)." During the process of economic development, there have been food safety problems, such as tainted milk powder, products with Sudan Red G, steamed buns dyed with colorant, and other contaminated foods; and quality problems with engineering projects like the occurrence of bridge, building, and road collapses. Facts have told us that unmoral behavior cannot help companies to improve efficiency and profits; on the contrary, once immoral behavior is uncovered, companies will face the risk of collapse. Therefore, it is necessary for companies to develop the sense of responsibility and the awareness of moral capital. Only under the constraint of morality can companies really realize their social responsibility instead of just talking about it, thus obtaining a high efficiency and more profits as well as promoting the rapid economic development of China. In short, we cannot superficially and rashly deny the existence of "moral capital."

References

Adam, S. (1994). *An inquiry into the nature and causes of the wealth of nations (I)* (p. 310; translated by G. Dali & Y. Wang). Commercial Press.

Aristotle. (1992). *The nicomachean ethics* (p. 2; translated by Huang Litian). China Social Sciences Publishing House.

Becker, G. S. (1996). *The economic approach to human behavior* (p. 5; translated by Y. Wang & Q. Chen). Shanghai Sanlian Bookstore.

Bernard, M. (2002). *The fable of the bees: Or, private vices, public benefits* (p. 28; translated by J. Xiao). China Social Sciences Publishing House.

Bourdieu, P. (1997). *Cultural capital and social alchemy: An interview with bourdieu* (translated by B. Yaming). Shanghai People's Publishing House.

Buchanan, A. E. (1991). *Ethics, efficiency, and the market* (p. 31; translated by L. Shenbai & D. Xie). China Social Sciences Publishing House.

Douglass, C. N. (2002). *Structure and change in economic history,* (p. 21; translated by Y. Li). Commercial Press.

Douglass, C. N. (2005). *Structure and change in economic history* (p. 21; translated by Y. Li). Commercial Press.

Douglass, C. N. (1994). *Institutions, institutional change and economic performance* (p. 84). Shanghai Sanlian Bookstore.

Douglass, C. N. (1991). *Structure and change in economic history* (p. 50; translated by Y. Chen et al.). Shanghai Sanlian Bookstore.

Douglass, C. N., & Thomas, R. P. (1988). *The rise of the western world* (p. 1). Huaxia Publishing House.

Fukuyama, F. (1998). *Trust: The social virtues and the creation of prosperity* (translated by P. Zhihua). Yuan Fang Publishing House.

Hu, Z. et al. (1994). *Human-centered product design in China* (p. 7). Guangzhou Publishing House.

Keynes, J. M. (2001). *The scope and method of political economy* (p. 8; translated by G. Dang & Liuhui). Huaxia Publishing House.

Lei, L., & Liu, Q. (1999). *Modern business operation decision—The application of the game theory* (p. 221, 222). Tsinghua University Press.
Li, Y. (1995). *Ethical issues in economics* (p. 3). Beijing Sanlian Bookstore.
Lin, N. (2005). *Social capital: A theory of social structure and action* (pp. 3, 16–18; translated by L. Zhang). Shanghai People's Publishing House.
Lionel, R. (2000). *The nature and significance of economic science* (p. 120; translated by Y. Zhu). Commercial Press.
Liu, G. (12 July 2001). UN Launches "Moral Indexes". *Beijing Youth Daily,* Version 7.
Lu, X. (1999). *Walking out of "Jungles"–Contemporary business ethics* (pp. 17–18, 46), Hubei Education Press.
Lynn, S. P. (2004). *The cornerstone of high-performance businesses* (pp. 25–26, 215–221; translated by D. Yang et al.). China Machine Press.
Machiavelli. (1996). *The prince* (p 95). Pan Handian, Commercial Press.
Mao, Y. (2003). *The moral prospect of the Chinese (Version II)* (p. 141). Ji'nan University Press.
Marshall, A. (1994). *Principles of economics* (I) (p. 35). Commercial Press, 1994.
Marshall, A. (1981). *Principles of economics* (I) (p. 157). Commercial Press.
Marx, K. (2001). *Capital* (Vol. I), *Collected Works of Karl Marx and Friedrich Engels* (p. 180, Vol. 44). People's Publishing House.
Plato. (1994). *The republic* (p. 170; translated by Guo Binhe and Zhang Zhuming). Commercial Press.
Qin, F. (2000). The Significance and Key Matters of Corporate Capital Expansion. *Tribune of Study,* (7).
Russell. (2003). *A history of western philosophy (II)* (p. 18; translated by He Zhaowu and Joseph Needham). Commercial Press.
Sen, A. (2001). *On ethics and economics* (pp. 13, 82–83; translated by Y. Wang & W. Wang). Commercial Press.
Sen, A. (2000). *On ethics and economics* (p. 13; translated by Y. Wang & W. Wang). Commercial Press.
Sison, A. G. (2005a). *The moral capital of leaders* (p. 56; translated by W. Ding & M. Ding). Central Compilation & Translation Press.
Sison, A. G. (2005b). *The moral capital of leaders* (p. 3, 7, 28, 41, 50, 56, 121, 217; translated by W. Yu et al.). Central Compilation & Translation Press.
Theodore, W. S. (1990a). *Investment in human capital* (p. 19, 68, 71, 93; translated by Z. Wu et al.). Beijing Institute of Economics Press.
Theodore, W. S. (1990b). *Investment in human capital* (p. 1; translated by Z. Jia & W. Shi). Huaxia Publishing Press.
Theodore, W. S. (1990c). *Investment in human capital: The role of education and of research* (pp. 6, 23–24; translated by B. Jiang & H. Zhang). Commercial Press.
Wang, C. (Ed.). (1999). *On Chinese famous brands* (p. 67). People's Publishing House.
Wang, H. (1997). *The practice of capital management* (pp. 117–120). China Industry and Commerce Press.
Wang, X. (2011). On the economic value of morality. *China Social Sciences,* (4).
Wang, X. (2009). Criticism of prisoner's dilemma game theory from the perspective of economic morality. *Jiangsu Social Sciences,* (1).
Wang, X. (2002). *Economic Morals* (p. 85). Chapter III Moral Capital and Business ethics. People's Publishing House.
Wang, X. (2000a). Moral capital. *Jiangsu Social Sciences,* (2).
Wang, X. (2000b). Moral capital. *Jiangsu Social Sciences,* (3).
Wang, X. (1999). The mission of ethics in the context of economic globalization in the 21st century. *Morality and Civilization,* (3).
Wang, X. (1994). *Economic ethics in China* (pp. 129–130). China Commercial Publishing House.
Wang, X., & Yang, W. (2002). The second study on moral capital. *Jiangsu Social Sciences,* (1).
Weber, M. (2000). *"Objectivity" in social science and social policy* (p. 8; edited by Han Shuifa, *Collected Works of Max Weber* (I), translated by Han Shuifa and Mo Xi). China Radio and Television Publishing House.

Weber, M. (1992). *The protestant ethic and the spirit of capitalism* (p. 85; translated by X. Yu, W. Chen et al.). Shanghai Sanlian Bookstore.
Weber, M. (1987). *The protestant ethic and the spirit of capitalism* (pp. 33–34; translated by Yu Xiao et al.). Sanlian Bookstore.
Wei, P. (28 March 2000). The relationship between ideological and political work and productivity development. *People's Daily*.
Wen, J. (28 September 2008). Q&A at world economic forum. *People's Daily*.
Yaoming, G. (2012). Questioning the concept of moral capital. *Philosophical Trends,* (11).
Zhang, H. (7 January 2002). The great influence of credit rating. *Global Times*.
Zhang, J. (1999). Morality: A significant variable in the study of *economic acti*vities and economics. *Social Sciences in China,* (2).
Zhang, R. (2000). The typical characteristics of new economic development. *Researches on Economics and Management,* (5).
Zhao, S. (1999). *An international comparative study on the human resource management and development of companies* (p. 3). People's Publishing House.
Zhao, Y. (1998). The theory of social capital: A review. *Social Sciences Abroad,* (3).
Zheng, C. (5 July 2012). *Morality is in danger of "Instrumentalization,". Social Sciences Weekly.*

Chapter 3
The Traditional Theory of Moral Capital in Chinese Intellectual History

Abstract This chapter primarily narrates the economic morality, especially the economic roles played by morality developed in the traditional intellectual history of the Chinese, providing thought resources for businesses to create and accumulate moral capital.

3.1 Moralism[1]

According to moralism, morality prevails over the economy or rationality and is superior to benefits. Moreover, morality is the end of the economy, while the economy is the means of morality. Some moralists even thought that interests could be sacrificed for the sake of rationality.

3.1.1 Ethical Economic Morality before the Emergence of Confucianism

1. In the Xia and Shang dynasties, economic morality was only sparsely embodied in some legends relating to the economy and morality and did not reflect the rational self-consciousness of the subject. Some traditional ideas, such as "no labor, no food", and "frugality is a virtue," actually truly reflect the life condition of people at that time, and largely, they are pretexts of later generations. The Western Zhou Dynasty saw the prime of China's slavery. Under slavery, natural economy developed rapidly, and correspondingly, economic morality was cognized and understood consciously by the ruler.

The rulers of the Western Zhou Dynasty drew the conclusion that it was the corrupt rulers who did not understand agriculture and the hardship of farmers, and who only indulged themselves, which caused the fall of the Shang Dynasty. As the *Book of Documents·Against Luxurious Ease* points out, "born with silver spoons in their mouths, they were not aware of the hardships of farmers, but just indulging

[1] *Economic Morality in China*, China Commercial Publishing House, 1994, p. 9–58, with corrections and deletions herein.

X. Wang, *On Moral Capital*, DOI 10.1007/978-3-662-45544-9_3

themselves," which led to the destruction of the Shang. Drawing lessons from the previous dynasty, the rulers of Western Zhou put pressure on agricultural development and the livelihood of farmers. King Wen of Zhou "wore the cloth of common people and worked in the fields himself." He supervised agricultural production "from morning to night, and even had no time for eating."[2] King Cheng of the Zhou "led tens of thousands of farmers to sow seeds in vast fields."[3] It can be said that the great success made by the Western Zhou in agricultural development is closely connected with the concern and participation of the ruling class.

Knowing the hardships of farmers, the rulers of Western Zhou called on people to live a better life through diligence and frugality. As recorded in the *Book of Documents Great Announcement*, Duke Zhou once said, "God rewards the diligent." In addition, he himself was an excellent example of diligence and industriousness. The *Book of Rites* clearly points out that people should "work hard to acquire wealth." Besides, the ruling class advocated the lifestyle of "living a frugal life"[4] and "not indulging in travelling, entertainment, playing, and hunting."[5] The rulers took King Gaozong and King Zujia of Shang who "understood the hardships of average people and thus always put their interests first" as their examples. At the same time, they used King Zhou of Shang as a warning for he "indulged in wine and women" and "amusement,"[6] which finally infuriated God and average people and led to "the destruction of Yin as the punishment of God."[7]

Private businesses started to emerge in the Western Zhou. Duke Zhou allowed people of the perished Yin to "transport goods far with ox carts to do business to make money" to "support their parents."[8]

When people just started becoming conscious of the significance of economic activities in their daily life and society, it is praiseworthy that the rulers of the Zhou held such moral ideas as "being aware of the difficulties in farming," "realizing the hardships of the average people," advocating diligence and frugality and opposing indulgence, and doing business to support one's parents. Rui Liangfu, King of Rui, can be labeled as the founder of ethical economic morality for he directly revealed the relationship between morality and the economy. He said, "Wealth comes from everything and shall be owned by everyone.[9] If it is possessed by the minority, disasters will follow consequently." It can be said that the rulers of Western Zhou originally put forward the philosophy of ethical economic morality.

It is worth pointing out that the economic morality claimed by the rulers of the Western Zhou only applied to the aristocracy. At that time, slaves were just "tools", "commodities", or "property" that had nothing to do with morality at all. In Western

[2] *Book of Documents·Against Luxurious Ease.*

[3] *Classic of Poetry·Eulogies of Zhou·Praise.*

[4] *Discourses of the States·Discourses of Zhou (II).*

[5] *Book of Documents·Against Luxurious Ease.*

[6] *Book of DocumentsNumerous Officers.*

[7] *Book of Documents·Announcement about Drunkenness.*

[8] *Book of Documents·Announcement about Drunkenness.*

[9] *Discourses of the States·Discourses of Zhou.*

Zhou, rulers like Duke Zhou advocated economic morality and put it into practice (since the development of morality was limited by a division between classes, in the social context that slaves can be transacted, doing business to support parents could only be the morals of slave owners). However, slave owners (the aristocracy) did not always follow moral norms in economic activities. Particularly, when their positions were consolidated, they started to throw their weight around to plunder wealth and indulge themselves. The aristocracy "lost ambitions, wasting their life in one party after another."[10] Moreover, due to the in fights and growth of selfish desires of the ruling class, immoral behavior, such as unreasonably levying tax and corvee as well as unfairly distributing wealth and rights, started to occur.

2. In the Spring and Autumn Period, when slavery realized its transition to feudalism, utilizing the implementation of iron farms and farm cattle as well as the progress of irrigation and water conservancy greatly promoted agricultural productivity as well as the reform of socio-economic relationships. As a result, a more complex social class structure was formed. On the one hand, due to the increase of productivity, large-scale collective agricultural production, which was under the supervision of slave owners in Western Zhou, was replaced by small-scale household agricultural production. Later, as the transacting of free land emerged, the ownership of pieces of land was transferred from the ruling class to a small number of landlords and a large number of small landowners. On the other hand, the progress of agricultural production promoted industrial and commercial development. In addition to state-owned handicraft organizations and family handicraft businesses, private small-scale handicraft businesses are also materialized. In a society with more and more complex socio-economic relationships as well as structures, ideas, and concepts about economic morality, started appearing. Insightful ideologists like Guan Zhong, Zip Chan, and Yan Ying put forward many valuable ideas and concepts about economic morality, which laid a foundation for the development of Confucian economic morality philosophy.

Guan Zhong (approximately 730–645 B.C.) was the prime minister of the State of Qi, the biggest power in the Spring and Autumn Period. He was known for his great accomplishments in administering the state. He divided the people of the Qi into four categories, namely, scholars, farmers, workers, and merchants, and arranged them to live and work in different areas: "scholars in quiet and comfortable places, workers in state-owned organizations, merchants in markets and farmers in fields."[11] According to Guan Zhong, such an arrangement has many advantages. First, it provides convenience for people to work and makes them always focus on their work—with relatively permanent occupations and residences, people will engage in certain professions for generations, during the process of which, "experience and skills are passed from one generation to another," which improves efficiency. Second, it helps people to concentrate on their professions, so they will not think "grass is always greener on the other side of the fence."[12]Moreover, it helps

[10] *Classic of Poetry·LesserCourt Hymns.*

[11] *Discourses of the States·Discourses of Qi.*

[12] *Discourses of the States·Discourses of Qi.*

people to develop noble morality. For example, when scholar families live together, "they will share sadness and misfortune, as well as happiness and fortune. Since they live as neighbors for generations, even when there is war, they can fight side by side while cooperating well with one another."[13] Another significant idea put forward by Guan Zhong is taxation. According to him, "tax shall be levied according to the degrees of fertility of land," so that farmers' enthusiasm can be aroused. He also put forward the moral principle of "tax shall be moderate" because "the productivity of land and man is limited, but the desires of the ruling class are unlimited. To meet unlimited desires with limited productivity, if the balance cannot be kept, there will be conflict… When tax is levied and used moderately, even a small state will be in prosperity and peace; but when tax is levied and used immoderately, even a big state will be in danger."[14]

According to Guan Zhong, in the process of social production and social life, "a competent ruler must know how to govern people through punishments and rewards," in order to arouse the enthusiasm of his people.[15] Then, how to make such punishments and rewards to play their roles effectively? First, "the regulations of punishments and rewards must be abided by, so that people will trust the ruling class."[16] If "the achievements and contributions that people make are not awarded," and "those committing crimes are not punished,"[17] "the rewards promised by the ruling class will not be believed by people," and "punishments also cannot deter people."[18] In this way, punishments and rewards cannot play the roles of encouragement and constraint. Second, rewards and punishments must be just. If "those without contributions are rewarded" and "those committing crimes are pardoned," people's enthusiasm will be destroyed. What's worse, it will encourage people to be free riders and even endanger social security.

Aside from the above, Guan Zhong insightfully pointed out that indoctrination is very important in arousing the enthusiasm of people, which is significant to economic morality. First, indoctrination builds the obedience of people, which is conducive to economic and military development.[19] Therefore, it is needed to "indoctrinate those who prefer leisure to work so as to promote economic development and those who are craven to be brave so as to promote military development." Second, indoctrination improves human quality fundamentally.[20] According to Guan Zhong, "indoctrination is completely different from administrative orders. It is like the clouds of autumn, so remote that it arouses our compassion; like the clouds of summer, so motionless that it penetrates our minds; like the bright moon in the clear

[13] *Discourses of the States·Discourses of Qi.*

[14] *Guanzi·Development of Rights.*

[15] *Guanzi·The Ruler and His Subjects (II).*

[16] *Guanzi·Self-discipline.*

[17] *Guanzi·Seven Relations between The Ruler and His Subjects.*

[18] *Guanzi·Legislation.*

[19] *Guanzi·Extravagance.*

[20] *Guanzi·Extravagance.*

sky, so quiet that it touches our hearts, and like flowing water, so modest that it makes us miss it and long for it."

According to Guan Zhong, harmony is the precondition of indoctrination. He said, "When the relationships between a ruler and his subjects, and between the ruling class and average people are not harmonious, even if the country looks peaceful superficially, it will certainly be in danger."[21] Then, how does one build a harmonious relationship? Guan Zhong believed, "Developing the moral quality of the army promotes the cooperation and unity of the people. Cooperation and unity lead to coordinative action, which then leads to harmony. Where there is ubiquitous harmony, there will be no fights and conflicts."[22]

Focusing a lot on the research of social economy, *Guanzi*, while advocating ethical economic morality, also promotes utilitarian economic morality. However, the two kinds of economic morality appeared as rivals. In fact, they coexisted harmoniously, making the philosophy of economic morality even more objective and practical.

A famous proposition of Guan Zhong is "only when social and individual wealth is abundant, would people follow formality and be aware of honor and disgrace."[23] It indicates that the moral sense of man is largely determined by the degree of economic development and benefit creation. Of course, the expansion of social and individual wealth is not without limits. Guan Zhong believes, "it's reasonable to be not too rich or poor" for "the very poor has no the sense of shame"[24] and "poor people can hardly be governed."[25] Moreover, "the very rich also can hardly be governed"[26] for the "rich people are too rich to work on behalf of the ruler for money."[27]

It can be said that Guan Zhong, consciously or unconsciously, noted the relationship between economic development and morality. He sensed the economic significance of morality and justice as well as how the economy and interests constrain human moral sense. Having obvious limitations due to the then historical context and class division though, his ideas and concepts were still of great social and practical significance at that time. Guan Zhong's understanding of the relationship between the economy and morality is still useful for us in developing today's economic and moral life and utilizing the economic functions of morality.

Another representative ideologist in the Spring and Autumn Period was Zichan (Gongsun Qiao, 574–522 B.C.), the youngest son of Zheng Chenggong, King of Zheng. Zichan ruled the State of Zheng for over 20 years. It seems that Zichan was a utilitarian, for he thought that it is difficult for man to be stoical, so man's desires shall be satisfied as much as possible instead of being controlled. In his view, when

---

[21] *Guanzi·Situation.*

[22] *Guanzi·The Art of War.*

[23] *Guanzi·Indoctrination of People.*

[24] *Guanzi·Extravagance.*

[25] *Guanzi·State Administration.*

[26] *Guanzi·Extravagance.*

[27] *Guanzi·State Reserves.*

human desire is satisfied, man can achieve success easier. In fact, he was a moralist who focused more on the moral requirements of economic activities. First, Zichan opposed governmental interference in market pricing.[28] For him, "commodities shall be priced by the market based on the consensus of parties involved." Second, he claimed that morality is the basis of socio-economic life. He said, "I heard that it's loyalty and goodness rather than authority that reduce resentment. It is easy to muzzle average people, but it's like blocking the course of a river: once the levee bursts, the consequence is catastrophic. So, it's better to listen to the criticism like diverting the water."[29] Third, valuing economic morality, Zichan advocated frugality and opposed extravagance. He said, "Royal and frugal officials have followers while haughty and extravagant officials have opponents."[30]

From the above, we can see that the concepts of Zichan concerning economic morality primarily served his ruling. However, it is also true that Zichan, at the same time of acknowledging human desire, also advocated rationality in his life. Confucius also acknowledged the necessity of pursuing interests, but he stressed that it must be moral and reasonable. It can be said that Confucius was affected by Zichan to some extent.

Rui Liangfu, King of Rui in the late Western Zhou, is considered as the pioneer who put forward the idea of ethical economic minority. He believed that if the majority of social wealth is in the hands of the minority, then "there will be a lot of disadvantages," so "wealth shall be distributed equally in society."In addition, the one who really expounded the idea is Yan Ying (approximately 590–500 B.C.), an ideologist in the Spring and Autumn Period.

His most famous idea regarding economic morality is that "the obtainment and amount of wealth shall be judged by moral standards, that is, the amount of wealth shall be limited in scope: once it's out of scope, it's harmful, and as long as it's in scope, it can sustain its expansion."[31] Yan himself put the idea into practice. When the King of Qi granted him 60 towns with fertile land, he firmly declined. He said, "The reason that I rejected your award is not because I hate wealth; on the contrary, it's because I'm afraid of losing wealth. Wealth is like a piece of silk cloth—silk cloth is limited by its dimensions, wealth should also be limited. Too much wealth will lead to disasters. I dare not to have too much wealth, for it has exceeded the limit."[32] According to Yan, "interests obtained on the basis of morality make people's lives better" and[33] "who values morality will obtain interests… and who abandons morality will lose interests."[34]Such ideas of Yan later became the resources of the philosophy of ethical economic morality of Confucianism.

[28] *Records of the Grand Historian·Annals.*

[29] *Zuozhuan·The 3rd Year of Duke Zhao of Lu.*

[30] *Zuozhuan·The 3rd Year of Duke Zhao of Lu*

[31] *Zuozhuan·The 10th Year of Duke Zhao of Lu.*

[32] *Zuozhuan·The 28th Year of Duke Xiang.*

[33] *Discourses of the States·Discourses of Jin (I).*

[34] *Discourses of the States·Discourses of Jin (II).*

By advocating "moral development wealth limitation", Yan naturally held that people should live a frugal life rather than unlimitedly satisfying their desires. He strongly opposed the immoderation of the ruling class, for "it consumes a lot of labor and money,"[35] and thus would certainly add the tax and corvee burden of average people. He thought the ruling class should "wear hats which are solemn but not decorative, and wear clothes which keep them decent and warm rather than making them look good,"[36] so "clothes do not need to be dyed, and hats do not need to be engraved."[37] The reason is the ruling class should "put the benefit of average people ahead of theirs" and "be strict to themselves and tolerant to average people."[38]

Opposing excessive wealth and "satisfying unlimited desires," Yan claimed that "wealth shall be equally distributed"[39] to develop people's morality.

According to Yan, morality is the basis of economic development. Limiting the obtainment of wealth with moral standards is a kind of moral philosophy more profound than the previous ones, thus was of great ideological and theoretical significance at that time. However, in the autocratic system at that time, Yan's ideas of equally distributing social wealth and limiting the extravagance of the ruler would only be good wishes. They could not be put into practice in the ruling class.

3.1.2 Ethical Economic Morality of Confucianism in the Late Spring and Autumn Period

The late Spring and Autumn Period is "an age of turbulence" in which rulers extorted excessive taxes and levies, and dukes fought with each other. As a result, the ritual system collapsed. Confucius, founder of Confucianism, and his followers cared greatly about the economic reform and the benefits and desires of average people.

Confucians highly praised the rituals of the Zhou Dynasty. They viewed "formality and morality" as the basis of social relationships, the standards for obtaining "interests" and "desires", and the principles of economic management. Therefore, ethical economic morality holds a very important position in the theories of Confucianism. In Chinese intellectual history, economic ideas of Confucianism always tend to be ignored, as if Confucianism is only about morality. However, this is wrong. In fact, Confucianism combined the economy and morality from the perspective of moralism, creating previous ideological wealth for the development of the theory of economic morality or that of moral economy.

1. Confucius (511–479 B.C.) was the founder of Confucianism. Based on the achievements made by previous ideologists in economic morality, he made

[35] *The Annals of Yanzi·Inner Chapter·Expostulation (II).*

[36] *The Annals of Yanzi·Inner Chapter·Expostulation (II).*

[37] *The Annals of Yanzi·Inner Chapter·Expostulation (II).*

[38] *The Annals of Yanzi·Inner Chapter·Expostulation (III).*

[39] *The Annals of Yanzi·Inner Chapter·Questions I (III).*

improvements and systematic conclusions. Confucianism primarily considers socio-economic activities and economic issues in the scope of morality.

Confucius expounded the philosophy of economic morality based on the relationship between interests and morality. He thought, "Wealth and highness are desired by man, and poverty and lowliness are loathed by man".[40] Moreover, "wealth, as long as it is in a reasonable and moral way, can be pursued by even the lowly."[41] We can see that, according to Confucius, it is natural for people to desire wealth and loathe poverty. In fact, Confucius held that making people rich and satisfied is the basic requirement to govern a country.

However, we must see that, for Confucius, the above ideas were established on the basis of morality (rituals and righteousness); otherwise, they were unacceptable. "Confucius seldom speaks of interests." It does not mean that Confucius advocated that people should live a poor life; in fact, it is just an abbreviated expression of his idea of "putting morality ahead of interests." Essentially, it is improper to speak of "immoral interests," and there is no need to speak of "moral interests."

The moralism contained in Confucius's ideas regarding economic morality is mainly embodied in his understanding on the relationship between interests and morality. He held that "interests grow from morality."[42] This means that interests obtained in a moral way are rational and legitimate; otherwise, they are irrational and illegitimate. He also said that morality arouses people's enthusiasm for work. "If the ruler follows rituals, average people will respect him; if the ruler is moral, average people will obey him; and if the ruler is credible, average people will trust him. Such a ruler will attract a lot of people who even carry their children to work for him." It is also recorded in *Great Learning* that[43]"a moral ruler will attract people to come. With more people, more land will be reclaimed; with more land, more wealth will be created; and with more wealth, more things could be done for social prosperity."

Second, Confucius thought that interests and wealth could only be obtained in a moral way. He said, "Wealth and highness are desired by everyone, but a gentleman will refuse to obtain them in an immoral way; poverty and lowliness are loathed by everyone, but a gentleman will not try to get rid of them in an immoral way."[44] He also said, "A country without morality, despite its wealth and highness, is still shameful."[45] Confucius once said humorously, "Eating plain food, drinking just water, and pillowing on the arm to sleep—I enjoy this kind of simple life. I don't care at all about wealth and highness obtained in an immoral way."[46] In short, Confucius held that interests and wealth could only be obtained in a moral manner.

[40] *The Analects of Confucius··Ethics and Benevolence.*

[41] *The Analects of Confucius··Transmission.*

[42] *Zuozhuan·The 2nd Year of Duke Cheng of Lu.*

[43] *The Analects of Confucius·Zilu.*

[44] *The Analects of Confucius·Ethics and Benevolence.*

[45] *The Analects of Confucius·Taibo.*

[46] *The Analects of Confucius·Transmission.*

Confucius developed earlier systematic theories concerning the unity of morality and interests, which guided people to have a correct understanding on the relationship between morality and interests at that time. In addition, it greatly affected later studies on economic morality.

It is worth pointing out that Confucius's understanding of the relationship between morality and interests, to a great extent, is an empirical conclusion of social life; thus, it is not and cannot be dialectical, but just a mechanical investigation on life. He also said "gentlemen value morality, while petty men value interests,"[47] and one time when his disciple Fan Chi asked him about how to farm, he called Fan Chi "a petty man." In this sense, morality and interests are opposite. Confucius did these to maintain the images of the ruling class and intellectuals and stress the importance of morality in life, but these contradict other internal thoughts and theories of Confucianism. Putting morality and interests at opposite positions actually seriously affected later generations in a negative manner.

In the age of Confucius, unequal wealth distribution was one of the main reasons of social turbulence. Confucius thought, "Interest-oriented behavior will cause the resentment of others."[48] Therefore, he claimed, "It's necessary to worry about unequal wealth distribution rather than poverty; to worry about social instability rather than a small population."[49] According to Confucius, poor people can still find peace and happiness in poverty without complaint; and the number of people does not affect them in following rituals. Unequal wealth distribution and social instability are against morality and are the sources of social turmoil. Confucius's ideas regarding wealth distribution played an important role in enlightening later generations to cognize and study the economic inequality and social conflict caused by unequal wealth distribution. For example, in the peasant movements in the history of China, "economic and political equality" was repeatedly put forward. We must see that Confucius's understanding on wealth distribution, limited by historical context, also exerted negative effects on social development. Particularly, the idea of "people can still find peace and happiness in poverty without complaint" eased class contradictions to maintain the interests of the exploiting class by guiding the poor to think that they were born to be poor, which could not be changed.

In the late Spring and Autumn Period, business activities started to play an increasingly important role in socio-economic activities. Confucius supported business activities and viewed business behavior from the perspective of morality. Zang Wenzhong, a senior official of the State of Lu set up six customhouses in Lu. Confucius criticized that Zang was "heartless," for his behavior had prevented the development of free trade. The economist Hu Jichuang thought that Confucius's attitude toward business was globally unique in ancient times. He wrote, "In China, in more than 2000 years after the late Warring States Period, commerce was disdained. Therefore, Confucius's attitude toward commence is quite unique (Jichuang 1981a)." He raised the following question: "Why did Confucius, at the same time

[47] *The Analects of Confucius·Ethics and Benevolence.*

[48] *The Analects of Confucius·Ethics and Benevolence.*

[49] *The Analects of Confucius·Chief of the Ji Clan.*

of strong opposition from Confucians and scholars that were engaged in agriculture and industry, take a supportive attitude towards business activities?" According to him, "the only possibility is that in the late Spring and Autumn Period, commerce developed rapidly, and rich merchants, like scholars, also didn't directly participate in productive labor, becoming members of the exploiting class (Jichuang 1981a)". Besides, in the emerging merchant class, many people had penetrated the intellectual class. These objective conditions forced Confucius to change his attitude towards commerce." However, Confucius's attitude toward commerce cannot be understood by separating it from his thoughts like "interests grow from morality"[50] and "interests are obtained for the interests of average people."[51] Rational and legitimate business activities are beneficial for all parties involved; therefore, they "should be conducted" and are "moral behavior."[52]

Given the historical context, Confucius's conscious combination of business activities with morality is original and extremely valuable. Even today, in a socialist market economy, it is still significant for enlightenment.

Confucius's views on consumption, well define his understanding of the relationship between morality and economic activities. According to Confucius, consumption cannot be separated from morality. He wrote, "Consumption, no matter high or low, shall meet the requirements of formality and morality." That is, formality and morality determine what should or should not be consumed. According to Confucius, "gentlemen should live a simple material life" and "should not be ashamed of poverty." However, he also believed officials should live a comfortable life. He once said, "I was once a senior official, so I shall not travel by foot," for according to him, travelling by foot is too frugal that it is against formality.[53] He pointed out, "as long as formality is followed, it's better to be frugal than extravagant."[54]

In the modern economy, Confucius's understanding on consumption is still of significance. Consumption, material or spiritual, shall be constrained by rationality in any era and any case. Irrational consumption behavior, in essence, is corruptive.

The theoretical basis of Confucius's philosophy of economic morality, which focuses on "morality prevails over interests," is the perfection and rational existence of man. In Confucius's ideas concerning the relationship between morality and economic activities, including economic management, we can clearly see this.

"Man," in the system of Confucianism, does not mean an individual, or a human in the sense of biology. It means man in a relationship (such as the relationship between a ruler and his subjects, between a father and his son, between a husband and his wife, or between brothers), and man in a group (such as in a country or a family). As Confucius said, "man is benevolent." Only in a relationship, especially the relationship between a ruler and his subjects, between a father and his son, and between a husband and his wife, could man acquire the meaning of his existence. Therefore,

---

[50] *Zuozhuan·The 2nd Year of Duke Cheng of Lu.*

[51] *The Analects of Confucius·Yao Spoke.*

[52] *The Analects of Confucius·Questions of Xian.*

[53] *The Analects of Confucius·Those of Former Eras.*

[54] *The Analects of Confucius·Eight Lines Of Eight Dancers Apiece.*

to realize optimal economic management and the optimal purposes thereof, and ultimately realize the perfection of man himself, Confucius put forward the concept of human-centered and moral economic management.

Confucius advocated the management concept of "human-centered management" or morality-based management. First, "human-centered management" means love and respect people based on such principles as "caring about the interests of others while pursuing self-interest" and "what you do not wish for yourself, do not do to others." It requires administrators and their followers to respect and care about each other, so that administrators can work smoothly and their followers can work full-heartedly with pleasure. Second, "human-centered management" means sincerity and cooperation. *The Doctrine of the Mean* states, "Sincerity, as the basis of everything, is the most precious virtue of a gentleman. Man with sincerity can, not only perfect himself but also help others to be perfect. Self-perfection is of benevolence, and the perfection of others is of wisdom. Moral improvement includes self-improvement and the improvement of others." This means that sincerity, at the same time of promoting self-spiritual development, can also help build the morality of others. This concept, as the primary element of successful management, is very significant for the development of economic management. The essence of economic management is man management, and human quality directly affects economic activities and economic development. The *Doctrine of the Mean* says, "Treat people and things with sincerity. Sincerity will be embodied, and as the embodiment becomes more and more obvious, sincerity will be promoted, affecting and finally indoctrinating more people. Only the most sincere man can indoctrinate the world." With sincerity, individuals in economic activities can cooperate harmoniously. Third, "human-centered management" means integrity. Confucius once said, "Like carriages without wheels cannot move, man without integrity can do nothing." Integrity is the basis of the economic man; man without integrity cannot obtain the trust and support of others.

Based on the concept of "human-centered management," Confucius thought the essence of management is man management. First, man management is realized on the basis of morality. According to Confucius, "decrees and punishments constrain people but cannot develop their sense of shame; but morality and formality can not only develop people's sense of shame but also their loyalty."[55] Therefore, administrators shall "administrate based on morality" and "put words into action before saying them."[56] Second, man management means appointing capable and moral people. Confucius once said that Duke Ling of Wei was an immoral man, and the reason why Wei did not fall is that he had "Zhongshu to manage his talents, Zhu Tuo to manage his ancestral temple, and Wangsun Jia to manage his army."[57] Confucius actually implied an immoral ruler will lead his country to destruction, or we can say that an immoral administrator cannot successfully manage his followers. According to Confucius, before appointing a person, it is necessary to "observe the personality,

[55] *The Analects of Confucius·The Practice of Government.*

[56] *The Analects of Confucius·The Practice of Government.*

[57] *The Analects of Confucius·Duke Ling of Wei.*

way of action, and purpose of action of the person."[58] Third, man management means self-management. Confucius held that "self-cultivation" is the precondition of managing others. Therefore, administrators shall "speak less and do more"[59] and "learn more to constrain themselves with rituals."[60]

In the field of economic management, Confucius put forward the ideas of "benefit others without harming self-interest"[61]and "use labor according to the seasons."[62]

Confucius thought, "Petty men value interests."[63] Petty men must be paid to work and take services, for "interests stimulate petty men."[64] To "benefit others without harming self-interest," laborers must create a certain amount of economic benefits for themselves. Although Confucius distinguished gentlemen from petty men to maintain the interests of gentlemen, it is undeniable that promoting productivity with benefits and focusing on the interests of laborers are the important moral means in economic management.

"Use labor according to the seasons" means asking people to provide free labor in the slack season so that agricultural production will not be affected. In this way, the interests of laborers are maintained, and human resources are reasonably used. Therefore, "use labor according to the seasons" is a rational means of economic management.

Superficially, it seems that "benefitting others without harming self-interest" and "using labor according to the seasons" focus on interests rather than morality, but in fact, the former stresses that "harming self-interest" is immoral and the latter means respecting the interests of laborers. Thus, they are important measures to harmonize the relationship between administrators and their followers.

2. Mencius (approximately 389–305 B.C.) of the Warring States Period is considered as the most famous Confucian after Confucius and a representative of the "doctrine of good human nature." Based on Confucius's philosophy of economic morality and the doctrine of good human nature, Mencius made further progress in development. He said he had mastered the essence of Confucianism and took inheriting and developing Confucianism as his mission.

Mencius's philosophy of economic morality was built based on the relationship between morality and interests built by Confucius, but it was extremely partial to morality. Although Confucius "seldom speaks of interests," he did not avoid speaking of interests. It can be seen from his ideas like "interests grow from morality," "put morality ahead of interests," and "interests are obtained for the interests of average people." Unlike Confucius, Mencius thought it is immoral to speak of interests. The following is recorded in *Mencius*: "One day, Mencius went to visit King Hui of Wei. King Hui said, "You travelled far to come here, you must have

[58] *The Analects of Confucius·The Practice of Government.*

[59] *The Analects of Confucius·Studying.*

[60] *The Analects of Confucius·The is Yong.*

[61] *The Analects of Confucius·Yao Spoke.*

[62] *The Analects of Confucius·Studying.*

[63] *The Analects of Confucius··Ethics and Benevolence.*

[64] *The Analects of Confucius·Yanghuo.*

opinions that are beneficial to my country." Mencius replied, "Your Majesty, I think we should not talk about interests. We should talk about benevolence and morality." The king always asks, "What's beneficial to my country?" Senior officials always ask, "What's beneficial to my family?" Average people always ask, "What's beneficial to me?" If everyone pursues interests, the country will be in danger. In a country with 10,000 chariots, the senior official that kills the king must have 1000 chariots; and in a country with 1000 chariots, the senior official that kills the king must have 100 chariots. It is because the senior official puts interests ahead of morality, so he kills the king to satisfy his desires. However, a moral person will certainly never abandon his parents, or kill the king. So, I think we should just talk about 'morality.'" The following is also recorded in *Mencius*: "One day, Mencius met Song Keng who planned to persuade the kings of Chu and Qin to stop fighting.[65] Mencius asked, "How do you plan to persuade them?" Song said, "I will tell them of the interests that they will lose by fighting." Mencius said, "It's great that you are trying to stop them from fighting, but I'm afraid you will use the wrong method. In this way, the kings stop fighting because of interests, so do their officers and soldiers. In a country, if subjects serve the king for interests, sons serve fathers for interests, and younger brothers serve elder brothers for interests, they are connected by interests instead of morality, and the country will certainly fall… Therefore, it is wrong to speak of interests'."[66] In the view of Mencius, in a country where people are connected by interests, the country will perish, so people must be connected by morality.

From the above we can see that Confucius only opposed "immoral interests" while Mencius opposed not only "immoral interests" but also "interests gained at the cost of losing morality" which will lead to the destruction of a country. Compared to Confucius, Mencius did not understand interests as a whole. His views focused more on morality with too much human interference on for-benefit behavior; thus, they are less dialectical. Of course, during the Warring States Period when kingdoms fought fiercely for interests, it is of great historical significance to stress the importance of morality.

In fact, Mencius did not oppose people pursuing all interests. From his proposition about "morality" and "property," it can be seen that Mencius supported people to pursue rational and legitimate interests. According to Mencius, only when people live a good material life will follow moral codes and be compliant to the ruler; otherwise, people will not follow moral codes. Mencius said, "Fire and water are essential for people's lives.[67] When someone knocks at others' doors for fire or water and no one refuses, there must be sufficient water and fire. In a country where grain is as sufficient as water and fire, people will naturally follow moral codes."[68] He also said, "If people are not able to support their parents, wives, and children, suffering from poverty in good years and facing the threat of death in bad years, all

---

[65] *Mencius·King Hui of Wei (I).*

[66] *Mencius·Gaozi (II).*

[67] *Mencius·Dedication(I).*

[68] *Mencius·Dedication(I).*

they could think is how to survive instead of supporting their family, let alone following moral codes."[69] When people are "struggling for survival," it is impossible to govern them with morality, even with punishments. As Mencius said, "If a ruler punishes his people who commit crimes due to poverty, he is framing his people. How could a benevolent ruler frame his people?"[70] This is quite true. As Mencius said, "Without a certain amount of property, scholars will follow moral codes, but common people will not. Without the constraint of morality, people will violate the law and discipline."[71]

According to Mencius, when people have a certain amount of property, "old people can wear silk cloth and eat meat, and common people are warm and fed," and they will follow moral codes. Then, what is considered as a certain amount of property? Mencius said, "If mulberry trees are planted around a house of about 5 mu (an ancient unit of area) and women raise silkworms with mulberry leaves, old people can wear silk cloth. If five hens and two sows are raised with enough time and energy, old people can have meat to eat. If fields of 100 mu are plowed, a family of eight can be fed."[72] He also said, "If mulberry trees are planted around a house of about 5 mu, old people can wear silk cloth. If chickens, pigs and dogs are raised with enough time and energy, old people can eat meat. If fields of 100 mu are plowed with enough laborers, a family of eight can be fed. If people are indoctrinated to be filial to their parents and love their brothers, old people do not need to work. In a country where old people wear silk cloth and eat meat, and common people are warm and fed, people will certainly obey the ruler."[73]

Unlike Confucius, Mencius thought that when people have to make a choice between material interests and morality, if the material interests are necessary for survival, people should choose material interests. The following is recorded in *Mencius*: "A man of the State of Ren asked Luzi, 'Formality and food, which is more important?' Luzi said, 'Formality'. The man then asked, 'Formality and wife, which is more important?' Luzi said, 'Formality'. The man refuted, 'If abiding by formality means suffering from hunger, and otherwise, one is fed, must he abide by formality? If abiding by formality means being single, and otherwise, one can have a wife, must he abide by formality?'He couldn't answer these questions. The next day, Luzi went to the State of Zou to consult Mencius. Mencius said, 'It's not difficult to answer these questions. The hypothesis of these questions is extreme which does not adapt to general conditions. According to his logic, a short wooden stick can be taller than a house, and a carriage of a feather can be heavier than a small piece of gold. If one can avoid suffering from hunger or have a wife by violating minor moral codes, of course he should do it. Go and ask him, "If you have to break your brother's arm to have food, will you do it? If you have to hold your neighbor's

[69] *Mencius·King Hui of Wei (I).*

[70] *Mencius·King Hui of Wei (I).*

[71] *Mencius·King Hui of Wei (I).*

[72] *Mencius·Dedication(I).*

[73] *Mencius·King Hui of Wei (I).*

wife to have a wife, will you do it?"[74] From here, we can see that Mencius had a practical and profound view on the relationship between interests and morality. Although Mencius put forward the idea that "people with a certain amount of property will follow moral codes" for the benefit of the ruling class, he, consciously or unconsciously, realized the internal logical relationship between interests and morality. According to Mencius, only when people could keep themselves warm and fed would it then be possible to govern people with morality. This idea is of great historical and practical significance. People's understanding of morality is limited by economic development and the condition of material life to some extent. Fundamentally, people's moral consciousness changes as economic development. Mencius did not hold that morality always comes before interests, which indicates that morality and interests are not opposites of each other, namely, it is wrong to think we must give up interests for the sake of morality, no matter the circumstances.

Mencius's understanding of the relationship between morality and labor is a partial and specific interpretation of his idea that "it is immoral to speak of interests". A famous opinion of Mencius concerning the relationship between morality and labor is "those who work with their brains rule and those who work with their brawn are ruled. Those who are ruled support others and those who rule are supported by others. This is a general rule."[75]This opinion is well-grounded. It follows the passage of "Like various craftsmen cannot work while farming, officials cannot administrate while farming. Officials have their duties, so do common people. Besides, the daily necessities of people are provided by various craftsmen. If everyone makes all he needs himself, everyone will be exhausted." At that time, scholars in the ruling class did not do physical labor, and only common people did physical labor. Therefore, his understanding of the relationship between morality and labor was obviously affected by class division.

A profound analysis of the above opinion of Mencius can help us understand today's relationship between morality and labor. In the view of Mencius, "working with brains" means not only brainwork but also following formality and morality, namely, having the consciousness of compassion, shame and refusal as well as the ability to distinguish right from wrong. People working with brains are actually "scholars who have the consciousness of formality and morality."[76]It is partial to say that only scholars have the consciousness of formality and morality, but the idea of governing people with formality and morality is still significant to enlightenment today, though it stood for the interests of the governing class.

"Those who work with their brawn are ruled" can also be understood deeply from another perspective. Guided by the thought that man is born good-natured, Mencius held that morality is good, while interests are evil. He pointed out that moral quality is the standard to distinguish good from evil. "He who rises at the rooster's crow and addresses himself earnestly to the practice of morality is a disciple of Shun. He who rises at the rooster's crow and addresses himself earnestly

[74] *Mencius·Gaozi (II).*

[75] *Mencius·DukeWen of Teng (I).*

[76] *Mencius·Lilou (II).*

to the pursuit of interests, is a disciple of Zhi. If you want to know what separates Shun from Zhi, it is simply this: the interval between the thought of interests and the thought of morality."[77]For Mencius, it is evil to act for interests. Since people working with "brawn" are petty men who value interests and work for the sake of interests, they can only be ruled.

It is true that Mencius put forward ideas for the interests of the ruling class—they demonstrate it is legitimate for the ruling class to "rule people" and reasonable for average people "to be ruled." However, the idea that people and countries shall be governed by formality and morality is of important academic significance, even today. It is enlightening to think about the development of modern society.

In the ideological system, we will find that Mencius's idea of "those who work with their brains rule and those who work with their brawn are ruled" is contradictory to some extent. In fact, some contradictions demonstrate that Mencius's opinion on the relationship between morality and labor can be used for reference. First, superficially, it seems that Mencius only maintained the interests of the ruling class, but actually, he also noticed the evil of the ruling class, which put the country in danger.[78] He said, "If everyone pursues interests, the country will be in danger. In a country with 10,000 chariots, the senior official that kills the king must have 1000 chariots; and in a country with 1000 chariots, the senior official that kills the king must have 100 chariots. It's because the senior official puts interests ahead of morality, so he kills the king to satisfy his desires. However, a moral person will certainly never abandon his parents, or kill the king. So, I think we should just talk about morality." He also pointed out that some rulers fought cruelly internally and exploited average people for self-interest that "they themselves have meat in the kitchen and strong horse in the stable, but average people suffer from hunger and even death." In the view of Mencius, such rulers are not scholars with formality and morality, which they need to regain. Second, according to Mencius, people working with brawn are certainly not gainful, for "one who doesn't do things he has the heart to do is benevolent, and one who refuses to do things he can do is moral." For example, one is benevolent if he doesnot do anything that will harm others; and one is moral if he refuses to steal or be looked down by others.[79] It can be seen that Mencius's understanding of the relationship between morality and labor is different from Confucius's—he profoundly discussed the relationship among labor, formality, and morality, and interests, which is of great academic significance.

Mencius's concepts about economic management were built on morality. From the perspective of governing a country, Mencius held that administrators must put justice first instead of self-interest; otherwise, the country will be in danger. Therefore, rulers shall govern people with morality, which, according to Mencius, is the way to govern a country. He said that a benevolent ruler would be unbeatable. Xia, Shang, and Zhou were built because of benevolence and perished because of the loss of benevolence. "A ruler without benevolence will lose the country, a duke

[77] *Mencius·Dedication(I).*

[78] *Mencius·King Hui of Wei (I).*

[79] *Mencius·Dedication(II).*

without benevolence will lose the state, a senior official without benevolence will lose the ancestral temple, and a scholar or a common person without benevolence will lose his life."[80]Only with benevolence and morality could a ruler win in "all aspects, including the obedience, of his people."

According to Mencius, the core of management is man management with the management of human thought as the priority, and the precondition of human thought management is governing people with morality and benevolence. If "people of the ruling class do immoral things, they are spreading their immorality to average people."[81] In this way, the ruling class cannot get the obedience of average people and govern average people. Maybe the ideas of Mencius were not incisive and systematic, but Mencius indeed inherited and developed the thoughts of Confucius. In today's society, economic and corporate management activities cannot be considered as merely economic activities. The reason is, if the morality of managers and laborers is not developed to a certain level, management, no matter in what form, is passive, and it is hard to develop the enthusiasm and initiative of man. Therefore, whether morality can play a full role in economic activities directly affects the speed and quality of economic development and corporate construction.

Xunzi (approximately 310–238 B.C.) was a representative of the "doctrine of evil human nature" of Confucianism. Based on Confucius's philosophy of economic morality and real conditions of social morality and the economy, Xunzi further developed the macroscopic and microcosmic perspectives.

Xunzi focused on the study of economic issues, which is a characteristic of his academic thoughts. He specifically wrote *National Wealth*to discuss the feudal economy and originally put forward the proposition of the morality of national economy as the basis of his system of economic morality. He advocated national wealth but held that the affluence of average people is the precondition of the affluence of a country. "When people are poor, the ruling class is poor; when people are rich, the ruling class is rich. Fields are the fundaments of wealth, and granaries are the terminals of wealth. People's farming, according to the seasons in an orderly and harmonious way, is the source of wealth, and taxes levied, according to ranks, are the branches of wealth. Certainly, a wise ruler would prudently maintain a harmonious and steady political situation. At the same time, the ruler would save expenses and expand sources, regulating the incoming and outgoing of wealth. In this way, wealth will roll in like water, and the ruler does not need to worry about national wealth. When both the ruler and his people are too affluent to store wealth, the national economy and people's livelihood reach their peak."[82] We can see that at the same time of stressing the importance of enriching people, Xunzi also expounded the significance of increasing productivity while reducing expenses.

Clearly, the above idea of Xunzi puts the issues of "people's wealth" and "people's livelihood" at the height of the proposition, illuminating the essence of Xunzi's economic morality philosophy. Its academic value and practical social significance

---

[80] *Mencius·Lilou.*

[81] *Mencius·Lilou.*

[82] *Xunzi·National Wealth.*

can only be evaluated appropriately from the perspective of historical and social development.

To further expound the idea that people's wealth is the basis of national wealth, Xunzi sternly pointed out that if a country tries to accumulate national wealth by sacrificing the interests of people, or even exploiting people, it can never become rich, and will even perish. He said, "A great king satisfies the material needs of his people, and a duke satisfies the material needs of scholars. In a dying country, the king satisfies the material needs of officials who actually govern the country for him. In a ruined country, the king only satisfies the material needs of himself. In a country where the king is extremely rich and national wealth is abundant, but people are poor, the foundation of the country is weak. As a result, it's unable to defend or attack, and cannot avoid the fate of destruction."[83]Xunzi clearly emphasizes that the economic development of a country cannot be realized at the cost of people's interests. Only when average people are affluent could the country be affluent, thus realizing the prosperity of the whole country.

Holding that people's wealth is the foundation of national wealth, whether consciously or unconsciously though, Xunzi insisted on the principle that national interests prevail over people's interests. According to Xunzi, national wealth is the precondition and purpose, and people's wealth is the means and condition. Such economic morality philosophy, which unifies national wealth with people's wealth consciously, is one of the important intensions of the doctrines of Pre-Qin Confucians. No matter how the feudal rulers understood and applied it, or to what extent it was cognized and put into practice, it is undeniable that Xunzi's understanding of the interest-morality relationship exerted great influence on the economic and social development of China.

Xunzi's understanding of the interest-morality relationship directly affected his understanding on the relationship between interests and morality. Supporting the pursuance of interests and discussing interests and morality in the same breath, Xunzi put forward his unique opinion regarding the interest-morality relationship as a branch of Confucianism. According to Xunzi, "both interests and morality are pursued by man. Ancient sages like Yao and Shun couldn't prevent people from pursuing interests, but under their rule, morality prevailed over interests; tyrants Jie and Zhou couldn't prevent people from pursuing morality, but under their rule, interests prevailed over morality."[84] Xunzi corrected and developed Confucius's and Mencius's thoughts, which particularly stressed morality instead of interests. Theoretically speaking, Xunzi made a fruitful discussion on the relationship between the economy and morality. He did not divide gentlemen and small men with the pursuance of interests and morality, or put interests and morality at opposite positions. In fact, Xunzi's understanding of the interest–morality relationship is a theoretical summary of his idea of "people's wealth is the foundation of national wealth"; therefore, if he undervalues or disdains interests, his idea would be groundless theoretically and socially.

[83] *Xunzi·How to be a Ruler.*

[84] *Xunzi·Great Strategies.*

It is true that Xunzi once said, "The period in which morality prevails over interests is of peace and prosperity; while the period in which interests prevail over morality is of turbulence," but this does not mean that Xunzi opposed the pursuance of interests—he just opposed "interests-before-everything." From another perspective, since Xunzi was a Confucian, it is natural for him to put morality ahead of interests.

Xunzi thought that man is born with desires, which is why he held that man's material needs shall be met and interests shall be pursued. He said, "Man is born with the desire for food when he is hungry, with the desire for warmth when he is cold, with the desire for rest when he is tired, and with the desire for gains rather than losses."[85] Specifically, he pointed out, "It's natural that people like seeing beautiful things, hearing beautiful sounds, eating delicious food, pursuing interests and living comfortable lives,"[86]and "It's human nature that man wants to eat good food, wear good clothes, travel by carriage or horse, accumulate wealth, and never be satisfied."[87]

Since having desires is a physiological function of man, and satisfying desires is a part of human nature, there is no need to restrain or suppress desires that are against human nature and morality. Xunzi demonstrated that "when human nature, including desires is connived without limits, there will certainly be conflicts",[88] and "man is born with desires. When desires cannot be met, man will pursue; when the pursuance of desires is not limited, there will be conflicts; when there are conflicts, there will be social turbulence; and when there is social turbulence, there will be poverty."[89]It can be seen that Xunzi thought social turbulence is caused by the restraint and suppression of desires. Although this idea is quite different from the thoughts of Confucius and Mencius, it is of profound significance for economic morality. If man's desires cannot be satisfied, his enthusiasm for work is low, and interpersonal conflicts will occur.

Creatively, Xunzi understood human desire by combining it with economic development, interpersonal relationships and morality under the guidance and constraint of morality. At the same time of claiming that desires are rational, Xunzi consciously extinguished desires themselves from the requirements of satisfying desires. Xunzi did not advocate the immoderate pursuance of desires, for he knew very well that immoderate desires are also the source of social turbulence. To realize the moderate pursuance of desires, Xunzi put forward the idea of "guiding the pursuance of human desire," so that human desire can be met to the highest degree. According to him, "Desires cannot be completely satisfied, but can be almost completely satisfied. Desires cannot be completely suppressed, but can be controlled… Therefore, people can satisfy their desires almost completely, or control

[85] *Xunzi·Do not Judge by Appearance.*

[86] *Xunzi·Evil Nature.*

[87] *Xunzi·Honor and Disgrace.*

[88] *Xunzi·Evil Nature.*

[89] *Xunzi·Formality.*

their desires."[90] The ideas of "satisfying desires almost completely," "controlling desires" and "guiding the pursuance of desires" are a specific and profound interpretation of Xunzi's understanding of the interest-morality relationship and also are relatively appropriate theories expounding the relationship between the economy and desires, between the economy and morality and between interests and morality.

Based on the proposition that "man is born with desires," Xunzi logically put forward the idea that wealth should not be distributed equally, which, according to Xunzi, is rational. Xunzi thought if wealth were distributed equally, people's desires would be essentially the same. Moreover, in case of short supply, there would be conflicts. He said, "If people have the same power and ranks, and the same likes and dislikes, in case of short supply, there will be conflicts." Therefore, "people's wealth and ranks should be different so that they are governed in a better way."[91] Xunzi wanted to point out that only when wealth is distributed unequally, people of different ranks will be satisfied differently and coexist in harmony. It seems to be inconsistent with Xunzi's ideas regarding economic morality mentioned above, and obviously, Xunzi said them to protect the interests of feudal hierarchy. After putting forward the idea of unequal wealth distribution, Xunzi pointed out that the rich and the poor are convertible. He said, "Is it possible for lowly people to become noble, for stupid people to become smart, and for poor people to become rich? The answer is yes, and the way is to study."[92] This means, by learning formality and culture, poor people can become rich; if the descendants of rich nobles do not study, it is possible for them to become poor.[93] This idea is of special significance, for compared with the thoughts of early Confucians, it shook and even broke the fatalism of "man is born to be poor or rich." From the perspective of moralism, we can see that Xunzi's economic morality philosophy is more advanced than those of previous Confucians. Originally, Xunzi connected the ability to get wealthy with the study of formality and culture, though in a simple and stiff way. Xunzi actually considered formality and morality as the preconditions of economic development and interest obtainment, which enlighten us to observe and analyze the moral and economic phenomena in China.

Xunzi focused a lot on socio-economic development, especially the relationship between economic development and morality. Based on the philosophy of economic management morality, Xunzi made progress from many unique perspectives.

First, Xunzi held that in social production and economic management activities, in terms of skills and physical strength, morality plays a more important role in promoting social production and economic management. He said, "Farmers are skillful in farming, but they cannot be agricultural management officials, merchants are good at doing business, but they cannot be market management officials, craftsmen are proficient in making instruments, but they cannot become instrument management officials. There are people who are not skillful in the above sectors but can

[90] *Xunzi·Rectification of Names.*

[91] *Xunzi·How to be a Ruler.*

[92] *Xunzi·Examples of Confucians.*

[93] *Xunzi·How to be a Ruler.*

manage such sectors. The reason is that some are good at skills while others are of high moral quality. The former can be the experts of a certain sector, while the latter can be management of many sectors."[94] That is to say, workers do professional work in a certain sector, while gentlemen do the management of many sectors.

It is impossible for Xunzi, who was born in the late Warring States Period, to scientifically expound the logical relationship between morality and social production and economic management activities. Regardless, Xunzi's thought that morality prevails over physical strength reveals the importance of formality and morality in management, and was of important academic value and practical significance at that time.

Second, according to feudal hierarchical relationships between the ruler and his subjects, between officials and their followers, between the seniors and the minors, and between the noble and the lowly, as well the characteristics of the feudal economy, Xunzi put forward the ideas of "social collaboration on the basis of hierarchy" and management with morality, which promoted management and production. According to Xunzi, when everyone plays his certain role in society, the society as a whole forms and people in society can be well managed. He said, "Fire and water possess a spirit but no life, grass and trees possess a life but no awareness, birds and animals possess awareness but no sense of morality. Only humans possess spirit, life, awareness as well as a sense of morality, and hence are the noblest beings in the world. Humans are not as powerful as cattle or as fast as horses, but cattle and horses are used by humans, why? The answer is humans cooperate with each other. Why are humans able to cooperate with each other? The answer is hierarchy. How is this realized? The answer is morality. When a hierarchy is established on the basis of morality, people will cooperate with each other, which enables them to be strong enough to fight against alien forces, to settle down with stability, and to manage all things according to the law of nature, creating interests. Therefore, it's a hierarchy and morality that improve human productivity."[95] From this we can see Xunzi's belief that only when a hierarchy is established could people abide by moral codes and thus increase human productivity.

Compared with the economic management philosophies of Confucius and Mencius, Xunzi's view is more appropriate and profound theoretically. As stressed by Xunzi, "People live in groups. Without a hierarchy, there will be conflicts. Where there are conflicts, there will be social turbulence. Where there is social turbulence, people will fall apart. When people fall apart, they become weak. When they are weak, they cannot fight against alien forces." Besides, "conflicts cause social turbulence which then leads to poverty."[96]

It is worth noting that the idea of "social collaboration on the basis of hierarchy" advocates the importance of the feudal patriarchal system and hierarchy. Xunzi stressed that the ruler and average people are at different ranks. He claimed that the ruler must have supreme power, noble position and abundant wealth, for

[94] *Xunzi·See Through Fake Appearance.*

[95] *Xunzi·How to be a Ruler.*

[96] *Xunzi·How to be a Ruler.*

the ruler "needs gorgeous ornaments to unify the people, needs wealth to manage his subjects and needs power to suppress violence."[97] For the management of average people, Xunzi did not think that average people should naturally be governed because of their low social status. In fact, he thought the ruler should govern his people by improving their living standard and increasing productivity. Xunzi said, "Reduce agricultural taxes and tariffs, cut down the number of merchants, seldom levy a corvee, and avoid effecting agricultural production. In this way, the ruling class and average people are all rich."[98] Xunzi also said, "Only when measures are taken to improve people's standards of living, people can live a rich life. If people are rich, then fields will be fertile. If fields are fertile, then grain yields will be greatly increased. The ruler should levy as stipulated in the law, and average people should live a frugal life as stipulated in formal norms. In this way, spare grain will be piled like mountains, and there is too much grain that some of it must be burned because there is no more space to store it. Consequently, gentlemen do not need to worry about the food supply. A ruler who knows how to save and how to make his people live a good life will certainly be considered as a sage of benevolence and morality, and his wealth will grow naturally. On the contrary, if the ruler does not know how to save and enrich his people, then his people will be poor. If people are poor, fields will be infertile, which will lead to a sharp decline in yield. In this case, even if the ruler desperately exploits his people, he still cannot be very rich. If the ruler does not follow formality and morality, then he will certainly be considered as a fatuous and immoral ruler."[99] Xunzi wanted to outline the importance of morality in economic management. If the ruler cannot enrich his people, or even exploit his people, his people will not be obedient, and consequently, production activities will become unordered economic activities. In this way, "things cannot be used rationally and accidents cannot be handled properly. Without advantageous natural conditions and the support of people, the country will fall into tragic plight"[100] in which daily necessities are in short supply and people are suffering from poverty.

After all, economic management is about man management, which was realized by Xunzi, consciously or unconsciously. According to Xunzi, the ruler should "care for his people who work for him." He said, "Caring for people and using them is better than using people without care… Caring for people without using them is better than caring for people and using them."[101] Then, how does one care for people and use them? According to Xunzi, the first thing is "levying as per the number and ability of the people."[102] Xunzi also thought that a ruler should, at the same time of requiring people to work, allow them to rest in order to revitalize. This is a rational moral means in economic management.

[97] *Xunzi·How to be a Ruler.*

[98] *Xunzi·National Wealth.*

[99] *Xunzi·National Wealth.*

[100] *Xunzi·National Wealth.*

[101] *Xunzi·National Wealth.*

[102] *Xunzi·National Wealth.*

Even today, Xunzi's philosophy of economic management, theoretically and practically, is still of great significance as a reference. A lot of modern economic management practices has proved that moral means is an important element in modern economic management or corporate management. Without moral means, all kinds of management, including economic management, are incomplete, or even unqualified.

Third, Xunzi claimed that formality and law are complementary. He said, "The means to govern a country are law and formality."[103] He thought that formality is the primary means in management and law plays a supplementary role. He also thought that the combination of law and formality is more effective than law or formality alone. In his view, formality has the power of "making people to work without rewards" and "making people to obey without punishments."[104] "Without formality, man cannot exist, things cannot be done and countries cannot be at peace." Attaching importance to governing by formality,[105] Xunzi also advocated governing by law. [106] He said, "Formality, a code of conduct, works as a standard in governing a country as the scale to weight, the rope and ink to make straight lines and the compasses and batten to make curves."

As for how to govern with both law and formality, Xunzi put forward a very incisive view— "the key element in governing a country is man rather than law." He said, "there are rulers who cause social turbulence, but there is no country that is certainly in turbulence; there are people who can govern a country well, but there is no law that is certainly effective in governing a country."[107] In other words, according to Xunzi, man is the precondition of governing a country as well as the existence and functioning of law. Xunzi said, "Governing by law is the start of politics, and gentlemen are the foundation of governing by law. Therefore, with gentlemen, no matter how brief the law is, it's effective; without gentlemen, no matter how well-established the law is, it cannot keep the order of society, and will even create chaos."[108] The value of the view lies in Xunzi's realization that the essence of management, no matter in what forms, is man management—how to manage man and how to use man to manage. Without human resource development, management (especially state management) will be nothing but empty talk.

Xunzi's proposition of combining law and formality in governing a country is the further development of Confucian management philosophy as well as the confirmation and application of Legalism. Legalism focuses too much on the force of law but ignores the power of formality; while Confucianism focuses too much on the power of formality but ignores the force of law. By combining law with formality, Xunzi perfected the philosophy of management morality for Confucianism, making formality and morality play a better role in management with the supplement of law.

---

[103] *Xunzi·Chengxiang.*

[104] *Xunzi·Do not Judge by Appearance.*

[105] *Xunzi·Self-cultivation.*

[106] *Xunzi·Dominance of Rulers.*

[107] *Xunzi·Morality of Scholars.*

[108] *Xunzi·Morality of Scholars.*

3.1.3 Ethical Economic Morality Philosophy in the Western Han Dynasty

1. Jia Yi (200–168 B.C.), a disciple of Xunzi, was a famous politician and a writer of the Western Han Dynasty. Jia held that wealth is a precondition for the peace of a country, and formality as the foundation. He expounded ethical economic morality philosophy appropriately.

In the early Western Han Dynasty, some thought that after 30–40 years of development since its foundation, the regime was "stable and in order."[109] Jia held an opposite view. He thought the Western Han's regime looked stable, but in fact, it was as dangerous as "sleeping on firewood that has been ignited."[110] Based on an analysis of the destruction of the Qin, he pointed out that "seizing state power is different from consolidating state power."[111] He said, "Shang Yang abandoned formality and morality just for territory expansion. Two years after the implementation of his new law, the social morality of the Qin grew worse and worse." [112]Therefore, to realize the long-term stability of a country, it is necessary to change from[113] "governing by law and punishment," as taken by the Qin, to "governing by formality and morality,"[114] in order to "unite the whole country."[115] According to Jia, "in a country governed by formality and morality, formality and morality will develop; while in a country governed by punishment, punishment will develop. The development of punishment increases the discontent of people; while the development of formality and morality increases the content of people."[116]

According to Jia, to govern a poor country, formality is not enough—economic development is essential to realize the affluence of the country and its people, which is the foundation of national stability. Agreeing with the view of "only when social and individual wealth is abundant would people follow formality and be aware of honor and disgrace" put forward by Guan Zhong, he said, "I've never heard of a country with poor people that can be well governed."[117] Therefore, wealth is a precondition of national stability.

Jia logically combined the ideas of "national wealth," "formality and morality," and "national stability," which played a unique role in developing the economic morality philosophy of Confucianism in terms of ways of thinking and theory. According to Confucius, economic issues are only the appendants of morality—issues concerning the economy, interests, and wealth were all discussed in the scope of

[109] *Collected Works of Jia Yi·Strategies of National Stability.*

[110] *Collected Works of Jia Yi·Strategies of National Stability.*

[111] *Jiazi·Passing Qinzhong.*

[112] *Collected Works of Jia Yi·Strategies of National Stability.*

[113] *Book of Han·Biography of Jia Y.*

[114] *Book of Han·Biography of Jia Yi.*

[115] *Book of Han·Biography of Jia Yi.*

[116] *Collected Works of Jia Yi·Strategies of National Stability.*

[117] *Jiazi·No Reserves.*

morality. Mencius almost followed the thought of Confucius, but he focused more on the importance of morality. Xunzi was different. Compared with Confucius and Mencius, he understood the interest-morality relationship from a different perspective—at the same time of focusing on the study of economic issues, Xunzi investigated social issues by combining human desire with economic development and combining interpersonal harmony with moral development. However, the problem is that the thoughts of Xunzi lack an elaborate demonstration. In fact, Xunzi's perspective of thinking is more enlightening than his basic views. As a disciple of Xunzi, Jia developed the thoughts of Xunzi.

Advocating "governing with formality" and "wealth is the basis of national stability," Jia considered the livelihood of average people.[118] He thought that average people should have "enough food and a certain amount of savings" for "national grain reserves and financial resources are the lifeblood for the existence of a country and the material support for the development thereof. Abundant grain reserves and financial resources are the guarantee of success, no matter in offense or defense. They are essential in making the enemy succumb band attracting allegiant people from afar."[119] For Jia, the affluence of average people is not only an economic issue but also a political and moral issue concerning how to reconcile public interests and arouse the enthusiasm of average people to build and defend a country. Therefore, Jia thought that for a ruler, "it's meritorious to make his people live a rich and happy life, and it's blamable to make his people live a poor and bitter life."[120]

Economic management is like corporate management. The priority of management is arousing the enthusiasm of people. The realization of which requires not only orders and ideological education but also measures which promote people to live a rich and happy life. Interests are a basic element that arouses the enthusiasm of people.

Advocating that wealth is the foundation of national stability, Jia firmly opposed extravagance and waste, which are immoral in his view. He thought that poverty is caused by "the lack of production and the rampancy of extravagance and waste."[121] He said, "If the silk weaved by 100 persons cannot meet the desire of one rich person, how could average people keep themselves warm? If the farmer has to work hard to fill the stomachs of 10 persons who do not work at all, how could average people keep themselves fed? When average people suffer from hunger and cold, it's impossible that they do not commit crimes."[122] For this reason, Jia advised, "Farmers should engage in farming, feeding themselves and more people. Moreover, merchants and idlers should go farm."[123] Albeit impractically, his idea is still of great historical significance.

[118] *Collected Works of Jia Yi·On the High Price of Grain.*

[119] *Collected Works of Jia Yi·On the High Price of Grain.*

[120] *Jiazi·Governmental Policies (I).*

[121] *Collected Works of Jia Yi·On the High Price of Grain.*

[122] *Collected Works of Jia Yi·Strategies of National Stability.*

[123] *Collected Works of Jia Yi·On the High Price of Grain.*

2. Dong Zhongshu (179–104 B.C.) was a great Confucian in the Western Han Dynasty. At the same time of inheriting the Confucian thoughts and ideas of the Pre-Qing Period, Dong put the theories of the Yin-Yang School into his study. Based on the above, he established an idealist and quite religious Confucian system that takes the theories of "the unity of Heaven and man" and "the interaction between Heaven and man" as the basis and "the principles of feudal moral conduct" as the core. It can be seen from his interpretation of economic morality that there are developed and rational views as well as distorted and irrational ones.

According to Dong, "Heaven is the ancestor of all things,"[124] and "nature is the origin, or the ancestor of man, and that's why nature and man are so alike."[125] To demonstrate his proposition of "the unity of Heaven and man," Dong stressed that man is a copy of nature. He said, "man's head is round, like a vault; man's hair is like the stars; man's eyes and ears are like the sun and the moon; man's mouth and nose are for breath, like wind and air; man's mind is full of knowledge, like gods; man's belly contains a lot, like all things. All things grow from the earth, and that's why man's body below the waist is earth. Man's waist is like the boundary dividing Heaven and earth. The part above the neck, where the spirit is noble and solemn, is like the state of Heaven. The part below the neck, rich and lowly, is like the soil. Man's foot, approximately quadrate, is like the shape of the earth."[126] He also said, "Man's body is formed by the law of nature; man's blood and vital energy are formed by the will of Heaven; man's morality is formed by the rules of Heaven; man's likes and dislikes are the warmth and coolness; man's joy and anger are winter and summer; man's missions are seasons. Man's joy, anger, sorrow, and happiness are like spring, summer, autumn, and winter. Joy is spring, anger is autumn, happiness is summer and, sorrow is winter. Heaven helps man. Thus, man's emotions and essence are given by Heaven. Therefore, giving and acceptance are determined by Heaven."[127] In the view of Dong, man, from the body to spiritual activities, is the embodiment of Heaven. In short, no Heaven, no man. In this way, morality, naturally, is required by Heaven. Dong said, "Heaven represents the highest benevolence" and "man receives instructions from Heaven, and man's benevolence comes from Heaven." Therefore, "man's morals in behavior are the morals of Heaven and earth."[128] Then, what are the morals of Heaven?[129] They are "ruler–subject morals, father–son morals, and husband–wife morals"[130], and the "five virtues of benevolence, morality, formality, wisdom, and integrity."[131]

---

[124] *Luxuriant Dew of the Spring and Autumn Annals·Testamentary Charge.*

[125] *Luxuriant Dew of the Spring and Autumn Annals·Predestination.*

[126] *Luxuriant Dew of the Spring and Autumn Annals·Man is the Copy of Nature.*

[127] *Luxuriant Dew of the Spring and Autumn Annals·Predestination.*

[128] *Luxuriant Dew of the Spring and Autumn Annals·The Integration of Nature, Earth and Man.*

[129] *Luxuriant Dew of the Spring and Autumn Annals·Man is the Copy of Nature.*

[130] *Luxuriant Dew of the Spring and Autumn Annals·Morality.*

[131] *Luxuriant Dew of the Spring and Autumn Annals·Countermeasure (I).*

Since man is the copy of Heaven, man shall live according to the moral requirements of Heaven. If man acts as required by Heaven, luck will fall on people; while if man acts against the will of Heaven, disasters will fall on man as warnings.

The idea of "interaction between Heaven and mankind" put forward by Dong is clearly interpreted in his economic morality philosophy. To promote morals and virtues, which, according to him, reflect the will of Heaven, Dong changed the Confucian proposition that "morality prevails over interests" into "morality is noble while interests are lowly," and interpreted the interest-morality relationship in a mysterious way.

According to Dong, morality and interests are two attributes given by Heaven to man. Since they mean different things for man, they have different importance. "Man is created by Heaven with the attributes of morality and interests. Interests are for physical needs, while morality is for spiritual needs. Without morality, man will not feel happy; without interests, man will not feel easy. Formality nourishes the spirit while interests nourishes the body. The body is inferior to the spirit; therefore, morality is more important than interests."[132] Dong pointed out that sages value morality more than interests, but small men "value interests more than morality."[133] He also said, "When people all value interests, a trend forms like water flowing down, and it can only be stopped by the dam of indoctrination. If the dam of indoctrination is solid, the spread of evil thoughts will be stopped, but if the dam of indoctrination is broken, evil thoughts will flow out, and even cannot be stopped by punishments."[134] Then, how does one indoctrinate people? According to Dong, people can be indoctrinated by "benevolence and morality."[135]

Dong's views, like "morality prevails over interests" and "indoctrinate people with morality and benevolence," are not new. They were put forward to ensure the supreme position of moral codes, which protected the interests of the feudal constitution, and provide a mysterious force to push forward the promotion of feudal morals and virtues.

In Dong's economic morality philosophy, there are two points that reflect his knowledge and ideological creation based on Confucianism. First, although "taking interests lightly," Dong did not oppose pursuing interests without damaging feudalism. According to Dong, since interests are necessary to meet man's physical needs, and man's body is given by Heaven, it must be the will of Heaven to allow average people to pursue certain amounts of interests, and the ruler must follow the will of Heaven. He specially put forward the idea of "enrich people before indoctrinating them,"[136] which is an important precondition of indoctrinating people. Average people are practical—when they are suffering from anger and coldness, it is hard to govern them and not practical to ask them to follow formality and morality. Although it is impossible to prevent people from pursuing interests, according

[132] *Luxuriant Dew of the Spring and Autumn Annals·Materials Needs Prevail Over Morality.*

[133] *Luxuriant Dew of the Spring and Autumn Annals·Materials Needs Prevail Over Morality.*

[134] *Book of Han·Biography ofDong Zhongshu.*

[135] *Book of Han·Biography ofDong Zhongshu.*

[136] *Luxuriant Dew of the Spring and Autumn Annals·Benevolence, Morality and Law.*

to Dong, the behavior of pursuing interests must be limited in a certain scope. Dong pointed out, "Too much wealth makes people arrogant while too much poverty makes people anxious. Poverty and anxiety make people steal while wealth and arrogance make people irritable. These are natural. From human nature, sages saw the source of turbulence, thus they developed different codes of conduct according to human nature. Such codes of conduct make rich people satisfied with their wealth so that they will not be arrogant and make poor people satisfied with health maintenance so that they will not be anxious. With such codes, wealth will be affluent, and society will be stable, thus making it easy to govern the country. In today's society, moral institutions have been abandoned, people indulge in pursuing interests, and desires cannot be satisfied. In this way, the king will complain about the lack of wealth, and average people will be tormented by poverty. When the rich become greedier, they will be more immoral; when the poor are tormented by poverty, they will commit crimes. Such a society can hardly be governed."[137]

Second, Dong considered the interests of average people. On the one hand, he asked the rich not to compete for interests with average people. He said, "The rich, with great financial strength, compete with the average people for interests." "The rich have a lot of slaves and servants, and numerous cattle and sheep. They expand property and business and accumulate wealth without limit by oppressing the poor", and thus "the poor become poorer and poorer." Therefore, Dong put forward the idea of "not compete for interests with average people."[138] His reason is "Heaven creates all living things equally: those with sharp teeth do not have horns and those with wings only have two feet, namely, one cannot have all advantages. In ancient times, officials were paid without doing physical labor or doing business—they had big advantages, so they can't have small advantages anymore. It's the same as how Heaven creates all living things. Though, in today's society, there are people with big advantages who still try to get small advantages, and that's why average people are living a miserable life."[139] On the other hand, from the perspective of morality and justice, Dong originally put forward the idea of "limit the land of landlords to make sure that average people have a certain area of land." He said, "Although it's not practical to implement the ancient pubic-shared land system, it's possible to realize a relatively equal land distribution." He also advocated "the free trade of iron and salt," that is, abolishing the state-run system of iron and salt.[140]

Dong's economic morality philosophy is closely connected with his interpretation of "Heaven" and "the will of Heaven." According to him, it is the will of Heaven that the king should govern his people. As he said, "Man is created by Heaven with a good nature that is not used by man. Therefore, Heaven chooses a king to guide people to use their good nature."[141] The king governs his people by "first, prudently abiding by the will of Heaven; second, indoctrinating his people so

[137] *Luxuriant Dew of the Spring and Autumn Annals·Institution.*

[138] *Luxuriant Dew of the Spring and Autumn Annals·Institution.*

[139] *Book of Han·Biography ofDong Zhongshu.*

[140] *Book of Han·Livelihood (I).*

[141] *Luxuriant Dew of the Spring and Autumn Annals·Investigation into Knowledge.*

that they will follow their human nature; and third, building a legal system which stipulates superiors and inferiors to prevent unrestricted growth of desires. As long as the three things are put into practice, the country will be stable."[142] This can be logically understood as follows: not accepting rule and slavery is "going against the will of Heaven." If a king fails to understand the will of Heaven and people fail to follow the will of Heaven, then "the country will decline. Heaven will warn man with disasters at first. If man doesn't correct his behavior, Heaven will warn man again with abnormal phenomena. And if man still doesn't change, he will be punished."[143] If a country goes against the will of Heaven, Heaven will warn it with disasters; if people go against the will of Heaven, people will be punished.

What's the management following the will of Heaven? According to Dong, it is as such: "the king follows the instructions of Heaven, dukes follow the instructions of the king, a son follows the instructions of his father, subjects and concubines follow the instructions of the king, and a wife follows the instructions of her husband. These are the mandates of Heaven."[144] The management principles are the three moral relationships between ruler and subject, father and son, and husband and wife, and the five virtues of benevolence, morality, formality, wisdom and integrity.

One characteristic of Dong's philosophy of management morality is moralized management. In other words, moral principles are the basis of management. According to Dong, all kinds of social management, such as economic management and production management are all subject to the signs of warning given by Heaven. The views of Dong regarding management morality, which seem very religious and superstitious, helped the ruler govern the country essentially. Regardless, his views on management requiring teamwork and norms are still of great significance. This is the first time (after Mencius made the point that management is essentially about man management) that the logical relationship between management and man was discussed theoretically, which is a breakthrough in the history of management, especially the history of economic management.

3.1.4 Ethical Economic Morality Philosophy in the Song and Ming Dynasties

As the Confucian idealist philosophy of the Song and Ming Dynasties were formed, the ancient philosophy of the ethical economic morality philosophy ended. The economic morality philosophy of the Song and Ming Dynasties, which was established based on Confucianism and absorbing the theories of Buddhism and Taoism, advocates heavenly principles and disdains human desire, pushing moralism to extreme heights.

142 *Book of Han·Biography ofDong Zhongshu.*

143 *Book of Han·Biography ofDong Zhongshu.*

144 *Luxuriant Dew of the Spring and Autumn Annals·Obedience.*

1. Zhou Dunyi (1016–1073) was a representative of the Lianxi School of the Northern Song Dynasty and became the founder of the Confucian idealist philosophy of the Song and Ming Dynasties. On the basis of Confucianism, Zhou absorbed some views of Buddhism and Taoism. Due to this reason, his ideas, which interpret the relationships between morality and the economy and between morality and interests, all deliver a clear opinion: morality is much more important than the economy and interests. He developed the Confucian idea that "formality prevails over interests," which was popular in the Pre-Qin Period and totally abandoned the idea of combining interests with formality to interpret issues regarding the economic morality advocated by Xunzi and Jia. This is one "mistake" made by Zhou in his academic research. However, given the ideological foundation of Zhou's philosophy, this "mistake" is inevitable. Even though, as the founder of the Confucian idealist philosophy of Song and Ming Dynasties, he "greatly developed Confucianism," establishing an irreplaceable academic position.

Zhou's fundamental economic morality philosophy is manifested in his understanding of the interest-morality relationship, the basis of which is his view on the formation of morality. Zhou said, "'When all living creatures were coming into being, each creature obtained its special life in changes," thus reality formed. Integrity is the purest and kindest thing. Therefore, "the change from yin to yang and from yang to yin is the law. The continuous development of yin and yang is benevolence, which is the origin of reality.' The ideas of 'yuan' ('origin') and 'heng' ('smooth') interpret the emergence and growth of reality; and of 'li' ('harmony') and 'zhen' ('insistence'), the development of reality. How great *The Book of Changes* is! It explains the origin of life."[145] Zhou affirmed that "reality" is derived from 'qian' and 'yuan', but he overstated the functions of "reality." He thought that "reality" exists in all things, and the development process of all things. According to Zhou, "reality" is the "basis of five virtues (benevolence, morality, formality, wisdom, and integrity) and[146] the origin of all walks of life." "Reality" is the extreme level of morality.

Then, how to reach the moral quality of "reality"? According to Zhou, to acquire reality, people must "desire nothing," meet the requirements of morality and justice, and disdain interests.[147] He said, "Morality and justice are the noblest virtues in the world."[148] Therefore, "gentlemen must desire nothing, be moral and just, control anger, and correct mistakes."

Aside from the idea of "formality prevails over interests," Zhou also inherited Confucius' idea of "enjoy a simple but moral life." He said, "Wealth and rank are desired by many, but Yanzi was an exception. He enjoyed his simple but moral life. Why? In the world, the most treasured things are morality and justice, which are different from materials. Morality and justice give us inner peace, with which, we will feel content, and can view wealth and poverty rationally. In this way, man integrates with nature. That's why Yan Hui was praised next to Confucius as a sage."[149]

---

[145] *Tong Shu·Reality (I).*

[146] *Tong Shu·Reality (II).*

[147] *Tong Shu·Teachers and Friends(I).*

[148] *Tong Shu·Control of Anger and Desires.*

[149] *Tong Shu·Yanzi.*

In terms of the understanding of the interest-morality relationship, Zhou did not make a creative contribution, but he expounded management morality from a special perspective. Zhou pointed out that "moderation is the basis of national stability and harmony is the way of interpersonal communication. With moderation and harmony, all things will flourish in the harmony between Heaven and earth."[150] According to Zhou, "moderation" and "harmony" are the basic means in political, social, and even production management. "When Heaven and earth are in harmony, all things will flourish." Only when "people live in harmony" could[151] "the government be good and the people live in peace," and could everything go smoothly. "Moderation is the extreme level of management."[152] Zhou's idea further strengthened and supplemented Confucius's idea of "harmony values the most," and thus is of great theoretical significance for the improvement and development of the philosophy of management.

How are "moderation" and "harmony" realized in management? According to Zhou, "To become a sage, one must be benevolent, moral, moderate, and just."[153] Therefore, "the sages care for all things with benevolence and indoctrinate average people with morality. When the will of Heaven is followed, everything will develop smoothly. When morality is developed, average people will be indoctrinated."[154] That is to say, when the principles of benevolence, morality, moderation, and justice are applied in management, people will live in harmony, and things will go smoothly.

Aside from stressing the management principles of benevolence, morality, moderation, and justice, Zhou insightfully put forward the proposition of "govern by law." He thought that to ensure the promotion of morality, it is necessary to make use of law and punishment. In many cases, morality is ensured by law and punishment. Zhou also held that the enforcement of law in a just way is moral. This idea, which is very creative, was necessary for the development of management morality, especially economic management morality, and won Zhou a position in the history of the economic morality philosophy.

2. Zhu Xi (1130–1200) was an important representative of the Fujian School in the Southern Song Dynasty. Based on a systematic analysis of Confucian doctrines, Zhu inherited the Neo-Confucianism developed by the philosophers (and brothers) Cheng Hao and Cheng Yi. At the same time, he absorbed some Buddhist and Taoist thoughts. Building a vast objective idealist system, Zhu epitomized Confucian doctrines in the Song Dynasty.

Except for his views on the interest-morality relationship, Zhu did not build a theoretical system of economic morality, which seems out of proportion to the vast Confucian ideological system built by him. Zhu thought, "The interest-morality relationship is the primary proposition of Confucianism."[155] The interest-morality

[150] *Tong Shu·Teachers.*

[151] *Tong Shu·Happiness (II).*

[152] *Tong Shu·Happiness (I).*

[153] *Tong ShuMorality.*

[154] *Tong ShuNaturalization.*

[155] *Collected Works of Zhu Xi*, Vol. 24.

relationship is the core of economic morality. According to Zhu, "Interests grow from morality. As long as behavior is moral, interests will appear. Interests come along with morality."[156] He also said, "For people who do not care about interests, as long as they follow their way, interests will arise naturally."[157] Zhu thought that the economy and interests are the elements of morality. Therefore, it is proper to say that Zhu centered his views on the moral economy rather than economic morality.

Zhu maintained that all things are brought into being by the union of two universal aspects of reality: "qi" ("vital force") and "li" ("rational principle" or "law"). According to Zhu, "li", which is spiritual as the origin of all things, is about philosophical methods and the metaphysical life, while "qi", which is material, arises from the movement of "li". "Li" and "qi" are inseparable, for "there is no 'qi' without 'li', and no 'li' without 'qi'",[158] but "li" dominates "qi". Zhu's theory of morality was built based on his interpretation of the heavenly principle. First, he thought the heavenly principle, in essence, is a moral entity, while the essence of morality is the embodiment of the heavenly principle. The concept of morality exists independently from the economic relationship, the material life and the social practice. Second, he thought that the heavenly principle is holy, acting as the standard to judge good and evil. Zhu said, "There are only right and wrong 'li'; right 'li' is good while wrong 'li' is evil."[159]

According to Zhu, "when 'li' and 'qi' coexist in harmony, man exists,"[160] for "li" forms the spirit of man, while "qi" forms the body of man. Since "qi" is different, man is born to be good or evil. Zhu thought that desires are evil. As the wants of man, desires fall into legitimate desires and illegitimate desires: material desires, such as the "desire to eat when one feels hungry and the desire to drink when one feels thirsty" are legitimate, while the desire to see, to hear, to speak, or to do indecent things is illegitimate. Zhu called "illegitimate desires" as "human desire." In this way, the heavenly principle and human desire become opposites. According to Zhu, "for everyone, when the heavenly principle exists, human desire dies, and when human desire exists, the heavenly principle dies."[161] Therefore, "sages earnestly indoctrinate people to understand the heavenly principle so as to eliminate human desire."[162] Zhu also thought that "scholars must be free of human desire and faithfully follow the heavenly principle."[163]

Zhu understood the interest-morality relationship according to the relationship between "li" and "qi". Zhu thought that benevolence and morality are the heavenly principle, while interests are human desire. According to his claim of "following the heavenly principle and eliminate human desire," behaviors, such as "only caring

[156] *Zhuzi's Language Category,* Vol. 68.

[157] *Zhuzi's Language Category,* Vol. 68.

[158] *Zhuzi's Language Category,* Vol. 13.

[159] *Zhuzi's Language Category,* Vol. 4.

[160] *Variorum of Zhuzi,* Vol. 5.

[161] *Zhuzi's Language Category,* Vol. 13.

[162] *Zhuzi's Language Category,* Vol. 12.

[163] *Zhuzi's Language Category,* Vol. 12.

about interests," "pocketing gold falling on the ground from another person's pocket," and flattering or catering to others, or "playing fast and loose for promotion"[164] should all be eliminated.

Based on the proposition of "morality is good and interests are evil," Zhu thought people must "put morality ahead of interests." Of course, as I mentioned above, Zhu did not completely oppose the pursuance of interests—interests subject to morality and growing from morality are acceptable. As Zhu said, "Where there is morality, interests exist naturally; where there is principle, success exists naturally. If one only cares about interests, there may be no interests at all."[165]

Admitting the existence of legitimate interests reflects the reason that Zhu is considered a great scholar. Besides, he combined morality and interests in the scope of Confucian doctrines, attempting to reveal the essential relationship between them, which further developed the interest-morality relationship understood from the perspective of Confucianism. However, we also need to see that, for the interests of the ruling class, Zhu advocated Confucius's idea of "gentlemen value morality while small men value interests" and took eliminating human desire as the primary purpose of indoctrinating people.

Zhu did not oppose legitimate human desire. He was eager to see national stability, but in fact, he saw people suffering from hunger and a society charged with instabilities. To change the conditions, he put forward a series of practical ideas regarding economic morality.

First, the government should take the basic interests of average people into account when developing policies concerning financial revenue and expenditure as well as grain reserves. In terms of financial revenue and expenditure, he held that the government should spend according to revenue, rather than "levying average people according to governmental needs." He put forward the idea of "levy people with extra money and subsidy those in poverty in order to narrow the gap between the rich and the poor."[166] In terms of grain reserves, he suggested that "community granaries" could be built in rural areas. Through the operating mode of timely and recycled lending, "mass death caused by starvation" and grain deterioration can all be avoided.

Second, landlords and tenants should depend on each other to realize social stability. Zhu said, "Many farmers rent fields from landlords, and in the season of seeding, they rent grain from landlords to sow and return grain in the season of harvest. Tenants depend on landlords to make a living and vice versa. Therefore, they must depend on each other to exist."[167] Zhu also pointed out, "Tenants should not violate landlords, and landlords should not bully tenants."[168]

To realize the above claims, Zhu specified the responsibilities of landlords and tenants. "Landlords, as long as financially capable, should try to provide relief to

[164] *Zhuzi's Language Category,* Vol. 27.

[165] *Zhuzi's Language Category,* Vol. 37.

[166] *Collected Works of Zhu Xi*, Vol. 25.

[167] *Collected Works of Zhu Xi*, Vol. 100.

[168] *Collected Works of Zhu Xi*, Vol. 100.

tenants, preventing them from suffering of starvation," for in case of farmer immigration caused by starvation, "fields will be barren and both landlords and tenants will suffer."[169] He also thought that landlords should sell or lend their surplus grain to tenants, and tenants should "in case of starvation, borrow grain from landlords rather than illegally obtaining grain from landlords,"[170]which would lead to severe punishment.

Obviously, Zhu stood on the side of landlords. Landlords benefitted a lot from such concepts, but farmers' rights of pursuing equality and fighting against the feudal rule were deprived. Of course, seeing the roles played by farmers in agricultural production, Zhu also put forward some ideas and suggestions to protect the interests of farmers. Those ideas and suggestions were of great economic significance, and an important addition to the theory of the ethical economic morality philosophy.

It is worth noting that Zhu considered harmonious interpersonal relationships and social stability as the preconditions of economic development. Although it is a common proposition in the study of ethical morality, Zhu gave some practical, relevant opinions of considerable value.

In some sense, the academic value and practical significance of Zhu's economic morality philosophy are comparable to those of his Neo-Confucianism idealist system. His economic morality philosophy is still of great significance of enlightenment in developing the moral philosophy of the socialist market economy and promoting the development of the socialist market economy effectively.

Viewing the ethical economic morality philosophies in the history of China, we can make the following conclusions.

First, the ethical economic morality philosophy focuses on the functions of benevolence, morality, and rationality in economic management. It seems that the direction, method and speed of economic management are all determined by morality. However, without economic significance and interest value, morality will be a mere abstract concept. While for economic management and interest creation, moral significance and functions are also of great significance. Therefore, it is important to value the economic significance of morality and rationality. However, we cannot consider morality and rationality as the foundation of economic management, for in this way, they will finally lose their economic significance and interest value.

Second, the ethical economic morality philosophy opposes "immoderately satisfying desires" and advocates frugality; opposes immoral interests and advocates moral interests; and opposes "human desire" and advocates that "interests grow from morality" is the basic principle of ethical economic morality philosophy. Although the ethical economic morality philosophy held "morality prevails over interests" and "human desire should be eliminated," it faced real social conditions (to some extent), which promoted the establishment and enhances the practical significance of the economic morality philosophy objectively. However, we shall also see that it is very limited to the study of economic issues in the scope of morality. To

[169] *Collected Works of Zhu Xi*, Vol. 99.

[170] *Collected Works of Zhu Xi*, Vol. 99.

establish a moral economy discipline, the logical start shall be economic interests, let alone building an economic morality discipline.

Third, the ethical economic morality philosophy stresses the moral means applied in the process of economic management and focuses on the moral quality and harmonious interpersonal relationship of managers. It claims "management by morality and benevolence." As for the working approaches and means of the ethical economic morality philosophy, they are undoubtedly of great theoretical and practical significance. The ethical economic morality philosophy not only affected the economic and management theories and practice in ancient China but also affected foreign theories and practices concerning economic development and corporate management. Even today, it still plays a significant role in the economic development and corporate management of the socialist market economy.

3.2 Utilitarianism[171]

The utilitarian economic morality philosophy is the opposite of the ethical economic morality philosophy. It claims that the economy prevails over morality, that interests are more important than justice; that interests are the foundation of social morality; that the precondition of justice is interests or benefiting man; and that "realizing the mutual benefit" is the "way to be a sage-king", and the "way to govern a country."

3.2.1 The Utilitarian Economic Morality Philosophy Came into Being as the Establishment of Mohism, Legalism and Taoism in the Pre-Qin Period

1. Mohism and Confucianism are two opposite schools coexisting in the Pre-Qin Period. Mohism confronts the social-economic life, focuses on the existence of interests and goes strong on defining morality with interests. Mozi (approximately 468–376 B.C.), an ideologist and a politician of the Warring States Period, is recognized as the founder of Mohism. Putting morality ahead of interests, Mozi put forward his economic morality philosophy, which, although seen as a major rival to Confucianism, was actually of great theoretical and practical significance.

Mozi was up in arms against Confucius's idea of "seldom speak of interests." He called on people to "pursue interests and eliminate evil."[172] Unlike Confucius, who

[171] Originally titled as Traditional Chinese Utilitarian Economic Morality Philosophy, *Economic Morality in China*, China Commercial Publishing House, 1994, pp. 59–98, with corrections and deletions herein. This paper has been included in Moral Capital and Business Ethics (*Selected Works of Wang Xiaoxi*), People's Publishing House, 2009.

[172] *Mozi·Universal Love.*

put morality and interests at opposite positions, Mozi did not ignore the importance of interests. According to Mozi, "morality matters the most"[173] and "a country with morality will develop and without morality will be in turmoil."[174] Therefore, morality is the real "treasure of all." Moreover, in the scope of the utilitarian ideological system built by him, he united morality with interests. He thought anything benefiting man is moral and anything not benefiting man is immoral; therefore, "morality is interests."[175] According to Mozi, interests are the precondition for the existence of interests, and without interests, morality is incomprehensible. Thus, interests are defined by morality. Mozi essentially equated morality with interests, which he used as a basis to unite morality and interests. In fact, "morality is interests" is a metaphysical theoretical proposition that ignores the logical relationship between morality and interests. Regardless, compared with Confucius, Mozi had a more realistic and rational view on the interest-morality relationship—Confucius focused on the functions of rationality, while Mozi tried to reveal the essential intension and value orientation of rationality, which is more advanced.

First, the proposition of "morality is interests" clearly shows the moral orientation and end of utilitarian, and was of great value for the development of moral ideology in ancient China. Unfortunately, the proposition has long been ignored, and the study on the orientation and the end of morality has seldom been touched. Although morality was used by the ruling class as a means to stabilize the regime, the correct orientation and the logical end of morality were abandoned. As a result, the economic significance and material end of morality were never (and of course could not possibly be) really embodied.

I believe that Mozi's understanding of the interest-morality relationship, especially his conscious cognition on the orientation and the end of morality, makes us think about the reality of the socialist market economy. Only when we fully understand the orientation and the end of morality in the context of present social reality, we could really understand the position and the functions of socialist morality and use it in a social construction.

Second, at the same time of stressing that morality is equal to interests, he pointed out, "Those who work survive while those who do not work cannot survive." For him, labor is of great importance. He said, "If average people work hard, there will be enough wealth"[176] and "If average people do not work hard, there will be no enough wealth."[177] He also said, "Why do farmers work so hard to plant grain, trees, and vegetables and store as many beans and seeds of grain as they can? The answer is that they believe as long as they work hard, they can feed themselves and become rich; otherwise, they will be poor, and even hungry. Why do women work so hard to spin and weave cloth and silk? The answer is that they know that as long as they work hard, they can keep themselves warm and become rich; otherwise, they will

[173] *Mozi·Morality Matters the Most.*

[174] *Mozi·Gengzhu.*

[175] *Mozi·Classics (I).*

[176] *Mozi·Will of Heaven (II).*

[177] *Mozi·Against Music (I).*

be poor, and even cold… If farmers are lazy to plant and women are lazy to weave, it is my understanding that the country will lack of wealth."[178] According to Mozi, people can only acquire wealth by labor. In addition, he thought, "Those who try to get something for nothing" must be condemned or punished. Mozi creatively unified morality and interests through labor, which is quite valuable.

Third, Mozi advocated frugality and opposed extravagance. Mohists enjoyed the hardships of life, which is an embodiment of utilitarianism. According to Mozi, frugality itself is the realization of morality. Mozi thought frugality means consuming to meet necessary human needs. "Ancient sage-kings ate simple food as long as it can tonify the 'qi' and build the body." "Ancient sage-kings wore azure clothes in the winter as long as it's light and warm, and ko-hemp clothes in the summer as long as it's light and cool." "When boats were needed to travel across a big river, ancient sage-kings built boats as long as they were large enough for use." "Ancient sage-kings built simple palaces, as long as walls could keep wind and coldness out, roofs can keep rain and snow out, rooms were clean enough for sacrifice, and internal walls were tall enough to separate men from women."[179] Mozi opposed the extravagant funerals held by the nobility. At that time, "when the nobility died, the coffins are heavy, the burial objects are expensive, the clothes are large in number and complex in decoration, and the tombs are big," which "cost a lot of labor and money."[180] In addition, there were still average people who "spend all their money to hold extravagant funerals."[181] Mozi thought people should follow the ancient sage-kings to hold simple funerals. "Coffins were only 3 cun (an ancient unit of length) in thickness to contain the rotting corpses; only 3 pieces of clothes were used to cover the bodies; and tomb pits were only 3 chi (an ancient unit of length) in length and width, and shallow in depth that their bottoms didn't reach underground water, the tops can just prevent the odor from emitting out."[182] It can be seen that Mozi advocated such a frugal life that people's basic needs are met. According to Mozi, the extravagance and waste from a portion of people will affect the life and even existence of the rest. We can deduce that utilitarians opposed hedonism. In my opinion, although the proposition of "morality is interests" is partial to some extent, it limited the pursuance of interests in the scope of rationality to unify morality and interests, which is of great significance. Modern bourgeois utilitarians who equate utilitarianism with hedonism should be ashamed.

2. The core of Legalism is law or morality ensured by law. Due to this reason, the economic morality philosophy was rarely of concern. In my opinion, the Legalist economic morality philosophy is utilitarian, for Legalists thought that pursuing interests is a human nature, and all kinds of interpersonal relationships are built based on interests.

---

[178] *Mozi·Against Predestination (III).*

[179] *Mozi·Frugality (II).*

[180] *Mozi·Simple Funeral (III).*

[181] *Mozi·Simple Funeral (III).*

[182] *Mozi·Simple Funeral (III).*

Li Kui (approximately 455–395 B.C.) of the Pre-Qin Period is known as the founder of Legalism. Li Kui's thoughts regarding the interest-morality relationship are mainly embodied in his proposition of "agriculture is the basis of all." Li Kui held that wealth primarily grows from the production of agriculture, and "destroying the production of agriculture will lead to poverty."[183] "Engraving and weaving destroy the production of agriculture. As a result, people will suffer from starvation."[184] "If the king focuses on the handicraft sector, his people will be extravagant and his country will be poor." Despite Li Kui's expressed opposition to the handicraft sector, his physiocracy formed the essential weight to his understanding of the interest-morality relationship from the perspective of utilitarianism. Li Kui stressed that agricultural productivity is determined by the efforts paid by farmers. He said, "If famers work hard, then fields will be very productive; otherwise, the yield will be very low."[185]

To protect agricultural production and the interests of laborers, Li Kui claimed that the price of grain must be moderate, for "if the price of grain is too high, the interests of non-farmers will be damaged, which will lead to the departure of non-farmers; however, if the price of grain is too low, the interests of farmers are damaged, which will lead to the poverty of farmers."[186] Therefore, the price of grain shall not be too high or too low. A wise king should find a balance so that "the needs of people can be appropriately met and the price of grain can be reasonable… Even in case of natural disasters, nonfarmers will not be forced to leave their homes by high grain price."[187]

Shang Yang (approximately 390–338 B.C.) was a reformer of the Warring States Period and a representative Legalist in the Pre-Qin Period. As a great reformer, Shang developed an economic morality philosophy deeply marked with the characteristics of his age and class. From the perspective of the emerging feudal landlord class, Shang held that pursuing self-interest is a human nature. He said, "It's natural that man seeks food when feeling hungry, seeks rest when feeling tired, seeks happiness when feeling sad, seeks honor when feeling disgraced… Man is born with the desire for interests… Disgrace and hardship are hated by average people, and honor and leisure are desired by average people."[188] Shang thought man's self-interest could be used to "weaken average people" and "strengthen the country." He said, "Weak people make the country strong, and a strong country has weak people; therefore, the way to strengthen a country is to weaken average people"[189] for "average people honor the nobility when they are disgraced, respect officials when they are weak and work for money when they are poor."[190]

---

[183] *Book of Han·Livelihood.*

[184] *Liu Xiang, Garden of Anecdotes·Rhetorical Question.*

[185] *Book of Han·Livelihood.*

[186] *Book of Han·Livelihood.*

[187] *Book of Han·Livelihood.*

[188] *The Book of Lord Shang·The Calculation of Land.*

[189] *The Book of Lord Shang·Weakening the People.*

[190] *The Book of Lord Shang·Weakening the People.*

Shang's understanding of the interest-morality relationship demonstrates the ideology of a reformer representing the interests of the emerging landlord class. Based on the proposition that self-interest is a human nature, Shang profoundly analyzed the self-interest of average people. However, due to his class, Shang did not respect and guide the self-interest of average people from a rational perspective; instead, from an irrational perspective, he took use of the self-interest of average people to serve the ruling class. This is a typical demonstration of egocentric utilitarianism standing for the interests of the ruling class.

As a philosopher in the later Warring States Period, Han Fei (approximately 280–233 B.C.) epitomized the Legalism of the Pre-Qin Period. Han Fei believed, "Man acts for self-interest."[191] He said, "Everyone pursues interests and avoids losses" and "everyone desires interests and dreads punishment."[192] Han Fei stressed, "Pursue interests and avoid losses" is a human nature. In other words, man is born to be selfish and of self-interest.

According to Han Fei, all kinds of interpersonal relationships, the reconciliation of such relationships and moral or immoral emotional experiences are determined by man's nature of self-interest. He analyzed that "people serve their ruler not because of love, but the power of the ruler" and[193] "a ruler and his subjects are connected by interests instead of affection like the kinship between a father and his son."[194] Han Fei understood the parent–child relationship in the same way. He said, "When a boy is born, his parents congratulate each other, but when a girl is born, her parents kill her. No matter boys or girls, they are the children of parents, but boys are cherished and girls are killed. The reason is that parents do it for long-term interests. If even parents and children are connected by interests, why would others be any different?"[195] He also said, "If parents do not take good care of their young children, then after they grow up, their children will blame them. If grown-up children do not take care of their parents, their parents will blame them. Parents and children blame each other for self-interest."[196] Since ruler-subject and parent–child relationships are bound by interests, it is certain that other relationships are built based on "self-interest" and "calculations." Han Fei further explained, "Yuliang loved horses for he needed to ride, and King Goujian of Yue loved his people for he needed his people to fight for him. Doctors are dedicated in treating patients not because of love, but money. Carriage makers want people to be rich so that they can sell more carriages, and coffin makers want people to die early so they can sell more coffins. Carriage makers do not do it because of benevolence but self-interest; and coffin makers do not do it because of hate but self-interest."[197] We can see that in

[191] *The Book of Lord Shang·Waichu (Left I).*

[192] *The Book of Lord Shang·Difficulties (II).*

[193] *The Book of Lord Shang·Six Oppositions.*

[194] *The Book of Lord Shang·Waichu (Left I).*

[195] *The Book of Lord Shang·Six Oppositions.*

[196] *The Book of Lord Shang·Waichu (Left I).*

[197] *The Book of Lord Shang·Beinei.*

Han Fei's view, since man is born to be of self-interest, interpersonal relationships are actually the exchange of interests.

Since interpersonal relationships are built based on calculations and the exchange of interests, it is natural that some will sacrifice the interests of others to obtain more interests. As an ideological representative of the feudal landlord class, Han Fei put forward the proposition of "the average people shall be poor." He said, "Laozi once said that as long as people are content, they will not feel ashamed and will not be in danger. Laozi was the only one who could do it. Average people are not Laozi, so it's wrong to think that satisfying their desires is the way to govern a country. King Jie of Xia, although owning everything, was still not content with his power and wealth. A king can make his people rich, but it's impossible for his people to be as rich as him. If even King Jie of Xia was not content, how can we expect that of average people? Therefore, it's impossible to govern people by satisfying their needs."[198] Han Fei wanted to express that average people are obedient and serve the ruling class when they are poor. Han Fei inherited Shang's egocentric utilitarianism standing for the interests of the ruling class, which is different from the utilitarian economic morality philosophy of Mozi. It can be said that Han Fei combined economic morality with political morality with "calculations," which is the essence of the economic morality philosophy of the ruling class. One idea attributed to Han Fei is his belief that people are in conflict when the population is big. He said, "In ancient times, men didn't farm and women didn't weave, but people kept themselves fed with fruits and warm with hides. They didn't work hard but were amply supplied, leaving them free of conflict; they were not rewarded or punished, but they lived in harmony. The reason is that their population was small. In today's society, it's common for a couple to have five sons. If each son has five sons, then the couple will have 25 grandsons. As the population grows, people will start to be in conflict. It's not because they are evil—it's caused by the lack of resources."[199] Han Fei is very partial in attributing social turmoil to population growth, but this is fundamentally wrong in principle. However, we must admit that Han Fei's combination of the phenomenon of "conflicts among people" with population is reasonable. When growth of wealth falls behind the growth of population, due to the limitation of moral quality, a series of social problems will occur. In fact, it is irrational that a country's material and financial sources cannot support its population. China's birth control policy is an objective requirement of the socialist economic morality philosophy. From this point of view, we must say that Han Fei's idea is valuable.

As for the relationship between consumption and morality, Han Fei held that "extravagance leads to disasters." He said, "If a king indulges in decorating his palace, women and pets for entertainment, it's a disaster for the king. Subjects decorate the palace, women and pets of the king to satisfy the desires of the king at the cost of increasing the burden of taxation on average people. They do it for self-interest, and their behavior is called raising disasters."[200] He also said, "If a king is fond

[198] *The Book of Lord Shang·Six Oppositions.*

[199] *The Book of Lord Shang·Five Pests Harming the Society.*

[200] *The Book of Lord Shang·Eight Political Conspiracies.*

of enjoying luxurious buildings, carriages, clothes and playthings at the cost of exploiting his people, he will lose his country."[201] Such ideas were put forward to persuade the ruling class and thus were significant at that time. It's true that Han Fei's interpretation of "raising disasters" is shallow and limited, and it barely worked in persuading the ruling class, but the idea that extravagance is the source of disasters, a new understanding of the relationship between consumption and morality, provided an ideological pro-condition for Legalists to develop the proposition of "prevent corruption by law."

Upon being put forward by Han Fei after man entered the age of civilization, "extravagance is the source of disasters" has continued to exist as a social phenomenon. Even in this day and age, extravagance is still opposed as an immoral phenomenon.

3. Yang Zhu (approximately 400–335 B.C.) was an ideologist in the early Warring States Period. His economic morality philosophy is extremely utilitarian. As one of the early representatives of Taoism in the Pre-Qin Period, Yang developed an economic morality philosophy, which obviously differed from those of Laozi and Zhuangzi by being naturalistic instead of "utilitarian".

The core of Yang's economic morality philosophy is "self-interest" and "self-regard." Yang said, "Bo Cheng and Zi Gao didn't want to sacrifice their self-interest to benefit the country, so they quit their jobs and became farmers. Yu the Great didn't acquire self-interest at the interests of his people, so he became seriously ill. Ancient people didn't sacrifice self-interest to benefit the country, or sacrifice public interests to benefit themselves. As long as no one sacrifices any of his interests for the benefit of his country, a country is governed."[202] Yang tried to demonstrate the importance of interests by taking Bo Cheng, Zi Gao and Yu the Great as examples. He thought, "Man should protect self-interest" without any cost. Mencius once said, "Yang refused to benefit the country by sacrificing any of his interests."[203]

Guided by the thought of "self-regard," Yang claimed, "Man should protect self-interest and not be burdened by material desires"[204] and "treat materials lightly" for the sake of realizing "immortality." However, paradoxically, Yang also claimed that man should "do what they want without control,"[205] to "listen to, watch, smell, speak and do what they want."[206] The reason is the real "immortality" is about satisfying material and spiritual desires, even it means life will be short; otherwise, no matter how long a man should live, he won't be immortal. Yang also said, "No matter how long one can live, he will ultimately die. No matter sages or devils, they will die and decay the same. What's the difference?"[207] Therefore, man should "follow his will" and "satisfy his desires."

---

[201] *The Book of Lord Shang·Omens of Destruction.*

[202] *Liezi·Yangzhu.*

[203] *Mencius·Dedication (I).*

[204] *Huai Nanzi·Silunxun.*

[205] *Liezi·Yangzhu.*

[206] *Liezi·Yangzhu.*

[207] *Liezi·Yangzhu.*

According to Yang, man lives to satisfy his own needs and desires, so man should obtain any interests beneficial to him and not care about the interests of others.

Strangely, Yang's advocacy of self-interest and self-regard is accepted widely. Why?[208] There are several possible reasons. First, Yang claimed that the human body and wealth are owned by the public, not by individuals, and a moral man must share his body and wealth with others. He said, "Our bodies do not belong to ourselves, but since we are living, we should protect our bodies. Materials do not belong to ourselves, but since we are using them, there is no need to abandon them. Our bodies are the subjects of our life, and materials are the subjects of supporting our life. We protect our bodies and materials, but we cannot occupy them; otherwise, we irrationally occupy human bodies and materials, which belong to the public. Only sages can refuse to irrationally occupy human bodies and materials which belong to the public; only moral noblemen can share their bodies and wealth with the rest of the world." This view was praised and promoted by the ruling class. Second, Yang put forward the ideas of "self-interest" and "self-regard" and claimed that man should enjoy his life, which certainly was supported by the rich. For the poor living a hard life, they were eager for immortality and enjoyment; thus, they did not oppose Yang's opinion.

4. During the Song Dynasty, influenced by the economic reform launched by Wang Anshi, a relative mature theoretical system of utilitarian economic morality philosophy gradually came into being.

Wang opposed the idea that "a Confucian official should be ashamed of managing money." In his view, managing money is moral. If the government is not involved in economic management, inevitably, rich farmers, rich workers, and rich merchants will exploit average people and poor farmers. Therefore, managing money is necessary.

Wang's economic morality philosophy is similar to that of Mozi, but there is still a difference. Mohists equated interests with morality without distinguishing them or understanding their dialectical relationship. Wang developed utilitarianism as well as the understanding of the relationships between interests and the morality of Mohism. He said, "The pursuance of mutual benefits is moral and requires morality" and[209] "to attract talents, money is needed; to manage money, morality is needed."[210] Wang emphasized the unity of interests and morality: morality acts as the means and interests as the ends. Therefore, only upon the unity of interests and morality could social stability and national prosperity be realized.

Wang's understanding of money management and the morality-interest relationship were opposed by people holding different opinions during its application, but they played a positive role in society at that time. Wang limited the pursuance of interests with morality and interpreted morality with interests. This was significant in guiding and supervising the further development of Confucianism as well as promoting production and improving the living standards of people.

208 *Mencius·DukeWen of Teng (II)*

209 *Continuation of History As A Mirror*, Vol. 219, 1st month, 4th year of Xining Period.

210 *Collected Works of Wang Linchuan*, Vol. 70, the Department of Finance.

Wang's doctrines concerning the morality-interest relationship act as a reference for the development of China's socialist market economy. In some sense, the market economy is a utilitarian economy, the development of which requires morality as an important means. China developed the socialist market economy primarily for the purpose of strengthening the country, enriching people, and stabilizing the society. However, essentially, the socialist market economy is a competitive economy that requires the guidance of morality to promote economic development. Without the participation of morality, the socialist market economy will certainly turn into a free economy built in the private ownership system. As a result, immoral phenomena, such as unfair competition and fraudulence will occur. Therefore, we can say that the socialist market economy is also the socialist moral economy. On the one hand, the development of the socialist market economy cannot ignore the interests of the country, people, and social progress, which are the essential intension thereof. Without such essential intension, a market economy cannot be called the socialist market economy. On the other hand, the socialist market economy is a conscious and orderly rational economy. Its management is constrained by law as well as morality. Therefore, moral development not only provides a correct value orientation for the development of the socialist market economy, but also strengthens the inner force for the development of the socialist market economy.

Wang's understanding of the morality-interest relationship stresses the unity of interests and morality, namely, morality exists in the process of interest creation. This view of Wang can be seen in his understanding of the morality-interest relationship and money management, as well in the policies and reform measures made by him.

Wang launched the economic reform for the purpose of restraining land annexation and equalizing resource and wealth distribution. In a deeper sense, Wang claimed that the wealth and land of average people cannot be deprived, and the power of rich farmers, rich workers, and rich merchants should be limited to protect the legal rights of the majority. As a representative of small and medium landlords in the Northern Song Dynasty, Wang put forward political and economic ideas standing on the side of morality, which promoted the embodiment of the utilitarian economic morality philosophy. This is very creative and praise worthy for that very time. The following passage well reflects the economic morality philosophy of Wang. He said, "Heaven appointed your majesty as a sage-king. When you send your people to the border to defend the country, they obey your order even it means sacrificing their lives. Why? It's because you protect their interests. You issued policies to equalize wealth and land, so that the rich cannot oppress the poor, and the strong cannot bully the weak. Now the rich annex the land of the poor. They have more wealth than the nobility, but the poor are dying on the street. Your majesty, don't you think you should be responsible for it to some extent? What's your return to your people who sacrifice their lives for you?"[211]

Wang implemented the *Act of the Grain Supply* to prevent rich and powerful merchants from "monopolizing the power of the grain supply by taking advantage

[211] *Continuation of History As A Mirror*, Vol. 240, 11th month, 5th year of Xining Period.

of the difficulties of the country." Thus, "in some extent, the government can take the power of the grain supply back. In this way, the grain can be distributed equally, transport costs can be saved, and the burden of farmers can be relieved. As a result, the wealth of the government and people may be sufficient."[212]

Wang also implemented the *Law of the Government Acquisition* and the *Law of Government Loan*. The government charged a lot of interest after the implementation of the laws, which directly led to the increase of state revenue, though Wang denied it. Moreover, on the one hand, objectively speaking, land annexation was controlled, which aroused the enthusiasm of farmers and increased the efficiency of their production. On the other hand, grain prices were stabilized, which promoted fair market competition.

The *Act of Pay for the Corvee* was implemented to justify the economic burden of people. Before the implementation of the act by Wang, the corvee system was very complex and unjust. Big landlords, such as officials and monks, and most urban residents were free from the corvee, and a heavy corvee was mainly undertaken by yeomen and small and medium landlords. However, once such people undertook the corvee, they may face miserable conditions where "families are ruined and fields are sold". In *A Brief History of Chinese Economic Thoughts (II)*, Hu Jichuang notes, "At that time, undertaking the corvee was considered as a dangerous and hard thing, for sometimes, people undertaking the corvee could not rest until their families were ruined. Escorting was the hardest job. Once, an escort sent 35 g of gold to a place over 500 km away. However, since officials of the treasury deliberately made life difficult for him, he couldn't come back home for over a year; thus, he suffered a serious economic loss. To escape from the corvee, many people would ask their widowed mothers to marry again, or 'ask their widowed grandmothers to marry again, or to live separately with their mothers', or 'give some of their fields to others' so they would not be considered as upper-class farmers. The cruelest thing is that in families with a father and a son, the father would hang himself so that the son didn't need to undertake the corvee." To reduce the occurrence of such irrational phenomena, Wang put forward the idea that people can pay for their corvee. According to the *Act of Pay for the Corvee*, officials, monks, and rich merchants that were free from the corvee before must pay a corvee subsidy. In addition, to relieve the burden of small and medium landlords and poor farmers, small and medium landlords were allowed to pay for the corvee as escorts. Moreover, poor farmers were exempted and free from the corvee, so that "farmers can have time that is equally distributed between farming and the labor force."[213] The act also stipulates that the "payment for the corvee shall be decided by the difficulty of the corvee," which made minor officials, whose income was mainly derived from bribes, live by salary.

The economic reform launched by Wang covered many aspects, and a series of new acts were made. From the perspective of morality, first, Wang strongly opposed the monopolistic behavior, which harmed the interests of average people and

[212] *Collected Works of Wang Linchuan*, Vol. 70, the Department of Finance.

[213] *Collected Works of Wang Linchuan·Five Things.*

farmers, such as land annexation and speculation, thus trying to equalize economic power and economic interests. Second, Wang opposed the existence of privilege in the economic sphere. He claimed that despite one's position and wealth, everyone should undertake economic responsibility, especially the responsibility of the corvee. In addition, the methods and amount of the corvee should vary with one's position and wealth. In this way, some feudal privileges would be limited, and the socio-economic life would be more just. Third, Wang's idea of money management was put forward in order to build a wealthy and strong country. It protected the interests of the country and the majority.

From the above, we can see that although Wang was known as a reformer and a politician, he also developed a relatively mature utilitarian economic morality philosophy. It can be said that his idea of economic reform and a series of measures taken by him are filled with moral spirit—morality existed in the planning and implementation of the reform as a precondition and an end.

From historical data, we can see that in the history of China, all economic reforms, despite the extent of reforming, contain profound moral ends. Although reforms were carried out by the ruling class for their own interests in the class society, to achieve results, they were, more or less, certainly related to the interest of average people, the reconciliation of some interpersonal relationships, interest relationships, and class relationships. Therefore, economic reforms were always, more or less, accompanied by moral change or development.

3.2.2 The Utilitarian Economic Morality Philosophy in the Song Dynasty

Li Gou (1009–1059) was an ideologist and a Confucian of the Northern Song Dynasty. He called himself a "devout follower of Confucius and Mencius,"[214] but he thought separating interests from morality was wrong. He said, "Should we speak of interests? Since we cannot live without interests, why shouldn't we speak of interests?"[215] He criticized Mencius' idea of "it's wrong to speak of interests." According to Li, people follow moral codes for the sake of interests. He said, "Mencius once said it's wrong to speak of interests. I believe this is extreme. Moral behavior is always accompanied by interests. In his book, he mentions repeatedly that King Tang of Shang and King Wu of Zhou expanded their countries from small areas, doesn't this mean a lot of interests?"[216] Li's understanding of the interest-morality relationship is essentially the same as Wang Anshi's view. They absorbed the utilitarian thoughts of Mohism, and thus actually improved Confucian doctrines.

When explaining the social phenomena that "people cheat each other and compete intensely like robbers" to pursue interests and satisfy desires,[217] he quoted the

[214] *Collected Works of Li Gou*, p. 296.
[215] *Collected Works of Li Gou*, p. 326.
[216] *Collected Works of Li Gou*, p. 326.
[217] *Collected Works of Li Gou*, p. 173.

idea of "pursuing interests in moral ways" put forward by Confucians in the Pre-Qin Period. He stressed that benevolence and morality are the preconditions for the pursuance of interests; otherwise, interests and desires will stand equal against greed and extravagance. Therefore, interests can only be pursued based on "ranking and morality."

Li agreed with the Confucian's idea of "national interests first" and thought that national interests are principal interests. He said, "Sagacious kings and wise gentlemen will place economic development as the priority."[218] I think this is a rational conclusion made by Li based on this practice. Only in a rich and strong country could people become rich and strong. Therefore, national interests are principal interests and are above all. For today's China, the highest moral goal should be developing the national economy and strengthening national power, thus ultimately benefiting average people.

Li understood the relationship between morality and the economy from a unique perspective.

As for land distribution, Li thought if the majority of land resources are in the hands of the rich, while farmers have no land at all, agricultural production will certainly be affected. He said, "The poor are landless, but the rich have vast land. Although the rich have retainers, who, living a comfortable life, are unable to do the farming. So, the rich hire poor people to farm for them. But, the fact is, those crafty poor people choose to do business, living an idle life; while the rest travel far to be tenants. When a small number of farmers work on the vast land, the yield is bound to be low. In the event of natural disasters, the loss will be extremely high due to a lack of labor force."[219] To improve the yield of land and equalize land distribution, Li came up with the idea of limiting the possession of land—"each one can only possess the area of land that it can farm."[220] When "land annexation is not allowed," "the price of land will certainly fall" and "when land is distributed equally, people can be self-sufficient." Upon the realization of equal land distribution, "both the labor force and land are efficiently used, and consequently, the yield will be high enough to meet the need."[221]

Li also put forward a series of economic reform ideas. In terms of grain trade, he held that grain should be purchased in bulk and poor people should buy grain at places that are near; meanwhile, he criticized the jobbery and falsification of corrupt officials and stressed the importance of protecting the interests of poor people. In terms of the salt trade, he held that salt shall be sold by the government to merchants who then sell salt at various places, for in this way, "the government will not lose interests," the quality of salt is guaranteed, the price of salt is low, the purchase of salt is convenient and corruptions, such as jobbery, can be effectively reduced. In terms of the tea trade, he opposed governmental monopoly and supported free trade, for it

---

[218] *Collected Works of Li Gou*, p. 133.

[219] *Collected Works of Li Gou*, p. 135–136.

[220] *Collected Works of Li Gou*, p. 136.

[221] *Collected Works of Li Gou*, p. 136.

can increase tax, assure tea quality and stabilize tea prices, realizing the trifecta-win of the government, merchants and buyers.

The fiscal policies put forward by Li well reflect his philosophy of economic morality. When making policies, he always put the interests of average people first, trying to protect their interests. He actively called for the reduction of average people's tax burden, thinking moderate taxation can not only ease the economic burden of average people but also promote agricultural production. He said, "Normally, in a family, the husband can farm to feed the family with a surplus, and the wife can weave to warm the family with a surplus. If such a family cannot get rich, the reason maybe that, internally, there is an expenditure on wedding or illness; externally, there is expenditure on tax."[222] Therefore, "tax should be levied according to the tax payer's ability."[223] "If the yield is very low, the tax should be exempted." In this way, the enthusiasm of farmers will be aroused.

Li held that merchants should make profits legitimately, namely, goods are produced and transacted in an honest and moral way, and merchants making profits legitimately should be encouraged. He said, "Why should we hate those who possess the same resources as others but become rich due to their wisdom, hard work and frugality while obeying the orders of the king? If we hate them and tax them heavily, they will be poor, and the economic development of the country would regress. Is this beneficial to the king? That's why former kings didn't tax them heavily. It would be a great pity if we just go against the rich in spite of interests that they bring to society. Who would do this?"[224] Compared with previous ideologists who thought all economic activities should be repressed, Li saw the difference between making profits in a moral way and making profits in an immoral way. Li's idea tells us that not all rich people are immoral petty men, which applies to any era. However, at the same time, we must see that in a society adopting private ownership, since resources and power are in the hands of the exploiting class, exploitation is indeed a characteristic of the rich, and immoral rich people do really exist widely.

Li thought as long as wealth is acquired through hard work and fair competition, then it is considered legitimate and shall be supported. Of course, it cannot be put on par with today's idea of "some people should be allowed to get rich before others so that these people would lead the way to common prosperity for all," but they share the same view on morality, that is, prospering from hard work in a honest and fair way. Therefore, the opinion of Li is still of historical value.

Today, in the socialist market economy, the policy of "some people should be allowed to get rich before others so that these people would lead the way to common prosperity for all" well reflects the combination of socialist utilitarianism and socialist morality. When wealth is acquired through the management of integrity and hard work, the creativity and moral quality of the rich are contained in production and management. Moreover, in a society dominated by public ownership and collectivism, the prosperity of a part of people will, objectively, inspire others to

[222] *Collected Works of Li Gou*, p. 82.

[223] *Collected Works of Li Gou*, p. 75.

[224] *Collected Works of Li Gou*, p. 90.

improve their abilities and adjust their economic goals, thus gradually becoming prosperous. This is a concentrated expression of socialist justice in the economic sphere. Therefore, allowing some people to get rich first for the end result of common prosperity is a strategic means and also a strategic goal for the economic development of today's China. This is also the economic pursuance of socialist morality.

Li supported legitimate prosperity, but not extravagance. According to him, if the rich, who are affluent materially and spiritually, live an extravagant life without supporting the poor, their consumption is immoral and the relationship between the rich and the poor will be tense.

Reflecting simple equalitarianism, Li's idea was not practical in his time. In today's society, prosperity through hard work is quite common. In such a context, should the rich help the poor? How? These questions are social issues as well as moral issues. I think that Li's idea, though simple and superficial, is still of significance in terms of reference. Indeed, it is the freedom of the rich to decide how to use their money, but it is also a moral issue. Rational consumption develops the moral quality of the rich, and at the same time, maximizes the social benefits of wealth and improves consumers' quality of social life. When the rich use their money to support social production and social welfare, their moral quality is improved and the social and economic benefits of their wealth are optimized.

Based on his utilitarian economic morality philosophy, Li came up with the idea that "parasitism" is immoral. He considered monks and Taoists, redundant officials, witch doctors, fortunetellers, prostitutes, and entertainers as parasites, for they consume without producing the necessities of life. Li thought that a temple-based economy is not beneficial to improving people's material and spiritual life. Therefore, he was against people becoming monks or Taoists, and the construction of temples. In his view, temples should be wiped out gradually. It is very creative and bold for Li to put forward this predictable and revolutionary idea, which typically reflects his utilitarian economic morality philosophy.

Ye Shi (1150–1223) was a philosopher of the Southern Song Dynasty who epitomized the utilitarian doctrines of the Yongjia School. His utilitarian economic morality philosophy was very representative of the times. Unlike Wang Anshi and Li, who discussed the value of utility in the scope of morality, Ye Shi represented pure utilitarianism.

Ye Shi thought utility is consistent with morality. On the one hand, holding that sagacious kings and wise subjects must be good at economic management, he pointed out, "Economic management doesn't mean heavy taxation." According to him, in the hands of gentlemen, "the money of a country is managed for public benefits" which is thus moral; but if money is managed by petty men, then it is heavy taxed. He said, "Economic management is different from heavy taxation, but today's people have confounded them. In fact, since the destruction of Zhou (due to the loss of morality), people have been equating heavy taxation with economic management. Some good officials acquire wealth from people in a skillful way without leaving people in poverty. However, it is still not economic management. Due to the above reasons, gentlemen avoid being involved in economic management, which then falls into the hands of petty men. In this way, gentlemen, though being moral, keep away from economic management; while petty men, being immoral, take use of economic management, acquiring as much wealth as they can. The king, as a gentleman, also does not participate in economic management. He gives the power of economic management to petty men, taking it for granted. In this way, the people suffer and the country is defamed. When could it come to an end?" On the other hand, Ye Shi thought land should be distributed to farmers to "make sure there are no poor farmers."[225]He held that by occupying land, farmers would follow the moral code. He said, "In the past, farmers were encouraged to reclaim land. In this way, tax was increased and farmers could undertake the corvee. However, in today's society, farmers are landless and hopeless. Brainless ones become tenants or servants; and smart ones become merchants or robbers. No matter in what way, they are homeless." He also said, "If land is not distributed to farmers, large area of land is wasted, and tax drops. In addition, landless farmers will gather together to rob, and naturally, morality is lost."[226] It is true that Ye Shi came up with the idea for the interests of the feudal ruling class, but his view that production development improves human morality is very valuable. This idea typically reflects Ye Shi's utilitarian economic morality philosophy and is of practical significance even today.

In the socialist market economy, moral development is determined by many factors, but economic development is the primary one. To some extent, the development of the national economy and the improvement of people's standard of living play a decisive role in improving people's moral quality.

Ye Shi held that morality coexists with interest, but profits must be acquired in an immoral way. He said that the idea of "the righteous putting friendship ahead of interests and the sensible disregarding any benefits" put forward by Dong "sounds rational at first, but is actually flawed" and is "agreed by Confucians as just useless empty talk."[227]

In conclusion, in the view of Ye Shi, the value of morality is embodied in interests; in other words, without interests, morality will be "just useless empty talk."

In a series of economic propositions of Ye Shi, we can see his economic morality philosophy.

First, Ye Shi held that levying heavy tax is immoral. He said, "In the heyday of the Song Dynasty, the fiscal revenue was twice that of the Hang and Tang Dynasties. After the Xining and the Yuanfeng Periods, many treasuries were set, payment of the corvee was abundant, and grain reserves were several times of those before the Zhiping Period. After the currency reform launched by Cai Jing, national reserves were further increased." In addition, "since the army of the Nyuzhen (an ancient Chinese ethnic group) tried to cross the river, national reserves have increased. In the Xuanhe Period, national reserves were doubled and were much more than today's."[228] According to Ye Shi, "heavy taxation," which is "levied" by cheating the people, is immoral.

[225] *Collected Works of Ye Shi*, Vol. 3, p. 656.

[226] *Collected Works of Ye Shi*, Vol. 3, p. 652.

[227] *Study Notes*(I), p. 324.

[228] *Collected Works of Ye Shi*, Vol. 3, p. 773.

Second, Ye Shi held that financial expenditures should be kept within national revenue, which should be acquired rationally without harming the interests of the people. He said, "People are the foundation of a country. If tax is levied irrationally, people's interests are harmed. If expenditures exceed revenue, the country is harmed."[229]

Third, Ye Shi advocated frugality and "the control of desires." He thought a sagacious king should never "impose heavy taxes on people to meet personal desires" like the First Emperor of Qin and Emperor Wu of Han.[230]

3.2.3 The Utilitarian Economic Morality Philosophy with Capitalistic Characteristics Emerging after the Late Ming Dynasty

1. Taizhou School, whose economic morality ideology standing in a relation of opposition to traditional orthodoxy ideology, developed the utilitarian economic morality ideology reflecting the requirements of capitalism.

Wang Gen (1483–1541), a philosopher of the Ming Dynasty, is known as the founder of the Taizhou School. The school mainly studied issues relating to the interests of average people, such as cooks, merchants, bricklayers, woodcutters, farmers, and employers. He thought, "Sages are concerned with issues relating to average people."[231] Therefore, he called his doctrines as "practical doctrines for average people."[232]

Wang's economic morality ideology is mainly reflected in his view on land ownership. He thought that unequal land distribution is irrational, and only when land is equally distributed could sustainable agricultural development be realized. He said, "The king offers land to dukes, during the process of which, marsh-grassland are divided. When land is divided into pieces, all pieces of land, though varying in size, have borders. Therefore, when equally dividing grassland, it is also necessary to define borders. The locations of borders shall be recorded so that no dispute will arise over any border in the future." For example, "a piece of marsh-grassland with an east–south length of about 25 km, a south–north width ranging in a certain scope, and a total area of 50 zong (an ancient unit of area) is divided into several sections (except for official fields and grain fields), and each section covers 540 mu. In each piece of land, there are more than 1500 people, and each one occupies a certain area, including marsh-grassland, an ash yard, a homestead, fields, and a graveyard. In addition, all the information is recorded and printed. In this way, even if the owner of

[229] *Collected Works of Ye Shi*, Vol. 3, p. 634.
[230] *Collected Works of Ye Shi*, Vol. 3, p. 634.
[231] *Collected Works of Wang Xinzai*, Vol. 1.
[232] *Collected Works of Wang Xinzai*, Vol. 3.

the marsh-grassland leaves, according to the information recorded, no disputes over the marsh-grassland will occur in the future."[233]

Of course, Wang did not mean equally distributing the land of feudal landlords. In his plan of equal marsh-grassland distribution, official fields and grain fields are not included. What's more, the fact is that at that time, many marsh-grasslands were ownerless, and during the process of distribution, the interests of the feudal landlord class would not be harmed.

Wang's idea of equal land distribution (actually marsh-grassland distribution) was of positive significance. First, it advocated that average people should occupy a certain area of land so that the problem of unequal property distribution can be eased. Second, objectively, it made full use of the existing labor force to promote agricultural development, improving the standard of living for the poor.

He Xinyin (1517–1579), an ideologist of the late Ming Dynasty, served as a representative for the Taizhou School. He held that it is normal that man has desires, so it is wrong to think human desire is evil. According to him, man's desire to listen, to watch, to smell, and to feel should be appropriately met, and he even thought that the king should "have the desires of average people (Jichuang 1981b)".

Based on the idea that the king should have the same desires of average people, He Xinyin came up with another idea that the king and average people should be equal. According to him, human desire means not only personal material desires but also the desires for a collective life. This view was of important theoretical significance among the doctrines of the Taizhou School.

It is worth stating that He put forward a humanistic economic morality view that "man is the foundation of wealth for wealth is created by man." Although in his idea, "man" means "man" as the foundation of wealth, not "man" with the modern intension, it is still praiseworthy that He found the roles played by man in wealth creation, which was of important and practical significance.

Today, the important and practical value of a "human-centered economic or corporate development" and its significance for socioeconomic development have been proved by history. It can be said that if a company ignores the economic significance of man and human quality and the positions of them in production, it will certainly lose the opportunities of development. Therefore, even the economic morality philosophy of He is not systematic, his idea that "man is the foundation of wealth" was a very valuable economic proposition and was of important significance of enlightenment.

Li Zhi (1527–1602) was an ideologist and a littérateur of the Ming Dynasty. He was known for criticizing traditional feudal ethics. It can be said that his utilitarian ideas are a summarization of the doctrines of the Taizhou School, and his economic morality ideology can be called a rudiment of capitalist economic morality ideology.

Li Zhi thought the pursuance of self-interest is a human nature, and man acts for self-interest. He said, "Man is born to be of self-interest. To pursue self-interest, man will act; otherwise, man has no motivation to act. Farmers, pursuing the

[233] *Collected Works of Wang Xinzai*, Vol. 2.

harvest in autumn, will work hard in the fields; homemakers, pursuing the accumulation of wealth, will spare no efforts to manage households; intellectuals, pursuing academic degrees, will strive to study hard; and officials, pursuing money and promotion, will follow the orders of the king. Confucius was a sage, but without his high position, he certainly would not have stayed in the State of Lu for even one day. Therefore, the pursuance of interest is a human nature; that's not an assumption. Hearsay about one that is not of self-interest is just fictional and cannot be trusted."[234] Li Zhi also said, "It's natural and wise that everyone pursues interests and avoids losses."[235]

Since it is natural and wise that everyone pursues interests and avoids losses, it is legitimate for people to pursue material interests. According to Li, even sages desire wealth, for "wealth and power are necessary for heroes and sages to make great achievements."[236] Therefore, "people desire for materials and beautiful persons, work and study hard, accumulate wealth, buy fields and houses for the welfare of their offspring, and practice geomancy for the luck of their offspring. People gather together for common interests."[237] Li believed that self-interest and desires are the common requirements of average people as well as sages, and "it's moral to face this fact."[238]

Li Zhi further pointed out, "Behavior relating to food and clothing are moral, and other behavior has nothing to do with morality. Man's moral activities are closely connected with material life; therefore, food and clothing are the motivation and ultimate goals of all kinds of human behavior."[239]

In Li's utilitarian economic morality ideology, "human equality is the foundation of production" is another important idea. He also held that upon human equality, man has the right to realize self-development at will.

From such ideas of Li Zhi, we can see the emergence of capitalistic ideas. Feeling the pulse to times, Li came up with an economic morality ideology that went against traditions. What makes his ideas valuable is that, consciously or unconsciously, he observed the relationship between morality and interests during a social and economic transition, and, from a new perspective, he expounded the concept of human-centered economic development as put forward by He Xinyin.

In conclusion, the economic morality ideology of the Taizhou School was of epoch significance. In particular, it put forward the extraordinary creative idea of human equality and expounded the important roles it played in economic development. It is true that some ideological systems of the Taizhou School are defective or utopian, and some even defend the rich; however, generally speaking, the doctrines of the Taizhou School are still of very important historical significance.

---

234 *A Collection of Books·Morality and Confucius Subjects (II).*

235 *Book Burning·A Reply to Dengming Government.*

236 *Collected Works of Li·Wisdom from the Past (I).*

237 *Book Burning·A Reply to Dengming Government.*

238 *Book Burning·A Reply to Procurator Di.*

239 *Book Burning·A Reply to Deng Shiyang.*

2. With the emergence of capitalist production relations and the spread of Western scientific knowledge among some feudal literati and officialdom, some enlightenment ideologists put forward new utilitarian ideologies.

The Yan-Li School developed a utilitarian ideology as Taizhou School, but it focused more on interests relating to people's daily life. Followers of the school represented by Wang Yuan held, "The pursuance of morality is for interests and only interests can reflect morality."[240]

Yan Yuan (1635–1704) was an ideologist and an educator of the early Qing Dynasty. His one key proposition is "humanistic pragmatism." He said, "With the mercy of Heaven, through reclamation, equal land distribution and irrigation system construction, the country is rich; through training average people to be soldiers and officials to officers, the country is strong; through talent cultivation and indoctrinate people with classics, formality and music, the country is peaceful."[241]In this case, building a rich and strong country is the ends and national peace is the means.

The idea of "equal land distribution" well reflects the economic morality ideology of Yan Yuan. He stressed, "Land should be shared by all."[242]

Li Ta (1659–1733) was an ideologist of the early Qing Dynasty. His economic morality is mainly reflected in the following two aspects: first, he held that wealth is created by agricultural and industrial activities, but commerce cannot produce wealth; thus, it cannot be put in front of industry. He said, "Agriculture keeps people fed and warm. Industry is not as important as agriculture, but all goods are manufactured by industry, so it is also essential. However, commerce has nothing to do with wealth creation but the transfer of wealth, so it is not as important as industry. Besides, employees engaging in commerce tend to be humble and employers tend to be arrogant. Therefore, it's wrong to put commerce in front of industry."[243] From this, we can see that Li confirmed the status of farmers and workers in economic activities. Second, he realized that "in today's society, the land of the poor has been robbed by the rich, making the poor live in misery," so "the primary policy of benevolence is realizing equal land distribution to narrow the gap between the rich and the poor."[244]

Wang Yuan (1648–1710) was a follower of the Yan-Li School. In terms of land ownership, he held that "the public ownership of land is the best choice, followed by equal distribution, and land limitation is the worst choice."[245] He said, "Those who possess land must farm it themselves and cannot hire others to substitute them. People who farm land themselves are farmers, and others are scholars, merchants and workers. Those who do not farm, like scholars, merchants and workers, especially officials, cannot have land. Officials, despite their ranks, cannot possess land,

240 *Criticism of The Four Books.*

241 *Chronicle of Xizhai* (II).

242 *National Administration*, Vol. I.

243 *Pingshuding*, Vol. 1.

244 *Strategies for National Peace*, Vol. 2.

245 *National Administration*, Vol. I.

and only farmers can."[246] Wang advocated equal land distribution so that landlords cannot hold land in their hands and farmers will never be landless. Although rather utopian, it is indeed a concentrated expression of Wang's understanding of the interest-morality relationship.

Huang Zongxi (1610–1695) was an ideologist and a historian of the transitional period from the Ming Dynasty to the Qing Dynasty. As an enlightened ideologist that openly opposed feudal power, Huang held that "man is born of self-interest,"[247] and it is irrational that "one doesn't pursue self-interest."

According to Huang, any behavior infringing on private interests and property is "very immoral". In terms of land distribution, he opposed the limitation on land possession and equal land distribution, for "it's immoral to seize private land."

Huang held that industry and commerce promote economic development. To develop industry and commerce, it's necessary to "change old customs, clear up confusion and suppress extravagance."

Huang held that industry and commerce promote economic development. To develop industry and commerce, it's necessary to "change old customs, clear up confusion and suppress extravagance."

Gu Yanwu (1613–1682) was an enlightenment ideologist of humanistic pragmatism. He held that the pursuance of self-interest is the premise of state administration. He said, "It's natural that people are of self-interest. Three generations ago, it was accepted that the pursuance of self-interest is rational. Sages make use of this human nature—using the selfness of people to realize public interest."[248] Hu thought only when the private ownership of property is realized could production be promoted.

Gu supported the development of commerce. In his view, it is wrong to restrain commercial development, for once the interests of merchants are harmed, production will be affected; therefore, relatively free trade should be advocated. When talking about the salt trade, he said, "Every year, the salt tax collected from Huainan and Huaibei reaches more than one million liang (1 liang = 50 g) of silver, where does it come from? It's from merchants making salt. In the barren coastal area, people live a hard life. Regardless, they still pay over one million liang of silver. Due to the failure of the currency law, the preferential policy for salt manufacturers was canceled. Therefore, except for the salt tax, salt merchants can just feed their families with a surplus. If they cannot make a profit, they will be homeless and cannot even keep themselves fed and warm… Therefore, without profits, merchants will become stranded… Besides, merchants can only make a small profit. If they are bankrupted, the rich merchants will be poor, and the poor ones will have no choice but to die. Although faced with a heavy tax, salt merchants are still reluctant to do other businesses as they are closely tied to salt making. If they are left with no room, we cannot levy over one million liang of silver to support the army."[249]

[246] *National Administration*, Vol. I.

[247] *Waiting for the Dawn·How to be a Ruler.*

[248] *Collected Works of Tinglin*, Vol. 1.

[249] *Pandect for the Pros & Cons about the Social, Political and Economic Conditions of Ming*, Vol. 28.

In conclusion, the ideologies of enlightenment ideologists are concerned more with the interests of average people, and thus are of important historical and practical significance. Although they thought man as being of self-interest and advocated private ownership, their ideas were put forward for the interests of society and average people, and the peace and prosperity of the country. Therefore, in the enlightenment period, the utilitarianism of enlightenment ideologists was always closely connected to patriotism.

3. In the social context of semicolony and semi-feudalism, bourgeois reformists came up with utilitarian ecologies containing both traditional Chinese thoughts and Western thoughts.

Kang Youwei (1858–1927) was an enlightenment ideologist of capitalist reformism in modern China. Young Kang was influenced by Western bourgeoisie and the growing bourgeois reformism in China. Later, he developed a new ideology, which marked the disintegration of feudalism and the emergence of capitalist enlightenment thoughts.

Kang held that interests could turn into morality, and "morality means meeting current human needs." He said, "Since national conditions have changed, the way to govern the country also needs to be changed. Generally, the society will transfer from a fairly well-off society to a society in great harmony."[250] "Morality prevails over interests, but interests can change morality."[251] He also said "morality means meeting current human needs." "Formality and morality change as the change of times. Today's new formality and morality, though never mentioned by the sages in the past, meet today's human needs. In the past, people's basic needs were only related to food, clothing, houses and instruments, and sages were concerned with developing formality and morality. However, with social development, mats have been replaced by tables and doudengs (ancient wooden containers) have been replaced by ceramic plates. Mats and doudengs, which had become a part of civilization due to their long history, have also been abandoned. Likewise, fire has been replaced by electricity, and manpower has been replaced by machines. As long as changes are practical, they are moral. Some people stick to the past, thinking it's moral; but actually, they are blocking the way of development, which is against the morality meant by the sages."[252]

Kang opposed the asceticism advocated by Buddhism. He pointed out, "Human desire ceaselessly grows and the way of state administration should thus constantly change." Therefore, it is necessary to develop the economy according to the actual needs of people and give them the freedom to "pursue easiness and avoid hardship." He said, "People desire wealth and hate poverty, so the government should provide guidance and support, such as introducing machines in agriculture, industry and commerce, helping them to get rich. People desire easiness and hate hardship, so the government should encourage the construction of hotels, restaurants and entertainment venues. People desire safety and hate danger, so the government should

[250] *A Collection of Japanese Books*, p. 1.

[251] *Preface of An Investigation on Confucius Doctrines of Reform.*

[252] *Collected Works of Kang Nanhai*, Vol. 8, p. 17.

arrange security personnel at public places, such as ships, cars and roads. People desire more information and hate isolation, so the government should encourage the establishment of schools and newspaper firms. Things benefiting and entertaining people, such as the museums, zoos and fairs, no matter from home and abroad, should be provided to people. People's desires, such as joy and freedom, should be satisfied; while things hated by them, such as heavy taxes, cruel punishments and a poor environment should be removed."

To develop capitalism, Kang came up with ideas defending bourgeois rights. First, he held that man is born with emotions. "Man is born with seven emotions, namely, joy, anger, sorrow, fear, love, hate and desire, which thus should be followed."[253] In addition, "it's natural that everyone in the world pursues life's pleasures and hates hardships."[254]Second, he pointed out, "All men are created equal." He said, "All men are created equal by Heaven, but sages claimed that only rulers are created by Heaven and average people are created by men. The fact is everyone is created by Heaven."[255] He also said, "Man is born good-natured. King Wen of Zhou was a sage, but he was also born good-natured, as average people; therefore, all men are equal in human nature. With the same human nature, King Wen can be a sage, so average people can also be sages through hard work and study."[256]

In *The Great Harmony*, Kang describes the economic morality in his society of great harmony. First, wealth is owned by everyone, everyone works and there is no inequality. "Land is publicly-owned and thus is not tradable." [257] "Industrial property, such as manufacturing plants, railways and ships, regardless of their scales, are owned by the public rather than individuals."[258] Second, "In the society of great harmony, since there are no countries, severe punishments like military punishments are not needed; and since there are no rulers, rebellions will not happen." "In a society of peace, there are no punishments but professional regulations and rules."[259]At the same time, since "the whole life of man, from birth to death, is supported by the government,"[260] "crimes like burglary, fraud, illegal possession, deception, tax evasion, threats, plunders, dispossession, extortion, absconding, gambling or murder will not occur."[261]

Kang's society of great harmony is utopian. He advocated the cancellation of private ownership, but his ideological basis is the bourgeois theory of human nature, which determines that his ideas, no matter how good they are, can never come true.

Kang's economic morality ideology essentially reflects the interests and psychology of the bourgeoisie. Given the social situation at that time, his ideology

[253] *Collected Works of Kang Nanhai*, Vol. 8, p. 8.
[254] *The Great Harmony*, p. 6–7.
[255] *Kang's Study of Spring and Autumn Annals*, Vol. 6 (I), p. 31.
[256] *Collected Works of Kang Nanhai*, Vol. 8, p. 7.
[257] *The Great Harmony*, p. 240.
[258] *The Great Harmony*, p. 246.
[259] *The Great Harmony*, p. 283.
[260] *The Great Harmony*, p. 193.
[261] *The Great Harmony*, p. 280.

still played an active role. His idea "morality means meeting current human needs" provided a theoretical basis for the development of capitalism from the perspective of morality. According to Kang, "current human needs" mean "the needs of the bourgeoisie." The concept opposes the Confucian idea of "morality prevails over interests," while also differing from the utilitarian idea of "morality is interests." With a wider intension, it is of important and practical significance. In the socialist market economy, behavior, which is in favor of the development of productivity, the enhancement of comprehensive national strength and the improvement of people's standard of living, should be considered as moral behavior, and thus should be advocated.

Tan Sitong (1865–1898) was a modern ideologist and a left-wing radical of the bourgeois reformism. His economic morality ideology, which was developed during the process of anti-feudalism, contains some specific characteristics.

Tan came up with the idea of "communication." In his view, all things coexist because of the existence of benevolence. All things, only when being connected by benevolence can exist rationally and then develop. Tan explained that the principal element of communication is benevolence, which, in essence, is the foundation of communication. "Communication determines the existence of benevolence, while benevolence lays the foundation of communication."[262] Therefore, "benevolence is communication."[263]

In Tan's view, "benevolence" and "communication" are essential for economic development. He held that the circulation of wealth creates profits for both the rich and the poor, and international trade is beneficial to both foreign merchants and China. According to Tan, communication is the precondition to obtain interests. If the communication in international trade or the relationship in production and management is cut off, social and economic development will be hindered.

Tan interpreted "benevolence" and "communication" from an original perspective. Based on traditional utilitarianism and absorbing the interest-morality ideas of moralism, Tan developed a practical guiding ideology for the economic development of modern China. However, we should also notice that there is an evident defect in his ideology: his communication lacks basic principles in the economic sphere—given the wide gap between China and the West, communication without principles will, objectively, damage the development of the national capitalistic economy.

To meet the requirements of capitalist development, Tan opposed the traditional idea of "restrain extravagance and advocate frugality." On the one hand, he thought that extravagance is beneficial to social development. He said, "I know the disadvantages of extravagance. However, the advantages of extravagance are much more than its disadvantages. Some people's pursuance of luxuries creates opportunities for farmers, workers and merchants to make profits. The King of Chu lost his bow, and Confucius said the lost bow would benefit the one who found it. A woman lost her favorite milfoil hairpin and felt sad, but the one who found it would not benefit

[262] *Collected Works of Tan Sitong*, Vol. 1, p. 11.

[263] *Collected Works of Tan Sitong*, Vol. 1, p. 45.

from it. The rich have the most national wealth, so it is better for them to consume a lot, creating opportunities for average people to make a profit."[264] On the other hand, he thought that the advocacy of frugality would hinder social and economic development, for, according to him, it will affect matters, such as "sericulture," and "silver and gold mining" related to people's livelihood. He said, "The more frugal people are, the poorer and more ignorant they are, and the lesser their social wealth is.""Frugality leads to poverty," "in this way, poverty will spread from one village to the whole country, and China, a country with 400 million people and 260,000 species will fall into extreme poverty." In the society of great harmony assumed by Tan, the relationship between morality and the economy contains "public ownership of land" and "the equality between the rich and the poor" and the disappearance of the concept of "country." A society of great harmony has "no borders, wars, suspicions, trickeries, rejections or inequality."[265]

In essence, Tan followed the economic morality ideology of Kang, but his ideas of "benevolence" and "communication" are original. During the process of socio-economic development, whether such ideas can be put into practice will directly affect the quality and speed of economic development.

Yan Fu (1853–1921) was a modern ideologist and a bourgeois scholar who systematically analyzed the economy. His economic morality ideology is typically considered utilitarian.

Yan held that morality and interests are not opposite, for morality does not exist without interests. According to Yan, morality is "long-term and real interests," and therefore "interests and morality are united." He said, "The separation of interests and morality hinders socio-economic development. Mencius once said it's immoral to speak of interests, and Dong Zongshu held that the righteous put friendship ahead of interests and the sensible disregard any benefits." "After the rise of the theories of evolution, people realized that morality doesn't exist without interests. It was first put forward by economists, such as Adam Smith. In the world, there are the superficial and the fatuous, but there are no real petty men. Why? Petty men only see interests, but they cannot see long-term interests as gentlemen." "Therefore, in the theories of evolution, interests do not mean the interests understood by the superficial, the fatuous, or the petty. Actually, only when interests are united with morality could people benefit from it and follow the moral code, thus enabling society to evolve."[266]

In the view of Yan, since interests and morality are united, it is natural for people to pursue interests. To acquire "long-term and real interests," one needs maximum freedom in individual economic activities. He said, "Wealth is created by man. To maximize the productivity of man, it's necessary to give him freedom to prevent him from being restrained… If the government, limited by partial thought, issue policies to restrain the freedom of man, his productivity will be lowered."[267] "Essentially,

[264] *Collected Works of Tan Sitong*, Vol. 1, p. 40.

[265] *Collected Works of Tan Sitong*, Vol. 1, p. 69, 85.

[266] *The Wealth of Nations*(II), p. 25 (note).

[267] *The Wealth of Nations*(VI), p. 6 (note).

the wealth of a country means the wealth of its people. If the government wants to enrich its people, at first, the people must be able to make profits themselves, while the pre-condition of which is giving people freedom."[268]

Yan's idea of freedom creates profits was of important practical significance for capitalistic economic development. Yan realized that wealth is created by average people, and in order to make them fully realize their creativity, it's necessary to give them the freedom in economic activities, or "the productivity of man will drop".

Yan put forward systematic moral concepts concerning taxation. He thought that tax should be levied according to people's ability and should be used on people last. He said, "Tax is not levied to meet private needs, but to benefit the public; therefore, the amount of tax is determined by the needs of the public. If no tax is levied, a country will lose the power to run, and people will suffer. However, tax must be levied according to the ability of people—if people are economically inept, even a small amount of tax will be a burden for them. To improve people's ability to pay tax, the priority is creating opportunities for people to make money and have a surplus."[269]

As for consumption, Yan advocated rational consumption, which means restraining extravagance without affecting production. He thought it is unreasonable to oppose frugality. As he said, "According to Taoism, frugality is a virtue conducive to socio-economic development, but some people oppose the idea of frugality. I really cannot understand."[270]

Liang Qichao (1873–1929) was a bourgeois reformist ideologist in the period from the late nineteenth century to the early twentieth century. His economic morality ideology is closely connected with his era.

As a utilitarian, Liang divided people into "interest creators," who directly participated in the production of creating interest, and "interest sharers," who did not directly create interest. He thought that it is better for the former to be greater than the latter. Such a division is superficial and general. It is of positive significance that he put playboys, beggars, and stealers into the category of the latter, but he also put some whose professions were despised by the society at the time, such as teachers, into the latter category. This is improper and even wrong. Liang's idea of "power for interest creation" well reflects his understanding of the interest-morality relationship. He thought that there are two kinds of power for interest creation: "one is physical power and the other is psychological power, and the latter falls into intelligence and morality."[271] Liang clearly pointed out that the productive process and productive interests are determined by human intelligence and morality.

Even today, the idea is still of significance for enlightenment. The development of the socialist market economy and the improvement of modern corporate institutions require culture, knowledge, and technology, but more importantly, require

---

268 *Poem and Articles of Yan Jidao*, Vol. 1, p. 19.

269 *The Wealth of Nations*, p. 19 (note).

270 *The Wealth of Nations*, p. 63 (note).

271 *Collected Works of Liang Qichao*, Vol. 13, p. 48.

man's correct views of the world, of life and of value. Only when intelligence and morality are well combined could they effectively promote economic development.

Of course, Liang understood the intension of "morality" in the scope of the bourgeoisie. Therefore, he thought egoism is a principle of the capitalist economy, for egoism drives the development of socioeconomic development, and thus advocated the private ownership of land. He said, "Human egoism drives economic development. Human desire is the reason of human economic behavior, and the economic desire of man is about possessing and controlling wealth."[272] "Therefore, economic behavior is conducted on the basis of property ownership. To acquire or enhance ownership, man will follow economic norms. In this way, naturally, national wealth is increased, and this is the result of egoism. Thus, the private economy is closely related to the national economy."[273]

Liang Qichao did not agree with Yan's understanding on the morality of consumption. He advocated extravagance and opposed frugality. On the one hand, he thought that frugality would not only hinder national economic development but also discourage people from working hard. He said, "I hate misers the most. They accumulate wealth for their offspring by taking advantage of others, and with a lot of money though, they seldom consume to promote economic development. Such people are pests and sinners in society."[274] "If one could support himself with 6 g of silver a day," then "after having that amount of silver, he would do nothing more. Even if he actually could make much more money, if the extra money is useless to him, of course he would not spend more effort."[275] On the other hand, he held that extravagance is beneficial to national economic development. As he said, "Confucius once said that resources should be used rather than being abandoned. Nature provides abundant resources for man to meet his needs. Resources are inexhaustible. The more we use, the more they will be created, which then form a virtuous cycle. And that's why the more extravagant Western people are, the richer they are, and the less the abandoned resources are."

Liang actually supported the rich to promote production through consumption. However, without principles, extravagance will turn into the corruption of morality. His understanding of frugality is negative. In fact, "frugality" should be understood as "rational consumption" which should be promoted as a traditional virtue of China.

From the utilitarian economic morality ideologies developed in modern China, we can see that its basic thoughts are much wider and profounder than those of traditional Western utilitarian economic morality ideologies, especially modern Western utilitarian economic morality ideologies, and some profound concepts and propositions are still of important theoretical and practical significance. In the history of China, although utilitarian economic morality ideologies did not have

[272] *Collected Works of Liang Qichao*, Vol. 32, p. 24.

[273] *Collected Works of Liang Qichao,* Vol. 32, p. 25.

[274] *Collected Works of Liang Qichao*, Vol. 1, p. 9.

[275] *Collected Works of Liang Qichao*, Vol. 1, p. 4.

a dominant position and wider influence as ethical economic morality ideologies, they still played positive roles in economic development.

First, the utilitarian economic morality ideology focuses on interests, holding that morality does not exist without interests, and "morality means meeting current human needs." Although some propositions are metaphysical, their ideological frame is rational. Even today, separating morality from interests or considering interests as a reference to understand morality is against the historical materialism. In fact, interests, as a basic condition for individual and social development, as the embodiment of individual and social value, should be the power motivation of human behavior, and the intension of social development. Besides, legitimate interests themselves reflect morality for they are acquired through moral means. Therefore, during the process of socioeconomic development, interests and morality are both the ends and the means.

Second, some utilitarian economic morality ideologies put interests in front of morality and even hold that morality is incomprehensible without interests. This confuses the dialectical relationship between interests and morality, and belittles the position of morality. In fact, morality, as a kind of value orientation and an economic means, directly affects and even controls man and society's acquisition of interests. Only "beasts" will pursue interests in immoral ways.

To promote the growth of the socialist market economy continuously, economic development is the core, and education (primarily ideological and moral education) is the foundation. Morality powers and promotes socioeconomic development, and ultimately determines the interest creation and development of the socialist market economy. Considering interests as the ends and measurement standard of all behaviors is the embodiment of vulgar and irrational utilitarianism.

Third, the utilitarian economic morality ideology generally focuses on national interests and wealth. Although in modern China, "country", in the view of ideologists at that time, meant a feudal autocratic country or a capitalist country, their ideas are still of important significance for enlightenment. In a socialist country, humans are equal and the government represents the interests of people. In this case, national interests and wealth are the biggest interests with the highest moral quality. All measures to develop the socialist market economy should be taken as national interests, for the prosperity and strength of our country is the greatest happiness for all.

3.3 Idealism[276]

The idealistic economic morality ideology contains such typical ideals as the ideal society, human equality (the king and average people farm together to support themselves), equal interest distribution without exploitation and absolute equali-

[276] Originally titled as Traditional Idealist Economic Morality Ideology of China, *Economic Morality in China*, China Commercial Publishing House, 1994, P99–106, with corrections and dele-

tarianism. The establishment of Physiocracy in the Warring States Period marks the formation of the idealistic economic morality ideology in China. The founder of Physiocracy was Xu Xing, who, with his unique ideology, built a position in the time when various ideologies boomed. Although Physiocracy almost disappeared after the death of Xu, as a school, it was revived at the perfect time. In fact, it penetrated the ideologies of other schools, leaving a deep impression. In particular, Physiocracy affected later Confucianism, Legalism and the Yin-Yang School to different degrees. From the ideas of the representatives of such schools, we can see the intension of Physiocracy.

The idealistic economic morality ideology of Physiocrats represented the interests and requirements of small producers, and falls in the social ideal school. The idealistic economic morality ideology advocated that all people, including the king, should directly participate in productive labor to support themselves. Xu not only depicted the blueprint of an ideal society but also tried to turn his idea into reality. He organized dozens of disciples to establish an experimental commune like Utopia, in which he idealized the backward productivity and means of production and put it into practice. Xu's ideology reflects small farmers' love for labor and their wish of removing exploitation of the ruler and the capital evasion of merchants. However, unable to get rid of such oppression, they could only turn good and positive social ideals into fantasies.

There are many reasons for the formation of the idealistic economic morality ideology with Physiocratic characteristics. The primary reasons are wars, which are caused by annexation, heavy taxes imposed by states and commercial frauds. At that time, this made a great number of small farmers live in extreme misery, and simultaneously forced many impoverished slave owners into poverty, thus becoming small producers. For this reason, a small number of literate people, such as Xu, became the ideological representatives of small producers. This group of people developed an idealistic economic morality ideology featuring an ideal society with human equality, just transactions as well as anti-commercial exploitation and fraud. The representatives of Physiocracy mainly include Xu, Zhao Guo, Si Shengzhi and Zhao Xinchen.

Physiocracy formed and developed in a unique way. During the Warring States Period, it came into being through two sources. One is the thoughts of Shennong (Yan Emperor), which is strongly idealistic. The other is the thoughts of "agricultural officials," which is authentic and focuses on agricultural technology. However, during the development of Physiocracy, there were no internal divergences. After the Qin and Han Dynasties, Physiocracy specially focused on the study of agricultural production technology. During that period of time, famous agricultural works such as *Shennong*, *Hou Ji* and *Yelao* coexisted. The famous historian Ban Gu of the Eastern Han Dynasty once said, "Originated from the thoughts of agricultural officials, Physiocracy advocated that people should focus on agriculture to keep them warm and fed (Gu n.d.)." Ideologist Liuzi of the Northern and Southern Dynasties

tions herein. The paper has been included in Moral Capital and Business Ethics (*Selected Works of Wang Xiaoxi*), People's Publishing House, 2009.

also attributed Physiocracy as originating from the thoughts of agricultural thoughts. He wrote in *Liuzi·Nice Schools* that “books like *Nongzhe*, *Shennong*, *Yelao*, *Zaishi* and *Sisheng* discuss agricultural technology. With developed agriculture, a country, as well as each household will have grain reserves, and in this case, formality and morality will develop well.” During the process of social development, China has grown into an agricultural power, and this fact is related to the development of Physiocracy to some extent. The ideas and thoughts changed as the change of time and the requirements of the ruling class. The political opinions of Xu are essentially quite different from those of the feudal landlord class of different times. Feudal literati and officialdom looked down on agricultural production, thinking farming and gardening are done by petty men, and thereby did not concern people engaged in agricultural research. For this reason, outstanding representatives of Physiocracy could not be recorded in books, and their books could not be listed as classics. Thanks to a controversy between Xu and Mencius, the dialogue between them was recorded in *Mencius*, which enabled later generations to learn the ideas belonging to Xu. Regardless, Physiocracy still left us with a rich heritage. From the Han Dynasty, Physiocratic thoughts were concerned and absorbed by more and more schools, and rulers attached more importance to agricultural management and technology.

3.3.1 The Economic Morality Ideology of Xu Xing

Xu Xing (date of birth and death unknown) was born in the Chu State during the Warring States Period. He had dozens of disciples, thus his Physiocracy occupies a small school. In the Pre-Qin Period, various schools all claimed that their doctrines originated from the thoughts of previous sagacious kings to demonstrate that their existence is the will of Heaven. For example, Confucianism originated from the thoughts of Yao and Shun, Taoism from the Yellow Emperor, Mohism from Xia Yu. Similarly, Xu claimed that the doctrines of Physiocracy originated from the thoughts of Shennong. His ideas were mainly recorded in *Mencius·Duke Wen of Teng (I)*. Mencius once said that “Xupreached the thoughts of Shennong,” thus his ideology is called “Physiocracy.” During the Warring States Period, Physiocracy was a small school but also the most radical school. The economic morality ideology of Xu is mainly manifested in three aspects, namely, human equality, just transactions as well as anti-commercial exploitation and fraud, which stood for the interests of a great number of small farmers.

1. Human equality (the king and average people farm together to support themselves) means that in a society, everyone, including the king, should directly participate in productive labor to support himself. This opposed exploitation and denied hierarchy. According to Xu, in order to become sagacious, rulers should also participate in productive labor as farmers while governing the country; and a ruler who supports himself by exploiting farmers cannot be called a sage. Xu opposed exploitation. He held that the ruling class should not impose taxes on average people or build warehouses to store grain and property, or they are “exploiting average

people to support themselves." This idea reflects the thoughts of agricultural socialism and the ideology of the small farmer class in a certain historical context. From the thoughts of the small farmer class grew a kind of extreme equalitarianism which requires everyone to participate in productive labor, such as weaving mats, making straw sandals, and farming. Xu put such requirements into practice. He, in person, led his disciples to weave mats, make sandals, and farm. Xu's ideas, which call for equality and justice, were special but also idealistic at that time, and thereby were criticized by Confucians represented by Mencius (Zhao n.d.).

2. Equal transaction is also a main idea of Xu. Grain and part of handicrafts could essentially meet their needs. For tools needed for daily use that they could not produce, like iron farm tools and hats, they would obtain them through transactions. In the view of Xu, such transactions are mutually beneficial, for there exists no exploitation between farmers and handicraftsmen—they exchange on an equal basis and benefit from each other. Xu held that through an equal transaction, both parties involved in a transaction would obtain interests, thus increasing the productivity level; otherwise, agricultural production would be hindered.

3. The third main idea of Xu is anti-commercial exploitation and fraud. Xu and his disciples all hated vary much commercial exploitation and fraud at that time. His disciples said, "By following the ideas of Xu, food prices would be stable and there would be no fakes. Merchant would not cheat even children. Cloth of the same length, linen and silk of the same weight, grain of the same volume, and shoes of the same size would be sold at similar prices." That is to say, when the types, sizes and weights of goods are the same, their prices cannot be adjusted at will. Then, how to set prices? Who can supervise and punish violators? According to the disciples of Xu, if people understand the doctrines of Xu and put his doctrines into practice, they will, consciously, not cheat each other, and as a result, the county would become a moral country desired by everyone (Zhao n.d.).

3.3.2 The Economic Morality Ideology of Physiocrats Recorded in Lyu's Spring and Autumn Annals

The four articles of *The Promotion of Agriculture, Land Utilization, Study of Soil* and *Study of Seasons* in *Lyu's Spring and Autumn Annals* relatively and completely expound the economic morality ideology of Physiocracy. The political ideas of Xu Xing are quite different from those of the feudal landlord class of different times. Influenced by Confucianism that existed as the dominating ideology for a very long time, feudal literati and officialdom looked down on agricultural production, thinking farming and gardening are done by petty men. Due to this reason, Physiocrats and their works were always ignored. For example, Shennong (containing 20 articles) and Yelao (containing 17 articles), which were written in the Warring States Period, were lost in the early Tang Dynasty. Regardless, the thoughts of Physiocracy still deeply affected other schools, including Confucianism, Legalism, and the Yin-Yang School and were recorded in the works of such schools. For example, Xu

Xing's idea of "the king and farmers should farm together" was changed into the rite that "the king leads subjects to farm before the start of spring farming." What's more, "after Emperor Wen of Han adopted the suggestion of Jia Yi, the rite had been followed until the destruction of the Qing Dynasty" (Sihe 1981). Of course, after the Qing Dynasty, the ruling class were not concerned with agriculture for agricultural development, but to realize its political goals. As *Lyu's Spring and Autumn Annals·The Promotion of Agriculture* says, "Agriculture is not promoted for agricultural development, but political goals." It is clear that the ruling class considered agriculture for the political and economic interests of the emerging landlord class.

1. Farmers are tied to land for national stability. To make better use of the characteristics of the farmer to serve the ruling class, the ruling class took measures to tie farmers to land. There were the following three advantages: first, very simple, farmers were easily utilized in stabilizing the border and the regime of the ruler; second, having land as property, farmers were unwilling to migrate, and thus the social situation was stable; and third, less self-interested, farmers would abide by the law. On the contrary, if farmers left land and became merchants, there would be the following three disadvantages: first, some would disobey order, thus lowering the fighting ability of the army; second, as they did not have land as fixed assets, they would leave in the face of disaster; and third, being crafty, they would take advantage of the flaws of laws and regulations.

2. There are moral requirements of Physiocracy. First, to make people stick to agricultural production, Physiocrats restricted long-distance marriages with patriarchal institutions to prevent farmers from leaving the land. Second, they developed "five bans" to promote Physiocracy, namely, "farmers are banned from fertilizing frozen land; children are banned from gardening; weak people are banned from farming; farmers are banned from changing professions; and merchants are banned from changing professions." Moreover, "activities, such as lumbering, hunting and fishing were only allowed during certain periods. In busy seasons, construction and conscription were not allowed. Physiocrats also held that people should not wear fur hats so that they would not waste time when hunting, and marriages and sacrificial rites should be held in a frugal way. Third, Physiocrats held that farmers should work hard to create more wealth. They even proposed, "Farmers can only stop working when they are old, sick or dead." Moreover, "a good farmer can support nine (9) persons and a bad farmer can support five (5) persons." "If a farmer can support ten (10) persons and six (6) heads of livestock, then he really makes use of the land." They also forbade farmers to be hired to do work in other sectors. Fourth, they advocated that men should farm and women should weave to meet the needs of each other. According to Physiocrats, people above 1.58 m must work in agriculture, industry or commerce to "plant grain, make tools or sell goods." Moreover, cities are filled with merchants, so that they are unsuitable for farmers in the long-term.

The idealistic economic morality ideology can be concluded as follows:

First, the idealistic economic morality ideology of Physiocracy, though not comparable to dominating schools, such as Confucianism, Legalism, and Taoism, put forward special ideas regarding building an ideal society, especially an ideal agriculture-based society, creating precious ideological wealth for the ideological development of China. As fantastic as it may seem, the morality ideology of Physiocracy could not develop given the backward productivity and feudal autocracy. Therefore, it could not be widely accepted, and naturally, its doctrines and experiments were bound to fail.

Second, the morality ideology of Physiocracy, though only an ideal ideology, was advanced to some extent. It opposed autocracy, exploitation and inequality, objectively standing for the interests of small producers. A rational design for future social life, the morality ideology of Physiocracy, more or less, enlightened the development of other schools and the emergence and development of peasant movements. Its ideas like human equality and just transactions, which are considered as traditional concepts concerning the interest-morality relationship, are of profound historical significance.

Third, the morality ideology of Physiocracy, after all, was developed for the interests of small producers. As fantastic as it was about the future, it was not built on a profound understanding of the process of social development (which, limited by time and class, it is objectively impossible); it is only an expectation for an empirical formula of social life. Therefore, the absolute equalitarianism advocated by Physiocracy, even though it was advanced for its time, became a negative idea for social development in the end.

3.4 Economic Morality Ideology in Modern China: Transition of Modernity[277]

In the transitional period from Ming to Qing, with the emergence and development of the capitalist production relationship, traditional doctrines led by ethical economic morality ideology[278] were challenged. Particularly, after 1840, due to the evasion of foreign capitalism, China did not and could not realize the transformation from feudalism to capitalism. Under the control of foreign capitalism and imperialism, China's capitalism developed its unique understanding of the interest-morality relationship in the special economic and social context. Some bourgeois scholars accepted and spread Western bourgeois economic, political, moral, and social doctrines, among which, economic doctrines had the biggest influence. Due to this reason, the modern economic morality ideology of China contains a lot of Western elements. It is worth noting that some national bourgeois industrialists absorbed

[277] Originally titled as Economic Ethical Ideology in Modern China: Transition of Modernity, *Jiangsu Social Sciences*, Issue 6, 1996.The paper has been included in Moral Capital and Business Ethics (*Selected Works of Wang Xiaoxi*), People's Publishing House, 2009.

[278] In the history of China, influential economic morality ideologies include the ethical economic morality ideology, the utilitarianeconomic morality ideology, idealistic economic morality ideology and naturalistic economic morality ideology, among which, the most influential and long-lasting one is the ethical economic morality ideology.

Western economic and management thoughts from abroad and put them into practice, which is a unique embodiment of the modern economic morality ideology of China.

It can be said that in the semicolonial and semi-feudal society of modern China, capitalism experienced deformed development. In this special period, deeply influenced by traditional economic morality doctrines while simultaneously accepting Western economic morality doctrines, some bourgeois scholars and industrialists developed economic morality ideology reflecting two kinds of economic morality doctrines, the special social form of modern China, and their own understanding of the interest-morality relationship. Existing in a historical transition period, the economic morality ideology in modern China promoted economic development, and even in the continuously growing socialist market economy, it is still of important significance for enlightenment.

3.4.1 Morality-Interest Consistency

According to the ethical economic morality ideology, interests are subordinate to morality—interests can only be acquired in moral ways; otherwise, it is immoral. Therefore, essentially, the ethical economic morality ideology opposes the pursuance of interests, except for moral interests. In the interest-morality relationship, interests or the economy is/are the only element of morality. The utilitarian economic morality ideology, which stands at the opposite side of the ethical economic morality ideology, interprets the interest-morality relationship in another extreme way. Representatives like Wang Anshi and Li Gou held that "interests can turn into morality and vice versa"[279] and "to attract talents, money is needed; to manage money, morality is needed."[280] That is to say, to pursue interest is to pursue morality, and morality does not exist without interests. In the view of utilitarians, interests and morality are separated.

From the above, we can see that in the history of China, the relationship between interests and morality was never interpreted in a rational manner. In fact, in the feudal society, which lasted for over 2000 years, the idea that "morality prevails over interests" was always dominant.

In modern China, as the progress of social history and the influence of Western economic and moral thoughts, the interest-morality relationship was interpreted comprehensively and profoundly to some extent.

First, modern enlightenment ideologists clearly pointed out, "The pursuance of morality is for interests, and only interests can reflect morality."[281]

Li Gou pointed out, "The primary policy of benevolence is realizing equal land distribution to narrowing the gap between the rich and the poor."[282] In other words,

---

[279] *Continuation of History As A Mirror*, Vol. 219, 1st month, 4th year of Xining Period.

[280] *Collected Works of Wang Linchuan*, Vol. 70, the Department of Finance.

[281] *Criticism of The Four Books.*

[282] *Strategies for National Peace*, Vol. 2.

preventing the pursuance of interests is immoral. Of course, for enlightenment ideologists, "interests" mean "self-interest". Huang Zongxi held, "Man is born to be of self-interest"[283] and it is irrational that "one does not pursue self-interest". Therefore, any behavior infringing on private interests and property is "very immoral". We can see that enlightenment ideologists admitted man's self-interest and advocated private ownership. At that time, such ideas played an active role in arousing the awareness of the public, opposing feudal autocracy, and promoting social progress. In the socialist system, the interest-morality relationship is understood in an all-round and dialectical way. In a socialist society, people's awareness and realization of personal interests directly affects, or even directly reflects the realization of collective interests. Moreover, the satisfaction of the personal interests of everyone, in many cases, reflects the moral consciousness and quality of the whole society. This is an important ideological precondition for the development of the socialist market economy.

Second, deeply affected by Western utilitarian thoughts, modern bourgeois reformists, on the one side, stressed that "man cannot live without wealth; even God cannot save people from hunger without grain in hand" Chi (n.d.); and on the other side, pointed out that morality is needed to prevent people from conflicting interests—"competition for interests leads to conflicts, which then lead to turbulence; therefore, morality is needed to realize national peace. Interest and morality can exist together Chi (n.d.)." In the socialist market economy, objectively, interests are pursued, but the "interests" herein include both public interests and personal interests, which are, then, united in the socialist economic system. We must realize that the unity of public and personal interests require the reconciliation of morality. Only when interests are acquired, based on the socialist moral requirements, could the unity of the public and personal interests be realized. If vicious desire growth is allowed, then the socialist market economy will certainly lose its advantages, and development of the market economy will face deforms.

Some bourgeois scholars, absorbing both ancient Chinese ideologies and Western ideologies, put forward the ideas of "morality means meeting current human needs" and "morality guides the pursuance of interests." Kang Youwei held, "Morality means meeting current human needs." He said, "Since national conditions have changed, the way to govern the country also needs to be changed. Generally, the society will transfer from a fairly well-off society to a society in great harmony." "Morality prevails over interests, but interests can change morality." He also said, "Morality means meeting current human needs." "Formality and morality change as the change of times. Today's new formality and morality, though never mentioned by the sages in the past, meet current human needs. In the past, people's basic needs were only related to food, clothing, houses and instruments, and sages were concerned with developing formality and morality. However, with social development, mats have been replaced by tables, and doudengs (ancient wooden containers) have been replaced by ceramic plates. Mats and doudengs, which had become a part of civilization due to their long history, have also been abandoned. Likewise, fire has

[283] *Waiting for the Dawn·How to be a Ruler.*

been replaced by electricity, and manpower has been replaced by machines. As long as changes are practical, they are moral. Some people stick to the past, thinking it's moral; but actually, they are blocking the way of development, which is against the morality meant by sages."[284] Kang Youwei discussed the interest-morality relationship profoundly. He interpreted "morality" as "meeting current human needs." It opposes the Confucian idea of "morality prevails over interests" and differs from the utilitarian idea of "morality is interests." The idea of "morality guides the pursuance of interests" is the interpretation of the interest-morality relationship made by Tan Sitong from another perspective. It not only improves the economic morality ideology in modern China but also reveals morality's functions of reconciliation and guidance. Kang Youwei held that all things coexist because of the existence of benevolence. All things, only when being connected by benevolence, can exist rationally and then develop. He explained that the principal element of communication is benevolence, which, in essence, is the foundation of communication. "Communication determines the existence of benevolence, while benevolence lays the foundation of communication."[285] From the modern perspective, Tan's idea means to develop the socialist market economy, it needs to establish correct socialist moral concepts and value orientation, and at the same time, develop a noble moral standard to judge what should and should not be done. Only in this way can the socialist market economy develop orderly and quickly.

Third, the modern bourgeois reformist ideologist Liang Qichao studied the interest-morality relationship on a deeper level. He held that there are two kinds of power for interest creation: "one is physical power, and the other is psychological power; the latter falls into intelligence and morality." Liang clearly pointed out that the productive process and productive interests are determined by human intelligence and morality. It is valuable that Liang understood morality, which was always considered as the value orientation and the standard to judge good and evil during the process of interest creation as an important means and a support for the pursuance of interests. In the process of continuous socialist economic development, if we lose morality, we lose the correct view of the world, of life and of value. As a result, the market economy will be disorderly with fraudulence and speculation here and there. An invisible hand of evil will push the socialist market economy to the edge of corruption. Therefore, putting aside the limited thoughts caused by time and class, we will see that his understanding on "interest"-"intelligence"-"morality" is still of important enlightenment and practical significance in the socialist market economy.

3.4.2 Economic Development for Public Interests

In China's feudal society, which lasted for over 2000 years, Confucian moral doctrines were followed in both ideology and social practices. Confucian moral doc-

[284] Collected Works of Kang Nanhai, Vol. 8, p. 17.

[285] *Complete Works of Tan Sitong*, Vol. 1, p. 45.

trines advocate "morality" which protects the interests of feudal patriarchal system and hierarchy and opposes the pursuance of "human desire." Those who protect the interests of the feudal social system are sages and gentlemen; while those who pursue self-interest are immoral. It can be said that in the feudal society, hypocritical "suprematism" unified the ways of thinking and the ways of man, thus the whole society was "cast into" the same mode of existence. The end of economic development is to improve people's standard of living; however, in the feudal society, morality was the end of economic development, and the economy was the means of morality. With the emergence of the capitalist production relationship, the transition of modern society, and the collision of Eastern and Western economic morality ideologies, enlightenment ideologists started to criticize feudal ethics earlier than modern ideologists. They made the concept of "man" abstract and set it free from the shackles of the feudal-patriarchal relationship and moral doctrines, trying to give "man" a proper social position. Li Gou of the Taizhou School thought that everyone is of self-interest, and man acts to pursue self-interest. He said, "Man is born to be of self-interest. To pursue self-interest, man will act; otherwise, man is not motivated to act. Farmers, pursuing the harvest in autumn, will work hard in the fields; homemakers, pursuing the accumulation of wealth, will spare no efforts to manage households; intellectuals, pursuing academic degrees, will strive to study hard; and officials, pursuing money for promotion, follow the orders of the king. Confucius was a sage, but without his high position, he certainly would not have stayed in the State of Lu for even one day. Therefore, the pursuance of interest is a human nature, that's not an assumption. Hearsay about one that is not of self-interest is just fictional and cannot be trusted."[286] Huang Zongxi of the Yan-Li School also though that "man is born to be of self-interest."[287] Moreover, enlightenment ideologists pointed out that it is rational that man is of self-interest, and pursuing interests and avoiding losses is a human nature. Li Zhi said, "It's natural and wise that everyone pursues interests and avoids losses."[288] "Wealth and power are necessary for heroes and sages to make great achievements."[289] In the late period of the feudal society of China, it required considerable courage and insight to put forward such ideas. Although such ideas are essentially the products of a certain age reflecting the ideological trends of the age, objectively, they provided a theoretical precondition for the development of capitalism and the emancipation of human nature, which is a requirement of capitalist development. However, facing stubborn feudal autocracy and ingrained feudal ideologies, such ideas cannot turn into reality without completely overturning feudal autocracy. Regardless, as anti-traditional theories called for the emancipation of human nature, such ideas provided a basis for the fundamental transition of the economic morality ideology.

Kang Youwei stressed the rationality of man's material desires. He said, "Man is born with seven emotions, namely, joy, anger, sorrow, fear, love, hate, and desire,

[286] *A Collection of Books·Morality and Confucius Subjects (II).*

[287] *Waiting for the Dawn·How to be a Ruler.*

[288] *Book Burning·A Reply to Dengming Government.*

[289] *Collected Works of Li·Wisdom from the Past (I).*

which thus should be followed."[290] In addition, "among various kinds of human desire, food and sex are desired the most, for they are basic human needs; among various dislikes of man, death and poverty are hated the most, for they mean the suffering of the body."[291] Ya Fu, in his study of taxation, directly pointed out that the purpose of economic development is to benefit the public. He held that tax should be levied according to people's ability and should be used on people last. He said, "Tax is not levied to meet private needs, but to benefit the public; therefore, the amount of tax is determined by the needs of the public. If no tax is levied, a country will lose the power to run, and people will suffer. However, tax must be levied according to the ability of people—if people are economically unable, even a small amount of tax will be a burden for them."[292]

The great revolutionary leader Sun Yat-sen interpreted the idea of economic development for public interests in his San-min Doctrine (doctrines regarding nationalism, democracy, and people's livelihood). He pointed out, "Humans, though enjoying and suffering differently in society, all need to make a living. Therefore, man's behavior is limited by livelihood. With a good livelihood, man lives a good life; otherwise, man can hardly live."[293] Therefore, the livelihood of the public is the end and center of all economic activities. "Since the dawn of time, human beings have struggled to make a living."[294] In fact, "livelihood is the center of politics, of the economy, and of all historical activities; it's the center of all." [295]Sun Yat-sen put forward the economic proposition of "equalization of land ownership." In fact, he stressed the equalization of economic rights and opposed the exploitation upon average people. He pointed out, "Farmers account for the majority of the population of China"; "however, most of the grain they obtain with hard work is grabbed by landlords, and they could hardly support themselves with the remains. It's very unfair."[296] He came up with the idea of "restraining private capital" in order to suppress monopolies at the cost of public interests, and preventing the minority from manipulating the livelihood of the majority. In his view, if private capital is restrained, more capital can be used as public capital to prosper the public and the country. He said, "In a socialist country, public ownership means state ownership. Since the country belongs to its people, public ownership equals state ownership. The government uses public capital to create interests for the public."[297]

The economic morality idea of economic development for public interests held by enlightenment ideologists and Sun Yat-sen played a very important role in enlightening the public and arousing their awareness of overturning the monarchy. However, limited by social history and class, these new ideas could not turn into a

[290] *Collected Works of Kang Nanhai*, Vol. 8, p. 8.

[291] *Collected Works of Kang Nanhai*, Vol. 8, p. 10.

[292] *The Wealth of Nations*(IX), p. 19 (note).

[293] *Complete Works of Sun Yat-sen*, Vol. 2, Zhonghua Book Company, 1982, p. 510.

[294] *Selected Works of Sun Yat-sen*, Vol. II, People's Publishing House, 1956, p. 779.

[295] *Selected Works of Sun Yat-sen*, Vol. II, People's Publishing House, 1956, p. 787.

[296] *Selected Works of Sun Yat-sen*, Vol. II, People's Publishing House, 1956, p. 810.

[297] *Selected Works of Sun Yat-sen*, Vol. II, People's Publishing House, 1982, p. 521.

social reality. Regardless, they are still of important enlightenment significance for the development of the socialist market economy. The socialist market economy, according to its basic economic characteristics, is still a competitive economy. All in all, since the socialist system admits and protects the legitimate interests and pursuits of each person, the purpose of competition is to better satisfy people's interests while simultaneously promoting economic development. In fact, the management mechanisms and growth of the socialist market economy largely depends on the realization of man's self-interest. Therefore, the realization of everyone's interests is the primary goal of the development of the socialist market economy. In the socialist market economy, all economic activities are conducted for public interests and for collective interests, which reflect and protect public interests. Without such preconditions, all economic activities will be powerless. After the economic reform launched in 1979, central government leaders like Deng Xiaoping stressed repeatedly that people must benefit from economic development. This means that satisfying public interests is always the primary goal of economic development. Since the economic reform, Chinese people have been actively engaging in the development of the socialist market economy. The reason is that national economic development is closely connected to public interests, and from practice, people have realized that the improvement of productivity, the enhancement of comprehensive national strength and the increase of living standards are a dialectical unity. Therefore, always taking the satisfying of public interests as the primary goal of economic development is the basic principle of the socialist economic morality ideology as well as the power source for the development of the socialist market economy.

3.4.3 The Equality of Rights is a Prerequisite of Economic Development

The inequality of rights is a basic characteristic of patriarchal and hierarchical systems in the feudal society of China. In the feudal society of China, which lasted for over 2000 years, the productivity level was low and economic growth was very slow. One of the main reasons is the inequality of rights in social life. Li Gou, who was known as a fighter of anti-feudalism, profoundly analyzed the social problems hindering the economic development of the feudal society. He stressed that real human equality is the precondition of economic development, and of free human personality development, which enables people to consummate their talents as they desire. In fact, Li Zhi tried to find the theoretical basis for the development of capitalism, which was blossoming. Modern bourgeois scholars, based on the thoughts of Li Zhi, systematically interpreted the relationship between equal rights and economic development.

On the one hand, some scholars claimed that to realize the equality of rights, it is necessary to realize the private ownership of land, thus promoting the growth of wealth. Liang Qichao pointed out, "Human egoism drives economic development. Human desire is the reason for human economic behavior, and the economic desire of man is about possessing and controlling wealth."[298] "Therefore, economic behavior is conducted on the basis of property ownership. To acquire or enhance ownership, man will follow economic norms. In this way, naturally, national wealth is increased, and this is the result of egoism. Therefore, the private economy is closely related to the national economy."[299] In the view of Liang Qichao, the private ownership of land is the prerequisite to realize the equality of rights, and the desire for self-interest stimulates people to conduct economic activities. Of course, Liang understood the interest-morality relationship from the bourgeois perspective, but he denied feudal autocracy. He said that if man loses his rights, he cannot act freely, cannot control material social wealth, and cannot realize his desires, which means man will live in a passive state. In today's socialist market economy of China, the problem of ownership has been solved fundamentally, and people are the owners of social material wealth. However, there is still a problem. In the socialist market economy, different economic forms exist together, which lead to the coexistence of national ownership, collective ownership, and private ownership. How to optimize the relations among them is the problem. If the relations cannot be handled well, the management mechanism of the socialist market economy will be affected fundamentally. Therefore, the socialist market economy, which contains the equality of human rights and socialist morality, should be valued by the world.

On the other hand, as Sun Yat-sen stresses in his San-min Doctrine, equal rights determine the realization of democracy, which determines economic development. In the view of Sun Yat-sen, the realization of democracy means that average people become the owners of a country and that officials are servants. He said, "In a democratic country, average people are owners and officials are servants… Upon the foundation of the Republic of China, average people will become owners and the emperor will become a servant… Everyone knows that the Republic of China does not have an emperor. Then, who can become the emperor? In the past, only one person can become the emperor, but now, all 400 million people are emperors." "Only when 400 million people are equal in rights and obligations and in wealth distribution will real human equality be realized,"[300] arousing people's enthusiasm in revolution and production. In particular, Sun pointed out that an important content of the equality of rights is fair distribution, which can effectively arouse the enthusiasm of the people. Sun thought, "Farmers account for the majority of the population of China"; "however, most of the grain they obtain from hard work is seized by landlords, and they could hardly support themselves with what remains. It's very unfair."[301] He also said, "According to Adam Smith, when profits are evenly shared by the local government, capitalists and workers, it conforms to the distribution theory in economics. In my view, all profits are created by workers, but the local government and capitalists reap two thirds of the total and the workers, who are large in number, divide only one third of the total. Compared with capitalists, the income

[298] *Collected Works of Liang Qichao*, Vol. 32, p. 24.

[299] *Collected Works of Liang Qichao*, Vol. 32, p. 25.

[300] *Complete Works of the Prime Minister*, Vol. 1, p. 319.

[301] *Complete Works of Sun Yat-sen*, Vol. 2, Zhonghua Book Company, 1982, p. 510.

of each worker is so meager. In this way, the gap between the rich and the poor will be wider and wider, and the interests of average people are seized by capitalists." Sun held that unfair distribution means exploitation and inequality, and means that "democracy" cannot be realized and economic development is powerless.[302] Therefore, he put forward some measures. First, "all farmers should have land." "If all grain belongs to farmers themselves, they will certainly be willing to farm, and then more grain will be produced."Second, "land and capital belong to the public. For the distribution of interests, workers obtain their due interests as the return of labor; while the interests arising from land and capital shall be used for pubic interests. Capital cannot be monopolized to seize the interests of average people. This is the theory of interest distribution in the socialist economy, and in this way, the problem of interest distribution can be fundamentally solved."[303]

Sun Yat-sen's ideas of the equality of rights, including human equality and fair distribution, and his practical interpretation of the relationship between the equality of rights and economic development are still of important significance of reference for the development of the socialist market economy. In today's society, bureaucracy and corruption are still weakening the legitimate rights of people to different degrees; therefore, it is necessary to stress the equality of rights, and to stress that officials are the servants of people and people are the real owners of the society. In addition, it is necessary to strengthen the constraint and supervision over officials while realizing the real equality between officials and civilians. Otherwise, the socialist market economy will lose its support, and the public will lose their hope for the development of the socialist market economy. Unfair distribution has always been a concern of the public. Currently, unfair distribution still exists, and it is caused by many factors, such as history, institutions, concepts and the contradiction in distribution. Whether the whole society will attach importance to the issue and gradually solve it is the key for the success of the development of the socialist market economy. Ignoring this problem is the regret and the sin of history.

3.5 The Combination of Management and Morality

The self-sufficient natural economy and patriarchal and hierarchical systems of the feudal society of China determined that traditional management ideologies were developed from a macro perspective. Therefore, ideas and methods concerning self-cultivation, collective management, national administration, and world peace were put forward in a systematic but general way. Generally, economic management ideologies are contained in such management ideologies. Due to the absolute domination of agriculture and the underdevelopment of industry, independent economic management ideology never formed. However, it is worth noting that since the feudal society, feudal morality was the starting point and end of all, and

[302] *Complete Works of Sun Yat-sen*, Vol. 2, Zhonghua Book Company, 1982, p. 512.

[303] *Complete Works of Sun Yat-sen*, Vol. 2, Zhonghua Book Company, 1982, p. 515.

naturally, the economy and management were closely connected with morality. In particular, the management methods and principles in management ideologies were put forward from the perspective of morality. We must see that the combination of management and morality in the feudal society is a requirement of feudal autocracy; therefore, in some sense, morality mandated participation in social management as an instrument.

With the emergence and development of the national capitalist industry in modern China, modern ideologists and industrialists (while absorbing the scientific Western economic (corporate) management ideologies) also absorbed excellent traditional morals, which acted as management means in ancient China. In this way, the combination of management and morality was realized theoretically and practically.

First, human moral quality in economic (corporate) management is improved. The modern national capitalism representative Zhang Jian was a representative valuing the functions of man in corporate activities. In the view of Zhang, man is a moral man whose enthusiasm thus can be aroused by spiritual motivation Zhao (1993). This idea still works in today's corporate management. It has been clearly pointed out in modern economic (corporate) management theories that employees cannot be considered as mechanical money-making economic men, but moral men. Only with correct value orientations and noble moral consciousness could they devote themselves to corporate development.

Second, intangible corporate asset is expanded through integrity-based management. Zhang Jian held that the transactions between a company and consumers as well as between companies should be conducted based on "openness, fairness, and integrity Zhao (1993)," thus expanding the business scale. Gu Gengyu, the "King of Bristles," once said, "The absolute predominance of a company is built based on high product quality… In some sense, we rely on them (consumers) for a living. When we lose one consumer, we lose some profits; and when we lose a large proportion of consumers, we go bankrupt. We must fully realize the importance of integrity-based management (China Enterprise Association Ancient Management Concepts Research Society 1998)."

Third, the priority of economic (corporate) management is the management of man, the priority of which is winning the respect and loyalty of employees. Some modern entrepreneurs, influenced by Western management ideologies and traditional Chinese management thoughts, put morality-oriented management into practice. Industrialist Lu Zuofu, founder of Minsheng Industry Limited, was concerned very much with the interests of employees. He thought if he cared for his employees in their work and family, he could win the support of his employees, and the company thus would be promising. Industrialist Fan Xudong advocated virtuous leadership. One of his employees once said, "Mr. Fan faces much more difficulties than me, but he always helps me with complete sincerity. I will never forget his kindness. All I can do is trying my best to solve technical problems in return (Zhao 1993)." National industrialist Rong Desheng also advocated "morality-based management instead of regulation-based management." Through morality-based management, he aroused the enthusiasm of employees, which led to substantial profit growth.

It follows that compared with regulations and material motivations, spiritual motivation and moral leadership are more effective in corporate management.

The labor relations in the companies in modern China are essentially different from the relations between employers and employees. It had been determined by the socialist system that interpersonal relationships of a company should be democratic and equal, and employers should focus on arousing the enthusiasm of employees. Only in this way, the substantive characteristics of socialist companies can be embodied, and the vitality of companies can be increasingly enhanced. In a modern company, if the business owner only focuses on pursuing interests without caring for employees, the company will certainly fail in the end.

References

Chi, C. (n.d.). Technology of gold metallurgy. *Continuation of the Economy, 3*, 7.
China Enterprise Association Ancient Management Concepts Research Society. (1998). *New exploration of traditional Chinese management concepts* (p. 354). Enterprise Management Publishing House.
Gu, B. (n.d.). *History of the han dynasty·art and literature.*
Jichuang, H. (1981a). *A brief history of Chinese economic thoughts* (p. 43). China Social Sciences Publishing House.
Jichuang, H. (1981b). *A history of Chinese economic thoughts* (II) (pp. 384–385). Shanghai Renmin's Publishing House.
Sihe, Q. (1981). *A study of the history of China* (pp. 190–192). Zhonghua Book Company.
Zhao, J. (Ed.). (1993). *Intellectual history of China's economic management* (pp. 513–514, 540). Beijing University Press.
Zhao, J. (Ed.). (n.d.). *The general history of Chinese economic ideology* (Vol. 1, pp. 154–155).

Chapter 4
The Roles Played by Moral Capital in Business Operations

4.1 In What Sense Could Morality Become Spiritual Productivity?[1]

Marx's clear interpretation of "spiritual productivity" helps us realize the roles played by scientific morality as a kind of spiritual productivity in the development of social productivity, and at the same time, guides us to develop the socialist market economy.

4.1.1 Interpretation of Marx's Spiritual Productivity

According to Marxist historical materialism, "Productivity always means useful and specific labor productivity,"[2] productivity "comprises material and spiritual productivity." In the *Economic Manuscript of 1857–1858,* Marx wrote, "It is revealed by the simple definition of money that money, as a developed factor of production, can only co-exist with wage labor, where, money will not disintegrate the social form; instead, it becomes a condition of social form development and the driver of all productivity, namely, material and spiritual productivity." That is to say, spiritual productivity holds an important position among all kinds of productivity.

If we ignore or deny the existence of spiritual productivity, material productivity will be incomprehensible. The reason is "nature builds no machines, no locomotives, railways, electric telegraphs, self-acting mules, etc. These are products of human industry; natural material transformed into organs of the human will over nature, or of human participation in nature. They are organs of the human brain, created by the human hand; the power of knowledge, objectified. The development of fixed capital indicates to what degree general social knowledge has become a

[1] Originally titled as Morality and Spiritual Productivity*Jiangsu Social Sciences,* Issue 2, 2001 and *Ethics*, Issue 3, 2002. The paper has been included in Moral Capital and Business Ethics (*Selected Works of Wang Xiaoxi*), People's Publishing House, 2009.

[2] *Collected Works of Karl Marx and Friedrich Engels*, Vol. 23, People's Publishing House, 1972, p. 59.

X. Wang, *On Moral Capital,* DOI 10.1007/978-3-662-45544-9_4

direct force of production, and to what degree, hence, the conditions of the process of social life itself have come under the control of the general intellect and have been transformed in accordance with it. To what degree the powers of social production have been produced, not only in the form of knowledge, but also as immediate organs of social practice, of the real life process." In fact, material productivity exists based on the existence of spiritual productivity. "Without human beings as a 'subjective productive force' and the conceptual orientation thereof, productive forces will be 'dead productivity' rather than 'living social productive forces Wang (1998).'" As Marx said, "Human beings, as a productive force, are also natural objects, which are alive with awareness, and labor itself is the presentation of productive forces."[3] That is, without the penetration of spiritual elements, material productivity cannot become social labor productivity, but only materials. Therefore, departing from man and human spirit (consciousness), the means of labor and the subject of labor cannot participate in production, and thus cannot become factors of production.

The concept of spiritual productivity was put forward by Marx relative to the concept of material productivity. Therefore, spiritual productivity means "general productivity." It is a kind of science comprising knowledge, skills, and social wisdom.[4] Marx stressed repeatedly that science is also a productive force. He said, "The reproduction of constant capital takes fixed capital, raw materials and science forces as the premises. In this case, 'science forces' mean not only science forces themselves, but also the science forces which have been realized in productivity."[5]

Of course, general productivity or spiritual productivity as scientific forces will form or appear only after combining with material productivity. Therefore, in the theories of Marx, material productivity and spiritual productivity are supplementary and dialectically united.

4.1.2 Morality is a Kind of Spiritual Productivity

Since spiritual productivity means the scientific elements or scientific forces in productivity, morality is naturally a kind of spiritual productivity.

Sciences and scientific forces as spiritual productivity or general productivity, shall, naturally, include natural sciences and social sciences. When interpreting the concept of productive forces, Marx focused on the functions and positions of natural sciences in productivity, but he did not exclude social sciences in productivity.

---

[3] *Collected Works of Karl Marx and Friedrich Engels*, Vol. 23, People's Publishing House, 1972, pp. 228–229.

[4] *Collected Works of Karl Marx and Friedrich Engels*, Vol. 46 (II), p. 201, Vol. 26 (I), People's Publishing House, 1972, p. 422.

[5] *Collected Works of Karl Marx and Friedrich Engels*, Vol. 46 (II), People's Publishing House, 1972, p. 285.

He pointed out, “The development of productive forces, after all, originates from the social nature of labor in action, from the internal division of labor in society, and from the development of intellectual labor, especially natural sciences.”[6] In the view of Marx, intellectual labor, certainly, means more than natural sciences, or there is no need to stress “especially natural sciences.” In *Capital,* Marx pointed out clearly that “in any *one* line of production (e.g. in the production of iron, coal, machinery; in architecture; etc.), may again be partly connected with progress in the field of intellectual production, notably natural science and its practical application…”[7] Deng Xiaoping developed the theories of productive forces of Marx. He came up with the idea that “technology is the primary productive force” and pointed out clearly that sciences, of course, include social sciences. He even particularly stressed, “Marxism is a science.”

Natural and social sciences have their special economic and social values, respectively. Without the development of social sciences, it is hard for us to find out the purposes and significance of studying natural sciences. If we do not understand our existence and the significance thereof, it is impossible for us to develop noble value orientations and the spirit of struggle, and naturally, the development of natural sciences will be powerless.

In the field of social sciences, morality or moral science has its unique roles and functions. Ancient philosophers have already expounded the idea of “in social science, moral science is a core science and a purposeful science.” China has an intellectual history of more than 2000 years, during which, morality was obviously a main topic of study. Cai Yuanpei once said that the field of ethics, which studies moral science, is “the only developed science in China” with an “extremely wide scope of research.” He said, “In China, Confucianism is the dominant ethical ideology, and social sciences included in Confucianism are studied in the scope of ethics. Philosophical psychology was closely related to ethics and was considered as a premise of ethics. Ideas like governing by morality and governing by filial piety fall into the scope of political ethics; like filial piety, brotherhood, royalty, and integrity are more powerful than weapons, which fall into the scope of military ethics; like cracking down on paganism, which falls into the scope of religious ethics; and like criticizing ancient articles and poems, which falls into the scope of literary ethics. The ethics of China covers a very wide rang Yuanpei (1996).” Cai Yuanpei told us that in the history of social sciences in ancient China, morality or moral science was always important.

Nowadays, morality or moral science is still a core and fundamental discipline of social sciences. The main reasons are, first, all social sciences take man and human society as the subjects of study, but morality or moral science studies the improvement and reconciliation of interpersonal relationship, which is the premise

---

[6] *Collected Works of Karl Marx and Friedrich Engels*, Vol. 25, People's Publishing House, 1972, p. 97.

[7] *Collected Works of Karl Marx and Friedrich Engels*, Vol. 25, People's Publishing House, 1972, p. 97.

for the normal existence and development of human society; while other social sciences only study a certain field or aspect of phenomena concerning man and human society. Second, morality or moral science is a theoretical discipline and an application discipline. It means that separated from social practice, morality or moral science tends to become preachment, and therefore, it is a typical and practical theoretical discipline. Third, morality or moral science is a "key" to open the door of other social sciences. Man and interpersonal relationships stand at the top of all subjects studied by social sciences; therefore, morality or moral science, which studies man and interpersonal relationships, is a basic theoretical discipline of other social sciences, and even the guiding discipline for the development of some social sciences.

From the above, we can see that spiritual productivity is general productivity as sciences, general productivity includes natural sciences and social sciences, and social sciences include morality or moral science; therefore, morality is a kind of spiritual productivity, and in a broad sense, morality is a productive force.

4.1.3 How Does Morality, as a Kind of Spiritual Productivity, Turn into Social Labor Productivity?

In the process of turning into social labor productivity, morality shows its unique functions and ways of embodiment.

Morality, as a kind of ideology, cannot directly penetrate the factors of production to play a part in most cases. However, it can affect laborers, determining their attitude toward labor and their ability to turn "dead productivity" into social labor productivity. Moreover, morality affects the way of existence of productive relations, thus affecting how the factors of production connect internally and the degree of their internal connection.

As I mentioned before, material productivity exists based on the existence of spiritual productivity. However, during the process of turning "dead productivity" into social labor productivity, morality, as a kind of spiritual productivity and an ideology, plays a unique role that cannot be played by other social ideologies.

First, morality as an ideology is the embodiment of objective rules concerning human perfection and the harmony of interpersonal relationships. Through academic analyses on social phenomena, especially social moral phenomena, morality shows people the "should be," which is free from the effect or interference of any subject or objective factor in social life. Meanwhile, morality demonstrates the relationship between the "should-be" morals and the improvement of the quality of life as well as between the "should-be" morals and social progress, showing people how to exist rationally in society and how to realize their rational existence. This is a premise for the agent to participate in production and for man and materials to fully play their roles in the increment of value. A man without morality serving as his soul will not try his best to activate dead productivity, let alone develop productivity.

Second, morality as an ideology is the science of value. It reveals the rational development trends of man, as well as the perfect development direction of society. If laborers, as the primary factor of production, can accept and grasp morality as an ideology, they will adapt to the requirements of social development, and develop a noble value orientation. In this way, man will certainly participate in production enthusiastically, fully play his roles, and actively develop and update tools and machines. On the contrary, with a low moral quality, people can only see short-term interest and self-interest, rather than long-term but bigger interests, such as the updating of fixed assets. Put it another way, the development of the means of production, which typically symbolize the level of productivity, relies on the development of human spirit, especially the spirit of focusing on productivity development out of the responsibility for the nation and society.

Third, morality as an ideology partly forms the superstructure. Although morality plays indirect roles in productivity development, sometimes, such roles are decisive. Mao Zedong once said, "It's true that productive forces, practice and economic foundation are generally decisive factors—it's admitted by every physicist. However, productive relations, theories and superstructures, in some cases, are also decisive factors, which must be admitted as well Zedong (1991)." It seems that the latter decisive factors cannot be considered as spiritual factors of production, but this is not true. The reason is that politics, law, religion, art, and philosophy as ideologies always, in different forms and to different degrees, influence the thoughts and ideas of laborers, thus influencing their lifestyles and attitude toward life. In addition, morality as an ideology, being a collection of theories indoctrinating people how to live a rational life, directly influences laborers' understanding of themselves and their attitude toward life as the primary factor of production.

Fourth, "in production, man is closely connected with both productive forces and also productive relations; and acts as both a factor of production and a factor of productive relations. Therefore, arousing the enthusiasm of laborers is of great significance for the development of productivity. To arouse the enthusiasm of laborers, it is crucial to solve interpersonal conflicts and to correctly handle the relationship between man's position in production and his material interests Guifang (1988)." To solve interpersonal conflicts and to correctly handle the relationship between man's position in production and his material interests, it is crucial to correctly understand the "should-be" morals.

In fact, the development of productivity itself depends on the rational connection and existence of the internal factors of productivity, namely, the rational combination between laborers and the instruments of labor as well as between laborers and the subject of labor. Only in this way productivity will develop normally. If the laborers become an appendant of the instruments of labor or if the instruments of labor and productive resources do not belong to laborers, the relationship there between is passive and irrational, which will seriously affect the existence and development of productivity. To realize the rational connection and existence of the internal factors of productivity, productive relations meeting the moral, and rational requirements of laborers need to be built, and the moral consciousness and quality of laborers need to be improved. People without moral consciousness can hardly understand and deal with the relationships between themselves and other factors of production. In fact, in the final analysis, how man and materials combine is, in some sense, how man exists and connects with others. In conclusion, laborers' understanding of morality as an ideology directly affects or restricts the development of productivity.

Therefore, morality as an ideology cannot exist or function without the "brain" of man. It exists and develops along with productivity in a special way.

Morality, as a character of man, will directly turn into productivity as long as man participates in production and plays his roles. Without the participation of man as "subject productivity," "dead productivity" cannot become social labor productivity. Without morality, man, as the primary factor of production, will stay passively in production, and be powerless and aimless when activating the energy of the means of labor and the subject of labor. In other words, "dead productivity" cannot be activated to the hilt.

First, to judge the development of productivity, the main marks are material, but human quality, especially moral quality is the decisive factor. "If man cannot exist as a real or perfect man, or if man exists as a passive or even reactionary 'existent', no matter how advanced the technical equipment is and how abundant the material resources are, his productivity can never be enhanced Wang (2000)." Therefore, "Only by fully realizing his existence and the significance thereof as well as clarifying a noble value orientation of existence could man build the spirit of constant self-motivation and create the core and basic conditions for productivity development Wang (2000)." That is to say, man's moral quality directly restricts the development of productivity.

Second, the level of productivity is not only measured by the factors of production themselves in a static way but also the functioning and results of the factors of production in a dynamic way. The latter requires the participation of man for other factors of production can only become productive with the participation of man. The functioning of laborers themselves, the instruments of labor and the subject of labor are closely related to the character of laborers—their responsibility for others and society. When the responsibility of laborers is strong, the functions of the instrument of labor and the subject of labor can be maximized. For example, when producing a product of labor, if the laborer devotes himself to production, then product quality is guaranteed, consumption is minimized and the socially necessary labor time is objectively shortened, which lowers product costs. Therefore, we can say that man's moral quality can directly create wealth, and morality is an important factor of productivity.

Third, laborers as a factor of production are a group of people; therefore, all behavior of labor is a group behavior. The development of productivity largely depends on the reconciliation and cooperation among laborers, and morality is the most important means and theoretical basis for the reconciliation and cooperation among laborers. In today's world, inter-laborer relationships, especially interest relationships, shall be reconciled based on the principles of justice and the unity of interests, which is the only way to maximize the enthusiasm of laborers. If the enthusiasm of laborers is destroyed, productivity itself will be affected first. Therefore, moral education, moral reconciliation, and moral development are necessary for the development of productivity.

4.1.4 Morality is the Premise to Discuss the Proposition of Spiritual Productivity

Probing into the proposition that moral is a kind of spiritual productivity or a kind productivity will surely broaden man's theoretical vision in the study of ethics, especially economic ethics, and at the same time, promote the fundamental theoretical research and practical application of ethics. To understand fully and discuss profoundly the proposition of "morality is a kind of productivity," and to maximize the functions of morality as a factor of production in economic development, it is necessary to discuss the proposition from the following perspectives:

First, the proposition that moral is a kind of spiritual productivity or a kind of productivity only means that morality, as an important part or factor of productivity, plays unique spiritual roles in the development of productivity. As mentioned before, relative to other factors of production, morality plays different roles in the development of productivity. The proposition by no means implies that morality is a kind of independent productivity; otherwise, we will become dualists or will violate Marx's basic philosophic view of "matter is primary and consciousness is secondary."

Second, in the proposition that moral is a kind of spiritual productivity or a kind of productivity, morality or moral science can be understood in two ways. First, morality or moral science means scientific morality, which not only correctly reflects the rules of moral life but also meets the requirements of social development. Second, morality or moral science changes with the change of times—it reflects or meets the requirements of social development of a certain period. Morals not required by times and corruptive morals cannot become the spiritual intension or factor of productivity; in fact, they will certainly hinder the development of productivity.

Third, morality is a kind of productivity means that morality plays its special roles in the development of productivity and acts as a kind of social labor productivity in the process of acting on material productivity. In this way, we can also consider guidelines, policies, politics, law, and even philosophy as the intension or factors of productivity. Of course, such intension or factors must be scientific theories or ideas, and must act on material productivity.

It needs to be stressed that although spiritual productivity manifests in different ways, unlike other kinds of spiritual productivity, morality, "especially socialist morality, as a rational rule or rational spirit, should penetrate into guidelines, policies, politics and law; otherwise, guidelines, policies, politics, and law will be unimaginable, or even backwards and passive Wang (1998)."

Fourth, "morality is the key to everything" is different from "the functions of morality are omnipresent." The former irrationally exaggerates the functions of morality, as if morality plays the decisive roles in the development of all sectors of society. Ultimately, it is possible that it may fall into the fallacy of psychic determinism. The latter means where there is man or interpersonal relationships, morality can play its role to different degrees. The full use of the functions of morality will help realize the better and faster development of all sectors of the society. The two essential or fundamental purposes of morality are realizing human perfection and building harmonious interpersonal relationships. As the two goals are realized gradually, society will gradually develop better and faster. To realize such goals, we must consciously push forward the moral education and development so that morality can comprehensively serve and act on the construction of the socialist society.

4.2 The Basis and Standard to Judge the Level of Productivity[8]

I put forward the concept of "moral productivity" for the first time in the *Introduction to Economic Ethics,*[9] where I demonstrate the proposition that morality is a dynamic productive force. In later papers, such as *The Second Study on Morality*[10] *is a Dynamic Productive Force* and *Morality and Spiritual Productivity,*[11] I try to illustrate the basis for the existence of moral productivity and its theoretical and practical values from various perspectives. My studies on moral productivity attracted the concerns of the academic circle. Some scholars questioned my opinions on papers or at academic meetings, and I responded in a timely fashion. There were also scholars, who, based on my opinion, conducted further and deeper studies. This sector is a further exposition of my opinion, and I would like to listen to the voices of my peers.

---

[8] Originally titled as *The Third Study on Morality is a Dynamic Productive Force*, *Studies on Ethics*, Issue 3, 2008 and *Ethics*, Issue 6, 2008. The paper has been included in Moral Capital and Business Ethics (*Selected Works of Wang Xiaoxi*), People's Publishing House, 2009.

[9] Jiangsu Social Sciences, Issue 1, 1994.

[10] Jiangsu Social Sciences, Issue 3, 1998.

[11] Jiangsu Social Sciences, Issue 2, 2001.

4.2.1 Morality Judges and Promotes the Development of Productivity

The core and foundation of productivity are laborers or labor force; therefore, production is a process in which man acts or play roles, and in which "subjective productivity" and "social labor productivity" are realized. In other words, "a single man cannot operate upon nature without calling his own muscles into play under the control of his own brain. As in the natural body head and hand wait upon each other, so the labor-process unites the labor of the hand with that of the head."[12] Therefore, "we understand productive forces or productivity as the sum total of the physical power and intelligence existing in the body, namely, the living body of a person, which is used when he produces a certain use value."[13] I have repeatedly pointed out that productivity contains the knowledge and intelligence of man, and in a broad sense, it contains the moral knowledge and moral quality of man.

Therefore, to judge the level of productivity, it is necessary to take laborers' moral quality and its functions into account. Moreover, the level of productivity shall be judged statically and dynamically, in this way, we can fully understand the indispensability of morality in the development of productivity.

Statically, the level of productivity is given. "Every productive force is an acquired force, the product of the previous activity. Thus, the productive forces are the result of man's practical energy, but that energy is in turn circumscribed by the conditions in which man is placed by the productive forces already acquired, by the form of society which exists before him, which he does not create, which is the product of the preceding generation."[14] Of course, it includes the form of social consciousness. The product of labor, which reflects the level of productivity the most, is the objectification of human behavior. "In the labor-process, man's activity, with the help of the instruments of labor, effects an alteration, designed from the commencement, in the material worked upon. The process disappears in the product, the latter is a use-value and Nature's material is adapted by a change of form to the wants of man. Labor has incorporated itself with its subject: the former is materialized, the latter transformed. That which in the laborer appeared as movement, now appears in the product as a fixed quality without motion. The blacksmith forges and the product is a forging."[15] Both labor and products are the externalization of the human spirit, static, or dynamic. Engels once said, "Labor includes capital, and the third factor that even economists have been aware of—I mean inventions and thoughts,

[12] *Collected Works of Karl Marx and Friedrich Engels*, Vol. 44, People's Publishing House, 2001, p. 582.

[13] *Collected Works of Karl Marx and Friedrich Engels*, Vol. 44, People's Publishing House, 2001, p. 195.

[14] *Collected Works of Karl Marx and Friedrich Engels*, Vol. 4, People's Publishing House, 1995, p. 532.

[15] *Collected Works of Karl Marx and Friedrich Engels*, Vol. 44, People's Publishing House, 2001, p. 211.

the spiritual element aside from the physical element of simple labor."[16] Marx later pointed out, "The development of productive forces, after all, originates from the social nature of labor in action, from the internal division of labor in society, and from the development of intellectual labor, especially natural sciences."[17] Undoubtedly, "inventions and thoughts," or "spiritual elements" mentioned by Engels, and "intellectual labor" by Marx all certainly contain the objectification or externalization of man's moral concepts and moral values. In this sense, separated from morality, which acts as the "soul" of laborers and products, laborers and products will be unimaginable, and the level of productivity will be the simple accumulation of matter with value as the basis.

The given level of productivity principally means the following: the technical content and functions of the means of labor; the understanding, development, and utilization of the subject of labor; and the overall quality and labor skills of laborers. First, for the technical content and functions of the means of labor, the advancement of the means of production mainly means its ability to control and change nature. During this process, questions like "how to control" and "why to control" will inevitably occur. The knowledge of social sciences, especially moral knowledge, by virtue of its normalization, can answer the question of "how to control" through rational and normative reconciliation, and answer the question of "why to control" through normative guidance. Thereby, it can be said that morality is the "connector" and "spiritual support" of advanced means of production. Marx once said, "Nature builds no machines, no locomotives, railways, electric telegraphs, self-acting mules, etc. These are products of human industry; natural material transformed into organs of the human will over nature, or of human participation in nature. They are organs of the human brain, created by the human hand; the power of knowledge, objectified. The development of fixed capital indicates to what degree general social knowledge has become a direct force of production, and to what degree, hence, the conditions of the process of social life itself have come under the control of the general intellect and been transformed in accordance with it; to what degree the powers of social production have been produced, not only in the form of knowledge, but also as immediate organs of social practice, of the real life process."[18] Second, for the understanding, development, and utilization of the subject of labor, from the perspective of morality, ecological consciousness directly affects the rationality of developing and utilizing the subject of labor; while from the perspective of social production, ecological ethics adjusts the rational relationship between man and nature during the process of social reproduction. The number of products can only partly reflect the level of productivity, and the improvement of product quality reflects not only technology but also the elements of value of ecological ethics.

[16] *Collected Works of Karl Marx and Friedrich Engels*, Vol. 3, People's Publishing House, 2002, p. 453.

[17] *Collected Works of Karl Marx and Friedrich Engels*, Vol. 46, People's Publishing House, 2003, p. 96.

[18] *Collected Works of Karl Marx and Friedrich Engels*, Vol. 31, People's Publishing House, 1998, p. 102.

Therefore, the "ecological cognition" and "ecological development" of the subject of labor are needed. In this sense, ecological consciousness "forces" the productivity to be more intensive and efficient. All the above, before man's ecological consciousness is roused, can only stay at the "upstart" stage of social production. Third, for the overall quality and labor skills of laborers, "without human beings as a 'subjective productive force' and the conceptual orientation thereof, productive forces will be 'dead productive forces' rather than 'living social productive forces Wang (1998)'." In addition, without man's moral concepts and moral behavior, the advancement and efficiency of productivity cannot be fully expressed, for advanced productivity must be used by man with advanced or scientific moral value orientation; otherwise, no matter how abundant and advanced the means of production are, productivity can hardly develop, and may even face disasters. Therefore, man as "subject productivity" is a key basis to judge the level of productivity.

Dynamically, the level of productivity should be considered as a process. The given level of productivity cannot be completely described by the given laborers and the means of production, for the product of labor, which reflects the level of productivity, is jointly created by labor and the subject of labor. During the process of understanding and operating upon the subject of labor, if we only look after short-term interests instead of long-term interests, focus on personal or small-group interests rather than collective (national) interests, or satisfy our needs at the cost of sacrificing natural ecology and social ecology, even if the product of labor looks abundant, the level of production will stagnate or even decrease to some extent due to irrational or even immoral overdevelopment of natural resources. Therefore, in this sense, static productivity needs to be considered as a part of the dynamic development process under the guidance of "social foresight" of a certain moral value.

From the dynamic perspective, the level of productivity largely depends on the mentality and morality of man. As I mentioned before, human behavior, thoughts, and morality are certainly involved in all material productive forces; otherwise, material productive forces or the level of productivity cannot be understood and correctly grasped. Moreover, the development of productivity means potential development and the trend of development, which require the participation of human thoughts and morality. On the one hand, thoughts and morality affect labor and labor efficiency, that is, the ideological consciousness and moral quality directly restrict the quality and efficiency of labor. It is unlikely that people without entrepreneurial spirit can realize high labor efficiency. Even if the means of production are advanced and abundant, without entrepreneurial spirit, production efficiency will be created at the cost of wasting the means of production. Marx said, "Man, as a productive force, is also a natural object or a kind of living matter with consciousness, while labor itself is the embodiment of such productive force on matter."[19] He also said, "The productive forces controlled by human beings are uncountable. The application of capital, labor, and science can infinitely improve the production capacity of land… Science makes it possible for man to control

[19] *Collected Works of Karl Marx and Friedrich Engels*, Vol. 44, People's Publishing House, 2001, p. 235.

more and more natural forces. Once such uncountable production capability is used by man consciously to create benefits for the public, the labor undertaken by man will soon be minimized."[20] Marx emphasized the functions of sciences (including social sciences), but with a great emphasis on the importance of "uncountable production capability is used by man consciously to create benefits for the public" for developing inexhaustible productivity.[21] On the other hand, the ecological awareness of man, developed from morality, determines whether potential productivity can fully play its roles. As mentioned before, from the macroscopic perspective, in the "process" of the development of productivity, immoderate resource exploitation will weaken and even destroy productivity. Therefore, the development of productivity, which seems like mere material activities, is essentially ecological or economic morality activities, which fundamentally determine the development of productivity. It can be said that even if immoral behavior ignoring or even destroying ecology can create benefits, the benefits certainly cannot last for a long time, and are very likely to be created at the cost of destroying the future development of productivity. Moreover, the development of productivity is constrained by some social institutions. Social institutions meeting the requirements of the development of productivity will promote the development of productivity; otherwise, the development of productivity will be hindered. Moral institutions are scientific and rational institutions, and the premise of the development of productivity. Marx described the relationship between institutions and science like this: "in a rational order which has gone beyond the division of interests as it is found with the economist, the mental element certainly belongs among the elements of production and will find its place, too, in economics among the costs of production."[22] Therefore, only by constantly enhancing the moral consciousness and improving morality-based social institutions could we constantly develop the social productivity.

4.2.2 Human Development and the Improvement of Interpersonal Relationships are the Important Indicators for the Level of Productivity

Although "productive forces are always useful and specific labor productivity",[23] it does not mean that productivity is independent from man. Marx clearly pointed out, "To develop human productivity, it's necessary to turn materials into scientific

[20] *Collected Works of Karl Marx and Friedrich Engels*, Vol. 3, People's Publishing House, 2002, pp. 463–464.

[21] Lenin highly praised the "voluntary labor on Saturday" event and extracted some statistical charts illustrating the multiple production efficiency brought by the "enthusiasm of morality". From such charts, we can easily find some "empirical data".

[22] *Collected Works of Karl Marx and Friedrich Engels*, Vol. 3, People's Publishing House, 2002, p. 453.

[23] *Collected Works of Karl Marx and Friedrich Engels*, Vol. 44, People's Publishing House, 2001, p. 59.

control over natural forces."[24] In fact, "the development of science, which is both conceptual and practical wealth, is only one aspect or one form of the development of human productivity, or the development of wealth."[25] Since man cannot be separated from interpersonal relationships, human productivity means the productivity cannot be separated from interpersonal relationships. Therefore, man, human development, and the development of interpersonal relationships are the important indicators of the development of productivity.

First, man is the foundation, content, and result of social production. To investigate the level of social productivity, the priority is, of course, investigating the development of man. "According to Marx, the process of social production, no matter under capitalism or communism, always takes man, the subject of interpersonal relationships, as the final product and result Novikova (1988)." In fact, "the reason why production is, first of all, called as social production, is that the production of society or man, who acts as the cultural and historical creature of society, is always the final result of production, and all of the rest—no matter the products, labor condition or even the direct productive process—are, after all, some elements—the instruments and equipment. In this sense, social production is always realized by man. In the process, 'man duplicates himself not only, as in consciousness, intellectually, but also actively, in reality, and therefore he sees himself in a world that he has created'. Therefore, it's not enough to just acknowledge that the mode of production plays the decisive role in the process of social development, we also must realize that man himself is the basis of social production Novikova (1988)." This opinion is reasonable. Man, naturally, is an indicator of the level of production. In this case, we must find out what the indicator of human development is. In my opinion, man as an important indicator of the level of productivity and human development are a special abundant field that we can investigate from both spiritual and material perspectives. Morality, intelligence, physical strength, mentality, and ability are the main content of investigation. I want to stress that man's moral quality is the basic and also core indicator of human development, for human intelligence, physical strength, and ability can only play their roles normally and effectively with the control and reconciliation of morality, and more importantly, man needs the guidance of a clear and noble value orientation to pursue and realize his goals in life. Therefore, social production needed by the times can certainly "produce" the moral man required by the times, and accordingly, the moral man required by the times can certainly create the social production needed by the times.

Second, man cannot be separated from interpersonal relationships. Since social production is "the production of social man," naturally, it is also the production of interpersonal relationships or social relationships. Therefore, to judge the level of productivity of a society, the harmony of interpersonal relationships, which reflects the developmental level of productivity from a unique angle, needs to be investi-

[24] *Collected Works of Karl Marx and Friedrich Engels*, Vol. 12, People's Publishing House, 1998, p. 251.

[25] *Collected Works of Karl Marx and Friedrich Engels*, Vol. 30, People's Publishing House, 1995, p. 539.

gated. In the process, we can also further observe the moral consciousness of man as an important indicator of the level of productivity and the roles that morality plays as a productive force. L. I. Novikova had rather original insight regarding the above. He said, "Improving the quantity and quality (the initial conditions only) of material wealth produced and constantly perfecting interpersonal relationships (or man himself) have become a development rule of social production under socialism. If we fail to realize that the growth and constant improvement of social production in a socialist society cannot be realized during the process that man has a better understanding and control of his social relationship and reproduce such relationship at a higher level, namely, man constantly changes and improves his social relationship, it's impossible for us to understand the growth and constant improvement of social production." He also said, "The formation of social production, which primarily aims at human development, marks that the boundary, which divides material production from conscious production, has been broken. Consciousness in advanced forms—science, art, morality and philosophy—has become an integral part of man's real social life, and a requirement for everyone to change society. High level of social consciousness, invigoration and a full life of average people are elements encouraging them to participate actively in social life. The more man can become the creator of his social relationship and the real subject of social development, the more man's spiritual activities are involved in his material activities. That is to say, human activities to promote social development include not only physical strength, but also mental development and tense mental activities Novikova (1988)." Novikova pointed out that the improvement of social productivity requires constant improvement of human quality and interpersonal relationships, and the realization of which, as stressed by Novikova, is closely related to the development of consciousness in its advanced form, including morality.

Third, productivity is a comprehensive concept containing various elements, and the combination of which, after all, is interpersonal relationship. Therefore, to judge the level of productivity, it is necessary to investigate the moral state of interpersonal relationships. I once pointed out in a paper[26] that the development of productivity itself depends on the rational connection and existence of the internal factor of productivity, namely, the rational combination between laborers and the instruments of labor, and between laborers and the subject of labor. Only in this way, productivity will develop normally. If laborers become an appendant of the instruments of labor, or if the instruments of labor and productive resources do not belong to laborers, the relationship there between is passive and irrational, which will seriously affect the existence and development of productivity. To realize the rational connection and existence of the internal factors of productivity, productive relations meeting the moral and rational requirements of laborers need to be built, and the moral consciousness and quality of laborers needs to be improved. People without moral consciousness can hardly understand and deal with the relationship between themselves and other factors of production. In fact, in the final analysis, how man and materials combine is, in some sense, how man exists and connects

[26] Morality and Spiritual Productivity, *Jiangsu Social Sciences,* Issue 2, 2001.

with others and how morality exists. Therefore, the level of productivity cannot be judged without considering morality.

4.2.3 Question the Questioning of "Moral Productivity"

Since coming up with the concept of "moral productivity," I have heard different voices—questioning and agreeing; nevertheless, both promoted the further study of my proposition. The questions were raised due to different disciplinary concepts, different understandings of theories or different research methods. To probe further the proposition of moral productivity, I will discuss several different understandings on some basic concepts.

First, what is productivity? Some scholars thought that "productivity is not a thing," but rather "the attribute of something." "In general, productivity is defined as the ability of laborers to change nature and obtain material means of livelihood in social production. As an attribute of man, productivity reflects the relationship between man and nature, and from the perspective of size, namely, the quantization of the relationship, productivity can be understood as a quantity of relationship, or, in the language of science, a kind of energy." Therefore, "productivity is an attribute of man as a special matter, and a kind of energy." According to the authors, if productivity is understood as a thing, namely, if man is a thing, if material elements directly relating to man, such as production and the subject of labor, are things, and if technology, organizational forms of production, management, education, social sciences, ethics, and morality are things, productive relations and the content of the superstructure are also things. However, this kind of thinking is wrong Hu and Li (2005). In fact, we must see that the authors transformed the concept of "the content of productivity" into "the concept of productivity." It is correct that productivity is an attribute or a kind of energy, but it is wrong to say that productivity is not a thing, and then make the conclusion that "productivity is neither a kind of matter nor a kind of spirit Hu and Li (2005)." In this way, productivity is abstracted into a virtual concept that cannot be seized. Nevertheless, the problem is what the carrier of productivity is, and where the attribute and energy in the process of productive labor come from. As far as we know, productivity falls into material and spiritual productivity. In fact, even the authors held that "productivity is an attribute of man as a special matter, and a kind of energy" and "energy attaches to material objects and thus is the attribute of matter Hu and Li (2005)." Therefore, productivity is certainly the productivity of something (matter or spirit), which can be demonstrated by Marx's concepts and propositions of "capital productivity," "personal productivity," "materialized productivity," "human productivity" and "productivity is the specific and useful form of labor." Of course, the authors also stressed that even though "we can only say that something has energy rather than something is energy." In actuality, "material" and "spirit" in the concepts of material productivity and spiritual productivity, in a certain discourse context, can be understood as "has energy" or "is energy." In this sense, energy is always the energy of matter.

Of course, it should be made clear that matter and spirit are not equal to productivity, that is, productivity is not matter or spirit itself. Before entering the productive process, the means of labor that primarily contain the means of production are just "deal productivity." However, after involving the process of production, with the operation of man as "subject productivity," matter and spirit will turn into the elements of production.

Second, how to understand the relationship between material productivity and spiritual productivity? Material productivity means (1) the ability to produce material products, and (2) the productivity of the means of labor which mainly contains the means of production to produce material and spiritual products. According to Marx, production is the reproduction of man and social relationships, including the production and reproduction of spirit and spiritual products. Spiritual productivity means (1) the ability to produce spiritual products, and (2) the productivity (primarily science, thought and morality involving the productive process) that guides and affects both material and spiritual products. It must be pointed out that material productivity and spiritual productivity are inseparable. As far as I know, no economist has ever considered spiritual productivity as a kind of independent productivity. In fact, only when science, thought, and morality as spiritual productivity play roles in the productive process (to activate the means of labor as dead productivity), could material productivity play roles as the social productivity of labor; likewise, spiritual productivity can only play roles after participating in production to guide or affect material and spiritual productions. Therefore, material productivity and spiritual productivity are two supplementary elements of production.

Third, is morality a kind of productivity? This has long been a controversial and theoretical issue. One opinion, which essentially questions the existence of moral productivity, is that moral productivity overemphasizes the functions of productivity, which shakes the foundation of the existence of historical materialism Li (2005). I think this is a wrong conclusion made from a wrong understanding of moral productivity. First, there is an opinion that moral productivity is not a kind of independent productivity, thus cannot play the role of productivity. My response is, as I have already stressed, moral productivity, as a kind of spiritual productivity, is not "independent" from the social productivity of labor, but rather a factor or element of productivity. In addition, as I mentioned before, material productivity is nothing but "deal productivity" without spiritual productivity, and spiritual productivity is useless empty talk without material productivity. Second, there is the opinion that since productivity ultimately determines social ideology, if morality is a kind of productivity, it means that social ideology determines productivity, which is wrong. My explanation is that the existence of moral productivity means human perfection and harmonious interpersonal relationships play unique and irreplaceable roles in the existence and development of material productivity, emphasizing the activity of morality in productivity. How does it "shake the foundation of the existence of historical materialism"? On the contrary, emphasizing the dialectical relationship and interaction between material productivity and spiritual productivity while highlighting the activity of moral productivity in certain discourse contexts is exactly the basic view and way of thinking of historical materialism.

4.3 Integrity is the Core Competitiveness of Economic Development[27]

Integrity is the basis, core, and condition of morality. A man with integrity must be a moral man, and in some sense, integrity is the synonym of morality. Therefore, studying integrity and its functions is an important way to understand moral capital.

In recent years, food safety scandals, such as tainted milk powder, clenbuterol, "gutter oil," steamed buns dyed with a colorant, and so on, happened one after another. While harming the health of consumers, these scandals destroyed many companies, affected the development of industry or even caused serious negative effects on the economy of a region or country. Behind such scandals are complex economic and social reasons relating to management, institutions, and even culture, and the primary reason is a lack of morality.

Integrity contains honesty and credibility. It can be said that in the intelligent history and economic practices of the world, integrity has always been a focus of attention. Confucius said, "Like carriages without wheels cannot move, man without integrity can do nothing," and "without people with integrity, a country cannot be governed." He considered integrity as the basis for man to live in society and for the administration of a country. Max Weber, when discussing the "elective affinities" between Protestant ethics advocating asceticism and the rise of Western capitalism, quoted Franklin as saying, "credit is money," to demonstrate the logistic relationship between "honesty, credit, and money." Francis Fukuyama, based on the empirical study of the social trust of some regions and countries, expounded the roles played by trust in economic development and made the conclusion that the degree of social trust of a society is an important cultural element affecting its economic development. The history of economic development has told us an "iron law"—integrity leads to prosperity and the loss of integrity leads to decline.

Integrity and economic development are inseparable. In today's increasingly growing socialist market economy, integrity has become the core competitiveness of economic development.

First, integrity is an increasingly developing special resource in the socialist market economy. (1) In the socialist market economy, the production, sales and after-sales service of products are guided by the free price mechanism of the free market. In this sense, the market economy is also called the free market economy. In such an economy, what and how it operates are decided by the operator, and with whom to cooperate as well as the way, the goal, and the direction of cooperation are also decided by the operator. It is easy to imagine that without integrity, such a free economy will be filled with fraud and cheating, and naturally, the free market cannot be really realized. Therefore, a well-established moral system (including integrity) is needed to guarantee and promote the sound development of the socialist market economy, thus realizing a real free economy. In this case, integrity is the indispensable link to maintain the socialist market economy. (2) In the social-

[27] *Guangming Daily,* Nov. 22, 2011, fully reprinted in *Xinhua Digest*, Issue 3, 2012. This section is partly modified herein.

ist market economy, socialized mass production is not a purely material economic process comprising input, output, and benefits, but the cooperation of stakeholders who form a "chain." In such a chain, if any stakeholder loses his integrity, the whole economic order will be destroyed, hindering economic development. (3) The market economy is a rule-of-law economy, which cannot be realized without the trust between the government and companies, between one company and another, between companies and employees, and between employees and the government; otherwise, the goal of the rule of law will be unclear, and the process of the rule of law will turn into a formality. In this sense, integrity development is the foundation of the development of the socialist market economy.

Second, integrity determines the moral image of a company and is the core competitiveness of a company to develop against fierce market competition. Largely, the speed of economic development depends on the benefits of companies, which are determined by the sales of products and services, and the sales of products and services rest with the integrity-based operation of companies. This has been proved by the cases—success and failure—of a lot of companies at home and abroad. For a company, if integrity penetrates into the entire process of product design and production to best meet the real needs of consumers in daily life and production while commitments are fulfilled during the process of sales and service to realize integrity-based sales and service, then undoubtedly, the company will, at the same time of winning the trust of consumers, continuously expand its market share. On the contrary, if a company, no matter how famous it is, loses its integrity in product design, production, sales or after-sales services by cutting corners, adulteration, exaggerating product functions, and making empty promises, its reputation will be seriously damaged. Consequently, its sales and profits will drop, which may ultimately lead to the collapse of the company.

Third, integrity is an important approach to lower the costs of economic transactions. Economic development is closely and relatively related to the content, types, and frequency of transactions. It can be said that the more the content and types are, and the higher the frequency is, the higher the benefits are. However, such a relation has a high requirement on integrity. In a transaction, all parties involved pursue the maximization of profits. In this case, without trust, the parties involved will block information which should be published, wasting a lot of energy and resources to access information. Some would even destroy the normal channel of economic information, like stealing or making up economic information, which gives rise to more "friction consumption," lowering economic efficiency, and the speed of economic development. On the contrary, with the participation of integrity, meaningless consumption will be reduced, and what's more, an integrity-based business environment will form, attracting various economic resources. In other words, integrity can not only lower transaction costs to increase economic benefits but also improve the investment environment, thus promoting efficient economic development.

We must see that although integrity is, evidently, the core competitiveness of economic development, due to the imperfection in the economic management mechanism and constitutions during the period of economic transition and some negative factors, such as the profit orientation and spontaneity of the market, to some extent, the importance and necessity of integrity in economic development are weakened. In recent years, many scandals caused by the lack of integrity have, to a certain degree, made people rethink the importance of integrity. However, to make integrity really play its roles as the core competitiveness of economic development, it is necessary to develop people's sense of integrity and related institutions first. That is, theories and institutions concerning integrity must be developed and put into practice, making integrity the real core competitiveness in economic development. In particular, to realize this goal, the following measures should be taken:

First, promote the concept of integrity in economic development to build a modern integrity-based economy. Integrity is not only a moral requirement but also a requirement of economic behavior. Economic integrity and economy with integrity are inseparable social phenomena. In economic development, an economy without integrity is lopsided, and thus is not a real economy. In recent years, theoretically or practically, "economic centralism" and "economic suprematism" are widely accepted in China. Then, from the "gross domestic product (GDP) centralism" in the macroscopic economic and social developments to the value orientations and business modes of companies that are developed to realize "profit maximization," and to the "theory of wealth priority" affecting personal behavior and social evaluation, we can, to a large extent, see the lack of morality in the theories concerning economic development. Therefore, in the development of the socialist market economy, it is necessary to make integrity penetrate every aspect of economic development. The ends and means of economic management, the design and manufacturing of products, the sales and services of products, and feedback and handling of consumer opinions should always be conducted in accordance with the concept of treating the public, customers, peers, and employees with integrity. Only in this way could the socialist market economy become a real integrity-based economy.

Second, build a social integrity system and improve corporate integrity management institutions. As a requirement of morality, integrity requires the ideas and consciousness of the economic agent to really play its roles. However, in the present complex socialist market economy, the ideas and consciousness of the economic agent alone are not able to build and improve an integrity-based economy effectively. In this case, it is necessary to institutionalize integrity in order to promote the formation of an integrity-based economy by virtue of the external coerciveness and the internal scientificity of institutions. Presently, the credit institution, which constitutes a key element of China's economic institutions, is an important paradigm to realize the moralization of economic institutions and is a crucial part in the development of an integrity-based economy. As long as a sound economic integrity system is built in society, integrity will become a principle that the economic agent and economic behavior must follow at anytime, anywhere, and in any condition. We should see that in the socialist market economy, companies are the primary economic agents, and corporate integrity is the core of economic integrity. Therefore, attention shall be paid in particular to strengthening the development and implementation of corporate integrity management institutions. The food safety problems occurring in recent years are fundamentally caused by the lack of integrity, and the main reason of which is the lack of sound corporate integrity management institutions. Just think, if well-established integrity management institutions are strictly implemented in the design, production, sales, and after-sales services, is it possible for tainted milk powder and clenbuterol to appear on the market?

Third, have the government, public, and media work together to supervise the development of an integrity-based economy. It can be said that in recent years, the lack of integrity in economic activities is largely caused by the lack of effective social evaluation and supervision mechanisms. If the economic agent is not condemned and punished for its lack of integrity, it will ignore the constraint of ethics during its pursuance of interests. Therefore, it is necessary to establish a sound integrity supervision mechanism so that the interests of economic agents holding integrity are protected, and of those losing integrity are damaged, thus building a positive correlation between integrity and interests. To realize the above, the government should take the lead in making comprehensive, systematic, and practical corporate and personal integrity records, based on which, corporate and personal economic activities can be evaluated. Besides, the government should fully play its role of supervision, timely disclosing and punishing economic agents losing integrity, thus increasing the cost of ignoring integrity. Moreover, the government should also call public and media supervision into play, so that the "top-down" government regulations and "down-up" public supervisions can work together. It is worth noting that unlike conventional media, emerging media represented by online media, by virtue of their efficiency, interaction, and anonymity to some extent, are not restrained by time, space, and environment, and have become a new force in guiding and supervising the development of economic integrity. In recent years, some serious moral crises were reported by online media first and the economic agents involved were punished last. Therefore, making full use of the functions of guidance, publicity, and supervision of emerging media is an effective approach to develop economic integrity.

4.4 Corporate Integrity and its Mechanism for Implementation:[28] Take Haier as an Example

Corporate integrity, as a key element of the core competiveness of a company and a basic disciple of business management, is a premise of corporate development. If we take the Haier Group as an example, we will find that "Haier," a world famous brand, is built based on the business concept of "Sincere Forever," and its strategic thinking and a series of strategic decisions taking integrity as the core.

[28] *Studies on Ethics,* Issue 6, 2003. It has been included in Moral Capital and Business Ethics (*Selected Works of Wang Xiaoxi*), People's Publishing House, 2009.

4.4.1 *Analysis of Corporate Integrity*

Integrity is a basic moral norm to maintain the contractual relationship between companies. Essentially, it is a kind of rational spirit of a company to fulfill its responsibility for customers, employees, peers, and society.

4.4.1.1 Integrity Toward Customers

Companies rely on customers for a living. Losing customers means losing profits. Without profits, a company cannot even exist, let alone develop.

For a company, its integrity toward customers should be manifested in the entire process of its business operation.

First, there is the human-centered product design. All products are for human use; therefore, products should be designed according to the real physiological, psychological, and social needs of man. Man's natural attributes should be taken into account in designing so that the new products can meet the technical needs of consumers. Moreover, according to man's aesthetic needs, artistic elements should be included in product design to meet the psychological needs of consumers. That is, products should be "safe, reliable, convenient, comfort, good looking, and economical Hu et al. (1994)." "According Haier, the technical content of a product should be judged by consumers rather than experts—the best technical content is the technical content accepted by consumers instead of the highest technical content Hu (2002)." Human-centered design is a principle of Haier. As one of its slogans goes, "You design it and we make it," Haier produces what consumers need. Within just 1 month, after launching the service of a custom-made fridge, Haier received orders of over 1 million fridges. It can be seen that human-centered product design and production means the maximization of profits.

Second, there are zero defects during the productive process. For business operation, product manufacturing is as important as product design. In the productive process, integrity is manifested with a high technological level and the complete consistency between product design and product manufacturing, which reflect the real sense of responsibility of a company. When product manufacturing is inconsistent with product design, the integrity of the company is partially lost. We must see that product design is a mental process, the results of which are ideas or concepts, and product quality is the final carrier of integrity. In the productive process of Haier, integrity can be measured by the "Six Sigma" (sigma is a statistical unit of the standard deviation from the average. The Six Sigma reflects the maturity of a process, in specific, the number of defects per million opportunities. The higher the sigma level is, the lower the error rate is Boton (2002)). According to the Six Sigma, only three to four defects per million opportunities are allowed, and the costs of defects should be borne by the producer itself (Mickle 2002). In other words, the products they bought are 100% qualified. For a company, "defective products are waste products," and defective products are the "natural enemy" of brand building. In 1985, 76 nonconforming fridges were found during quality testing. Haier CEO,

Zhang Ruimin, asked the person in charge to smash the fridges in front all employees and deducted his salary voluntarily. The case demonstrates a company's integrity toward consumers, which will, undoubtedly, greatly improve its market share.

Third, always fulfill after-sales service commitments. A company's integrity toward consumers does not disappear after products are sold. After-sales service commitments should be fulfilled by both the dealer and the producer.

Founder of Panasonic, Konosuke Matsushita, once said that "sales means service" and "a product not provided together with service, no matter how good it is, cannot satisfy consumers, and will lose its credibility Konosuke (1996)." Haier knows very well the importance of fulfilling service commitments, which actually played an essential role in developing "Haier" into a world famous brand. First, Haier originally put forward the ideas that "a company sells credibility rather than products" and "marketing is not about selling but buying Hu (2002)." Adhering to such ideas, Haier set the principles of zero product defects, zero consumer complaints, and zero consumer worry about after-sales service, while actively taking advice from consumers in order to improve product quality and service. Second, Haier always remains committed to the highest after-sales service standard and the optimal service mode. Its service standard is as follows: providing a detailed and friendly consultation service during and before sales; providing 24-hour home delivery service; providing installation service according to the requirements of consumers in time and place; providing onsite debugging and demonstration service so that consumers can grasp skills easily; and providing follow-up service and on-site service as well as replying to consumer questions within 20 h so that consumer would have "zero worry" about after-sales service. The service mode is as follows: "one result"—providing consumers with a satisfactory service; "two ideas"—eliminating the worries of consumers and leaving behind the sincerity of Haier; "three controls"—providing a service complaint rate below 1/100,000, a service omission rate below 1/100,000, and a service dissatisfaction rate below 1/100,000; "four completes"—complete recording of consumer opinions, complete handling of consumer problems, complete review of handling results, and complete feedback of handling results to the design, production, and operation departments. In this way, Haier provides service according to consumer needs with the scope of service covering the whole product market Guo (2003). Third, Haier holds that the relationship between a company and consumers is not the exchange of materials, but interpersonal communication. Claiming that "non-consumers are also God," Haier expands its service to non-consumers—it repairs products of other brands and even solves problems concerning the products of other brands. Haier puts forward ideas ahead of its time, which ultimately has won it more consumers and the market Hu (2002).

4.4.1.2 Integrity Toward Employees

Corporate integrity is a kind of corporate spirit and a corporate quality. Therefore, integrity is also required inside a company.

It can be said that integrity toward employees is the premise to realize integrity toward consumers. A company losing the trust of its employees will certainly lose the trust of its consumers and the society. It is impossible for a company without internal integrity to treat consumers with integrity.

Integrity toward employees should be first manifested as dignity equality. In a company, despite the product category or the property (state operated, private operated, or individual operated), employees are its owners and thus should be respected by management as well as regulations and policies formulated by them. In Haier, where a quality problem is detected, the corresponding responsibility is borne by the manager in charge, whose salary or bonus will also be deducted. In this case, employees' respect and trust for the company are built. Haier is like a big family in which all members are equal.

Second, all employees should have equal opportunities of creation and development. This is another innovation of Haier. Zhang Ruimin once said that the right way to discover talents is not promotion by manager, which, as a personal management system, is not normative and reliable, but competition, which is fair, just, and open Boton (2002). Accordingly, Haier developed a fair and rational personal management system—"the co-existence and dynamic shift of three kinds of employees." According to the system, as performance increases, a worker can progress from a worker during probation (temporary worker) to a qualified worker and then to an excellent worker; likewise, with the decrease in work performance, a worker will be demoted from an excellent worker to a qualified worker, and to a temporary worker. In this way, talents are discovered in practice instead of through the judgment of management. The position of a worker is not decided by management, but his performance. This personal promotion system, avoiding the phenomena of favoritism and the formation of cliques, can greatly improve the innovation and the sense of achievement of employees. "Haier is a sea" is a significant idea put forward by Zhang Ruimin. He thinks that every employee is a drop of water in the sea, and only when each one fully plays his roles could Haier act as a whole to realize its great goals. Haier provides all employees with the opportunities and platforms to create and develop, which, in turn, contributes to the prosperity of today's Haier. In Haier, even a common logistics worker is proud to be a member of Haier and of contributing to Haier.

Third, try to realize equal interest distribution. The direct goal of a company is to make profits, which requires employees to create profits. A consequent problem is the distribution of profits. Fair and just interest distribution is an important indicator of corporate integrity and vitality. In Haier, the salaries of workers, which are not fixed, are not decided by their superiors, but by their work quality and integrity, namely, both their work performance and the claim for compensation. This is the so-called market chain. Therefore, in Haier, interest distribution is an indicator of integrity and a chain of integrity linking Haier and consumers. Zhang Ruimin came up with the idea of the "trinity" of shareholders, consumers, and employees, that is, the company creates values to satisfy shareholders' desire of a high share price, consumers' desire of high-quality products with reasonable prices, and employees' desire of a higher income, which are the best embodiment of internal corporate integrity.

Fourth, turn each managed employee into a manager. A vigorous company must be a family in which every member is vigorous. Corporate management includes both macroscopic decision-making and microcosmic decision implementation. In Haier, employees at different positions and levels are required to think about two questions: how should they do their work? How should the company develop? Each employee has his/her qualifications and the right to voice his/her opinions, and in many cases, the voices of employees constitute the basis and content of Haier's operation decisions. After the Second World War, Panasonic managed to recover in a short time span. One of the main reasons is that Konosuke Matsushita talked independently with each employee, and based on the ideas of his employees, he developed the development plan of Panasonic. At the same time of winning the support of all employees, he successfully aroused the enthusiasm of employees. Compared with Panasonic, Haier arouses the enthusiasm of employees in a more practical and innovative manner. In Haier, "You are your own boss!" Since everyone is a boss, everyone is naturally an operator who must be responsible for the market, the company as well as his/her own innovation capability, performance and interests. In this case, the integrity of the company toward employees and of employees toward the company will certainly be greatly improved.

4.4.1.3 Integrity Toward Peers

Corporate competition is the basic way for corporate development to exist. In the context of rational operation, corporate competition should not rely on or be content with the law of "survival of the fittest." Considering peers as foes would only hinder corporate development. In an unhealthy competition without cooperation, information access, and mutual support, material, spiritual, and social resources will be wasted, and the interests of companies will be harmed at last. Konosuke Matsushita once said, "Common development with peers is the only way that leads to sustainable development." He also said, "For a company, sacrificing the interests of a partner to realize self-interest is unforgivable and will certainly lead to self-destruction in the end Konosuke (1996)."

Integrity toward peers first requires companies to not launch the dog-eat-dog price war (Konosuke 1996). When a price war develops to a certain degree, superficially, consumers will benefit; however, the interests of companies involved will be harmed, thus affecting expanded reproduction and harming social interests in the end.

Second, integrity toward peers requires companies to provide information and support to each other at the premise of protecting trade secrets. "In market competition, there are always rivals. However, companies that only see their rivals cannot have long-term development. One of the mistakes often made by operators is that they stare at the movement of their rivals and lose their own ways of development Hu (2002)."

Third, integrity toward peers requires companies to focus on business, the market and consumers. When companies that are related in an area work together to develop natural and social resources, while benefiting human beings and society, they will benefit their peers, consciously becoming the support or condition for the development of their peers.

4.4.2 Mechanism for the Implementation of Corporate Integrity

Integrity, as a corporate code of conduct and an indicator of corporate quality, reconciles and supports various forces, and means needed for the realization and formation of various processes.

4.4.2.1 Improve Corporate Institutions and Management Mechanisms

From the macroscopic perspective, corporate institutions are about property relations. As long as property relations are clarified, managers and their followers will really realize their roles and their relationship with the company, and really understand that corporate integrity is established based on "personal integrity." From the microcosmic perspective, only when various reward and punishment institutions and various disciplines are clarified could all employees clearly distinguish right and wrong corporate behaviors formally, and could integrity penetrate into corporate behavior through strict institutional management. Without strict institutions and disciplines, "zero product defects, zero consumer complaints, and zero consumer worry about after-sales services" can hardly be realized. Haier's "market chain" management institution and mechanism is one of the examples of the corporate integrity establishment in China. Internally, aside from strict disciplines, employees of related positions and levels have formed the market relationship and service relationship, and the income of every employee at every position comes from his/her own market. Employees providing consumers with effective service are paid as contracted; otherwise, consumers can claim for compensation. "Market chain" is about turning external marketing goals into internal goals, turning internal goals into personal goals, and turning the results of the market chain into personal income. In this way, the effects of external market competition are internalized. At the same time, through the information access and feedback realized through the market chain, "product competitiveness is determined by the potential needs of consumers, product development is determined by the difficulties met by consumers, and product quality standard is made according to customer requirements. Through such a virtuous circle, corporate integrity is realized both internally and externally Hu (2002)."

4.4.2.2 Zero-Distance Service and Zero-Distance Production

"The closer to consumers, the further from rivals Hu (2002)." The zero-distance service and zero-distance production has really shortened the distance with consumers. As a concept, Haier first holds that consumers buy solutions rather than products, and buy comforts rather than troubles. Following the marketing concepts of "Haier makes the earth safer" and "building a service brand is much more important than building a product brand," Haier provides solutions in both products and thoughtful services. For example, during an onsite service, a service card, a pair of shoe covers, a placemat, a duster, and a small gift are enough to make consumers satisfied and comforted. One time, in order to resolve the problems of consumers, service personnel went to Xiamen by air, which had never happened before. Second, Haier holds that the process of selling products is also the process of buying the opinions and advice of consumers. Through face-to-face trouble shooting and communication with consumers, Haier collects the feedback of consumers. Then, according to an analysis of the feedback, Haier develops products according to consumer needs, even if what consumers need are appliances of abnormal shapes, such as triangular fridges, or machines to wash sweet potatoes or lobsters. This is a zero-distance production. By treating consumer needs with integrity, Haier has increased its competitiveness and maximized its profits at the same time.

4.4.2.3 Enhance Education to Unify Concepts

Corporate integrity cannot form naturally, or be realized by virtue of institutions, disciplines, or empty talks, which are of no help.

First, integrity education is about developing a sense of responsibility of employees, so that all employees will be responsible for the country, for the society, for others, and for themselves, so that they will know that a life lacking the sense of responsibility is incomplete, or even meaningless, and so that they will realize that the degree of their sense of responsibility is directly related to the amount of corporate and personal interests. In addition, the education of the sense of responsibility will effectively develop the sense of honor and the sense of shame of employees, which will lay a solid conceptual foundation for the performance of commitments.

Second, integrity cannot be developed without the training of knowledge and skills. In this case, knowledge should include the knowledge of both social sciences, such as philosophy and natural sciences; otherwise, employees will become low-brow and brainless wage earners who cannot understand the world and cannot judge values; naturally, such employees cannot really understand the significance of integrity. At the same time, the training of skills is also very important. The realization of integrity penetrates into various aspects and levels of business operations, and without skills, employees are not able to produce high-quality products. As Zhang Ruimin said, "untrained employees are debts, while trained employees are assets." The knowledge and skills obtained by employees through training can create profits, and thus can be a growth point for profit. As long as an employee establishes a correct ideology and a high loyalty, he/she transforms from a debt into an asset Hu (2002).

Third, integrity development should be combined with the mechanism of rewards and punishments. A company is also a society. In the socialist market economy, employees are sophisticated and their value orientations are different. In this case, rewards are given to set good examples, helping employees to set clear objectives; while punishments are given to prevent behavior from harming integrity, ensuring that integrity as a rational intangible asset can fully play its roles. When Zhang Ruimin smashed 76 nonconforming fridges in front of all the employees and deducted wages—he not only educated the person in charge but also enlightened and stimulated all employees. The significance of education and practical effect are nothing less than several speeches or papers.

4.4.2.4 Business Leaders Play an Exemplary Role with Deeds Rather Than Words

The internal and external integrities of a company directly depend on the reliability of its business leaders. On the one hand, highly reliable business leaders will not only play the role of a demonstrator but also the role of a motivator and a guider. Famous US scholar, Lynn Sharp Paine, once pointed out, "It's very likely that the demonstration of organizational leadership is the most important element to establish and maintain organizational integrity. Obviously, corporate employees convey organizational ethical standards. Generally, individual behavior, which has a lot of rights, plays an important role in building the ethical image of a company, for the information conveyed by such behavior is much more explicit than that written in the ethical statement of the company Lynn (1999)." Business leaders treating employees and things with integrity can bring hope to employees, making them build a strong sense of safety and responsibility. On the other side, the integrity of business leaders can, objectively, prevent dishonest words and deeds from happening. Besides, the integrity of business leaders can also directly affect the integrity development of a company at large. As an entrepreneur said, "a business leader with integrity can develop a business leadership with integrity, a business leadership with integrity can develop a team with integrity and a team with integrity can produce products containing integrity."

To play an exemplary role, business leaders should take care of their employees in terms of their work and life. According to Zhang Ruimin, business leaders should follow the discipline of "three for one," namely, solving the problems of employees with enthusiasm, criticizing employees with sincerity, and doing ideological work with understanding to win the loyalty of employees. According to the principle, every employee can receive the help and care he/she needs at anytime, like living in a warm family in which members depend on each other Boton (2002).

4.4.2.5 Build a Government with Integrity by Virtue of Improving Laws and Regulations

Corporate integrity is affected by the social environment. In a society with a low level of integrity, companies can hardly turn integrity into practice. Therefore, the government, policy protection, and legal support are the important conditions for the realization of corporate integrity.

First, try to build a government with integrity. On the one hand, it is necessary to develop governmental integrity. At present, while reforming the practice of the governmental administration and enhancing the transparency of policies, the moralization of government functions is also needed to affect and guide the enhancement of corporate integrity. On the other hand, it is necessary to protect and promote the implementation of integrity development measures and the realization of integrity development goals with governmental power and concrete measures. For example, to strengthen the protection of property rights to ensure that the commitments made by the owner of the property rights to the market can be fulfilled and promote the establishment of the market credit system; to verify strictly the capacity of taking on the responsibility of companies in the market; and to examine, supervise, and guide incessantly the development of corporate integrity. On the other hand, the government itself should develop integrity, that is, conducting a people-centered administration, putting national interests first, enhancing the awareness of service and guidance, and overcoming bureaucracy and administrative omissions in order to promote corporate integrity and moral development while guaranteeing its own integrity.

Second, corporate integrity should be conscious corporate behavior, the continuity of which makes integrity the quality of a company. However, a sound corporate integrity development system cannot be formed spontaneously, or be built through persuasion, education, or guidance. Currently, legal restraint still plays an important role. On the one hand, legal restraint guarantees the improvement of a corporate credit mechanism and the performance of corporate commitments. On the other hand, through legal restraint, dishonest behavior will be punished, which warns those trying to break promises while protecting those holding on to integrity. In this way, a social environment encouraging the pursuance of integrity and cracking down the neglect or disregard of integrity is created.

4.5 Strategic Analysis on Corporate Morality and Its Development in Contemporary China[29]

Recently, my academic team and I carried out a nationwide corporate morality "mirror image" survey. Through sampling surveys, in-depth interviews with representative figures and on-site investigations, we collected highly reliable first-hand information. Based on this information, we developed a report generally depicting the corporate morality in contemporary China, which provides an important source of information and a theoretical basis for strengthening the development of corporate morality and improving corporate core competitiveness.

The first cohort of 12 companies surveyed includes China Minsheng Bank; the large-scale enterprise Chongqing Iron and Steel (Group) Co., Ltd. located in Western China; Henan Baixiang Food Group, Henan Honggaoliang Food Co., Ltd., Zhengzhou Sanquan Food Co., Ltd. and Zhengzhou Shuangjixing Furniture Co., Ltd. located in Central China; and Changzhou Minghuang International Hotel, Wujiang Kelin Environmental Protection Equipment Co., Ltd., Typical Sewing Machine Wanping Machinery Co., Ltd., Zhangjiagang Tiantai Top Textile Co., Ltd., Zhangjiagang Furui Special Equipment Co., Ltd. and Zhangjiagang Gangying

[29] *Social Science Front,* Issue 2, 2013, fully reprinted in *Ethics,* Issue 4, 2013.

Industrial Co., Ltd. located in southern Jiangsu Province. The 12 companies are state-owned, private, or individual enterprises from both developed and underdeveloped areas, with business covering the financial industry, heavy industry, light industry, mechanical industry, food industry, and service industry. To improve the credibility of the "mirror image" of corporate morality, we applied the sampling survey method and collected a lot of information, which generally reflects the objective condition of the corporate moral development in China. Based on the survey results and the existing academic research results, we made the following analysis of the corporate morality and its development prospect in today's China:

4.5.1 Achievements in Corporate Moral Development

The theoretical and practical developments of corporate morality has a short history of more than 20 years in China, during which, corporate morality experienced the change from passive to active development, and from abstract concepts to practice. This is also the process where moral productivity emerged and developed into important materials and spiritual resources and assets.

4.5.1.1 Evidently Increased Corporate Moral Consciousness

Corporate moral consciousness develops as the development of the consciousness of social responsibility. As early as 1923, the British scholar Oliver Sheldon came up with the idea of "corporate social responsibility" and clearly pointed out that morality is an element of corporate social responsibility. In the following nearly 100 years, many scholars and research institutions studied and identified the concept of "corporate social responsibility" from different perspectives and with different approaches, and corporate ethics and corporate morality always held important positions in their research. In addition, some claimed that morality is the foundation and core of "corporate social responsibility Zhang and Chen (2008)," while some scholars went as far to say that "promoting the standard of corporate social responsibility is, more generally, advocating the development of corporate social morality Xu and Yan (2007)".

The development of corporate morality and corporate consciousness of moral responsibility experienced the process from obscuration to consciousness (Xu 2007). Before the 1970s, when politics dominated social thoughts, corporate morality's position and functions were ignored in corporate development. At that time, social morality, separated from materials and interests, was only considered as an important basis and an approach to improve moral consciousness and expand the spiritual realm, but the basis, standard, and objective to improve moral consciousness and expand the spiritual realm were seldom discussed. Even now, some still hold that morality must be separated from materials and interests, or the nobility of morality will be irreverently treated, and morality will be used as an instrument, which is very dangerous. With the constant development and improvement of the socialist market economy, people have, based on the combination of theories and practice, realized that economic development cannot be interpreted or understood from the sheer material perspective. If we do not analyze economic phenomena from the spiritual perspective, especially the perspective of morality, we cannot correctly understand and deal with economic phenomena, let alone realize rapid economic development efficiently. This point can be clearly seen from corporate development. Founded on January 12, 1996, in Beijing, in accordance with the *Company Law* and the *Law of China on Commercial Banks,* China Minsheng Bank Corp. (CMBC) is the first nationwide joint-stock commercial bank with a non-public enterprise as its biggest shareholder. As of December 31, 2011, CMBC had RMB 2229.064 billion in total assets, RMB 1644.738 billion in total deposits, RMB 1205.221 billion in total loans and advances, RMB 27.920 billion in net profits, and a nonperforming loan ratio of 0.63 %, achieving an industry-leading performance. It set 32 branches in Beijing, Shanghai, Guangzhou, Shenzhen, Wuhan, Dalian, and Nanjing, one representative office in Hong Kong, with organizations reaching 590 in total. With rapid development, CMBC's great concern can also be affirmed by the public and the banking industry. It was awarded as "The Most Vital Enterprise in China," "The Best Online Bank," "Top 100 Vital Enterprises in China," "The Best Private Bank in Service," "The Best Retail Bank," "The Best Risk Control Bank in Asia," "The Best Marketing and Service Team" and the "Top 10 Commercial Electronic Financial Brands Favored by Consumers." In 2006, it topped the list of the "Top 100 Private Listed Companies in 2006" and ranked first among the 100 privately listed companies on the sub-categories of market value and social contribution. In 2009, it won "The Best Bank Providing Service to Small and Micro Enterprises" of China Business News Financial Value List; the "Trade Finance Achievements Award" from *The Asian Bank*; the "Innovation Award in Providing Financial Service to Small and Micro Enterprises in 2009" at the twenty-first Century Annual Finance Summit of Asian; and "The Most Respectable Bank in 2009." The performance of CMBC cannot be separated from its concept of "Serve the Public and Care for People's Livelihood." It can be said that its achievements made in terms of responsibility management, market responsibility, win–win development, green financing, and charity provided strong spiritual support for its development. In terms of responsibility management, according to the requirements of strategic transformation, CMBC continuously enhanced its compliance risk management, strengthened risk warning, and normalization guidance, improved the entire process management of product innovation and business operation, enhanced legal compliance training and compliance ability development, and lowered business risks. It also made breakthroughs in internal control project construction and the basic construction of daily risk control projects. Besides, through improving the anti-money laundering organizational institution and institutional system, organizing a professional anti-money laundering team, and optimizing an anti-money laundering supervision and reporting system, CMBC greatly enhanced its anti-money laundering risk control ability. As for market responsibility development, CMBC introduced three strategic management tools, namely, the "Voice of the Consumer," the "Six Sigma," and the "Balanced Scorecard," which played an effective role in enhancing its scientific and meticulous management. Through such management, at the same time of assisting corporations to grow bigger and stronger, CMBC also greatly improved its ability to provide financial service to small and micro enterprises, winning consumer satisfaction as a leading industry. In addition, its "banking service with agricultural features" played an active role in promoting rural and agricultural development. Win–win development includes the win–win for the bank–consumer relationship, for the bank–employee relationship, and for the bank–partner relationship. In terms of the win–win for the bank–consumer relationship, CMBC promoted product service innovation, collected ideas for bank development, built the "product analysis and innovation project team," improved existing products while developing new products and developed custom-made products and service according to consumer needs. For the win–win of the bank–employee relationship, by adhering to the principle of taking employees as the foundation of corporate development, CMBC protected the rights and interests of employees, improved the institutions of the labor union and the workers' congress, developed employee training systems and career development channels at different levels further, and assisted employees to realize self-development. Caring for the physical and psychological health of employees, CMBC specifically launched the "home culture" project, assisting employees to find the balance between work and life. In terms of the win–win for the bank–partner relationship, CMBC actively established strategic cooperation relationships with relevant governmental agents, business groups, suppliers, and research institutions to realize common development. Green financing means improving risk control via strategic planning and institution and procedural norm formulation, strengthening the credit granting to energy efficiency and emission reduction projects and the risk control of green credit, and controlling the credit granted to projects with high energy consumption, high pollution level, and excess in capacity. CMBC strongly supported projects relating to energy efficiency and emission reduction technology, clean coal technology, smart power grids, and renewable energy equipment manufacturing, thus building a market image of the green bank. In term of charity, CBMC took measures to manage and use its "charitable donation fund" effectively to strengthen its support further for charity projects. The Yanhuang Art Museum was opened as free to the public, and money was invested for appointed poverty alleviation projects and other projects creating considerable social benefits.[30]

The corporate morality survey results show that companies have an increasingly growing consciousness of social responsibility and self-moral development. About corporate moral development, we asked employees of the companies surveyed two questions: "Does your company have moral requirements for employees?""Has your company issued the code of professional ethics?" Results show that among the 12 companies, only two companies did not fill in the questionnaire and one company without its moral concept;[31] thus, for the remaining nine companies, an

[30] Data source: *Social Responsibility Report 2011,* China Minsheng Bank.

[31] Formula: the average percentage of nine companies = (the total number of employees of the first company x sampling percentage + the total number of employees of the second company x

average of 75 % of employees said "yes" while answering the first and second questions, respectively. To the question, "Do you think it's necessary for your company to develop and implement a code of ethics?"[32] an average of 87 % employees chose "It's necessary" or "It's necessary to some extent." See the graphs below for details:

1. "Does your company have moral requirements for employees?"

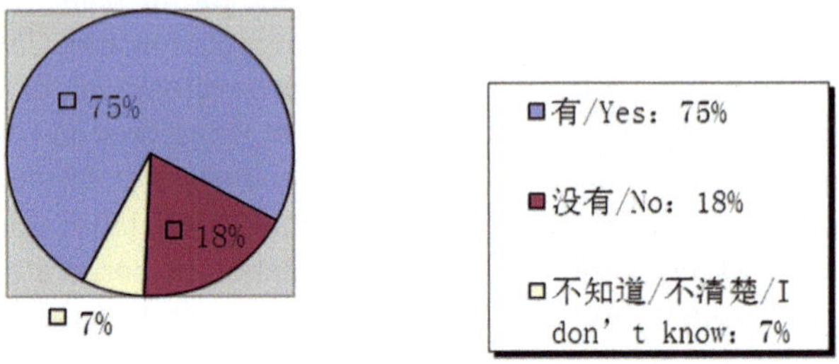

2. "Has your company issued the code of professional ethics?"

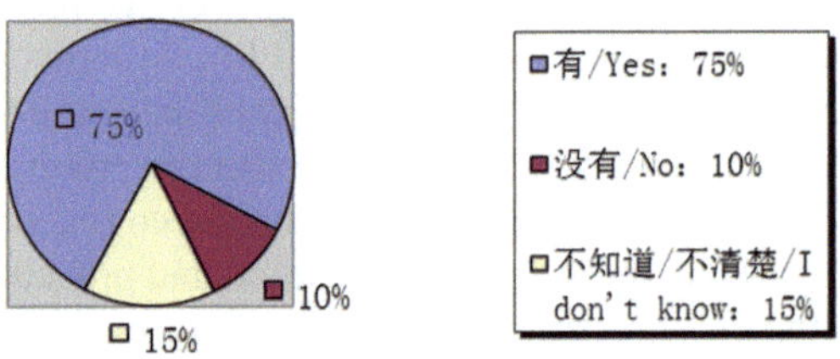

3. "Do you think it is necessary for your company to develop and implement a code of ethics?"

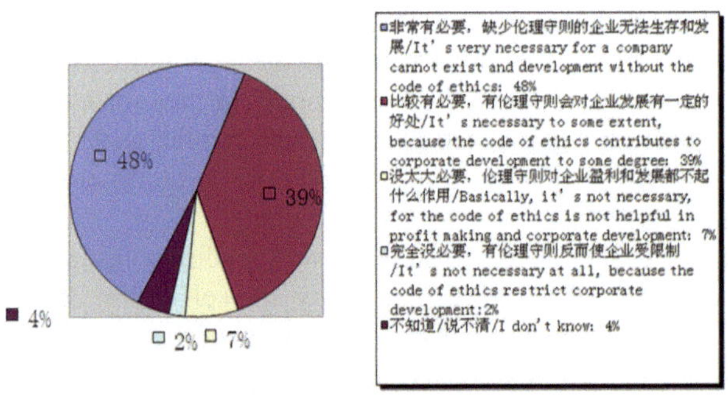

sampling percentage + … + the total number of employees of the ninth company x sampling percentage)/ the total number of the nine companies.

[32] By rights, the answers to the two questions should be either "yes" or "no", instead of having most respondents choose "yes" and a few respondents choose "no" or "I don't know". The reason is that, first, the respondents have different educational backgrounds which make them understand the same thing differently; and second, some employees do not know the relevant information clearly enough due to the company's lack of promotion.

4.5.1.2 Humanistic Care Has Become the Core Concept of Corporate Operations

For a company, its level of productivity and economic efficiency do not rest with its capital and technology, but rather its humanistic care, which acts as important basis and condition for the internal cohesion of the company and the cooperation between the company and its external stakeholders. A mercenary company that does not care for its employees and cooperators can never have long-term development. It can be said a company taking humanistic care as its core business principle will certainly obtain it due market share. The development of Jiangsu Province's Dan Niang Dumpling, to some extent, is the epitome of the theories and practice of humanistic care in China. Since its foundation in 1996, it has grown from a 30-m^2 store with six employees to the biggest and most widely distributed dumpling fast food chain enterprise in China, with the largest number of domestic company-owned stores. Currently, more than 5000 employees are serving it at more than 200 stores in more than 40 large- and medium-sized cities. Besides, with continuous business expansion, it has opened chain stores overseas. It was listed as one of the "Top 10 Famous Fast Food Chain Store Brands" several years ago. Adhering to the core discipline of "humanistic care," Da Niang Dumplings developed more than 100 kinds of products to meet the needs of consumers in different areas and of different consumption levels. On the one hand, with a clean, elegant, and comfort environment as well as an enthusiastic, efficient, and thoughtful service, it attracts a lot of consumers; on the other hand, by respecting employees and making their work enjoyable, it coheres employees together. This should be the secret that Da Niang Dumpling uses to hold its position against severe market competition.[33]

The survey results indicate that in China, companies have a growing awareness of the importance of humanistic care and corporate cohesion, which lead to growing corporate benefits. Changzhou Minghuang International Hotel is a good example. A famous catering brand in Jiangsu Province, the hotel covers a total area of about two hectares, including a business area of more than 20000 m^2, and approximately 220 employees, which provide comprehensive services, such as catering, accommodation, and entertainment to consumers. General Manager Yu Jianwen has a strong awareness of humanistic care, which not only attracts consumers but also coheres his followers together. According to Yu, the hotel attracts consumers with "tangible benefits" and "reasonable prices," and coheres employees by giving them a sense of belonging, sense of safety, and sense of honor, so that everyone lives with integrity. The hotel considers training as the biggest perks to employees. For example, it always arranges training for chefs to improve their professional skills instead of directly hiring better chefs. Besides, for the convenience of employees, the hotel specially built a long corridor linking the hotel and the dormitory. On the walls of the corridor are many pictures of employees, such as pictures from birthday parties and from outdoor training. Standing at the joint of the corridor and the hotel area

[33] The data of Jiangsu Province's Da Niang Dumpling come from Appendix IV of *Economic Benefits and Social Responsibility,* Dou Yanguo and Han Yun, Academia Press, 2007.

is a sink equipped with three taps providing drinkable hot, cold, and warm water to employees. Details like this well reflect the concern of the hotel for employees, bringing employees the sense of safety and belonging. No wonder there are many employees as couples who really take the hotel as their home.

The survey data indicate the importance of humanistic care and companies' growing concern for humanistic care. Among the companies, state-owned companies, food companies and companies with a high moral consciousness attached more importance to humanistic care, and some companies, though valuing the development of corporate morality, still needed improvement in humanistic care. To the question "Does your company arrange regular checkups for your employees," among the 12 companies, six companies (Chongqing Iron and Steel (Group) Co., Ltd., Wujiang Kelin Environmental Protection Equipment Co., Ltd., Changzhou Minghuang International Hotel, Typical Sewing Machine Wanping Machinery Co., Ltd., Henan Honggaoliang Food Co., Ltd., and Henan Baixiang Food Group) said that they do arrange regular checkups for their employees. An average of 73 % of respondents said they were able to access regular checkups. It can be said that compared to the condition at the end of the twentieth century, corporate humanistic care awareness has been improved greatly. The average data of the six companies are shown below.

Does your company arrange regular checkups for your employees?

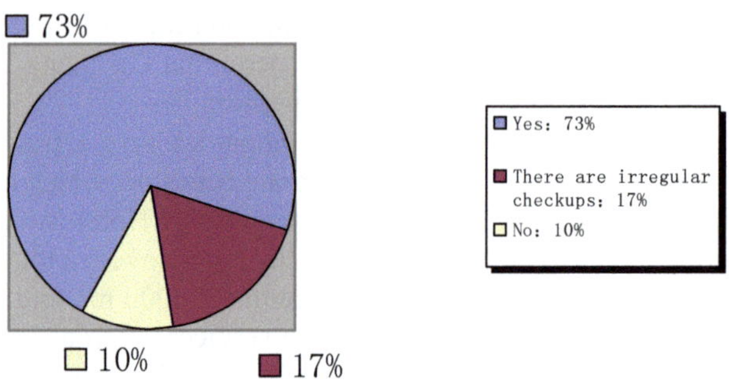

Although there were still some companies that did not arrange regular checkups for their employees, through the survey, we still saw an improvement. For example, some would hold meetings to ask for the opinions of their employees. Zhangjiagang Tiantai Top Textile Co., Ltd., Zhangjiagang Gangying Industrial Co., Ltd., and Zhangjiagang Furui Special Equipment Co., Ltd. often held such meetings.

Does your company often hold meetings to ask for the opinions of your employees?

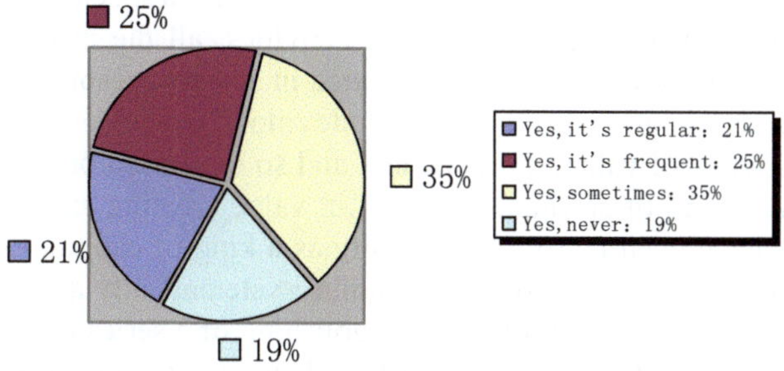

4.5.1.3 Integrity Ensures the Increase of the Corporate Market Share

From the corporate integrity development data (2005–2006) published by the China Enterprise Confederation (CEC), it can be seen that the increase of the corporate sense of integrity promoted the leapfrog development of companies. Among more than 500 respondents, "95 % consider corporate integrity as a strategic issue, 90 % view integrity development as a priority, 97 % adopt integrity as one of their core values, and 88 % hold that the increase of the level of corporate integrity is one of the decisive factors for corporate sustainable development." Some companies, such as Baossteel Group and Xizi UHC, through setting integrity development goals and integrity management departments to realize the penetration of integrity into the entire management process, successfully turned integrity into productivity, accelerating corporate development. [34]Our survey results also show that companies with good performance and growing profits all have developed and applied correct integrity concepts, and some companies, though with moderate performance, still hold that integrity is important for corporate development (Zhang 2008b). To the question "Do you think morality-like integrity will bring losses to your company," as shown in the graph below, among the respondents of 10 companies completing the questionnaire, an average of 54 % chose "No, it's good for corporate development," 39 % chose "Sometime it brings losses, but generally, it's beneficial," 2 % chose "Yes, mostly it brings losses to the company," and 2 % chose "Yes, it's of no help to the company at all."

Do you think morality-like integrity will bring losses to your company?

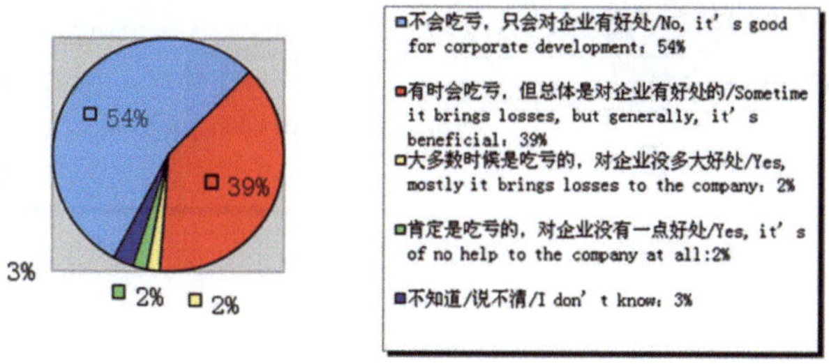

[34] The data of Jiangsu Province's Da Niang Dumpling come from Appendix IV of *Economic Benefits and Social Responsibility*, Dou Yanguo and Han Yun, Academia Press, 2007.

4.5.1.4 The Sense of Identity of Moral Capital is Improving

As a kind of productive spiritual resource, morality plays a special role in the course of creating values. I believe, in economic activities, all the moral elements that are helpful to create profits should be included in spiritual resources. As a kind of spiritual resource, morality specifically includes moral consciousness, moral realm, code of ethics, view of value, moral action, and so on. Based on the special effect of morality, as a kind of spiritual resource, in value creating and adding process, some scholars have even confirmed morality as a king of capital. Over the years, I have expounded the concept of moral capital systematically and quite a stir has been caused in academic circles with the publishing of a series of research results. In addition, it has attracted the attention of academic circles and corporate business departments with the presentation of different opinions. Some enterprises have consciously taken corporate morality as corporate business capital connotation and listed into the corporate development strategy and plan, so that some enterprises have put moral development as a top priority in operation. This is the leapfrogging progress of business administration and management ideas. In 10 investigated enterprises, the answers of employees from at least six enterprises (Chongqing Iron & Steel (Group) Co., Ltd., Zhangjiagang Tiantai Top Textile Co., Ltd., Zhangjiagang Furui Special Equipment Co., Ltd., Changzhou Minghuang International Hotel, Typical Sewing Machine Wanping Machinery Co., Ltd., and Henan Baixiang Food Group) are in line with the above. On the question, "Which do you think is essentially important to your company in the operation and management process, morality or profits?" 28 % hold the view that "certainly morality is important, and a company without morality will be cast aside and finally cannot earn money," while 26 % hold that "both are important, but the former is more important," and the total proportion of these two parts is 54 %. It is shown in the chart below.

Which do you think is essentially important to your company in the operation and management process, morality or profits?

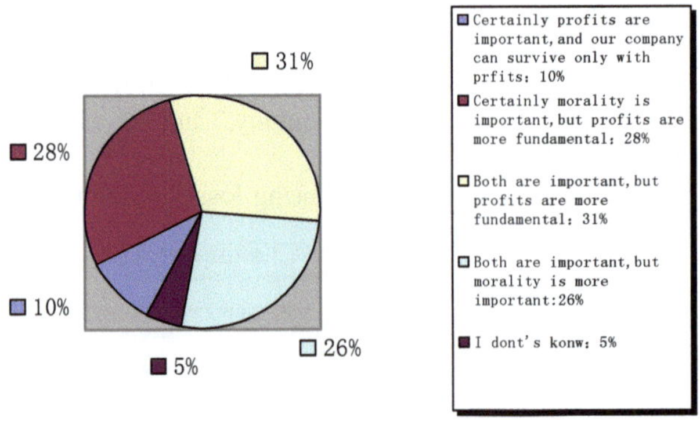

4.5.2 Loss of Corporate Morality and Analysis of Its Fundamental Cause

Although corporate morality has been accepted and emphasized by various enterprises of China, our corporate moral development is not ideal in its macro significance. On the basis of corporate morality investigation and research, I once analyzed three types of conditions for China's corporate morality and reached the following conclusion(s): first, there is moral consciousness: this means that enterprises are able to take morality as a tool to apply to production and operation activities by reason and pierce it through product design, production, and sales process in order to help improve product quality, accelerate sales speed, and increase more profits. However, such enterprises are very rare. China Minsheng Banking Corp. Ltd. and Haier Group are just two representatives. Second, there is a vague idea of morality: This means that enterprises sometimes think morality has a positive effect and sometimes think it is not beneficial to corporate development, and sometimes think it will bring losses. For uncertainty and ambiguity in concept, they lack a consistent behavior. In reality, there is a majority of such enterprises. Third, there is moral degeneration: This means that the enterprises get profits by whatever means necessary at the expense of damaging the interests of consumers or society. Enterprises recently revealed to have a "food problem" like the "Sanlu scandal," and "steamed buns dyed with colorant" are typical of such enterprises.

In fact, China's corporate morality and moral development cannot be belittled and should be taken seriously; otherwise, it will affect the competitiveness of our enterprises in international and domestic markets.

4.5.2.1 Representation of Chinese Enterprises' Moral Deficiency

1. The relationship between morality and business operation is unclear. Many enterprises are ambiguous to the meaning of morality in economic development. They always hold that economic activities are only related to input, output, efficiency, etc., but unrelated to morality. In theory, they cannot realize that economic activities certainly have spiritual content, and morality is the soul of economic activities in one sense; in practice, they have no idea of the effect of spiritual elements and do not know how rational morality as a tool plays its role in economic activities. For the question, "Do you think your company's assets include intangible asset elements (note: intangible assets refer to the economic values brought by corporate brand, reputation and etc.), at least 80.75 % of surveyed employees from two enterprises among the 12 investigated enterprises hold, "Yes, the intangible assets account for a small proportion," the surveyed employees from one enterprise hold, "Yes, the intangible assets account for a big proportion," and 46 % surveyed employees from two enterprises hold that "I don't know."
2. Seek nothing but profits and be wicked in operation. For years, many of China's enterprises have blindly sought after profits and benefits without considering people's health, reasonable interests, and even life. In particular, the media has

revealed that some food enterprises have "products with Sudan red G," "steamed buns dyed with colorant," "tainted milk powder," "toxic capsules" and other problems, indicating that these enterprises are unconscionable in operation. Even individual enterprises uphold the operation philosophy "we will suffer losses with morality, but profits without morality," which is harmful to others, themselves and the society.

3. Lack of honesty increases the friction consumption among enterprises and business costs. According to investigation data of "Corporate Social Responsibility Development in China 2007: A Report" published in 2008, "the enterprises are troubled by many behaviors of breaching promises, mainly including back money, default, infringement, false information, counterfeit and shoddy products, quality fraud, etc. In enterprises suffering from the above behaviors of breaching promises, back money accounts for 80 %, default accounts for 71 %, infringement accounts for 47 %, false information accounts for 31 %, counterfeit and shoddy products account for 28 %, and quality fraud accounts for 13 %. According to relevant statistics of related departments in previous years, direct, and indirect economic losses caused to China's enterprises due to a credit loss amount to approximately RMB 600 billion," "the losses caused by contractual fraud amount to approximately RMB 5.5 billion, and various losses caused by poor product quality or production and distribution of counterfeited products reach RMB 200 billion Zhang and Chen (2008)." This is what Zhou Xujun, Curator of Beijing Minsheng Modern Art Museum said, "The discreditable enterprises damage all the stakeholders and certainly, first and foremost, damage themselves."
4. The corporate leaders lack of the moral leadership concept. As some enterprises' leaders in China do not take moral management as an important leadership strategy, they often do not care much about the employees, so that employees' incomes and welfare are not reasonable. In the worse cases, some leaders even lack the respect for the personality of employees, seriously damaging their enthusiasm. In recent years, individual enterprises have witnessed continuous suicides by employees. Behind this, although there were complicated social causes, it could not be taken as one of important causes for enterprises to lack the care and respect to their employees and even managed people as a production machine, seriously damaging employees' enthusiasm. In fact, this also damaged enterprises' social reputation and would influence their economic benefits to some extent. Lately, facts have proved that with the improvement of corporate management, employees' loyalty has enhanced, corporate efficiency has increased obviously and at least, corporate internal friction consumption has been prevented.

4.5.2.2 Cause Analysis for Lack of Morality of China's Enterprises

(1) Corporate morality research falls behind the economic development speed.

China's corporate moral development is not ideal, and the problem is not all in enterprises themselves. With respect to the achievements of economic development since China's economic reform, the reason is that our theoretical research of corporate morality is relatively behind, and at least some theoretical problems have remained in a confused state up until now. For example, what is the form of China's corporate morality? What are the moral role characteristics and the moral responsibilities of enterprises, corporate leaders, and employees as moral subjects? How to perfect the integrity mechanism among corporate stakeholders? How does the rational morality as a tool play a special role in the course of getting more benefits and profits? How to make morality become an irreplaceable way of management? For all of these problems, no convincing high-level research results have been formed; therefore, without the guidance of well-developed corporate moral theory, corporate leaders and employees can only perform the moral responsibility in ambiguity or experience, thus playing a moral role, more or less. In fact, according to our investigation, more than 90 % of corporate leaders and employees have not read about or received professional theoretical training on existing theoretical studies of corporate morality.

(2) The leaders have a weak awareness of moral responsibility.

It should be mentioned that the responsibility for the problems of corporate morality that currently exist in China is mainly on the corporate leaders and not on the employees. If a leader has a strong awareness of moral responsibility, he will at least take administrative means to propagandize and perform the moral responsibility, and make moral requirements penetrate into the corporate production and operation processes. Thus, on the issue of corporate moral development, corporate leaders play an important role. In *The Moral Capital of Leader* Sison (2005) of Alejo G. Sison, he holds that leadership comes from morality, "Leadership is a two-way transformative and intrinsically moral relationship between a leader and his followers. The two parties, which are involved in a leadership relation (the leader and the followers), morally transform and elevate each other through their interaction. Thus, ethical leadership becomes the primary conduit through which not only persons, but also the organization for which those persons work become ethical. Leadership nurtures personal ethics, allowing it to grow and configure an auspicious organizational culture Sison (2005)." Sison stresses, "The core of leadership is ethics Sison (2005)" from the perspective of a leader's leadership. Moreover, Sison's expositions all indicate that a villainous leader will lose trust and authority. In fact, upon further thought, we can learn that if a leader lacks a moral force, he will have no appeal and will certainly lack abilities in moral analysis and organization. Furthermore, he will never discover the penetration mechanism of morality in economic development. Therefore, the economic activities under the jurisdiction of a leader without moral force will certainly weaken and even lose the effect of morality in itself. As a result, the "cask effect" will appear in corporate development for the corporate leaders' weak awareness of moral responsibility.

(3) Corporate morality is not widely popularized, the employees' understanding of it is superficial and it has a weak implementation force.

Most of China's enterprises have not received due education on corporate morality, and they have just seen or gained limited moral knowledge and behaviors from media. Other than insufficient theoretical research, this situation is attributed to three aspects: first, our facility is weak; second, the company leaders are unable to fully know morality and its roles, so they pay no attention to it; third, there is no special planning and guidance from governments. Therefore, employees have a superficial knowledge and understanding of corporate morality. Moreover, in most cases, morality is just kept untouched within the background of a company, while depleted of its authority and unique role. The investigation shows that in response to the question, "Are there corporate values, such as corporate vision, corporate mission, development philosophy, and corporate spirit, in your company?" 53.2% employees on an average of the 80% of the investigated companies said, "Yes, but I know little about them," while 15.47% on average answered, "I don't know" and "No." Therefore, though the moral concept and moral environment of the investigated companies seem not bad, they have not completely understood and mastered the corporate morality, greatly confining its moral role.

(4) Incomplete integrity mechanism

Integrity is essential to and badly needed by Chinese companies. Integrity contributes to the reduction of business costs of a company to some extent. Nevertheless, the truth is a lack of integrity has been a serious problem. Dishonesty, fraud, bad faith, and other behaviors have happened frequently during business operations, which is mainly attributed to the following four aspects: first, the credit risk has not yet been fully recognized and prevented, and many companies always know it only when their survival is threatened, they are about to close down or they have already closed down; however, at that point, it is often too late for any regret; second, integrity should be a code of conduct that the stakeholders should abide by jointly, but there has not been a set of supervision and restriction mechanisms available in China. A problem of the integrity chain will result in a chain of problems; third, China lacks an integrity management system for companies, especially the social morality of judging integrity, let along the publicly recognized "moral court"; fourth, the government has not yet formulated a set of complete policies and measures to reward and punish the behaviors of integrity and bad faith. Facts have proved that an incomplete integrity mechanism will result in the emergence of behaviors of bad faith from time to time, which will seriously corrupt social morality. A society lacking integrity should be a society with degraded morality, and a society full of moral risks and crises.

4.5.3 "An Entrepreneur Should Have the Blood of Morality Flowing Inside" and a Company Should Strive to Realize Its Moral Operation

"An entrepreneur should have the blood of morality flowing inside" is a very important strategic thought put forward by the former prime minister Wen Jiabao to Chinese enterprises. The moral consciousness of an entrepreneur is the precondition for a company to carry out moral operations smoothly, and maintain its international and domestic business competitiveness. According to a preliminary analysis on basic situations of China's corporate morality construction and investigation results of corporate morality, Chinese enterprises should carry out a construction movement of corporate morality, to make the corporate morality an important condition, factor, and driver for business operations.

4.5.3.1 An Entrepreneur Should be a Model for the Fulfillment of Moral Obligations and Comprehensive Quality

The consciousness of building corporate morality first stems from the moral consciousness of entrepreneurs. The outlook on life, the value outlook, and the moral outlook of an entrepreneur, who serves as a leader of a company, directly influence and restrict the strategic decisions of the enterprise, influence the life value orientation and labor attitude of employees, and influence various aspects of the company from production, sales, distribution of profits, etc. A leader of a company who lacks the moral concepts and moral consciousness should not be a qualified entrepreneur, as such entrepreneur is unable to completely achieve the double harvest of the enterprise in material and spiritual benefits, and to lead the enterprise to enhance its core competitiveness continuously. Therefore, the spiritual system of a company first needs to be supported by the entrepreneur. "An entrepreneur should carry the blood of morality."

The investigation shows that employees of a company generally place the hope of developing the enterprise on the leader. They hope that there will be a leader of high quality to lead them to strive for the maximum and best benefits of the enterprise. In the ten companies that received the questionnaire survey, their answers to the question, "Do you think the personal quality of the leader of a company has a significant influence on the atmosphere and environment of the enterprise?" had a high consensus, of which 55 % believed "Very significant, it has a direct influence," and 38 % believed "Comparatively significant, it has an influence to some extent," as shown in the chart below:

Do you think the personal quality of the leader of a company has a significant influence on the atmosphere and environment of the enterprise?

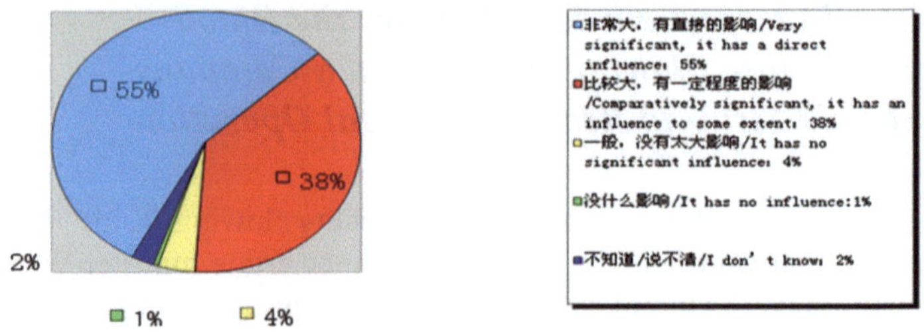

Therefore, an entrepreneur should stick to the following points:

1. Learn some knowledge of ethics, master some theories of morality, economic morality, and corporate morality, especially at the current stage; fully recognize the relationship between morality and the development of a company; and really understand the roles of economic morality and corporate morality; which serve as the important assets of the enterprise and promote a company's core competitiveness.
2. Convert the economic morality and corporate morality into specific working horizons and production factors, and always keep in mind the roles and infiltration of morality in the study and discussion of the enterprise's development plan and objectives, production process, marketing strategies, etc.
3. Insist on the moral institutionalization and institutional moralization in the enterprise. In the formulation and issuance of internal systems of a company, such as the wage system, the benefits system, the vacation system, the production management system, the work and rest system, and the employee training system, entrepreneurs should discuss and pay attention to the demands on improvement of life quality and career development of employees, on coordination of the internal interpersonal relationship of the enterprise, on the growth of the stakeholder's benefits, on the fulfillment of social responsibility, etc.
4. Adhere to daily people-oriented management, respect the personality of employees, allow them to work and live with dignity and fully mobilize their labor enthusiasm, thus affiliating the realization of the enterprise's business benefits to the maximum extent.

4.5.3.2 Strictly Abide by International Standards Like SA8000 According to Actual Social and Corporate Situations to Promote the Corporate Moral Development in an All-Round Way

1. Enlighten and affect corporate moral development with international standards. SA8000 requires companies to fulfill their social responsibility, primarily moral responsibility. SA8000 stipulates: first, respect human rights, particularly, child labor cannot be used, and policies and written procedures for remediation of children must be formulated; no use or support for forced or compulsory labor;

and respect the right to form and join trade unions and bargains collectively. Second, treat all personnel with dignity and respect; there should be zero tolerance of corporal punishment, mental or physical abuse of personnel. Third, compliance with laws and industry standards; formulate reasonable salary system; overtime is voluntary; and overtime paid at a premium rate. Fourth, develop enforcement regulations to ensure that welfare, safety, and health of employees are protected. Although international standards, such as SA8000, should be implemented according to the actual situations of China, we must see that fulfilling moral responsibility and realizing harmonious internal and external cooperation as per relevant international standards is an important condition for corporate moral development, and also an entry path for China to develop its own relevant standard.

2. Moral development in an all-round and all-level way. For China's companies, the first thing is (1) making certain the logical relationship between the economy and morality and between the company and responsibility through the combination of theories and practice; (2) building the concept that morality is a kind of spiritual property and capital; and (3) making morality fully play its unique rational roles as an instrument. Second, understand collective and personal moral responsibilities from macroscopic and microcosmic perspectives in the entire process of operation, and turn such responsibility into the code of conduct in design, manufacture, and sales. Third, strengthen the construction of moral institutions and the moral environment to create a strong moral atmosphere, so that morality can really become an indispensable part of corporate existence and development.

4.5.3.3 Improvement of the Integrity Mechanism[35]

Integrity, as a corporate code of conduct and an indicator of corporate quality, reconciles and supports various forces and means needed for the realization and formation of various processes:

1. Improve corporate institutions and management mechanisms. From the macroscopic perspective, corporate institutions are about property relations. As long as property relations are clarified, managers and their followers will really realize their roles and their relationship with the enterprise, and really understand that corporate integrity is established based on "personal integrity." From the microcosmic perspective, only when various reward and punishment institutions and various disciplines are clarified could all employees clearly know right and wrong corporate behaviors formally, and could integrity penetrate into corporate behavior through strict institutional management. In this way, it is possible that "product competitiveness is determined by the potential needs of consumers,

[35] Corporate Integrity and its Mechanism for Implementation– Take Haier as an example, *Moral Capital and Business Ethics,* Issue 6, 2003.

product development is determined by the difficulties met by consumers, and product quality standard is made according to customer requirements. Through such a virtuous circle, corporate integrity is realized both internally and externally Hu (2002)."

2. Enhance education to unify concepts. Corporate integrity cannot form naturally, or be realized by virtue of institutions, disciplines or empty talks, which are of no help. First, integrity education is about developing the sense of responsibility of employees, so that all employees will be responsible for the country, for the society, for others, and for themselves, so that they will know that a life lacking the sense of responsibility is incomplete, or even meaningless, and so that they will realize that the degree of their sense of responsibility is directly related to the amount of corporate and personal interests. Second, integrity development should be combined with the mechanism of rewards and punishments. A company is also a society. In the socialist market economy, employees are sophisticated and their value orientations are different. In this case, rewards are given to set good examples, helping employees to set clear objectives; while punishments are given to prevent behavior harming integrity from happening, ensuring that integrity is a rational intangible asset that can fully play its roles.
3. Business leaders should play an exemplary role with deeds rather than words. The internal and external integrity of a company directly depends on the reliability of its business leaders. On the one hand, highly reliable business leaders will not only play the role of demonstrator but also the role of motivator and guide. The famous US scholar Lynn Sharp Paine once pointed out, "It's very likely that the demonstration of organizational leadership is the most important element to establish and maintain organizational integrity. Obviously, corporate convey organizational ethical standard. Generally, individual behavior which has a lot of rights play an important role in building the ethical image of a company, for the information conveyed by such behavior is much more explicit that that written in the ethical statement of the company Lynn (1999)." Business leaders treating employees and things with integrity can bring hope to employees, making them build a strong sense of safety and sense of responsibility. On the other side, the integrity of business leaders can, objectively, prevent dishonest words and deeds from happening. Besides, the integrity of business leaders can also directly affect the integrity development of a company at large. As an entrepreneur said, "a business leader with integrity can develop a business leadership with integrity, a business leadership with integrity can develop a team with integrity and a team with integrity can produce products containing integrity."
4. The government, policy protection, and legal support are the important conditions for the realization of corporate integrity. First, try to build a government with integrity. On the one hand, it is necessary to develop governmental integrity, moralize government functions to affect and guide the enhancement of corporate integrity. On the other hand, it is necessary to protect and promote the implementation of integrity development measures and the realization of integrity development goals with governmental power and concrete measures. For example, to strengthen the protection of property rights to ensure that the commitments made

by the owner of property rights to the market can be fulfilled and promote the establishment of the market credit system; to strictly verify the capacity of taking responsibility of companies in the market; and to incessantly examine, supervise, and guide corporate integrity development. On the other hand, the government itself should develop integrity, that is, conducting people-centered administration, putting national interests first, enhancing the awareness of service and guidance, and overcoming bureaucracy and administrative omission, so as to promote corporate integrity and moral development while guaranteeing its own integrity. Second, corporate integrity should be conscious of corporate behavior, the continuity of which makes integrity the quality of a company. However, currently, to build a sound corporate integrity development system, legal restraint still plays an important role. On the one hand, legal restrictions guarantee the improvement of corporate credit mechanisms and the performance of corporate commitments. On the other hand, through legal restrictions, dishonest behavior will be punished, which warn those trying to break promises and protect those holding integrity. In this way, a social environment encouraging the pursuance of integrity and cracking down the neglect or discard of integrity is created.

4.5.3.4 Improve Labor Relations to Build Harmonious Companies

Corporate morality, in the final analysis, is about thinking good thoughts, doing good deeds, and harmonious cooperation, thus continuously increasing corporate benefits. In China, due to the difference in corporate type and nature, corporate internal labor relations are different and complex. In this case, companies must take labor relations seriously to reconcile ethical relations in labor and build ecological labor relations; otherwise, various conflicts will occur, affecting not only the cooperation among internal and external stakeholders but also industrial development and even social economic development. It can be said that improving labor relations is the primary goal of corporate moral development. Without increasingly improved labor relations, corporate morality cannot play its special roles in corporate operations. To improve labor relations, enterprises should pay attention to the following:

1. Satisfy reasonable interests and requirements of employees and stakeholders. When employees are treated with dignity, and their requirements and problems in work and life are concerned and reasonably met and solved, they will certainly devote themselves into serving the enterprise. If necessary, a company should sacrifice corporate interest to meet the interests of employees and stakeholders, in order to obtain their understanding and support.
2. Improve the mutual trust mechanism so that internal and external stakeholders can do business openly and equally, and problems can be solved in all sincerity and frankness. As long as mutual trust is strengthened, stakeholders will unite as one, maximizing corporate benefits.
3. Improve the management mechanism to realize democratic management and human-centered management. Companies should ask for the opinions of employees and stakeholders regularly, and accept their right to provide opinions and

suggestions. Meanwhile, the management behavior of corporate leaders must be supervised by all staff in order to avoid bureaucracy and paternalism.

4. Strictly abide by relevant national laws and regulations and protect the rights of employees and stakeholders. Particularly, corporate leaders should guarantee the development conditions of employees and stakeholders, giving them the sense of safety, of belonging and of achievement. Only in this way would employees and stakeholders completely devote themselves toward business operations, maximizing corporate benefits.

4.5.3.5 Establish the Ethics Committee

To prevent the shortcomings from occurring in business management, and to promote the transformation and development of modern corporate management institutions with a well-established moral management mechanism, it is necessary to establish an ethics committee. The ethics committee should undertake the following tasks:

1. Help companies to analyze and discover the intension and representation of corporate morality; to make certain how to improve corporate image constantly, especially moral image; and to make moral requirements consistent with the production and management of the business penetrates every aspect of production and management, that is, to turn the moral concepts and ideas into action plans and operating means.
2. Help companies to deal with and reconcile various internal economic and moral conflicts with both sincere emotion and reasoning under the constraint of institutions, thus solving conflicts and crises and developing strong moral relationships. Moreover, the ethics committee should study the interest demands and moral feelings of external corporate stakeholders, handle various factors of dissonance, and remove the possible or existing doubts and even grievances of stakeholders, thus strengthening the awareness of cooperation and realizing win–win or multi-win situations.
3. Study the intension and approaches of moral leadership that fits the business, and provide unique moral leadership concepts and approaches for the improvement of the art of leadership. In addition, it should also correct the moral mistakes made by leaders in leadership, making moral leadership an important moral asset or element of production of the business.
4. Study the content and measures for the construction of soft and hard environment to create a corporate environment filled with morality. First, make certain the business purpose, value orientation, moral responsibility, and moral institutions of the business, and create a strong atmosphere of public opinions through all-round publicity and education. In addition, it should also embody the respect and care toward employees in various aspects of employees' life and work and develop the moral consciousness of employees, making employees have the sense of satisfaction and the sense of happiness brought by morality.

References

Boton, M. D. (2002). *The best CEO in China in my eyes: The practice of management of Zhang Ruimin* (pp. 38, 128, 273–274; translated by G. Wen). Democracy and Construction Publishing House.

Guifang L. (1988). *On social productivity* (p. 106). People's Publishing House.

Guo, X. (Ed.). (2003). *The essence of Haier: Corporate culture and the performance of Haier* (p. 114). Democracy and Construction Publishing House.

Hu, Y. (2002). *Haier and made in China: Competitive strategies and core competence* (pp. 81, 123, 206, 237, 320–321, 353–354, 391). Hainan Publishing House.

Hu, Y., & Li, L. (2005). A new understanding of productivity. *Journal of Jiangxi Institute of Education*, (2).

Hu, Z. et al. (1994). *Human-centered product design in China* (p. 7). Guangzhou Publishing House.

Konosuke, M. (1996). *My life and management philosophy (I)* (p. 102, 187). Yanbian University Press.

Novikova, L. I. (1988). *The spiritual production. A social-philosophical aspect of the problem of spiritual activity* (pp. 79, 81, 316–317; translated by Q. An). Beijing Normal University Press.

Li, M. (2005). Overview on moral productivity. *Data and Communication*, (7 and 8).

Lynn, S. P. (1999). *Cases in leadership, ethics and organizational integrity: A strategic perspective* (p. 109; translated by J. Han et al.). Dongbei University of Finance and Economics Press.

Sison, A. G. (2005). *The moral capital of leaders* (p. 49, 50; translated by W. Yu & M. Ding). Central Compilation& Translation Press.

Wang, X. (2000). Moral capital. *Jiangsu Social Sciences*, (3).

Wang, X. (1998). The second study on "morality is a dynamic productive force". *Jiangsu Social Sciences*, (3).

Xu, L., & Yan, D. (Eds.). (2007). *The social responsibility of SMEs: Theories and practice* (p. 44). Science Press.

Yuanpei, C. (1996). *History of China's ethics* (pp. 2–3). The Eastern Publishing Co., Ltd.

Zedong, M. (1991). *Selected works of Mao Zedong* (Vol. 1, p. 325).

Zhang, Y., & Chen, L. (Eds.). (2008). *Corporate social responsibility development in China 2007: A report* (pp. 14–16). China Electric Power Press.

Chapter 5
Annex: Corporate Moral Capital and its Evaluation Index System

Corporate capital means productive resources participating in the productive process and creating profits or benefits such as money, materials, obligatory rights, corporate culture, and corporate spirits. Among them, corporate culture and corporate spirit, as intangible capital, are embodied as productive moral resources like the moral consciousness and morals of employees, morality-related institutions, and materialized morals.

Moral capital as an intangible productive resource is different from tangible corporate capital, such as money and materials, in some aspects. First, tangible capital like money and materials play their roles as capital after participating in the productive process and creating profits or benefits, but moral capital, manifested as the moral consciousness, morals, morality-related institutions, and materialized morals, starts to play its roles as capital as soon as productive activities happen. Second, during the productive process, in the case of economic depression or the adjustment of economic behavior, tangible capital, like money and materials, can withdraw from the productive process, but moral capital, manifested as the moral consciousness, morals, morality-related institutions, and materialized morals, always exists as long as economic activities exist. It guides and constrains tangible capital like money and materials during the productive process, and when tangible capital, like money and materials, withdraws from the productive process, it then supervises the rational withdrawal and the later reinvestment. In fact, during the process of business operations, moral capital always plays an active role of promotion. Third, moral capital cannot exist independently. It can only depend on physical capital to play its spiritual roles, and thus promote the formation of moralized physical capital. Physical capital can exist independently; however, the value of physical capital largely depends on the functioning of moral capital.

Moral capital, as a kind of intangible corporate capital, though, cannot be quantified, can be evaluated according to corporate moral behavior and moral phenomena. The indexes of corporate moral capital evaluation can be decided from the four aspects: (1) corporate moral concepts, namely, the understanding of corporate morality from the ideological perspective; (2) corporate moral institutions, namely, all man-related institutions reflecting the concern of a company for all personnel

X. Wang, *On Moral Capital*, DOI 10.1007/978-3-662-45544-9_5

(including stakeholders) transformed from corporate morality, cleaner production institutions, and so on; (3) the moral consciousness of business entities, that is, the moral consciousness of corporate leaders, employees, and corporate partners manifested as loyalty, care, and integrity; and (4) the moral demands of corporate production and management, namely, the corporate moral responsibility for consumers, and the purpose thereof during the process of production and management.

According to the above principles and the actual moral development situation of China, we can break up moral capital into application and operation indexes of different levels and categories. There are eight primary evaluation indexes: (1) corporate moral concepts and principles embodied in the moral realm and moral requirements that a company should have in production, operation, and management, and the concepts concerning the roles of guidance and management played by moral realm and moral requirements after penetrating production, operation, and management; (2) morality-related institutions embodied in corporate regulations regarding humanistic care and harmonious cooperation; (3) the moral environment embodied in the family-like harmonious interpersonal relationship environment in which employees are cared for and respected and the materialized moral environment filled with moral culture; (4) moral royalty manifested in the centrality and dedication of employees to the company; (5) product moral content manifested in the company's awareness of consumer needs in production, daily life, mentality, physiology, and morality and degree that the awareness is put into practice; (6) morality-based sales embodied in the initiative and degree to fulfill the commitments made by the company to consumers during the process of product sales; (7) social moral responsibility, namely, the obligations for the country, the society, sheers, employees, consumers, and any other stakeholders that should be fulfilled by the company; and (8) moral leadership and the leader's morality, namely, the moral quality of the leader and the humanistic care for employees and their families.

Among the eight primary indexes, moral concepts and principles are the core elements contained in the other seven indexes, and, for this reason, the eight indexes are connected more or less. It is worth pointing out that corporate moral capital is a comprehensive concept, thus it cannot be evaluated by a prominent index. In fact, a company with strong moral capital is certainly successful in moral development in various aspects and fruitful in corporate production and management, as well as the humanistic care for employees in life and work.

The eight moral evaluation indexes can be divided into 100 secondary indexes. Each index has a score range of 0–10, reflecting the existence or degree of the secondary indexes. The total points are 1000. Percentage = actual points/10.

Corporate moral capital evaluation table		
Primary index	Secondary index	Score
1. Moral concepts and principles	1. Corporate development purpose	
	2. Corporate awareness of social responsibility and goals	
	3. Corporate maxim	
	4. Corporate values such as integrity in operation	
	5. Corporate internal human-oriented management philosophy	
	6. Corporate code of professional ethics and requirements on employees' moral development	
	7. Corporate moral concepts concerning asset analysis	
	8. Corporate moral concepts concerning product design and manufacturing	
	9. Moral norms regarding business operations (service)	
	10. Leaders' work report or work arrangement including moral development	
	11. Just and fair interest distribution	
	12. Treat stakeholders in a fair and just way	
	13. Respect and protect the intellectual property	
	14. Employees are treated with integrity in work and life	
	15. Moral concepts of corporate leaders in decision making	
2. Morality-related institutions	1. Employee training institution	
	2. Checkup institution	
	3. Institution relating to overtime and raises	
	4. Maternity leave institution	
	5. Institution concerning leaders regularly or irregularly working with workers	
	6. Corporate financial disclosure institution	
	7. Corporate business performance reporting institution	
	8. Democratic life institution	
	9. Reward and punishment institution	
	10. Institution concerning the disclosure of corporate income and employees' income	
	11. Equal pay for equal work institution	
	12. Institution concerning not using child labor and protecting female employees	
	13. Promotion of publicity institution	
	14. Institution concerning the signing of the labor contract	
	15. Cleaner production institution	

Corporate moral capital evaluation table		
Primary index	Secondary index	Score
3. Moral environment	1. Promote corporate spirits through the network, newspaper and blackboard	
	2. Catchphrases or noble statues	
	3. Degree of harmony of interpersonal relationship	
	4. Degree of employee safety control	
	5. Degree of comfort of employees' workplace	
	6. Degree of comfort of employees' living environment	
	7. Environmental health and the physical exercise equipment and environment	
	8. Mechanism concerning quick response to accidents in production and employees' daily life	
	9. Atmosphere in which employees are respected	
	10. Degree of employees' accepting the company as a big family	
4. Moral royalty	1. Quantity or frequency of job-hopping	
	2. Employees' awareness of going through hard times together with the company	
	3. Enthusiasm of employees to advise in the case the leader makes mistakes in work	
	4. Degree of employees' accepting punishments	
	5. Employees' concern for the corporate development prospect	
	6. Employees' concern for the leader's moral quality	
	7. Employees' sense of ownership over the company	
	8. Refusal of commercial bribes	
	9. Employees' enthusiasm to participate in group activities	
	10. Employees' enthusiasm to work overtime	
5. Product moral content	1. Investigate consumer needs before product design	
	2. Human-centered and environment-friendly product design	
	3. Product manufacturing and product quality examination	
	4. Comprehensive product examination	
	5. Renewal of product design	
	6. Product safety	
	7. Product durability	
	8. Product appearance	
	9. Environment-friendly and economical product packaging	
	10. Disposal of nonconforming products	

Corporate moral capital evaluation table		
Primary index	Secondary index	Score
6. Morality-based sales	1. Product sales commitment	
	2. Human-centered product instruction	
	3. Product warranty	
	4. Rationality of the length of the warranty period	
	5. Human-centered after-sales services	
	6. Product recall institution	
	7. Warranty service	
	8. Supervision on consumer satisfaction with sales service	
	9. Investigate consumers' opinions to or preference for products	
	10. The authenticity, scientificity, and credibility of product advertising	
7. Social moral responsibility	1. Concern social assessments to products	
	2. Mechanism concerning the response and handling of customer complaints	
	3. Disclosure of product quality information	
	4. No accounting fraud	
	5. Pay attention to environmental protection	
	6. Participate in charity activities	
	7. Degree of integrity towards stakeholders	
	8. Pay taxes according to relevant laws	
	9. Operate according to legal requirements, protect national, and social interests	
	10. Unfair competition with rivals or friendly cooperation with rivals	

Corporate moral capital evaluation table		
Primary index	Secondary index	Score
8. Moral leaders, moral leadership, and the leader's morality	1. Management responsibility and commitments of the leader	
	2. The leader works on time	
	3. The leader always investigates or examines production and sales	
	4. The leader is concerned with work safety	
	5. The leader works together with workers	
	6. The leader calls the labor union into play	
	7. The leader corrects workers by education	
	8. The leader cares for disabled or sick employees	
	9. Reasons of dismissal	
	10. The leader visits sick employees and celebrates the birthdays of employees	
	11. Social insurance and medical insurance of employees are bought	
	12. The leader informs the families of employees about employees' condition in work, life, and study	
	13. The leader helps the families of employees to solve problems	
	14. The leader performs good in unity, democracy, and affinity	
	15. The leader holds regular or irregular meetings to ask for the opinions of employees	
	16. The leader does not discriminate female or disabled employees	
	17. The leader assesses employees in a just and fair manner	
	18. The leader knows internal social responsibility management standards, such as SA8000	
	19. The ethics committee is established or the moral affairs coordinator is appointed	
	20. Corporate moral capital evaluation is conducted annually	

Points (Percentage):

It needs to be pointed out that moral capital evaluation indexes vary with businesses due to the diversities of the latter. The moral capital stock of productive businesses can be evaluated as per the indexes above, but for service businesses relating to commodity trading, food and beverages, tourism, restaurants, and so on, in the scope of the eight primary indexes, content, presentation, and expression of secondary indexes are different to some extent; however, such indexes, no matter the business field, are set to realize the same purposes. For example, for the index of "product design," productive businesses primarily inject elements of morality into products in the process of product design, while service businesses provide moral services through the design of service projects. Nevertheless, they have a common goal—to maximize product performance. Another example is "moral environment." Large businesses, like societies or cities in scale, require a systematic moral environment, including software and hardware development, while small businesses, representatively service businesses, which operate only on a service platform, in one office building, or even in one office room, need a moral environment that fits their actual circumstances. In other words, if there is only an office building or even only one office room, the hard and soft moral environment shall be designed to be simple, focusing on a progressive cultural atmosphere, comfortable working environment, harmonious interpersonal relationship, and comprehensive and complete safety assurance. In the scope of "product morality content," some concepts are different in productive and service businesses in terms of intension and presentation forms; thus, they are not completely applicable to all businesses. For the commodity trading industry, product morality content is manifested in strict inspection regulations concerning purchasing, sales, and services and optimized service behavior in order to realize the highest cost-performance ratio, best service, and best product performance. For the food industry, it is about increasing the level of health, sensual pleasures, and the life quality of consumers at the premise of guaranteeing product safety and quality. For the tourism industry, it means having a strong sense of responsibility towards consumers during the process of designing tourism products in order to design the most scientific, economical, reasonable, and satisfactory tour routes for tourists. For the restaurant industry, product morality content lies in creating an environment as comfortable as home to guests through design and services. In particular, the moral capital evaluation indexes of emerging Internet businesses, due to their particularity, shall also include new integrity-based content and presentations that are designed based on the basic concepts of the primary, and, to the exclusion of the above, secondary indexes.

Likewise, the secondary indexes of moral capital evaluation also differ in content and presentation forms due to the different operating content, characteristics, and methods of businesses. For example, "cleaner production" often manifests itself as green production in productive businesses but as integrity and high cost performance in service businesses, especially Internet businesses. Of course, its conceptual goal of pursing goodness and morality remains unchanged in terms of content and presentation in both kinds of businesses. As for "product safety," different businesses have different requirements for safety in product design and production: Productive products focus on convenient and safe transport and utilization, tourism products focus on the safety of tourists' life and property when traveling, and food products hold food safety with the utmost importance. Taking the "product-recall institution" as another example, it is very specific for productive businesses, but for the tourism sector, though defective tourism products can also be recalled and replaced with qualified ones, it is still more about economic compensation and the improvement of tourism products.

In general, the commercial activities of modern productive businesses have covered the fields of production, sales, and service; therefore, in some sense, productive businesses contain service businesses. In this case, I think that the primary corporate moral capital evaluation indexes that are designed based on the moral requirements of productive businesses are applicable to all businesses in terms of basic concepts and scope. The content and presentation forms of secondary indexes vary with businesses. Be that as it may, all indexes, regardless of the diversity in businesses, are designed for the same purposes in moral capital evaluation.

I would like to make it clear that I designed the moral capital evaluation indexes with the following objectives: First, to help enterprises attain a complete and comprehensive understanding of modern corporate assets (capital), especially modern corporate intangible assets (capital), and to pay special attention to the understanding, development, and application of corporate moral assets (capital); second, to provide feasible indexes, regulations, and action plans for businesses to increase moral capital stock; and third, to enlighten businesses on how to develop an acute awareness of moral capital in the process of development and for a better development.

Index

X. Wang, *On Moral Capital*, DOI 10.1007/978-3-662-45544-9

MIX
Papier aus verantwortungsvollen Quellen
Paper from responsible sources
FSC® C105338
www.fsc.org

If you have any concerns about our products,
you can contact us on
ProductSafety@springernature.com

In case Publisher is established outside the EU,
the EU authorized representative is:
Springer Nature Customer Service Center GmbH
Europaplatz 3, 69115 Heidelberg, Germany

Printed by Libri Plureos GmbH
in Hamburg, Germany